the Unofficial Guide™ to Hot Careers

Shelly Field

IDG Books Worldwide, Inc.
An International Data Group Company

Foster City, CA • Chicago, IL • Indianapolis, IN • New York, NY

IDG Books Worldwide, Inc.
An International Data Group Company
919 E. Hillsdale Boulevard
Suite 400
Foster City, CA 94404

For general information on IDG Books Worldwide's books in the U.S., please call our Consumer Customer Service department at 800-762-2974. For reseller information, including discounts and previous sales, please call our Reseller Customer Service department at 800-434-3422.

ISBN: 0-02-863416-0

Manufactured in the United States of America

10 9 8 7 6 5 4 3 2 1

First edition

*This book is dedicated to my parents Ed and Selma Field,
who not only believed in all my dreams but helped them
come true; and to my sisters Jessica and Debbie, who
always cheered me on.*

Acknowledgments

I thank every individual, company, corporation, agency, association, and union who provided information, assistance, and encouragement for this book.

First and foremost, I acknowledge with appreciation my aquisition editor Randy Ladenheim-Gil for providing the original impetus for this book, as well as her support over the years. I consider myself extremely fortunate to have worked with Alex Goldman, the development editor for this project. My sincere appreciation goes to him for his guidance, patience, and encouragement. I also gratefully acknowledge the assistance of Ed and Selma Field for their ongoing support.

Others whose help was invaluable include: Ellen Ackerman; Advertising Club of New York; Advertising Council; Advertising Research Foundation; Advertising Women of New York, Inc.; Aerobics and Fitness Association of America; Julie Allen; American Advertising Federation; American Association of Advertising Agencies; American Association for Counseling and Development; American Society For Hospital Marketing and Public Relations; American Association For Music Therapy; American Academy of Actuaries; American Bar Association; American Chemical Society; American Chiropractic Association; American Dance Therapy Association; American Dental Assistants Association; American Dental Association; American Dental Hygienists Association; American Geriatrics Society; American Health Care Association; American Hospital

Association; American Association of Certified Public Accountants; American Institute of Chemists; American Meteorological Society; American Optometric Association; American Physical Therapy Association; American Society of Biological Chemists; American Society of Travel Agents; Joanne Anderson; Art Directors Club, Inc.; Barbara Ashworth; Association of Computer Professionals; Association of National Advertisers; Lloyd Barriger, Barriger and Barriger; Allan Barrish; Marguerite Berling; Beauty School Of Middletown; Eugene Blabey, WVOS Radio; Joyce Blackman; Steve Blackman; Robert Boone, Corporate H.R. Director, Isle of Capri Casinos; Keith Browne, Environmental Engineer; Theresa Bull; Business/Professional Advertising Association; Kim Butler, Trump Casino Resorts; Caryn Cammeyer, Advertising Research Foundation; Liane Carpenter; Eileen Casey, Superintendent, Monticello Central Schools; Mary Cawley; Casualty Actuarial Society; Andy Cohen; Bernard Cohen, Horizon Advertising; Dr. Jessica L. Cohen; Lorraine Cohen; Norman Cohen; Commission on Opticianary Accreditation; Community General Hospital, Harris, NY; Contact, Inc.; Jan Cornelius; Phyllis Cornell, Image Consultant; Crawford Memorial Library Staff; Meike Cryan; Clearinghouse Services, Contact Center, Inc.; Council on Chiropractic Education; Barbara Dankulich; Su Perk Davis; Daniel Dayton; W. Lynne Dayton; Carrie Dean; Linda Delgadillo; Direct Mail/Marketing Association, Inc.; Direct Marketing Educational Foundation, Inc.; Gina Damato; Jane Donohue; Donna Dossey-Aust, American Airlines Advantage Sales Reservationist; Scott Edwards; Dan England, UNLV; Valerie Esper;

Ernest Evans; Field Associates, Ltd.; Deborah K. Field, Esq.; Gale Findling, R.N.; Finkelstein Memorial Library Staff; Greg Fotiades; David Garthe, CEO, Graveyware.com; John Gatto; Sheila Gatto; Gerontological Society of America; George Glantzis; Kaytee Glantzis; Sam Goldych; Graphic Artist Guild; Grey Advertising; Gail Haberle; Joyce Harrington; Harris Home Health Services, Community General Hospital of Sullivan County, NY; Hermann Memorial Library Staff; David Hernandez, Community College of Southern Nevada; Hope's Corner, Bloomingdales, New York City; Jan Hopkins, R.N.; of Patricia Hopkins; Joan Howard; International Chiropractors Association; Jimmy "Handyman" Jones; Margo Jones; Bruce Kohl, Boston Herald.com; Tom Lagrutta; Liberty Public Library Staff; Lipman Advertising; Litson Healthcare; Ginger Maher; Dorothy Marcus; Robert Masters, Esq.; Richard Mayfield; McCann-Erickson; Lois McCluskey; Werner Mendel, New Age Health Spa; Phillip Mestman; Rima Mestman; Beverly Michaels, Esq.; Martin Michaels, Esq.; Monticello Central High School Guidance Department; Monticello Central School High School Library Staff; Monticello Central School Middle School Library Staff; Cindy Moorhead; David Morris; Sharon Morris; Donald C. Morse, Jr., Accu Search; Joseph Napolitano; National Association For Music Therapy; National Association of Alcoholism and Drug Abuse Counselors; National Association of Broadcast Employees and Technicians; National Association of Broadcasters; National Association of Life Underwriters; National Association of Realtors; Earl Nesmith; National Resource Center on Health Promotion and Aging; New York State Department of Environmental Conservation; New York State Department of Environmental Conservation, Law Enforcement Division; New York State Employment Service; New York State Nurses Association; Ellis Norman, UNLV; Peter Notarstefano; The One Club; Joy F. Pierce; Public Relations Society of America; Doug Puppel, Business Editor, *Las Vegas Review Journal;* Ramapo Catskill Library System; Doug Richards; Martin Richman; Michele Roberts, Travel Planners; David Rosenberg; Genice Ruiz; Saatchi and Saatchi Advertising; Iris Silver, Proprietor/Trainer Computrain; Raun Smith, Casino Career Center; Society of Actuaries; Society of Illustrators; Debbie Springield; Matthew E. Strong; Sullivan County Community College; Dana Swails; Thrall Library Staff; Anne Thum, R.N.; Marie Tremper; United States Department of Labor; Brian Vargas; Karen Waits; Carol Williams; John Williams; Marc Weiswasser; John Wolfe; Johnny World; WSUL Radio; WTZA Television; and WVOS Radio.

My thanks also to the many people, associations, companies, and organizations who provided material for this book who wish to remain anonymous.

Contents

The *Unofficial Guide* Reader's Bill of Rights

We give you more than the official line

Welcome to the *Unofficial Guide* series of Lifestyle titles—books that deliver critical, unbiased information that other books can't or won't reveal—*the inside scoop*. Our goal is to provide you with the *most accessible, useful* information and advice possible. The recommendations we offer in these pages are not influenced by the corporate line of any organization or industry; we give you the hard facts, whether those institutions like them or not. If something is ill-advised or will cause a loss of time and/or money, we'll give you ample warning. And if it is a worthwhile option, we'll let you know that, too.

Armed and ready

Our handpicked authors confidently and critically report on a wide range of topics that matter to smart readers like you. Our authors are passionate about their subjects, but have distanced themselves enough from them to help you be armed and protected, and help you make educated decisions as you go through your process. It is our intent that, from having read this book, you will avoid the pitfalls everyone else falls into and get it right the first time.

Don't be fooled by cheap imitations; this is the genuine article *Unofficial Guide* series. You may be familiar with our proven track record of the travel *Unofficial Guides,* which have more than two million copies in print. Each year thousands of travelers— new and old—are armed with a brand-new, fully updated edition of the flagship *Unofficial Guide to Walt Disney World,* by Bob Sehlinger. It is our intention here to provide you with the same level of objective authority that Mr. Sehlinger does in his brainchild.

The Unofficial Panel of Experts

Every work in the Lifestyle Unofficial Guides is intensively inspected by a team of three top professionals in their fields. These experts review the manuscript for factual accuracy, comprehensiveness, and an insider's determination as to whether the manuscript fulfills the credo in this Reader's Bill of Rights. In other words, our Panel ensures that you are, in fact, getting "the inside scoop."

Our pledge

The authors, the editorial staff, and the Unofficial Panel of Experts assembled for *Unofficial Guides* are determined to lay out the most valuable alternatives available for our readers. This dictum means that our writers must be explicit, prescriptive, and above all, direct. We strive to be thorough and complete, but our goal is not necessarily to have the "most" or "all" of the information on a topic; this is not, after all, an encyclopedia. Our objective is to help you narrow down your options to the best of what is available, unbiased by affiliation with any industry or organization.

In each *Unofficial Guide* we give you:

- Comprehensive coverage of necessary and vital information

- Authoritative, rigidly fact-checked data

- The most up-to-date insights into trends

- Savvy, sophisticated writing that's also readable

- Sensible, applicable facts and secrets that only an insider knows

Special Features

Every book in our series offers the following six special sidebars in the margins that were devised to help you get things done cheaply, efficiently, and smartly.

1. **Timesaver**—tips and shortcuts that save you time.

2. **Moneysaver**—tips and shortcuts that save you money.

3. **Watch Out!**—more serious cautions and warnings.

4. **Bright Idea**—general tips and shortcuts to help you find an easier or smarter way to do something.

5. **Quote**—statements from real people that are intended to be prescriptive and valuable to you.

6. **Unofficially…**—an insider's fact or anecdote.

We also recognize your need to have quick information at your fingertips, and have thus provided the following comprehensive sections at the back of the book:

1. **Glossary:** Definitions of complicated terminology and jargon.

2. **Resource Guide:** Lists of relevant agencies, associations, institutions, Web sites, etc.

3. **Recommended Reading List:** Suggested titles that can help you get more in-depth information on related topics.

4. **Important Statistics:** Facts and numbers presented at-a-glance for easy reference.

5. **Further resources:** More information to help you find a hot job.

6. **Index.**

Letters, comments, and questions from readers

We strive to continually improve the *Unofficial* series, and input from our readers is a valuable way for us to do that.

Many of those who have used the *Unofficial Guide* travel books write to the authors to ask questions, make comments, or share their own discoveries and lessons. For Lifestyle *Unofficial Guides,* we would also appreciate all such correspondence—both positive and critical—and we will make our best efforts to incorporate appropriate readers' feedback and comments in revised editions of this work.

How to write us:

Unofficial Guides
Lifestyle Guides
IDG Books
1633 Broadway
New York, NY 10019
Attention: Readers' Comments

About the Author

Shelly Field is a nationally recognized motivational speaker, career expert, and author of over 20 best-selling books in the business and career fields. Her books instruct people on how to obtain jobs in a wide array of areas including the hospitality, music, sports, and communications industries, casinos and casino hotels, advertising, public relations, theater, the performing arts, entertainment, animal rights, health care, writing, and art; and how to choose the best career for the new century. She is a frequent guest on local, regional, and national radio, cable, and television talk, information, and news shows and also does numerous print interviews and personal appearances.

Field is a featured speaker at conventions, expos, corporate functions, casinos, employee training and development sessions, career fairs, spouse programs, and events nationwide. She speaks on empowerment, motivation, gaming, careers, human resources; attracting, retaining, and motivating employees; customer service; and stress reduction. Her popular seminar, "STRESS BUSTERS: Beating The Stress In Your Work and Your Life" is a favorite around the country.

Field is a career consultant to businesses, educational institutions, employment agencies, women's groups, and individuals. President and CEO of The Shelly Field Organization, a public relations and management firm handling national clients, she has represented celebrities in the sports, music, and entertainment industries as well as authors, businesses, and corporations. For information about personal appearances or seminars contact The Shelly Field Organization at P.O. Box 711, Monticello, NY 12701 or log on to www.shellyfield.com.

The *Unofficial Guide* Panel of Experts

The *Unofficial* editorial team recognizes that you've purchased this book with the expectation of getting the most authoritative, carefully inspected information currently available. Toward that end, on each and every title in this series, we have selected a minimum of three "official" experts comprising the "Unofficial Panel" who painstakingly review the manuscripts to ensure: factual accuracy of all data; inclusion of the most up-to-date and relevant information; and that, from an insider's perspective, the authors have armed you with all the necessary facts you need—but the institutions don't want you to know.

For *The Unofficial Guide to Hot Careers,* we are proud to introduce the following panel of experts:

Warren Ladenheim is a Director at Peak Search, Inc., an executive recruitment firm in New York City specializing in Accounting and Financial recruitment. Warren has been in executive recruitment for eleven years. He is a Certified Public Accountant and began his career after attending graduate school at Baruch College, City University of New York, in National and Big-5 CPA firms. He has also been a Controller specializing in the real estate and financial service industries. Warren lives on Long Island with his wife and two children.

Jason R. Rich (http://www.jasonrich.com) is the author of several career-related books, including Job Hunting for the Utterly Confused (McGraw-Hill), the Unofficial Guide to Earning What You Deserve (Macmillan Publishing), and First Job, Great Job (Macmillan Publishing). He's also a weekly columnist for The Boston Herald's Sunday "Careers" section and continues to contribute articles to publications such as The Wall Street Journal's Managing Your Career and National Business Employment Weekly.

Hilary J. Bland worked in human resources, as an executive recruiter, and as a training and development consultant in the financial services industry. Hilary is a graduate of Mount Holyoke and holds an MA in Organizational Psychology from Columbia University.

Introduction

Are you happy with your life? How about with your career? It's hard to be totally happy with one if you're not satisfied with the other. If you're like most people, chances are you want to improve on your career and your life. The good news is you've taken the first step by reading this book!

You've already made one positive decision to improve your life by improving your career, simply by picking up this book. This is your chance to find the hot career you have always dreamed of having. This is your opportunity to determine what you want and finally get it. Now that you've made that decision, it's time to take some positive actions to reach your goal.

The *Unofficial Guide to Hot Careers* offers you the most useful and up-to-date advice on career issues and information on hot careers. Throughout the book, I'll help lead you on your journey to finding *your* hot career. It's important for you to know that what's hot for you might not be hot for someone else, and vice versa.

It's up to you to choose what *you* want to spend your life doing. You—and you alone—have to make that choice. Not your mother, father, sister, brother, best friend, or spouse. No one else knows *your* inner desires and hopes for the future better than you! Only you know what your true dreams and passions are. You know your special talents and skills. You know what would make you happy. You know what you're willing to do to get what what you want. It's up to *you* to go after it!

Each day that you don't take any positive actions or fear making a change is another day you won't have the hot job you deserve. Don't wait until it's too late. You don't want to look back over your life and say, "I wish I had done this" or "I wish I had done that." Read this book, get some ideas and advice, take some action, and do it now!

I know it can be frightening to make a change. We all get comfortable in situations and often feel rocking the boat isn't worth the risk. In your career, as in most of life, you might feel that while things aren't really good, they aren't that bad, either. You might be getting a paycheck, but really not have any job satisfaction. It's essential to understand that sometimes you have to take risks to make things better. Why shouldn't you have a hot career? You deserve the best.

I can't promise you life will get better if you take a risk. I can't even promise you'll get a better job immediately. The one thing I *can* promise you is that if you don't try to get what you want, you'll never get it. Take some positive actions or it will never happen.

What's in this book?

The first five chapters of the *Unofficial Guide to Hot Careers* are designed to help put you in the driver's seat. They provide the information to help give you the confidence to be in control of your career. These chapters offer you the inside scoop to finding, obtaining, and excelling in the hottest career around. They cover everything from determining what your dream job is to giving you techniques on how to prepare and obtain it.

Some of the areas the book covers include:

- Finding a hot career you can love
- Changing your career path
- Innovative ways to obtain hot job leads
- Networking
- Determining when to stay and when to leave a job
- Determining whether you have job burnout
- Savvy success strategies
- Methods to market and promote yourself
- Surfing the Net to a better job
- Assessing your skills
- Firing up your career
- Shining like a star in the workplace
- Telecommuting tips, flex time, part time, and job-sharing options

This book is chock-full of insider tips, techniques, and tactics to give you the edge over others. Want to learn how to determine what *your* hot dream job is? How about how to prevent others from destroying your dreams? Did you know you can visualize your way to a better career or make the job you have better? Check out Chapter 1 for some ideas.

Do you want to be the one to find the invisible jobs in the hidden job market before anyone else? How about how to increase your success with the classifieds? Do you know the savvy secrets of networking? Chapter 2 helps you learn about these areas, among others.

Are you confused about whether you should leave your current job or stick it out? Do you want to increase your chances of success when reentering the workforce? Do you know how to deal with unemployment? Are you suffering symptoms of stress and burnout from your job? Chapter 3 gives you the answers to these and other pertinent topics.

Want some innovative ideas on getting a potential employer's attention? Check out Chapter 4 and learn what eggs, chocolate chip cookies, fortune cookies, a dozen red roses, chocolate bars, and mugs with gourmet coffee can do for your career. Want to learn how to formulate your personal career plan or develop a Hot Job Journal? Chapter 4 covers those topics as well.

Do you want to fire up your stalled career? Would you like know more about what makes people succeed? Do you want to be the one to shine in the workplace? Chapter 5 gives you some ideas.

The new millennium offers a multitude of hot career options. Chapters 6 through 18 of *The Unofficial Guide to Hot Careers* offer you the inside scoop to finding, obtaining, and excelling in the hottest career around. One of them can be yours. All you have to do is go after it. These chapters covers a vast array of specific careers in many different areas. Maybe you'll see an area that interests you. Here's an idea of the type of careers we'll explore in this book:

- **Careers helping and healing others.** Check this section out if you're interested in working in health care, medical technology, fitness, or nutrition.

- **Careers working with seniors.** Check this section out if you're interested in caring for the elderly or helping them have more productive and satisfying lives.

- **Careers for retired workaholics.** Be sure to check this section out if you or someone you know is retired and wants to return to work.

- **Careers for talented and creative people.** Check this section out if your dream is to have a career in some facet of writing or in the arts.

- **Careers for great speakers and writers.** Check this section out if you have dreamed of working in the communications industry or want a career in the media.

- **Careers serving others.** Check out this area if you've been thinking about working in the hospitality or travel industry.

- **Careers in the sales and service areas.** Check out this area if you love selling in any capacity or you think you might want to work in a service sector.

- **Careers working in the information age.** Check out this area if you wish you could have a career working with computers, on the Web, or in information technology.

- **Careers in engineering, science, and technology.** Check out this area if you think you might want a career as an engineer, scientist, biologist, etc.

- **Careers everyone wants.** Check out this area if you want know more about areas such as customer service, entertainment, sports, or a home business.

Career areas often overlap. You might, for example, be interested in working in sales and find a career in the hospitality industry selling conventions. Or you might want to work as a scientist and find your hot career with a food manufacturer. You therefore might want to read through a variety of career sections.

The appendix section in the book offers you a wealth of information to help you in your search for the hot career of your dreams. A glossary defines any unfamiliar terms. The reading list provides you with books to look into for more information. Charts offer interesting statistics from the Department of Labor and the Bureau of Statistics regarding trends in jobs and the workforce.

One of the most useful resources in the appendix section is the comprehensive listing of trade associations and organizations. It gives you not only names, addresses, phone numbers, and fax and toll-free numbers, but also e-mail and Web addresses (when available). This list can help speed your search for information on specific jobs. With the click of a mouse, you can access trade associations and learn about their programs, conferences, membership requirements, and other resources.

How this book is different

The Unofficial Guide to Hot Careers is written in an easy-to-understand style. As a motivational speaker, career expert, and author of over 20 books in the career and business fields, I know what employers and employees are looking for. Over the years, I have spoken to thousands of people about career and workplace issues as well as specific careers in a multitude of career areas.

You deserve to be happy. Don't let it always be the other people you hear about who love their job. You can join them. Work is not supposed to be a punishment. If you find a career you love, you will wake up every morning with the anticipation of the coming day—and as a bonus you will get paid for it!

This book can help you find the hot career of your dreams for the new century. Put some time and effort into your quest. Let this book be your guide. While I can't personally speak to each and every one of you, hopefully you will be motivated and inspired by the words in this book to take the necessary actions to obtain the career you desire and dream about. I know you can do it. Good luck!

—Shelly Field

What Is a Hot Career?

GET THE SCOOP ON...
Defining your dream job ▪ Not allowing others
to destroy your dreams ▪ Setting career-related
goals ▪ Obstacles standing in the way of your
hot job ▪ Preparing yourself for a better career
▪ Making the job you have better

PART I

If You Get a Job You Love, You Have a Hot Career

Everyone wants a hot career. But not everybody has one. If you wake up every morning dreading work and unsure whether you can make it through your day, you are not alone. There are thousands of others who wake up with the same feelings.

There is a tremendous amount of job dissatisfaction today. But you can change that for yourself. There *is* something you can do about it. You can decide to find a job you love; when you are doing something you truly enjoy, you will have job satisfaction. What that means is that if you can find a job you love, you will be on the road to a hot career.

This chapter will help you determine what your dream job is—and what it is not. It will give you basic advice so that you can act now! We'll go over some of the exciting career areas so that you can begin to seek the hottest careers for you in the new millennium.

3

If you already have a job, you'll learn how you can begin molding your current job into a hot career for *you*. Even if you want to take your job and shove it, you'll learn how to beat that feeling and have a job and *love* it.

Your dream job...What do you want?

Most of us have an idea of what our dream job is. Unfortunately, for many of us, it's not the job we have. Dream jobs are something we talk about, think about, and wish we had—but don't. Dream jobs are for other lucky people. We envy those people, who have jobs they love. People who love their jobs are successful—not only in their careers, but in their lives. They possess an aura of total success, happiness, health, and prosperity. They have a circle of friends, volunteer to do things for others, and seem to have time for everything.

You might ask yourself how they can appear so centered with so much going on all around them. Especially when you may feel your job doesn't leave you time for anything. Your standard routine is waking up, going to work, coming home, cooking and eating dinner, perhaps watching a little television or helping the kids do their homework, going to bed, and starting all over again the next morning.

If your daily life sounds like this and the only good thing you can say about your job is that it helps to pay the bills, you definitely don't have a hot job. This is true even if your job is at the top of everyone's hot list of careers. The good news is, you too can be one of the lucky people, the ones with the great hot jobs and the successful, happy lives. You just have to do some planning and take some action.

> **"**
> I never did a day's work in my life. It was all fun.
> —Thomas Edison
> **"**

Dreams and nightmares

It's important to realize that everyone's dream job is unique. Everyone has different skills, talents, personality traits, and desires. What one person thinks is a great job, another puts at the bottom of the list of things he or she wants to do.

While I might think a career recording hit songs, traveling the country, and singing on stage every night would be the hottest job in the world, there are others who would think that living out of a suitcase and having to perform in front of thousands of people would be a horrible life. Your dream job might be teaching young people and helping them mold their lives. But this dream might be your best friend's nightmare. She might love working with food every day and dream of becoming a chef; for you, putting together dinner every night might be a chore.

Finding a job you love

Life is not supposed to be miserable. Neither is your job. In order for you to be generally happy, you have to wake up in the morning with a purpose. The purpose of life is not sleeping for eight hours so you can get up for 16 hours and do things you really don't like. You need to enjoy life, meet interesting people, spend time with your family and friends, and, unless you are independently wealthy, find a way to earn money. You're at your best when you have passion for the things you do, and that includes your job.

It's essential to assess what you want to do so you can determine what your dream job is. You can then work to achieve your goals. The world of work has changed tremendously over the years. The new millennium offers many choices that weren't available even a short time ago. As the new century

Bright Idea
One of the keys
to getting a hot
career is finding
a job you love, a
job you can be
enthusiastic
about.

progresses, there will be even more options for you to choose from.

There are thousands of jobs for you to choose from, some hot, some not. The hottest jobs are those in which you can use your favorite talents. Hot careers are available in every industry. You just have to know where to look.

What's your dream job?

If you could have your dream job, what would it be? You might have to think about this for a while. What would give you passion in your work, and in turn, in your life?

Determining what you want your career to be and where you want it to go is not always easy, but you have to think about it to make it happen. Sometimes it's easier to do this by first establishing what you *don't* like and what you *don't* want to do. This seems simple, but you probably haven't done it yet. Knowing what you don't want to do is as important as knowing what you do want. More than anyone else, you know what you don't like.

The following list will help you determine those things you don't like to do. Let this list be a beginning. Take a clean sheet of paper and add to it with your specific dislikes regarding your work life. Once you've identified some of the things you don't like to do, it's often easier to find out what you enjoy.

Unofficially...
Bill Gates loves
developing prod-
ucts. He probably
would·be doing
the same thing
as a hobby, even
if he didn't
own Microsoft
because to him,
it's fun.

- I don't like working with others.

- I don't like working alone.

- I don't like dealing with people all day. I am not a people person.

- I don't like getting up early in the morning to go to work.

- I don't like working the night shift.
- I don't like being stuck in an office all day.
- I don't like working with numbers.
- I don't like being on my feet eight hours a day.
- I don't like being outdoors in all kinds of weather.
- I don't like doing the same thing day after day.
- I don't like commuting to work an hour every day in each direction.
- I don't like making decisions.
- I don't like working as part of a team.
- I don't like being in charge.

Remember to add your own personal dislikes to this list. Now that you have determined some of the things that you don't like, let's work on what you enjoy doing.

First, get comfortable. Sit in a soft chair or lie on your couch or in bed, and daydream a bit. What can you see yourself doing? Imagine it for a while. Indulge your passions. Make yourself happy. What would you really like to do? Keep in mind that none of your ideas are foolish and let your imagination run wild.

Now that you have some ideas, ask yourself what has stopped you from getting your dream job up to now. Did people tell you that you couldn't do it? Did you lack confidence in yourself? Perhaps you needed more education or training and you didn't think you could afford it or you thought you weren't smart enough. Maybe you think you don't live in the right area for the type of job you want, or you don't have enough contacts in that field. These are just

Timesaver
Keep a pad of paper and pencil or pen close at hand to write down your thoughts. When your ideas are in writing, you can always go back to them. That way you won't have to start over, even if you are interrupted or only have short spurts of time to work on this.

In order to ➜ find the job you love you must determine your interests, know what you enjoy doing, and recognize your skills and personality traits.

FINDING A JOB YOU LOVE

Fill in the blanks of the following sentences.

In my free time, I enjoy going

_____

_____

_____

_____

In my free time, I like to

_____

_____

_____

_____

The last time I volunteered to do something, it was

_____

_____

_____

My hobbies are

_____

_____

_____

_____

My skills are

_____

_____

_____

_____

My best personality traits are

_____

_____

_____

_____

I enjoy being supervised

_____

I would rather supervise myself and others

_____

_____

_____

My current job is

_____

Prior types of jobs included

_____

_____

_____

_____

My best subject(s) in school was (were)

_____

_____

_____

_____

If I could have any three jobs I wanted they would be

_____

_____

_____

What steps can I take to get a job I will love?

_____

_____

_____

_____

_____

_____

_____

_____

_____

_____

_____

excuses. Don't let yourself or anyone else stop you from getting your dream job.

Don't let anyone burst your bubble

When you're excited, you share your ideas with a friend or a family member. Even though they may be trying to be supportive, sometimes friends destroy your dreams by pointing out all the possible problems you might encounter.

For example, they tell you that you don't have enough education to get the job of your dreams. Education is useful and very necessary in many jobs, but it's never a guarantee that you will—or will not—get a job. There are countless hot new jobs available for people who never went to college. Companies that say that they require education often take experience instead.

Other friends burst your bubble by telling you that you don't have enough money to start a home business (or a home based Internet business). Today, more and more people are starting their own businesses. Home businesses are growing by leaps and bounds. Not having enough money is not a good excuse.

People might tell you the economy is bad. Well, it might be, but the people who have money are still spending. Come up with a good idea and you'll get your share of the pie.

Others try to destroy your dreams by telling you you're a "pipe dreamer," that you need a dose of reality. But if you don't dream, you won't do anything with your life and you will stay in that same mediocre job you don't really care about. You'll never have a hot career. I can guarantee that if you don't try, you'll never get the hot job you dream about. The truth is, everything starts with a dream, including getting a new hot job!

Unofficially...
Henry Ford dreamed of building an automobile. Unofficially, it is said, people thought the idea would never work. What would have happened if Henry hadn't followed his dream?

Dream your own dream

So dream. What would make you happy? Make a list of your current and prior jobs and include what aspects of each you liked and didn't like. What are your special talents, skills, and personality traits? What gives you joy and makes you happy? If you know what skills and talents you enjoy using, you have a better chance at finding a more satisfying job.

Let's say you like to design and sew clothing. Consider becoming a seamstress, tailor, or fashion designer. Are you the one who is always volunteering to bake the cakes and cookies for school bake sales? Consider a home business baking and decorating cakes and other baked goods. Can you spend hours on the computer coming up with just the right designs for birthday cards, flyers, and stationery? Consider a job as a graphic designer. Are setting beautiful tables, choosing decorations, and arranging parties right up your alley? Consider becoming a party planner, wedding planner, or event coordinator. Even people whose main hobby is shopping can look into a hot career as a personal shopper.

Bright Idea
If you are creative enough, you can turn any hobby or volunteer activity into a business, career opportunity, or job possibility. It may or may not be very lucrative. Only you can decide what is most important to you.

Turning your dreams into reality

Once you know what your dream is, how can you turn it into reality? First of all, have faith in yourself. You must believe that you can make it happen. It's essential to focus on what you really want. Were you ever eager for something to eat, but not quite sure what you wanted? First you had a sandwich, then a salad; a little later you tried some pizza and a couple of cookies, some potato chips, and on and on. Finally, you had a hot fudge sundae and you were satisfied. You just kept eating until you could find the right thing.

However, if you had known you wanted a hot fudge sundae in the first place and you ate one, you probably would have been satisfied a lot sooner. If you know what you want in your career, it too will be easier to find and achieve.

Remember that you may have to *pay your dues.* Success doesn't always come on the first try. Most people who become movie stars or entertainers, for example, have to start in small theaters or clubs (or on local TV or in commercials). In the world of work, paying your dues may mean that you have to take a job that you don't like for a short time to obtain experience or training or to pick up skills before moving on to the job that you really want. One job can be a stepping stone to another in your career. You have to have patience and perseverance. With effort, you can have a fulfilling career so that you can enjoy going to work every morning.

At this point you may or may not know the exact career you want. Once you can pinpoint where you want to be, you're closer than ever to getting there. Let's look at what might stop you from getting where you want to be:

- *Have you been unable to find the job or career you want?* If you know what you want to do but haven't found that job yet, continue looking.

- *Did you find the perfect job but it wasn't offered to you?* If you found the job you wanted and didn't get it, don't despair. Even though it's hard to believe, things usually work out for the best. There's probably a better job waiting for you in the near future.

Unofficially...
Many people thought Estelle Getty, who played the mother on the TV sitcom *The Golden Girls*, was an overnight success. Getty, who always dreamed of being a successful actress, kept plugging away over the years in non-acting jobs and small acting roles until she got her big break, first in a Broadway play and then in the hit television series.

- *Do you have the necessary skills?* If you don't have the necessary skills for the career you're interested in, now is the time to get them. Check out skills needed for similar jobs by browsing through the later chapters of this book, looking in the newspaper classifieds, and checking out job sites on the Internet.

- *Do you have the required education?* Don't let lack of education stop you from applying for a job. As I mentioned earlier, often companies requiring education will take experience in lieu of educational requirements. Some will accept you if you make a commitment to acquire the necessary education.

- *Do you need additional training?* Look into training you might need for the career that you're interested in. If it's generic training, start now. However, don't go overboard. Training requirements often change quickly as technology changes, and many companies offer on-the-job training.

- *Do you need more experience?* Experience is sometimes a catch-22 situation. It's difficult to get experience if you don't have a job, and you often can't get the job without experience. You can gain experience through internships and apprenticeships. Another solution is to get volunteer experience. For example, if you want to work in advertising and public relations, volunteer to handle those duties for a local not-for-profit organization or community group.

- *Are you in a geographic area where jobs in your chosen field are not readily available?* This is a tough one, but if you're creative enough, you'll find a

Bright Idea
When you volunteer, you not only get experience, you also begin building a network of contacts.

solution. For example, you might locate your chosen position out of the area and see if you might work from home. You might also create a position with either the company you are currently employed by or a new corporation.

Answer these questions honestly. Then, take action to obliterate the obstacles. In order to get the job of your dreams, you need to assess what is required to obtain it, discover the problems, and break down the barriers.

No more Monday Morning Blues

Many people don't like what they do. Do you dislike your job? Perhaps there's nothing wrong with your job, but there really isn't anything right about it either.

Do you like your job? If you don't have a job you love, or at least like, you don't get excited about going to work—as a matter of fact you start to dread it. You go through the day like a robot doing your work but you have no real passion for it. You start to hope for the weekend and wish the rest of the week away. The end result for many is becoming a member of the Monday Morning Blues club.

Are you a member of that club? Here's how you can tell if you belong. Take a moment and think about something. When the alarm clock rings on Monday morning, do you start having that dialogue with yourself—"Oh, God, it's Monday. Only five more days until Friday…" —and that's how you get through your whole week? If so, you have the Monday Morning Blues. Actually, whatever day you start your work week can become like Monday if you don't like your job.

People who belong to the Monday Morning Blues club are also usually members of the Thank

Watch Out!
You can have what others consider the hottest job around, but if you don't like what you're doing it won't be so hot for you. Begin your plan now to take action in your career quest so you'll have a hot job that you love.

Bright Idea
Most of us are in a work environment for a good part of the day and for most of our adult life. For 8 or 10 hours a day, we might as well like what we do.

God It's Friday club. It's time to check out of the TGIF club! Wishing away five days of your week waiting for the weekend is not the answer.

Disliking your job—whether it's because you don't like the job in general or the people you work with, or you just don't like what you do—is not good for anyone. It puts undo stress on you, which in turn puts unnecessary stress on your family, friends, and coworkers. Additionally, if you don't like what you do, you won't be a good employee; and this will make it difficult to excel at your job.

Luckily, there is something you can do about it. There is no reason that you can't find and do something you like. Especially with all the new hot jobs out there ready for the picking. If you find a job you love and get a hot career, you can put an end to the Monday Morning Blues forever.

Take this job and love it

If you've ever had the Monday Morning Blues, this book will help you change all that. Instead of waking up and thinking how you wish you could take your job and shove it, I'm going to help you find a hot career so you can take your job and *love* it. Then you'll be able to hit the jackpot in the job market and get one of the best jobs around.

If you don't currently have a job, it can be frightening. You have no income coming in and you don't know what you're going to do, how you're going to pay the bills, and how you're going to make ends meet. You may have been downsized, laid off, or just plain fired. You might even have quit because you hated your job. Perhaps you've been taking care of your family and now you want to reenter the job market. You might be entering it for the very first time. Maybe you're retired and want to keep busy,

Watch Out!
You shouldn't dread going to work every day. It's not good for you and it's just not necessary. It puts you in a bad mood, it ruins your day, and conceivably could ruin the days of those who are unfortunate enough to have to come in contact with you.

Timesaver
For many, the Monday-Morning Blues begin on Sunday night. Try to put off worrying about Monday by doing something positive regarding your job search on Sunday evening. Update your resume, make phone calls, or write up a list of what you need to do the following week. This will save valuable weekday job-search time.

or you need the money or the social contact that work offers.

Whatever the reason, remember that you can be anything you want to be and do anything you want to do, you just have to be prepared to work at it. That might mean changing jobs, learning new skills, or creating a job or a business. If you don't know what you want to do, that's okay, you have time to figure it out.

If you can take your job and love it, you will always be a winner in the job market. There might be one or two aspects of a job that you probably don't enjoy as much as the others. The trick is making sure you have a job that has more positive aspects than negative ones.

Bright Idea
Keep an eye open for projects that need to be done and offer to handle them. It makes good career sense. You'll learn new skills, meet new people, gain career viability, and be seen as a team player.

Preparing for a hot career

Try to keep up with changes in the marketplace. If you are currently working, be aware of what's happening in your own company. While spreading gossip isn't good, listening to the office grapevine can be a great source of information. What do you hear is going on? What does the trade press say? Is your company moving ahead in the same direction it has been or is it changing course? What do you hear about other companies? Every change, no matter how big or small, could affect you and your career. Even staying the same in a changing marketplace can affect you and your job. Pay attention to what's happening so you can be prepared no matter what the changes.

In today's hot job market, it's essential that you're comfortable and competent using a computer. If you aren't already computer-literate, pick up the skills by taking classes at local high schools or colleges, vo-tech schools, libraries, or any other places they may be offered. Young people who have grown up with computers and technology are also great teachers. Or check the Yellow Pages under "Computers—training."

If you can, become adept at using Macintosh technology as well as PC. While PCs are more prevalent in the workplace, Macs also have their place. You can never tell when the ability to use either platform will put you a step ahead of someone else in the job market.

It's also a good idea to learn to use a variety of software programs, such as WordPerfect or Microsoft Word. Your local or college library may offer videos and books on using the various software packages to help you learn on your own. Video stores may also be a source of rentals to pick up techniques and tips on some of the more popular software programs. If you prefer to learn in a class, schools, colleges, and other computer education specialists may offer the classes you want.

Today, the ability to surf the Internet is also crucial. Whether you are searching for a job, researching information, checking out statistics, or just having fun, you need to get online. Don't panic if you don't have a computer at home. Today many local libraries are online and allow cardholders to use their on-site computers free of charge. Many local colleges also offer similar services, either for free or a nominal fee.

Keep abreast of trends that might affect your career by watching television. Local, regional, national, and international programming provide useful information. Whether you're viewing news broadcasts, business and financial shows, information, or talk and variety programs, you can always learn something. Talk radio can also offer some

Timesaver
A number of search engines on the Internet have news watcher features. This enables you to obtain current news articles from their database of newspapers or magazines online on any subject you specify

Moneysaver
Many people aren't aware that temp agencies offer classes in some of the main software programs. They use the classes to ensure that they have a stable of people ready to send out for jobs. These classes are usually either offered at no charge or for a minimal fee.

useful insights regarding marketplace happenings and emerging trends.

Visit your local library to read a variety of newspapers, magazines, and periodicals. Surf the Internet to find online newspaper and magazine articles regarding your industry or one in which you might be interested.

Don't fall behind. Keep up-to-date on new lingo and language associated with business in general as well as in your field. It's easier to talk shop if you're speaking the language!

Razor-sharp skills cut the competition

In today's ever-changing world, your skills need to be honed constantly. Other people are in the wings keeping their skills razor-sharp, so to remain competitive, you must too. Make an effort to learn something new every day. It doesn't have to be big, just something you didn't know when you woke up that morning. Whether you learn something new by a traditional method or by reading, watching, listening, or talking, never turn down an opportunity to pick up new information.

No matter what career you are considering, try to get the best training and experience you can. This might mean sacrificing time or money working with skilled people who are willing to teach you. Try to take advantage of any apprenticeships, internships, and sound advice offered to you by experts. Every time you're asked to handle a new responsibility or given a different job, look at it as a gift from Lady Luck!

In addition, try to find a mentor, a person who will help guide you in your career goals. A mentor will be very helpful in your career and a good source of contacts. He will be a supportive force in moving you from level to level in your chosen field.

Moneysaver
If your employer offers training, seminars, courses, educational reimbursement, or tuition assistance, take advantage of them. It's not possible to learn too much.

You are not the only one who needs a mentor. Offer to be a mentor to someone else: a coworker, youngster, or older person just reentering the workforce. It doesn't matter who, as long as you are sincerely offering to help that person. You might be tempted to say you are too busy. You don't even have time to get your own career on track—but make the time. After all, you're expecting someone else to be your mentor and to give up her time. While you shouldn't be helping someone else just to help yourself, in helping open doors for others, you often open up doors for yourself as well as feel personal satisfaction. When you improve the life of another, you improve your own life.

Setting specific goals

Be as specific as you can when setting your career goals. Make them clear and concise, especially to yourself. Some people find it easier to reach their goals if they develop a series of goals; others just work toward one goal. It's important to remember that goals are not cast in stone. As you change, they can—and should—change.

A goal also shouldn't be "I want to make a million dollars in some job and I don't really care which one." Money is a good motivator, but you need not only a specific goal, but a plan of action to help you get there. Instead your goal might be to make a million dollars selling real estate, or as a recording artist, author, doctor, lawyer, salesperson, software designer—wherever your interest lies.

It's easier to develop specific, clear, and concise goals by writing them down. You might want to get a notebook that you keep just for working on your career. Jot down new goals as you think of them. Write down where you think you might want to be in

Bright Idea
Update your resume now! Always have a few perfect copies ready in case you come across that perfect job. Don't wait until you need one and have to rush around, perhaps leaving things out by mistake or making errors.

Watch Out!
Your goal should not just be that you want a job. Anyone can get a job doing something. Make your goal more specific: perhaps to get a job in the field of your choice. If you don't focus on the type of job you want, you probably won't get one you like.

your career in the next six months, year, two years, five years, and the distant future. Don't worry about situations changing. You can always adjust your goals to suit what's going on in your life at that moment.

When working on your goals, remember that there are general work-related goals and specific work-related goals. Here are some possible general work-related goals. Use this list to help you get started on defining your goals:

- Getting a promotion by the end of the year
- Obtaining certification for a specific job
- Starting a new career
- Starting a home business
- Becoming a manager or executive
- Changing career fields

Here are some examples of more specific work-related goals. These goals will depend on what you want to do:

- Writing and selling a book
- Getting a job as a reporter at a newspaper
- Becoming a pediatric nurse
- Managing a retail store
- Working with computers
- Becoming a teacher

Your next step is to determine how to achieve these goals—your *actions*. Actions are what make your goals achievable. Write down those actions in your notebook so you can refer to them later. You might not do them all, but they will give you a feeling of power. Seeing what you need to do helps you take the necessary action to get what you want.

Some examples of work-related actions include:

- Starting a new job search
- Networking daily or weekly with new people
- Making new contacts
- Reading the classifieds daily
- Updating your resume
- Going on "practice" interviews
- Updating your skills
- Learning new skills
- Continuing your education
- Getting a degree
- Finding a mentor
- Reading a book or periodical about your chosen field
- Assessing your skills
- Taking a class or seminar in business
- Taking a seminar, class, or workshop in a hobby which you might relate to your career
- Spending 30 minutes a day developing a business plan
- Developing a marketing plan for you and your career
- Volunteering to gain experience in your field

Visualize what you want and make it happen

Visualize what you want. Think about each step you need to take to get where you want to go and see the end result in your mind, and you stand a better chance of success.

Do you want to sell real estate? Visualize it happening. Do you want to be a recording artist?

Visualize yourself making a record. Do you want to work for a newspaper, magazine, or write a book? Think of yourself working at the computer and doing it. Have you thought about a job in health care? Imagine yourself with patients. Do you want to work in an advertising agency or public relations firm, teach in a school, or work in the hospitality industry? Whatever your dream, visualize it, think about it, and the act of visualization will help make it happen. Make a commitment to your dream and stick to it. Without this commitment, your dream will turn into a bubble that will burst.

If you don't know what actions you can or should take, a reverse visualization exercise sometimes works. To do this, you need to visualize starting from the point where you want to be, and going back to the point where you are now. Use this exercise to determine what actions may help you to achieve your goals.

For example, begin by visualizing the job you want. Think about where you'd like to work—your environment, the office decor, the buzz of coworkers, and the excitement of the day. The more details you can add, the better. Now put yourself in the picture. Imagine what you are wearing—the outfit, the colors, the accessories. Think about how you feel on the job; the happiness and excitement you have doing your job. Think about driving in your car to work that first day. Keep visualizing in reverse. Think about getting dressed in the morning. Remember the alarm buzzing and how you couldn't wait to get up.

Keep visualizing. Hear the telephone ringing and see yourself answering to hear the news that you got the job! Think about hoping you would be hired, sending a thank-you note to the interviewer, going to the interview, answering tough questions and filling out applications. Recall finding out about the perfect job and sending your resume and cover letter.

Think about all the preparation you did to find your dream job. The skills you updated, the people you spoke to, the networking, the volunteering to get the experience you needed. Remember all the interviews you went on and the other jobs you applied for and didn't get. In retrospect, you know you were lucky because you now have the hot job you always dreamed about. This technique often works well in preparing an action plan and steps to take for any realistic goals you might set for yourself, whether career-oriented or not.

Finding the hottest careers

Whether you're planning a new career, just entering the job market, or changing careers totally, there is a hot career waiting for you. There are a treasure trove of hot careers for the new century; and later in this book we're going to talk more specifically about a lot of them. You, however, have to decide the hottest career for yourself. The job market today requires people with a multitude of talents and skills. You have to decide which of your talents and skills you want to showcase.

Of course, it's important to watch the trends. But it's impossible to predict the future. So I'm going to help you find some ways to choose a hot job for yourself. That way, even if the economy, technology, or your circumstances change, you will be able to find something you enjoy and still earn a living.

Changes in technology will result in a wider spectrum of opportunities than ever before

Bright Idea
No matter what type of career you are interested in, you need to be comfortable using computers.

in almost every field, from information services, medical technology, the business world, communications, sales, science, engineering, computers, and education, to new home-based businesses. People careers are hot. Whether you're interested in working in the hospitality or travel industries, sales and service, health care, law enforcement, retail, food service, or teaching, you'll have the opportunity to work with others if that is what you choose.

Molding a hot career

Whatever career you are interested in, job satisfaction is essential. Dissatisfaction in the workplace can come from any number of things:

- You feel you are underpaid.
- You feel overworked.
- You aren't doing what you really want to do.
- You are no longer motivated in your job.
- Your job is not mentally stimulating.
- You don't get any (or enough) fringe benefits.
- You don't feel appreciated.
- You're not being promoted fast enough (or at all).
- There is no opportunity for advancement.
- You don't like your boss.
- You don't care for your coworkers.
- You don't like the commute.
- You don't feel you have job security.

   If you already have a job, one of the first things you should determine is if you can mold that job into one that is more fulfilling and satisfying. Sometimes all it takes is a little initiative and push on your part to do this. You can't expect your employer to do it for you. Sit down and think. Come up with an idea, and present it to your employer in a manner that he can't refuse to try. If it were your company, what would you do to make it better? What can you do to make it happen?

Here's one example. Let's say you're a secretary or an administrative assistant. While you enjoy the people you work with, you just aren't fulfilled with that job and the responsibilities. What can you do? You might talk to your supervisor and see if there are more challenging jobs in the company. If there are, fine. What if there aren't? What can you do? It depends on your skills and your aspirations, but perhaps you can mold a new career at the same company. Perhaps you want to be more creative. You like to write, and you do it well. You might suggest a company newsletter to boost employee morale or to let staff know what's going on in the company. It might be sent to existing and prospective clients. You might even do a prototype of the first issue on your computer at home. When an employer sees that you are willing to do an extra bit of work, she will give you additional responsibilities.

Let's say the newsletter idea works. Your employer might incorporate its development and preparation into your work responsibilities. You may be able to advance your career by putting it together, writing it, and editing it. You'll begin to learn more about your company and get to know other employees. This in turn can change your ho-hum job into something you like to do. Maybe it will be worth a raise or a bonus. One way or the other, you have a more interesting job, you have honed a skill, and you've accomplished something you can put on your resume and take with you to other exciting positions.

You might not be able to mold the job you have into something you enjoy more. Perhaps you're bored and burned out, or have other dreams and aspirations. At this point you might have to change jobs or even change your career. But before you do, answer some questions:

- Are you content with your career?

- Do you feel you are doing something worthwhile?

- What are the daily routines and tasks of your job doing to your hopes, dreams, and ambitions?

- Can you look back at your work life when you retire and say you were happy with what you did?

- Will you be able to say you have done and tried everything and lived all of your dreams?

If you could turn your career into one of the hottest jobs around, what would you want?

- More money

- Increased responsibilities

- More challenges

- More job security

- A more secure career field

- A better company to work with

- A better work environment

- Different hours

- Less commuting time

- Increased job satisfaction

Whether you currently have a job and want to change it, or you were downsized, laid off, or fired, or if you're just plain unemployed and looking for a new job and a new career, this is what we're going to

Bright Idea
It doesn't matter what you want in a hot career. It might be something I've listed or something you've thought up. Don't settle for less. You *can* have a better career!

try to do together. I will give you the information to find a job and a career that makes you happy.

Changing your career path

The millennium may bring upheaval. Companies are merging and being acquired in great numbers; others are forming alliances to become stronger in the marketplace. You need to be prepared now in case your company is sold, and the new owner decides to change personnel or job functions. In mergers, some people inevitably are let go and others are shifted to jobs they may not want.

Now is the time to take stock of what you have and what you don't have. Now is the time to decide what you want. Will you have to change jobs? Or will you have to change your entire career path? The answer is up to you.

You can't change your past, but you can change your future. You should not have to settle for a nowhere job and a nowhere life. You deserve more. You can enjoy your job and your life to the fullest. You can be happy. At the very least, if you take a positive course of action, you are doing something. Start changing your career path now for the better. Do it for you. Things might not happen overnight, but with some effort you can have a fulfilling hot job that you enjoy going to every morning.

Just the facts

- By thinking about what you want and arming yourself with an action plan, you *can* find a great hot job.

- To put an end to Monday-Morning Blues, determine your dream job—the work that you would love to do.

- To make yourself marketable, keep your skills up-to-date and razor-sharp.

- Set clear, concise, and specific goals for yourself.

- Hot jobs can be discovered in almost every career area. Be creative.

GET THE SCOOP ON...
The hidden job market ▪ Classifieds ▪
Using the Internet ▪ Job fairs

Chapter 2

Looking for Jobs in All the Right Places

Do you know where to find a job? Do you know where to start your job search? To many, the job search begins and ends with classifieds. People devour the classifieds daily hoping to find their dream job…and if they don't see it advertised, they just give up.

In the last chapter I discussed how to determine what your dream job is. This chapter will cover where to look for your hot new dream job so you don't have to *settle* for something you really don't want. Once you find your hot job, you're on your way to getting it.

There are many methods of job searching in addition to scanning the classified section of newspapers. This chapter will discuss them.

The hidden job market

There are literally thousands of opportunities for employment. Job openings are advertised in a variety of places or manners. These may include the following:

- Newspaper classifieds
- Display advertisements
- Store window signs
- Radio ads
- Television commercials
- Trade journals
- Periodicals
- Newsletters
- Internet Web sites
- Bulletin boards
- Employment postings
- Your college or technical school
- Job hot lines

It's important to realize that many jobs are not advertised. These positions are often referred to as the *hidden job market.*

Unofficially...
It's estimated that 80 to 85 percent of the jobs available today are not actively advertised.

The hidden job market covers every industry and many positions. The hidden job market is difficult to locate. Lists of jobs are not just sitting there waiting for you to find them. Why should you consider looking for the hidden job market?

- There's a lot less competition. As jobs are not actively advertised, hundreds of people are not sending their resumes to the same P.O. box.

- Positions in the hidden job market are often better jobs. The majority of the jobs in the hidden job market are not entry level. This does not mean that no such jobs are entry level. If you are creative enough, savvy enough, and see a need, you might be able to create a position for yourself even if you are only on the first rung of the career ladder.

- When you find the hidden job market, you have an edge over other job applicants who can't find it or don't want to waste their time looking.

- You often come recommended by someone who knew about the opening. This means you already have one foot in the door.

- When you are available, you make yourself convenient and immediately accessible to those who are seeking to fill a need or a position.

Filling jobs in the hidden job market

How are positions filled in the hidden job market? Here are a few ways:

- Employees may be promoted from within a company.

- Networking through contacts and connections.

- Applicants may send resumes or letters to be kept on file.

- Suitable candidates may place cold calls to a company at the right time.

- An employee working in the company may recommend candidates.

- Someone who knows about an opening may tell friends, relatives, or coworkers.

- Savvy job seekers may create positions to fill needs.

- Headhunters, search firms, or recruiting firms may be used.

- Companies may run recruitment events themselves.

In the last chapter we discussed the lucky people who have the hot jobs they love. Chances are that many of those lucky people found their dream jobs

Watch Out!
Some jobs that start out in the hidden market eventually may move to the public job market if they're not filled. The majority, however, are snapped up quickly. When you see or hear of an interesting opportunity, jump on it immediately before it becomes public knowledge.

through the hidden job market. They worked hard to find their jobs. Using the hidden job market is a skill that requires networking, research, drive, determination, and the ability to be creative.

Networking to find a hidden job

How can *you* find a job in the hidden market? There are many ways. Networking is one method. I will cover networking more completely in Chapter 4. At this point, however, it's essential to realize that networking is extremely important for finding great jobs.

In job hunting, as in everything else, it's not always what you know, but who you know. Being at the right place at the right time doesn't hurt either.

How can you network? You probably already have a long list of people you know. If you don't have a list, make one. You may be surprised to find that you know a lot of people. Get out there and meet more. You can never tell who might know about a possible opening.

The most successful network includes of a variety of people from all walks of life. These include:

- Friends (or friends of friends)
- Family members
- Friends of family members
- Coworkers
- Members of professional associations, clubs, or civic groups to which you belong
- Your dentist, doctor, or pharmacist
- Your hairstylist
- The butcher
- The checkout clerk at the local grocery
- The mail carrier or delivery person

Unofficially... Join your local chamber of commerce. Many have networking events where you can meet business people from your area. It's a great way to meet people who are active in the business community. Professional organizations are also great places to network.

- The waitress at your favorite restaurant
- The counter person at the local coffee or donut shop
- A teacher or professor
- Your child's teacher
- Your priest, pastor, rabbi, or members of your religious congregation
- Your neighbors

People you know are primary contacts in your network. Those you are referred to by others, such as a friend of a friend, are secondary contacts. Everybody you come in contact with can become part of your network.

The right place, the right time

Sometimes you hear about a job opening from an unlikely source. Perhaps you just happen to be at the right place at the right time. For example, your hairstylist may tell you that the customer who had the appointment before you was talking about how short-handed they were at her office because the company CPA was just fired. If you're looking for a job as a CPA, you're in luck! Or you might be having lunch with a friend at a local restaurant and the service is not as good as usual. Perhaps while your server was giving you the check, she apologized for the service and mentioned that the restaurant was more hectic than usual because the manager had just quit unexpectedly. If you were looking for a managerial position in the food and beverage industry, this might be a good opportunity for you.

The larger your network, the more opportunities you'll have in finding a job in the hidden job market. Who do you deal with every day, every week, and every month? Who do these individuals know

Bright Idea
If the company you are working for uses a package delivery service such as UPS, Federal Express, or Airborne Express, develop a relationship with the delivery person. These individuals know a lot about what's happening in businesses on their route, and they often know it first.

Bright Idea
Don't be afraid to ask people if they know of openings in their organization or who you might contact.

and deal with? All of these people may potentially know about your dream job. The more people who know what you have to offer and what you are looking for, the better. Tell people what your skills are and what kind of job you're after. Jobs in the hidden market are often filled by word of mouth and referral.

How else can networking, contacts, and connections help you? Asking for advice is always a good bet. Most people like to feel needed and help others. Some things you might say are:

- "I'm looking for a job working for a newspaper. Do you have any idea where I might get information for my job search?"

- "You were very successful in your job before you retired. I'm interested in working in the same field. When you have some time, could you spare 10 minutes to give me some advice?"

- "I'm looking for a job in fitness and nutrition. Do you know of any organizations or associations I should join to meet people who might be helpful in my job search?"

- "Do you know of any job openings in this field?"

- "Do you know of any other people I should talk to?"

Watch Out!
Make sure you aren't overstaying your welcome. While people are usually more than happy to help, they are busy too. If you ask for 10 or 15 minutes of someone's time, stick to it.

At the end of the interview, ask for the interviewer's card and ask if you may call if you have a question. After every interview or meeting, send a note, such as the one shown below, thanking the person you spoke to. In addition to showing good manners, this keeps your name and phone number in front of someone who might hear of an opening.

Before you start networking, it's important to know what you want. As we discussed in the first

---

Ruby Stratton
P.O. Box 123
Anytown, NY 12345
800-555-5678

Mr. Jim Edwards
Edwards & Edwards
421 Main Street
Anytown, NY 12345

Dear Mr. Edwards:

Thanks for taking the time to discuss opportunities working as a paralegal. I have already contacted Ms. Evans as you suggested and plan on meeting with her next week.

I appreciate your help and your time. I will keep you updated with my career.

Yours truly,

Ruby Stratton

---

chapter, make sure your goals are clear, so you can tell others exactly what you're looking for.

Remember that you need to take action to get results. So if you have to, push yourself to get out and about. Your activities don't have to be expensive or complicated. Your goals are to see, meet, and talk to more people so that you see what is happening outside your immediate circle. You might see a help-wanted sign or get an idea about finding your dream job. You don't need to go expensive places. You just need to do something. If you're changing careers, you need to meet new people in the career you're moving to. You can do any of the following simple things:

- Go to the grocery store
- Window-shop at the mall
- Go to a real estate agent's open house
- Go to a museum or library
- Take a class
- Visit a friend
- Volunteer at a hospital or school
- Go to a local theater production

Join professional associations, civic groups, and organizations you are interested in, and attend their meetings. Part of networking is becoming visible to others. When you go to meetings, don't just sit on the sidelines. Speak up and offer suggestions. Get involved. Volunteer for projects or to work on committees. For example, depending on your skills, you might offer to:

- Do publicity
- Handle the bookkeeping
- Make refreshments
- Run an event
- Organize a fund-raiser
- Serve on the membership committee
- Design brochures
- Take the meeting minutes
- Contact a business to cosponsor an event

The more visible you are, the more people will remember you and your skills. Then when someone hears about a job opening, your name will come to mind.

Spreading the word

If you aren't employed, or are in a job you aren't planning on staying in, don't keep your job search a secret. Tell everybody what you are interested in doing. Ask advice. Talk to people. The more people who know about your aspirations, the better your chance that someone might hear of an opening and refer you.

If you are employed, it can be difficult to make your job search public. What can you do? Even if you don't like your job, make yourself visible in your workplace. You might, for example, ask for additional responsibilities or ask to work on a project so that you will gain new skills or experience.

It may be acceptable to let your supervisor know how you are interested in advancing your career at the company. If he knows, your name might pop into his mind when a new position opens up.

Research the news

Do research and check out local newspapers. They contain a wealth of information that may be useful in your job hunt. Look through the entire newspaper. You can find:

- *Articles on new businesses.* New businesses mean jobs.

- *Blurbs on people who are being promoted.* Promotions mean openings.

- *Blurbs on employees who are retiring.* Retiring employees may mean openings.

- *Feature stories on companies in your area.* If you get creative, you might find a niche for yourself.

- *News articles with the correct names and titles of people working in area companies.* Consider giving them a call or sending a letter to see if you can set up an informational interview.

> **"**
>
> While working at a go-nowhere job in sales, I volunteered to do publicity and fund-raising for a local library. Eight months later, a member of the library board told me about a great job as public relations director for a local college where she was also a board member. She recommended me and I got the job.
> —Judy B.
>
> **"**

- *Blurbs about honors or awards business people receive.* Send a brief note of congratulations.

- *Stories about new products.* If there is a name in the story, you might call that person to inquire about opportunities.

- *News about companies being awarded contracts.* More business often means more job opportunities.

- *Profiles of business people in the news.* These give you the names of people and companies to contact.

In addition to dailies and weeklies, many places also have business journals that can be especially helpful.

You might call a person you read about. Tell them you noticed the article in the paper and you were wondering if they could use someone with your skills. If you do this, it's important to develop a script. Rehearse it, and be able to get your key points out quickly. Here's an example of how to get started. Read it over and develop your own script.

> *You:* Hello, Mr. Jones? My name is Brian White. I noticed the article in the paper about your promotion to sales manager of the Green Roof Resort.
>
> *Mr. Jones:* Do I know you?
>
> *You:* No, I just read the article and wanted to congratulate you...
>
> *Mr. Jones:* Well, thanks for calling. I appreciate it.
>
> *You:* I'm looking for a position in the hospitality industry in sales and was wondering if you might be interested in someone with my skills.
>
> *Mr. Jones:* Well, hiring is usually done through Human Resources, but at long as you're on the

Bright Idea
Build business relationships with others in your business community. If you learn that Mr. Jones of the XYZ company was elected president of the Kiwanis, drop him a note of congratulations at his workplace. You don't necessarily have to know him personally. Enclose a copy of the article. If you later contact him about a possible job, he will either remember your name or it will at least seem familiar.

phone, I may be looking for a sales representative.

You: Perhaps I could meet with you at your office tomorrow to discuss it...or would Wednesday be better?

Mr. Jones: Why don't you come by tomorrow morning at 10 with a copy of your resume.

You: Thanks, I'll be there. Let me leave you my phone number in case you have a scheduling problem. I look forward to meeting you.

You should also prepare a generic letter, such as the one below, that you can personalize and send to people whom you have read about. It can be as simple as "Congratulations on your new position." Or you might use the opportunity to congratulate them and begin selling yourself.

Classified ads: The pros and cons

Classified advertisements are one of the best ways to attract employees to job openings. When you are unemployed or looking for a new job, where is the first place you look? Chances are, you pull open the newspaper and check out the help-wanted section.

Are the classifieds the best place to go when job searching? There are pros and cons. You can't lose anything by looking, and you might find yourself a great job. However, you should not rely solely on these ads. For the most complete job search, use every possible avenue to look for good job opportunities.

There are some positions which are required by law to be advertised, including many government jobs. These are often advertised in the classifieds as well as through newsletters or job postings.

One of the major problems in applying for jobs advertised in the classifieds is the sheer number of

Timesaver
When you find pertinent articles, tear them out of the newspaper immediately, highlight them, and keep them in a filing system or folder. You'll save valuable time looking for the article later. Try to take some action within the week, such as writing a short note or calling for an interview.

Bright Idea
Many career centers have computers that you can use to type your resume and cover letters. Some have people that can help you if you're unfamiliar with computers or can't type. Look for career centers in schools, vo-tech centers, colleges, state labor department offices, and libraries.

Bill Johnson
125 First Street
Hometown, NY 10010
888-555-4567

September 23, 1999
Ms. Merry Cross
Vice President of Marketing and Public Relations
Green Roof Resort
Greentown, NY 10010

Dear Ms. Cross:

Congratulations on your promotion and new job! I am sure you will have a great deal of success in your new position. If you are seeking additional members of your marketing team at the Green Roof Resort, I would appreciate being considered. I am seeking a position in marketing, public relations, or special events.

I have held my current job as a marketing assistant at the River Shopping Center for the last two years. My degree, with a major in marketing and public relations and a minor in hotel administration, was earned at State College. Over the past two years, I have been responsible for the creation and implementation of special events and promotions at the Hometown Mall. As a result of my efforts, foot traffic at the mall has been tripled. Additional responsibilities include helping to develop advertising campaigns, writing press releases, and dealing with the media.

I would like to be on your winning team helping to make Green Roof Resort even better known than it is. I will call your office next week to discuss the possibility.

Once again, congratulations.

Sincerely,

Bill Johnson

responses they can elicit. A great job is advertised and everybody wants the job. This means that you probably will have a lot of competition in getting your application singled out and read.

Your goal in responding to a classified ad is first to get an interview and then to get the job. There are ways to boost your chances of success when using the classifieds in your job search. Here are some tips:

- If the ad specifies you must fax or send a letter and/or resume, make sure your material is neatly typed and presented. No one wants to read something that is difficult to understand. If you can't type, find someone who can to help you.

- Send a cover letter with your resume, whether or not one is requested. Tailor the letter to the job you're applying for.

- Proofread your resume and cover letter carefully to catch any grammatical and typographical errors. You might also want to give them to a friend to read.

- If possible, call the company and try to find out who will make the final hiring decision. If possible, send your letter and resume to that person's attention instead of to Personnel or Human Resources.

- If you're not sending your letter to the person who can hire you, wait two or three days before responding to a classified ad. Personnel often receives the greatest number of responses in the first couple of days after the ad appears. Yours will receive more attention if it comes in after the first batch.

Watch Out!
Never send your salary history with a job application, even if the ad specifies you should or your application won't be accepted without it. If they like you, they can often find the extra money to compensate you. If they know your salaries from past jobs, and they want to hire you, negotiating upwards may be difficult. If pressed, you might give a salary range that would be both acceptable to you and within the norms of your specific industry.

Timesaver
Keep copies of the advertisements you are responding to and of the letters and resumes you send. That way when people call to set up interviews or want to do phone interviews, you can refer to the ad and what you said in your letter.

■ Remember that classifieds specify what an employer wants; not necessarily what she will get. Apply for positions you are interested in whether or not you meet all the requirements.

The classifieds are usually largest in the Sunday papers, as opposed to weekday papers or other publications. National papers may also feature large numbers of ads on other days. For a complete job search using the classifieds, go through the entire classified section. Job titles differ from company to company. The duties of these jobs may be similar but their names may be different.

Large newsstands or bookstores like Borders and Barnes & Noble often carry the Sunday edition of newspapers from various cities throughout the country. Many libraries also have the Sunday editions of newspapers from other locations. This is helpful if you are searching for your hot job out of your area.

If you can't find the newspapers you are looking for, you can usually call the newspaper directly and order a Sunday subscription for a short period of time (for the length of your expected job search).

A hot job is just a mouse click away

The World Wide Web has changed the way we do everything. Today, you can find a new hot job from the comfort of your home (or the library) using your computer and the Internet. The World Wide Web holds a wealth of opportunities. You just have to know where to look and what you're looking for.

There are countless job sites full of databases containing job openings and opportunities. Some carry all kinds of jobs, while others are industry-specific. Some allow candidates to post online

Watch Out!
Be careful when replying to *blind ads*. Blind ads are classifieds that don't mention a company name. In responding to a blind ad, you could be applying to the same company you're working for!

resumes, read career advice, and participate in career chats.

Some of the more popular career sites are:

- The Monster Board (www.monster.com)

- Career Mosaic (www.careermosaic.com)

- Hot Jobs (www.hotjobs.com)

- Career Path (www.careerpath.com)

In addition, many companies have their own Web sites. A company's site usually contains that company's employment opportunities. In many cases, you can even e-mail (short for "electronic mail") a resume or job application.

Use the Internet to research information vital to your job search. You can find:

- Information about the industry or field you'd like to enter

- Information about specific companies

- Names and addresses of key people in companies

- Annual reports

- Company Web sites

- News stories and articles about companies and business

- News stories and articles about careers

- Career sites

- Employment opportunities

- Online business journals and newspapers

You can also learn about many large companies, check out their track records, and secure other useful information. Use a traditional search or try logging on to a business information site such as www.hoovers.com. This site will help you get

Moneysaver
You can save money and browse the Sunday classifieds from all over the country and the world for free. Log on to your computer (or a library computer) and search for a newspaper in the area you are researching. Most of the large city papers online also feature the classifieds.

Timesaver
Make it a rule to keep your job search file near your telephone. If people call, you'll be ready. You won't have to run around looking for the file and you won't sound flustered.

Bright Idea
To look up any-
thing on the
Internet, use a
search engine
(such as
www.yahoo.com
or www.
google.com).
Invest some time
in it. Treat the
search engine as
a computer pro-
gram that you
need to learn
how to use.

information on thousands of companies, as well as link you to specific company Web sites.

As no site holds every job, to do the most complete job search, surf around. Most search engines such as Excite, Yahoo, Netscape, and Infoseek offer career sites with valuable career advice, job postings, and links to other career sites and databases. Once there, you can look for more specific information.

With the help of the Internet, you can also access Usenet Newsgroups. These are similar to electronic bulletin boards where you can find a treasure trove of information. You can find job postings, advice, and discussions about topics related to your industry.

A prospect's paradise: Job fairs

Job and career fairs offer excellent opportunities to meet employers and recruiters who are actively searching for candidates to fill job openings. These events are virtual gold mines for job hunters. Opportunities at these fairs include:

- The opportunity to network
- The opportunity to learn about companies, employers, or industries
- The opportunity to learn about job openings
- The opportunity to meet with many potential employers in a short period of time
- The opportunity to be evaluated by numerous recruiters in one day

Timesaver
To save time
when searching
for a company's
Web site first try
using the name
of the company
in the address:
www.thename-
ofthecompany.
com. Although
this doesn't
always work, it
gives you a start.

There are a variety of job and career fairs. Events are put on by professional expo firms or sponsored by specific companies or industries, schools, colleges, or agencies, and each has its own value. Some are very large; others are small. Some feature a variety of employers and industries; others are industry-specific, focusing on hot careers such as health care or computer technology.

Depending on the job fair and employer needs, companies may offer positions from entry level to executive. Job fairs are a win-win solution for everybody. Employers need people and people need jobs. They put the two together for mutual evaluation.

Job fairs are often advertised in the newspaper, in business journals, and in industry publications. If you're looking for an industry-specific fair, call a large employer in that industry and ask someone in Human Resources where fairs are located. Schools, colleges, and labor departments can also help you locate upcoming fairs.

Many sponsors of job fairs offer seminars to help you prepare for the job fair. These are useful if you've never attended a job fair or if you're reentering the workforce and need to brush up on skills and techniques. Call before the event to see if any type of job fair preparation is offered. Job fairs may also offer seminars throughout the day on various careers and career-oriented topics. These are often interesting and give you the opportunity to pick up tips, tricks, and techniques that may be helpful in your job search.

In order to succeed at a job fair, it's essential that you prepare in advance. Follow these tips:

1. Dress for success. Potential employers will be evaluating you when they meet you. Their first impression may be all they remember about you. Dress neatly, conservatively, and professionally. Dress as you would for an in-person job interview.

Unofficially...
Don't be afraid to ask questions of potential employers to determine if you're interested in working at a specific company. Ask about what types of positions are available, what type of training is offered, career paths, the type of work environment, benefits, and so on.

2. Bring plenty of copies of your resume. Your resume should be typed perfectly with no grammatical errors. It should be printed on clean, unfolded 8 ½ × 11–inch paper. Make sure you bring enough copies so you can hand them out freely to recruiters at each booth you stop at. Keep copies neat in a large envelope or folder. If you don't use an attaché case or portfolio, the envelope or folder you carry your resume in will also be useful for material employers hand out.

3. Bring a couple of pens with you to fill out applications.

4. Get to the job fair early. These events often get very busy. If the fair begins at 9:00 a.m., you might want to arrive around 8:30.

5. Visit the booths of the companies or employers you are most interested in first. It's more difficult to talk to recruiters when there are a lot of people around.

6. Practice what to say, so you can quickly tell recruiters what your basic skills are and what type of job you want. The environment often gets quite hectic.

7. Contact someone at each booth you visit. Don't just walk up, grab some information, and leave.

8. From each booth you visit, obtain a business card with a name and phone number of someone you can contact later.

9. Visit all the booths that may have good opportunities. Don't just stop at one or two, go through an interview, and leave. The more interviews you have and contacts you make, the better your chance of getting the job you want.

At the job fair you may be asked to fill out applications and either be interviewed or pre-interviewed on the spot. Recruiters may also request that you make an appointment for an interview at a later date.

If you're offered a job on the spot, you have the option of accepting immediately or thanking them for the opportunity and saying you would like to call with your decision the next day. Either is acceptable. Calling the next day may give you a better chance to negotiate your salary and package.

Even if you're not offered a job, keep in contact with the recruiter. She may have other opportunities down the line that might be perfect for you.

Let them find you—Headhunters and employment agencies

Wouldn't it be great if someone called you and asked you if you were interested in interviewing for the hot job you've been searching for? Can't happen, you say. Think again. It can and does happen with the help of a headhunter.

Executive search firms work with client companies to find candidates with the right qualifications for specific job openings. The search firm uses a headhunter or recruiter to find the candidate. In small search firms, the recruiter may also be the owner of the company.

Recruiters work with their clients in a number of ways. Some work on a contingency. This means that the recruiter isn't paid a fee unless he finds a candidate who is hired by the client. Recruiters may be paid a retainer whether or not they find a suitable candidate. No matter which way the recruiter works, *you* are never charged. Recruiters or search firms earn their money from the client by receiving from

Unofficially...
A pre-interview gives potential employers the opportunity to see if you would be a good candidate for their company. During a pre-interview an employer usually doesn't go into a great deal of depth. He or she just makes sure you have the basic qualifications and may answer some of your questions. In many cases a generalist does the pre-interview and a specific department head handles the next interview.

Bright Idea
Remember to bring the names, addresses, and phone numbers of references with you in case you need to supply these on applications. Don't forget to ask people in advance if you plan to use them as references.

Bright Idea
Headhunters might call you at work and ask whether you know of anyone who might be a possible candidate. If you're not interested yourself but know of a possible candidate, refer them.

the firm the equivalent of a percentage (approximately 30 to 35 percent) of the first year's earnings of the individual they are placing.

How headhunters work

Headhunters contact people who are working in the industry in which they need to fill an opening and ask for referrals. They also call people who are currently working in a job similar to the one they are attempting to fill.

If a headhunter calls you at work and offers you a job you want, proceed quietly. Get his phone number and ask if you can contact him later when you're not at work. It's not a good idea to talk to the headhunter from your office, or to tell coworkers about the call at this point.

Recruiters will frequently target professional membership lists as well as people who are prominent in various organizations. The more visible you are, the better your chances of catching the eye of a headhunter. As I mentioned earlier, use your contacts, join organizations, volunteer, and look for opportunities to get your name in the news. It's perfectly acceptable to "toot your own horn" when you have accomplishments. Write and send announcements to your local paper and to radio and television stations when you have been promoted, received an award, or do anything noteworthy. Just as you might use this information about others in your job search, a recruiter might use it in his job.

Contacting recruiters

You might want to contact a recruiting consultant yourself. There are countless executive search firms located throughout the country. These companies are often advertised in the Yellow Pages of your local phone book under "Executive Search Firms,"

"Search Firms," "Executive Search Consultants," or "Executive Recruiters." To find recruitment firms or consultants who specialize in the industry in which you are interested, also check out trade journals and periodicals.

Once you find the firms you want to contact, send them a resume with a cover letter. If you don't hear from them in a week or two, give them a call. If you can, set up an interview.

Headhunters can be a boon to your career. Keep in contact with them at various recruitment firms even after you get your dream job. You never can tell, they might be able to help you again. Call occasionally just to thank them for helping you get a great job, to say hello, or to refer other candidates. Send holiday cards, short notes, interesting articles, and anything else to keep your name in their mind.

Employment agencies

Employment agencies are another avenue to consider when looking for your new hot job.

Agencies often advertise jobs in the newspaper under the banner of their agency. Check out the ads to see what type of jobs various agencies have. Some may specialize in certain industries or types of jobs. Remember that agencies only advertise a small number of their openings. They usually have many more available.

To find out what jobs are available, you usually must:

1. Make an appointment.
2. Bring in your resume.
3. Fill out an application.
4. Be interviewed by an agency representative.

Remember that you have to sell yourself—your skills and marketability—to the employment agency

Watch Out!
Because recruiters work for the client company, their loyalty lies with them, not you. Don't give any information to the recruiter that you wouldn't want an employer to know.

Unofficially...
Before you sign any agreements at an employment agency, find out who is responsible for the fee if they find you a job—you or the employer. In the best agencies, the fees are paid by the employer. Always ask first. Fees can be costly.

representative before you even interview with a potential employer. Always dress professionally when you go to the employment agency. If they feel you're qualified, they might set up an immediate interview with a potential employer.

Will cold calls work for you?

When you think of a cold call, you might think of one of those salespeople who calls you during dinner, trying to sell something. They don't know you, but they get your phone number and call you...and call you...and call you. Would you buy anything from them?

You might say no. But the fact is, if they were selling something you wanted, you might. Telemarketing is a fact of life because it pays off. When you make a cold call to a potential employer, you are selling yourself, your skills, and your services. Can you make them seem so great on the phone that you can get an interview? If you can, you have it made. Securing an interview on a cold call is a great achievement.

Some people insist they are just no good at this. I say, try. It may pay off big time. What's the worst that can happen?

What should you say? You might try starting a cold call with something like this:

Hello, Mr. Thomson? My name is Mary Jones. I'm not sure you're the right person to talk to about this. Can I take a moment of your time to run it by you so you can point me in the right direction if you're not? Thank you.

I have a bachelor's degree in Communications and I've been a staff writer for a number of newspapers. Does your company have

Bright Idea
Your first cold call is also a practice call—if anything goes wrong, you will learn from your mistake.

someone on staff who does corporate newsletters? Do you think they might be interested in someone who does?

At this point, Mr. Thomson may or may not be interested. If he is, ask if you can send him a resume and set up an interview. If he isn't or he says they have someone, ask if you can send a resume anyway and have it kept on file. Then, let two or three months go by and call again. You might also ask if he knows of other companies that might need someone with your skills.

You need to develop a list of people to call who might have openings or know of job possibilities. This list can come from a number of sources, including:

- The Yellow Pages of your local phone book
- Business listings in the newspaper
- Business people who you have read about in the newspaper
- Chamber of commerce listings of businesses
- Advertisements of businesses
- The Internet

The more calls you make, the more you increase your chances of success in getting potential interviews. Expect rejection when making cold calls. Not every person you call will want to talk to you. Just remember, it's not a personal rejection.

Creating the job that doesn't exist

As you learned in Chapter 1, some of the best jobs are those that didn't exist until enthusiastic, eager individuals with a little initiative created them. How can you create a job that doesn't yet exist? Think about it. What could you do for the company you

Unofficially...
If you can't get past the secretary, get creative. Call early in the morning before the secretary gets in, at lunchtime, or after hours. Keep calling, and you will eventually get through. If you get voice mail, leave a message with your name and phone number and say you'll call back later.

work for that isn't being done now? What could you do for a company you are interested in working for? Just because a job is not advertised doesn't mean that it doesn't or couldn't exist.

Come up with an idea, develop it in your mind, put it on paper, and then bring it to the attention of those who can use it. It doesn't have to be a new idea, it just has to be an idea that a company needs. For example, could the local radio station benefit from a promotion coordinator? Could a large business in your community need a concierge for their busy executives? Might there be a need for an event planner at a local hotel? Could a big corporation benefit from having an in-house chef to prepare lunches on site? What about a nutritionist or fitness trainer? Think of the possibilities and create your own job.

Just the facts

- Use available resources when searching for your hot dream job.
- Look for jobs in the hidden job market as well as those that are advertised.
- Networking increases your chances of finding a great job.
- Check out the Internet for lots of job search possibilities.

GET THE SCOOP ON...
Should you leave your job or stick it out? ▪
Making your job better ▪ Succeeding when
reentering the workforce ▪ Dealing with
unemployment ▪ Symptoms of stress
and burnout

When Is Your Career Hot Enough? Career Transition

Chapter 3

Is your career hot enough? Are you happy doing what you're doing? If the answer to either of these questions is "no," what should you do? What can you do?

This chapter will help you determine if your career is hot and what to do if it's not. Should you stay at your present job, try to reinvent your position, or quit and move on? Only you can answer these questions. This chapter will help you decide what to do and how to do it. It will also offer you some tips for success if your career is in a slump because you've been downsized, fired, or are reentering the workforce.

To go or not to go...that is the question

Many people stay in a ho-hum job simply because it's easier to stay than to leave. Does this sound like you?

There are risks to quitting your present job. Can you deal with the uncertainty and confusion? When

Bright Idea
Preparation and
planning are
your keys to a
successful career
change. If possi-
ble, prepare for a
change while you
are still
employed.

you think about leaving a job, you start asking yourself questions:

- What about your family?

- Can you afford to be unemployed for a period
  of time?

- If you are unemployed, what will you put on
  your resume to cover that gap?

- What would you lose if you left? Benefits, retirement plans, security?

What if you want job satisfaction and you don't
have it? Or worse than that, what if you hate your job
and it's making your life a living hell? You need to
do something, but what? You need a plan.

The pros and cons of your current job

To begin with, you have to clear your mind and
think about the situation rationally. To do this you
need to make a written list of the pros and cons of
your current job.

Your list of "pros" might include the following:

- You are employed.

- You have a steady paycheck.

- You have some benefits.

- You like some of your coworkers.

- You only have a 15-minute commute each way.

- You feel secure in your job.

- Your current employer offers in-house child
  care.

Now that you've determined what the pros of
your current job, decide what the cons are. Make a
written list of these too. Take your time. What don't
you like about your job? Your list of "cons" might
include the following:

- You don't see any chance of advancement.

- You don't like your boss.

- You don't like a couple of your coworkers.

- There is an office backstabber who is always taking credit for what you do and trying to get your job.

- Your job is too stressful.

- You're worried about being downsized.

- You hear via the grapevine that your company is being acquired and you don't feel very secure.

- You feel that you're not being compensated adequately for what you do.

- The commute is too long.

- The hours are too long.

- This is not what you want to do for the rest of your life.

- You have no passion for what you're doing.

- You aren't allowed to use your creativity.

- You are bored and burned out.

Bright Idea
Even if you're not sure whether you want to change jobs, it doesn't hurt to browse. Check out the classifieds, attend job fairs, and look at job postings on the Internet to see what's available (see Chapter 2). Depending on your situation, it might be critical that you keep your "browsing" a secret from your current employer. If this is the case, do your "browsing" on your own time, and don't use the computer/Internet access at work to conduct your research.

Staying or going

Now look at your lists. Is a weekly paycheck worth more to you than long hours? Is in-house child care worth more to you than not having any passion for your work? Is being so stressed that you're getting physically ill worth any job? Everything is a compromise. To make your choice, you need to decide what is important and what isn't important.

Retaining employees saves employers money. Employers, therefore, generally want to keep good employees. If you have a problem with your job, your supervisor might want to help. If you don't speak up and discuss the problem, he can't even try

Watch Out!
Don't make any final decisions about leaving your job when you are ill, depressed, or have other problems on your mind. It's difficult to think clearly when you're not at your best.

Unofficially...
While there are exceptions to every situation, in most cases you are not eligible to receive unemployment if you quit your job unless you do so for a specific cause such as harrassment. In these cases, it would be wise to have documentation to use in an unemployment hearing.

to change it. It's important to try to improve things before you decide to leave.

With that in mind, let's look at some of the "cons" on the list and see what you could do to negate them. Do you just *think* there's no chance to advance in your current job or is there really no hope? You might want to talk to your supervisor about advancement opportunities. Find out what she might think is holding you back. Could new skills, education, or training be helpful? You'll never know if you don't ask.

Working with a difficult boss can have consequences. People who deal with difficult bosses on a day-to-day basis frequently experience a range of both physical and emotional problems. Dealing with a difficult boss can make you unhappy at work as well as at home. If you don't like your boss but you like your job and the company, you might ask to be reassigned or transferred to another section of the organization. This isn't always feasible, but it's worth a try.

Consider meeting with your boss to discuss exactly what she expects from you. Simply explain that you want to meet her expectations and want to be sure you are on track.

There are a lot of people who leave jobs because they don't like their coworkers or the workplace politics. If you are working with a backstabber who is always taking credit for what you do, trying to make you look bad, and is after your job, the only thing you can really do is wait and hope people realize what the backstabber is doing. Stooping to his level makes you look bad every time.

If you feel that your job is too stressful, try some stress-reduction techniques or look for a stress-management program. Determine if the job is the source of stress or if there are other sources of stress in your life.

Realizing that stressed employees are never at their best, many companies are now concerned about stress in the workplace. Check with the Human Resources department at your company to see if they offer programs on stress management.

If you're worried about being downsized, or you hear your company may be acquired and you don't feel very secure about the future, you need to begin working on your plan to find a new hot job. That way you'll be in the driver's seat when and if it happens. Even if you don't want to leave, it's good to be prepared.

One of the big "cons" on many people's lists is feeling that they aren't being compensated enough. When you feel that you are underpaid, it starts a bad cycle. You get angry or you feel that if your boss doesn't think you're worth more, you should be doing less. You might even lower the standards of the quality of your work. This is not good for you, your career, or your employer.

What can you do? That depends. Have you asked for a raise? It's a simple solution, but when many people are asked this question, they answer no. Employers sometimes wait for *you* to *ask* before they'll give you a raise.

Before you ask for a raise, make sure you have all your facts straight. Prepare a presentation to your boss. Include the length of time you have worked at the company, your accomplishments, and anything else you think is pertinent. Don't discuss your personal financial situation. Having credit card debt, not being able to make ends meet, or your spouse just losing a job is not your boss's problem.

Bright Idea
One way to deal with a backstabber is to write regular memos to your supervisor detailing your ideas, work, and accomplishments. This may mean extra work, but it'll be worth it. Not only will it show your boss what work you're doing, it will provide documentation for raises and promotions.

Watch Out!
If your job is giving you so much stress that you're ill with headaches, pains in your chest, stomach problems, or other physical symptoms, get out as soon as you can. No job is worth getting sick over.

Bright Idea
If your boss tells you that you deserve a raise and that he wishes the company could afford to give you one, consider asking for other compensation such as increased benefits, extra vacation days, or a company car.

Make an appointment with your supervisor and go in calmly and confidently. State your case without whining. If you get a raise, great. If not, smile, tell your supervisor that you appreciate his time, and step up your job-hunting efforts.

Is one of the reasons you want to leave your current job because you're spending more time at work and less time with your family, or because you hate the long commute every day? Consider asking your boss if you can telecommute a few days a week.

If one of the big "cons" on your list is that you no longer have any passion for what you're doing, you're going to have to make a decision. Can you find a way to get passion into your current job? If so, fine. If not, it's definitely time to move on. In the same vein, if you recognize that the job you have is not what you want to do for the rest of your life, start looking for a new job. This is a tough situation because finding a hot job is much more complex if you don't yet know what you want to do.

Watch Out!
When discussing a raise, don't give an ultimatum such as threatening to quit if you don't get what you want. That may force you into looking for a job before you're ready. Imagine how good you'll feel if you have a job to go to when you tell your boss you're quitting.

Burned out and stressed out

Stress at work can sneak up on you. Everything is going well in your job, you're excited and working on projects, and all of a sudden it hits you slowly at first and then like a ton of bricks. How can you tell if you're burned out at work? Answer these questions:

- Have you been experiencing more headaches, stomachaches, rashes, or other ailments?

- Do things that used to excite you no longer interest you?

- Are you often irritable at work or at home?

- Do you get angry easily at work or at home?

- Do you lose your temper easily?

- Has your diet deteriorated?

- Do you eat too much or have you lost your appetite?

- Do you sleep too much or have trouble sleeping?

- Are you always tired?

- Have you started smoking (or smoking more)?

- Have you started drinking alcohol (or drinking more)?

- Have you started using drugs?

Everybody has a bad day or two. However, if you answer yes to more than a few of these questions for an extended period of time, you are headed for burnout if you're not already there. It's time to go! But plan your exit.

Job hopping

In today's world, people rarely stay with the same employer for 25 years. There is no shame in changing jobs or changing careers completely. Many successful people have multiple employers and careers during their lifetime. Changing jobs every three to five years is very different than hopping from job to job every few months.

People are often concerned, however, about job hopping. Job hoppers are those who frequently change jobs. If you held three jobs in two years for reasons other than promotions or layoffs you are a job hopper. Employers may be afraid to hire you. It doesn't matter if you have held numerous jobs because you were fired for cause or because you quit on your own. Job hopping frequently sends a negative message to prospective employers, who might think that:

> 66
> I had a decent job that I liked, but I knew there was no way I could advance my career there. I was working in an organization with a small staff and they had all been there for years. No one was leaving until they retired. I took some classes and landed a new great job.
> —Karen, Conference Manager
> 99

Watch Out!
While job hopping looks bad, don't turn down a job opportunity without considering it carefully.

- You're not committed to work.

- You're unreliable.

- You don't have any long-term career plans.

- As soon as they train you, you will leave.

- You don't get along with your coworkers.

- You aren't a team player.

Your departure

Unless your job is making you physically or emotionally ill or there is another serious problem, try not to quit until you either have another job or are at least closer to the end of your search. As noted previously, the best time to look for a job is while you are still employed. You'll feel better about yourself, and potential employers will see you as more of a commodity.

Many people think that they don't have time to hold down a full-time position and launch a successful job search. At least give it a try. When you're working you can network with colleagues, keep up with what's happening in your industry, and possibly hear about openings when they happen. If you find you need time to make and receive phone calls or go to interviews, take advantage of personal or sick days. If you quit to search for a job, some recruiters may think you were fired.

Here are some tips that may be useful in your departure:

Bright Idea
As you learned in Chapter 1, take time to develop a plan for your job search. Creating a plan with steps that you can follow helps you feel that you are in control and are doing something positive.

- Be discreet. It's not a good idea at this point to tell others in your workplace your plans of leaving. Wait until you formally tell your boss or supervisor.

- Once you find a job and accept it, write a letter of resignation. Never say anything negative

about your job, your boss, or your coworkers in
the letter.

- If your company has exit interviews, you can be
  honest about your reason for leaving. However,
  think twice before saying anything detrimental
  about anyone at your company. If you're leaving, what difference does it make if you think
  your boss is a jerk?

- Make sure you give appropriate notice. Offer
  your current employer between two weeks and
  30 days notice. Don't just quit and walk away
  from your current job.

- Never quit in anger. No matter how upset you
  get, don't just storm out. It hurts you more than
  anyone else.

- Don't burn your bridges. Try to leave your boss,
  your company, and your coworkers on good
  terms. You might need one of them as a reference.

Can you reinvent your job?

Things change in life. When these changes occur in
your career, will you be ready to take action? Let's
look at a few scenarios which might have occurred
at work:

- A job that was initially exciting is not exciting
  now. You need more.

- You have a job that's fine. There isn't anything
  wrong with it, but you don't get excited thinking about going to work.

- You feel your career is on a downward spiral.

- You feel bored and burned out or overly
  stressed.

Watch Out!
Just because
you're leaving
doesn't mean you
should stop
doing your job.
Continue working
and do your best
until your last
day. Leave a
good impression.

■ You've got so much work to do that you don't do anything else.

Is any of this familiar? If so, it might be time to reinvent your career. If you are creative, you might be able to revive your career and make it hot once again.

The following can make your current job hot again:

■ New challenges

■ New responsibilities

■ New training

■ Increased job satisfaction

■ Increased job fulfillment

■ A promotion

■ A new job within the company

Bright Idea
Instead of leaving your job, look for ways to improve it! All it may take to go from a lukewarm job to one that's hot are some new responsibilities or additional training.

In Chapter 1, I briefly discussed how you could mold the job you have into one that is more fulfilling and satisfying. When reinventing your career, you are expanding on that concept and taking a proactive approach.

Remember the example from Chapter 1, of the employee who was bored on the job and wanted to be more creative? From that need a company newsletter was born, along with a reinvented career for that employee.

If you want to revive your career in this manner, think about how you could improve or contribute more to your workplace. Some steps you might take to make your ideas a reality include:

1. Determine what you could do to make your current job better.

2. Take some time and think about ideas and develop concepts. Write them down as you go.

3. Look at any potential problems and come up with ways to solve them.

4. Determine how your idea or suggestion might make your workplace or company better or more productive.

5. Discuss the idea with a trusted friend, family member, or mentor to see if there are any holes or problems you might not have considered.

6. Put your plan in writing before you talk to your supervisor.

A great way to start reinventing your career is to talk to your boss. Management is interested in retaining valued employees. Either set up a special meeting to discuss your situation or discuss it during a periodic performance review.

When you meet, be calm, cool, and collected. Explain that while you enjoy working for the company and like your job, you are beginning to feel unchallenged. Ask your supervisor if she has any suggestions for revitalizing your career with the company. For example:

■ Are there opportunities for retraining?

■ How can you employ skills you have that are not currently used within your current job?

■ If you acquire new skills, what are the possibilities for promotion?

■ Is it possible for you to work on more fulfilling or challenging assignments?

■ Are there new positions opening up within the company that might utilize your skills?

During your meeting, go over your accomplishments and discuss what you'd like to accomplish in the future. After you discuss your career aspirations

Unofficially...
It's easy to get depressed when you think your career is on a downward spiral. When you're attempting to reinvent your career, it's especially important to try to remain as positive as possible. If you continue to take positive actions, your prospects will eventually improve.

with your supervisor, she may surprise you with some positive suggestions for your career.

While you might not feel like doing work-related activities after hours, during a low point in your career, it's a good idea to attend industry and association meetings. These offer opportunities to see colleagues, meet people, get new ideas, and network.

Getting back in the saddle

If you've been out of work, reentering the workforce can be difficult. There are a variety of reasons you might have been out of work for a period of time. These could include:

- You have been taking care of your children, spouse, or other family member.

- You have been fired.

- You have quit your job.

- You have been downsized.

- Your former company merged and you were laid off or let go.

- The headquarters of your former company moved across the country and you couldn't go with them.

- You retired and then decided you wanted or needed to work again.

- You have just graduated from high school or college.

The workplace can be a jungle, but there are ways to make it easier to fit in. Here are some basic tips to help you succeed in your new hot job:

- Always be professional. You represent your company. Make them proud of you.

- Be on time for everything. This includes your job, meetings, phone calls, deadlines, and assignments.

- Show up for work every day. People are depending on you. If you don't come to work, people will have to cover for you. If they don't, something won't get done.

- Return phone calls in a timely fashion.

- Answer e-mail messages promptly.

- Don't bring your private life to work.

- Don't complain constantly about how busy you are.

- Don't speak negatively about your boss, your coworkers, or your company. It always comes back to haunt you.

- Be a team player. Help your coworkers when you can.

- Do a little bit more than is expected of you.

- Don't get involved in office politics.

- Don't depend on your memory; write everything down.

- Be honorable and have integrity.

Following these tips will help you be more efficient and confident in your job and in your life.

Bright Idea
At work and during a job search, always be responsible and true to your word. If you say you are going to do something, do it.

Your reputation precedes you

Your reputation and image are important in the workplace. They can enhance your career or push it down the tubes. The first few days on any new job, people will form their image of you. Once that initial impression is formed, it's very difficult to change. Make sure you put your best foot forward and create the image you want to project.

Your image depends on a number of things:

- *The way you dress.* Your job will determine the type of clothing you wear. You may be required to wear a uniform, or you may wear street clothes. Whatever you wear, make sure it's clean, neat, pressed, and looks professional.

- *The way you speak.* Try to speak in a pleasant tone of voice. Don't yell or scream in the workplace. Don't curse or swear even if others are doing so.

- *The way you act.* The way you conduct yourself in your professional life is essential to your success. Always act professionally and treat others with respect.

Here are some suggestions on how to build a solid professional reputation that will be respected by superiors and coworkers:

Watch Out!
Be trustworthy. Make sure people can trust that you are telling the truth and are neither lying nor exaggerating.

- *Be dependable and trustworthy.* If you say you are going to be somewhere or do something, do it.

- *Be a team player.* Be helpful and demonstrate that you are willing to help others.

- *Be honest.* Of course you wouldn't take a computer home. But taking home office supplies, making long-distance phone calls on the office phone, or putting in for expenses that you didn't use or hours that you didn't work is stealing too.

- *Be ethical.* Don't compromise your standards. If you know something is wrong, don't do it.

- *Don't gossip.* Don't start it or continue it.

- *Don't use foul language.* If you do, people will remember your mouth, not what you say, no matter how important it is.

How do you fit in?

The first day on a new job is like the first day of school. You're probably excited as well as anxious, or even scared. The good news is these feelings go away after you get settled in. Some companies have orientation programs designed to make new employees' first few days more comfortable. If your new company doesn't, just relax and try to keep calm. There are usually one or two employees who will go out of their way to make you feel welcome. Be open to everyone.

Downsized or fired, you can still be a winner

Have you been downsized or fired? Almost everyone has lost a job at one time or another. Nowadays, it's more common than ever.

The feelings that accompany any job loss cover a spectrum of emotions. They include:

- Panic
- Fear
- Depression
- Anger
- Sadness
- Helplessness
- Hopelessness
- Desperation
- Insecurity
- Self-doubt

Your financial plan of action

You feel horrible. You're panicked. What are you going to do? How are you going to pay the bills? What are you going to tell your spouse and the kids?

Watch Out!
While the workplace usually breaks up into cliques, this is not the time to choose one. Get to know everyone before you decide where you belong.

Unofficially...
Even if you really didn't like your job, your boss, or your coworkers, you may feel like a failure if you're let go. Some people blame themselves. Others blame everyone other than themselves. Blame is not important—the fact is, you no longer have a job.

What about your house payments? Your car payments? Credit cards? There are a lot of questions. The best thing to do, no matter how difficult, is try to relax so you can think clearly.

One of the most frightening things about losing your job is the uncertainty of your financial situation. As soon as you find out about your change in employment status, check out your finances. Have you been living paycheck to paycheck? Do you have additional sources of income? Do you have money in the bank? You're going to have to make some changes. The smart thing to do is to cut your spending immediately. Cut back where you can. Look at your numbers and see if you can make it financially until you're employed again. It might make you feel better to make a list of all your necessary expenses on paper. These might include:

- Rent or mortgage
- Insurance
- Health care and medicine
- Food
- Car payments and expenses
- Gas, electric, and other utilities
- Credit cards
- Phone service

Add your other expenses to this list. Include at least minimum credit card payments. Now, write down the money you have on hand and money that will be coming in. This might include:

- Savings accounts
- Checking accounts
- Spouse's income (if applicable)

Bright Idea
Small changes in the way you live and spend money add up and make a difference in your finances when unemployed. Try watching movies on television instead of going out or renting them from the video store, using the library instead of buying books and magazines, taking advantage of free leisure time activities in your community instead of those which cost money or planning family picnics instead of trips to the local fast-food restaurant. Don't forget coupons when grocery shopping.

- Alimony or child support (if applicable)

- Other income (if applicable)

- Severance pay

- Unemployment income

Now add up both lists and see what the difference is. Will you have enough to survive for a month without financial hardship? Two months? Six months? A year or more? Hopefully, your job search won't take that long. In the meantime, what can you do?

Consider a part-time or temporary job. Either option has a number of benefits:

- They bring in money to help you pay the bills while you're looking for your new hot job.

- They may lead to full-time employment.

- They allow you to try out new fields.

- They give you time to work on your job search and go to interviews.

- They offer you the opportunity to network and make new contacts.

Maintain your composure

Even if you're expecting bad news, when you're told about your termination it will probably hit you like a ton of bricks. Your throat will feel like it went down into your stomach and you might have to catch your breath. It's essential that you keep your composure while you are in the workplace. Do not start screaming, crying, or begging for your job. The decision has been made. Keep calm. You'll have plenty of time to vent at home later. At this moment, your boss probably feels more uncomfortable than you. Use this to your advantage.

Bright Idea
If you are unemployed, you want to contact credit card companies and other creditors before they start calling you. In this way you can explain the situation and try to come up with a viable payment plan.

Watch Out!
Make sure that losing your job doesn't ruin your health. Take special care to stay fit, eat healthy, and get enough sleep every day.

Bright Idea
If you need a couple of minutes to get yourself together when you receive bad news, ask to be excused. Then return to your boss calm and collected.

Ask about a severance package. If none is offered, negotiate for one. If you are offered a package, find out what is included. This is no time to be shy. Negotiate for a better one. The worst that can happen is you won't be successful.

Severance packages differ from company to company and from job to job. They are not all the same. There are a variety of things you can ask for. That doesn't mean you will get everything, but here are some things you could negotiate:

- Money—try for one month's salary for every year you worked at the company
- Health and dental insurance
- Other types of insurance (life, disability, etc.)
- Pension
- Outplacement services
- Retraining
- Use of company secretarial services for a specified amount of time
- Use of company office or desk, phone, computer, and photocopy machine for a specified amount of time

Once you understand which of these might be in your severance package, try to get it in writing. You might be asked to sign a statement discussing your severance. Do not sign anything that you don't understand and make sure that what you discussed with your boss is included in the severance agreement.

Unofficially...
In the rare event that your severance is not covered by a confidentiality or non-compete agreement, you may be able to take clients with you or even set up business on your own.

Before you leave

There are a number of things you should do before you leave your present job:

1. If you haven't discussed a severance package or one is not offered, visit the Human Resources department to check out any benefits or money you may have coming. For example, find out how you can continue your health insurance, what your pension fund is worth and whether you're entitled to it, and whether you have any vacation pay coming.

2. Find out whether your company has outplacement programs. Take advantage of every opportunity. The most basic offer tips and techniques to help you brush up on your job search skills. Some companies also offer their terminated employees the use of offices, desks, and phones to help make their job search easier.

3. Whether you are being downsized or fired, talk to your supervisor about giving you a letter of recommendation. Try to get the letter before you leave the job.

4. If possible, tell coworkers you will be leaving. You don't have to go into detail. No matter how angry you are, don't bad-mouth your boss or the company.

Starting over

Here's a news flash for you: *Now* is the best time to look for a new hot job. Unemployment is low. Employers need good employees and are having problems finding them. With the current flurry of downsizing, mergers, reorganizations, and acquisitions, it's also easier to explain your current employment status. There are many very qualified people who have lost their jobs. Being terminated for these reasons holds no shame. If a potential employer asks your reason for leaving, you can simply say company reorganization or downsizing.

Watch Out!
Many people have a false sense of security, thinking they will never lose their job. But it can happen to anyone, so prepare yourself now.

Bright Idea
Always get the names, addresses, and phone numbers of two or three coworkers. That way if your company closes down, you'll have a name you can contact to verify you worked at a particular company.

Moneysaver
Don't let feelings of shame or embarrassment stop you from applying for unemployment benefits. Visit the unemployment division of your state's labor department at your first opportunity. Unemployment checks will help you survive until you find a new job. The unemployment office may also know of job opportunities.

Try to remain optimistic. Confidence is important in your job search, especially after you have been terminated. Look at your job search as an opportunity to find one of those new hot jobs you have heard about.

Treat your job search as your new temporary job. Don't slack off. Make sure you take positive actions every day to find the job you want. Keep a written record of each day's job search activities and accomplishments. These include:

- Developing, updating, and polishing your resume
- Asking people to see if you can use them for references
- Visiting the unemployment office for leads
- Assessing your skills
- Determining what job you want
- Scanning the classifieds
- Making phone calls to inquire about jobs
- Scheduling interviews and appointments
- Writing cover letters to send with resumes
- Learning new skills
- Networking
- Going to professional meetings
- Reading professional or business journals for leads

Climbing the career ladder

The goal of most people is to climb the career ladder to success in a job that they love. How does that happen? You need to set goals for yourself and then find ways to meet them. It's essential to make people aware of your career aspirations. You don't want to

Moneysaver
Find out where you can make inexpensive, good-quality photocopies. This can save you money when you need copies of your resume.

give the impression that you're after someone's job; but you do want to be sure that if openings become available, you will be considered.

Keep up on what's happening in your company. Are there opportunities? Don't depend on others to let you know what's happening. Make a concerted effort. Keep your ears and eyes open. Make yourself visible in your company as well as in the business community. Volunteer for assignments, offer to take jobs others don't want, and speak up at meetings. Similarly, go to meetings and events outside the office where you might meet people who need someone with your skills.

Bright Idea
Become friendly with someone in the Human Resources department. They often know of openings before they are announced.

Staying in the same company

Perhaps you like the company you work for, but you aren't happy with your job. Perhaps you aren't feeling challenged or maybe you want to use other skills. One of the best places to start a job search is in your own company. Look around you. What's available within your organization? Internal job progression is a wonderful method of making your career hotter.

The best time to attempt to move up is when you have done something positive. Did you just complete a major project successfully? Have you increased sales? Is productivity in your department up? Talk to your supervisor about your career aspirations. Find out what types of positions are on the next rung of the career ladder.

Moving on

If you've tried to move up the career ladder in your present company and don't see it happening, you're going to have to look elsewhere. You need to be discreet. If you apply for positions in competing

Bright Idea
A lateral move or a similar job at a larger company may ultimately help you in your quest to climb the career ladder. Larger companies have more jobs to offer, and one may lead to your dream job.

companies, be sure to tell them you are applying in confidence. While this doesn't guarantee your current boss won't find out you are job hunting, at least you're doing the best you can.

Remember that whether you are trying to move up or move out, similar job hunting skills are needed. Develop a plan and take action to make it happen for you.

Just the facts

- Only you can decide if you should stay in or leave a job you don't love.
- Make yourself visible in the workplace to advance your career.
- Job hopping can send the wrong message to potential employers.
- Reinventing your job can revitalize your career.

GET THE SCOOP ON...
Marketing yourself and your career ▪ Developing
a career plan ▪ More on networking ▪ Getting
people's attention ▪ Using the Internet

Savvy Search-and-Seize Career Strategies

Chapter 4

You can control the success of your career. You can be in charge. You can have the power. Do you want to succeed? If so, take control and do it now.

This chapter will help you begin to take a proactive approach to moving your career forward. Whether you want to climb the career ladder in your present field or change fields totally, positive actions ensure success. Sure, it takes a little extra time and effort. But your reward will be a better career. If you don't take these steps, you leave your career success to chance.

This chapter will also cover techniques to help you become more successful in your career. I'll show you strategies that will help make your career sizzle—whatever your job or industry. And I'll discuss how to sell yourself and develop and implement a career plan.

Market yourself: Become a hot commodity

Looking for a hot job? So are thousands of other people. Do you want to increase your chances of getting and keeping the hot job you want? Learn how to market yourself to become a hot commodity.

Have you ever noticed that every year there's a new hot toy? One that is so hot, you can hardly find it...and when you do, you have to pay dearly. Whether it's for your own child or the son or daughter of a friend or relative, in this context, most of us have dealt with the results of good marketing.

What can marketing do for you and your career? Depending on where you are and where you want to be, it can do a number of things. These include:

- Setting you apart from other job candidates
- Setting you apart from other employees
- Making you visible so potential employers will see you as a hot commodity
- Making you visible to superiors for promotions
- Helping you obtain the attention of head-hunters
- Obtaining the attention of superiors seeking to fill new positions
- Obtaining the attention of employers at other companies
- Opening up the door to new opportunities
- Making you feel better about yourself and your career

The five P's of marketing your career

What exactly does marketing mean? In the most general sense of the term, marketing is creating and finding markets and avenues to sell something. The five P's of marketing are:

1. Product
2. Price
3. Positioning
4. Promotion
5. Packaging

You might ask yourself, what does this have to do with me and my career? To answer that question, let's explore the possibilities of each of the five P's:

1. *Product.* In this case, *you* are the product. *You* are a package. This includes not only your physical self but your skills, talents, and ideas. Your package includes anything else that might be of value to your employer.

2. *Price.* Price has to do with the compensation you receive for your work. There is a range of possible earnings for any one job. Your goal in marketing yourself is to sell your talents and what you have to offer so that you will receive the best salary.

3. *Positioning.* Positioning means developing or creating innovative methods to fill one or more needs an employer might want filled. It also means differentiating yourself from your competitors, which in this case are other employees.

4. *Promotion.* Promotion means developing and implementing methods that make you visible in a positive manner—advertising yourself!

5. *Packaging.* Packaging is the way you present yourself.

Packaging the product

Many job candidates are passed over simply because they don't understand the concept of packaging themselves. When you're trying to sell yourself, you have to demonstrate that you have something special to offer. You must be able to illustrate that you can fill the employer's needs better than any other applicant.

Selling yourself doesn't stop when you get a job. To move up the career ladder, you have to continue selling yourself. You must make yourself clearly visible in the workplace. If you don't, others will get the jobs and the promotions you are hoping for.

The best marketing campaigns incorporate packaging to help sell the product. You want potential employers to see you in the most positive light. What does your package include? A great many things. Let's go over a few of them.

Your appearance: The first impression people have of you is usually based on your appearance. It doesn't matter what type of hot job you want, appearance is always important.

Appearance encompasses an array of items. Personal grooming is essential. Before you go to interviews, check that:

- Your hair is clean and neat.

- Your nails are clean. Also, keep in mind that unless you're going for a job in one of the creative areas, you shouldn't go to an interview with overly decorated nails.

- Your breath is fresh and clean, especially if you smoke.

- If you're a man, you are freshly shaved with facial hair such as mustaches or beards neatly styled.

■ If you're a woman, your makeup should look natural, not overdone. This is not the time to try out two-inch-long fake eyelashes, iridescent colors, or anything flashy.

Your attire: When you are interviewing or in situations where you may have contact with potential employers, always dress appropriately and professionally.

The fact is, you should always dress to impress, at the interview as well as once you get the job. Appearance is important to *all* employers.

What's appropriate for an interview? Men should opt for a suit and tie, or a pair of dress slacks with a jacket, dress shirt, and tie. Women have more options, including a suit, professional-looking dress, skirt and jacket, or a skirt and blouse. No matter what the season or how warm it is outside, women should wear stockings or pantyhose. Sneakers should not be worn by either sex at an interview.

If you look successful, you will feel successful, and this will give you a sense of confidence that others will notice. Even if your company's dress code is casual or you have casual Fridays, it's in your best interest to dress neatly and with a sense of style.

Your verbal communication skills: What you say and how you say it are essential parts of your packaging. Your communications skills can mean the difference between getting and not getting the hot job you've been dreaming about. Good communication skills can push you up the career ladder.

How would you rate your communications skills? Are they sloppy or polished? If your communication skills need some work, consider these tips to help improve them:

Unofficially...
Don't make the mistake of dressing down for an interview because the job you are going for has a casual dress code. What you wear is important. It shows the interviewer you are professional and interested in the job.

Bright Idea
What should you wear once you get the job? Look around to get an idea of what others in your workplace are wearing. If you want to move up the career ladder, check out what those a couple steps up the ladder are wearing and emulate them. Remember, you're trying to set yourself apart in a positive manner.

Watch Out!
Wearing perfume
or cologne can
be a problem at
an interview or
even on the job.
Many people are
allergic to vari-
ous scents. If
you insist on
wearing one,
keep it light.

- Listen to what others are saying. Listening helps you understand what others want and need. It's often difficult, especially at an interview when your mind is going in a hundred directions, to really listen to the questions and what the interviewer is saying. You might be busy thinking about the points you want to get across, or concerned that you're making a good impression.

- Make sure you understand difficult points. Ask for clarification if you don't understand something.

- Maintain eye contact when you are speaking to someone or they are speaking to you.

- Use body language to show that you are paying attention when others are speaking. A slight nod of your head, or leaning toward the person who is speaking, indicates you are listening.

- Think before you speak.

- Know what you want to say before you say it.

- Don't use poor grammar or slang. For example, don't use words like "ain't"; instead, say "are not" or "aren't." Don't say things like "He and me was working on a project together." Say, "He and I were working on a project together."

- Don't curse in the workplace. Actually, you should try not to curse at all. The problem is, if you curse a lot, you get used to the words and they come out involuntarily in the most inappropriate places.

- Don't use off-color language.

- Don't tell jokes or stories with racial or sexual overtones or innuendoes. Have respect for others.

Bright Idea
In an interview,
it's hard to know
the right answer
unless you know
the question, so
try to focus and
listen.

- Be polite and courteous. Don't interrupt when others are speaking.

- If you disagree, do so calmly without screaming, yelling, or screeching.

- Be respectful. If you don't know someone in a professional capacity, address that person by their title (Mr., Mrs., Miss, Ms., Doctor, etc.).

- Use a strong, confident tone when you speak. Practice modulation. You could record yourself speaking and play it back so you can hear what you sound like to others. Listening to yourself is often a scary experience. Most people don't like the way they sound when they first hear their own voice. Use this experience as a tool to improve yourself, not to beat yourself up. Change what you can and don't worry about the rest.

Your written communication skills: Depending on the type of job you're seeking, your written communication skills can be very important. At the very least, you should be able to develop a grammatically correct resume and write a good cover letter. Many people say they can't write, but the fact is, writing is a skill. If you put some effort into it, you can improve. Consider taking a writing class at your local community college or vo-tech school. If you're comfortable working on your own, visit the book store or library to find a couple of books on writing.

While a great deal of what you write will be done with a word processor or typewriter, sometimes you will have to handwrite something. Strive to write neatly and legibly at all times. This is especially important on job applications.

Bright Idea
If you're not sure about correct grammar, study a simple book on proper English to help guide you.

Watch Out!
Don't use first names until you are invited to do so. It may be misinterpreted as demonstrating a lack of respect.

Bright Idea
If you don't know if a woman is married or single, address her as Ms. It's also perfectly acceptable to ask her, or someone else, which title she prefers.

Bright Idea
If you are asked to fill in a job application, make sure you fill it in completely. Don't write remarks on the application such as "see my resume." While this might seem like extra work to you, many companies scan applications into a computer or code answers into a database. If your information is not complete, you may be excluded.

Your body language: The way you carry yourself is an important part of your packaging. Employers want to have confident people working in their organization. Here are some tips:

- Stand straight and tall without hunching over.

- When you meet someone, give them a firm (but not bone-crushing) handshake.

- Show interest when people are speaking to you.

- Make eye contact when you are speaking to someone.

- Try not to clench your fists. People will think you're stressed.

- Smile. People like to be around happy people.

Your demeanor: Courtesy is essential in the workplace and in life. Here are some tips to help you demonstrate a good demeanor.

- Arrive a few minutes early for interviews and appointments. Nothing can turn off an interviewer faster than a job applicant who shows up late, or worse, not at all. If you can't show up on time for the interview, what are the chances you will be on time for work?

- Thank the person or persons interviewing you for their time and consideration.

- Use polite expressions such as "please," "thank you," "excuse me," and "pardon me."

- Always send a thank-you note after your interview. Send it the same day or, at the latest, the day after your interview.

- Shake hands with people you meet in business situations.

Watch Out!
Remember the golden rule: Always treat people the way you would like to be treated. This is a very practical rule—people will treat you the way you treat them.

Your personality traits: What are your personality traits? Are they attractive to potential employers or will they be reason to choose another candidate? Look over this list to see if your personality traits would be an asset or a detriment to your employers:

- Do you appear happy?

- Do you appear calm?

- Do you appear to have a positive attitude?

- Can you deal effectively with others?

- Can you work as a team member?

- Can you deal effectively with stress?

- Do you seem argumentative?

- Are you a complainer?

Your skills and talents: The things that you can do comprise your skills and talents. These are what make you special. Skills can be learned and acquired; talent is what you are born with. You can embellish talent. Everyone has a different variety of skills and talents. I'll discuss assessing your skills and talents in more detail in the next chapter.

Tooting your own horn

Many people are embarrassed to promote themselves. They think that if they talk about their accomplishments or bring them to the attention of others, they're bragging. Is this you? If so, it's time to change your thinking.

When you promote yourself you should not be bragging. If you do it correctly, you are simply making yourself visible to get what you deserve. This is essential to your career success whether you have a job you love or are looking for a new one. When should you toot your horn? Here are some examples of when it is appropriate:

Bright Idea
Always strive to be on time for appointments, but if you find yourself running unavoidably late, call. Tell the secretary or person you are meeting that you apologize, but you have been delayed. Ask if it would still be convenient to come in 15 or 20 minutes late, or whether you should reschedule.

- When you get a new job or promotion
- When you are appointed to a new position
- When you chair an event
- When you receive an honor or award
- When you break a record
- When you graduate from school, college, or a training program
- When you obtain professional certification or licensing
- When you have a major accomplishment
- When you give a speech or are invited to speak at a professional conference
- When you appear on television or radio
- When you are elected to an office or take part in civic activities
- When you take part in activities with not-for-profit organizations
- When you have something published

You will get the most amount of exposure by channeling the information about your accomplishments to local newspapers and radio, television, and cable stations. Remember to include trade association newsletters and journals. Why would the media be interested in your story? It's simple. They need to fill space. A great many of those stories and announcements you see filling up the paper, hear about on radio, or view on television every day, are the direct result of press releases.

A press release is not an advertisement. You pay for ads; you don't pay to have a press release used in the media. Editors and producers use the information in press releases to develop stories or may just edit and print them.

Some companies have public relations departments that write and send press releases to the media on a regular basis. Promoting you, the individual, gets the company name in the paper and helps promote them too. If this is not an option, try calling the media yourself with your information. Ask to speak to someone in the editorial department. The problem with this method is you can't do it very often. When you call an editor, your news had better be newsworthy.

A better option is to become your own publicist and write a press release about yourself to send to the media. If you don't know how to write a press release, there are books available in the library and bookstores on the subject. Generally, a press release should be informative, interesting, easy to read, and contain, at the very least, the 5 W's. These are: who, what, when, where, and why:

1. *Who* you are writing about

2. *What* you are writing about

3. *When* the event occurred or will occur

4. *Where* the event occurred or will occur

5. *Why* it occurred and why it is relevant

The example below gives you an idea of what a simple press release looks like.

Here are some other pointers that might help you develop your press release and get the story placed:

■ Your press release should be neatly typed and double-spaced. Never send a handwritten press release.

■ Make sure your release is easy to read, using short sentences and paragraphs.

NEWS FROM:
KATHY CARTER
P.O. Box 111
Some City, NY 12345
Media: For additional information, contact:
Kathy Carter, 988-555-4567

For Immediate Release
Carter Selected General Hospital Employee of the Month

Some City, NY: Kathy Carter, a licensed practical nurse, was selected General Hospital Employee of the Month for February. She works on the 11:00 p.m. to 7:00 a.m. shift in the stepdown unit of the hospital. As a licensed practical nurse, Ms. Carter is responsible for patient care, including administering medications and treatments, monitoring patients for changes in condition, and documentation.

Associated with General Hospital since May 1996, Ms. Carter is a 10-year resident of Some City, New York, where she lives with her two daughters Meg and Debbie and husband Richard. She attended the High School of Art in New York City and the State University of New York at New Paltz. Her hobbies include baking, pottery, and creating stained glass.

"I joined the staff at General Hospital because I needed a change," said Ms. Carter. "Previously, I had worked at a very small hospital and wanted the experience and variety a large institution would bring me."

The qualities Ms. Carter admires most in fellow employees are the same qualities which led coworkers to nominate her Employee of the Month. "I admire a positive attitude and kind treatment of patients," she said. "The most satisfying part of my job is seeing that everything possible is done for my patients. I like to see patients are treated in the same kind manner I would want to be treated if I were a patient."

"I work as a part of a functioning team of doctors, nurses, and other staff," said Ms. Carter. I'm proud to be part of the team."

Ms. Carter's future goals include continuing her education. "I'm working on becoming a registered nurse," she said. "I enjoy working with patients."

The Employee of the Month is nominated by coworkers, physicians, volunteers, patients, and visitors, and selected by the EMPLOYEE CARE Committee. The EMPLOYEE CARE Committee gives recognition to outstanding members of the staff. At the end of each year, the 12 monthly nominees compete for Employee of the Year designation.

- Be sure to develop a title to use as a heading before your main copy. If you can make it catchy, fine; if not, just use the facts. For example: "Jones Promoted to Manager" or "Webber Named Employee of the Month."

- Use one or more quotes to help make your release more interesting. For example, if you are writing a press release about being named Employee of the Month, you might use a quote like: "I enjoy working with people," said Webber. "My colleagues and my customers are what makes this job so great."

- Make sure your grammar is correct.

- Check the release carefully for spelling errors. A spell-check program can help you flag many errors, but it's no substitute for a careful proofread.

- Have someone else look over your release for ease in reading and comprehension.

- Include either a date that the story can be used or the words "For Immediate Release." This is so the editor knows when he can release the information.

- Make sure all your information is accurate.

- Try to send your release to the editor of the specific department that will use your story; for example, Business Editor, Food Editor, or Money Editor.

- In order to build a continuing relationship with the media, it's a good idea not to call and bother them, asking when and if they will be using your releases.

Bright Idea
Don't forget to use a short, catchy heading or title on your press release.

Type the release on press release stationery that you can create on your computer. Your stationery should include:

- Words like "News," "Press Release," or "News From": should appear on your stationery. This differentiates your copy from an advertisement.

- A contact name and phone number so that editors can reach you for additional information. This should be separate from your main copy. For example: "For additional information, contact Jena Ward: 912-555-4567."

- The symbol "#" or "-30-" at the end of your release. This indicates to the editor that your release has ended.

There are also software programs on the market where you just type the information into a template. Microsoft Word, for example, has a simple press release template.

After you develop and write your press release, make copies and send them to the media. You might be able to get a list of your local media from your area's chamber of commerce or office of public information. If not, call the radio and television stations in your area and ask for their mailing address. You can usually get newspaper and magazine addresses directly by scanning the front or editorial page of the paper or periodical. Send press releases to the media on a consistent basis whenever you have news.

Other marketing and promotion strategies

How else can you market and promote yourself? There are many ways to make yourself visible in a positive manner. Consider these strategies:

Watch Out!
Whatever you choose to do, make the most of your efforts. Don't sit on the sidelines. Make yourself visible in a positive manner. Seize opportunities, or nothing positive will happen.

- Make yourself an expert on something. People will seek you out.

- Offer to write a periodic column for the newspaper on a subject with which you feel comfortable.

- Offer to write a periodic column for your company newsletter.

- Put yourself on the speaker's circuit. Offer to give speeches at civic and not-for-profit group events.

- Offer to be a guest on radio, cable, and television station news or information shows. Check out the stations and their programming to find where you would fit best. Send a letter with your idea and resume or background sheet to program producers.

- Join professional associations and volunteer to be on committees or to chair events.

- Join civic groups and not-for-profit organizations in whose platforms you are interested. Volunteer to be on committees or to chair events.

Your key to career success: A plan

You might be asking yourself: How do I do everything? What should I do? When should I do it? How do I know if I'm going in the right direction?

What you need is a plan. Start by becoming your own career manager. That means *you* will be in charge of your career. Don't leave the planning to someone else who doesn't care as much as you do. Don't leave it to chance. Managing your career will put you in the driver's seat. Take control and make it happen. As a career manager, you are responsible for developing your career plan.

Sit down and seriously think about your career and the direction you want it to take. Prepare your plan in writing. Get out a pencil and paper or sit at your computer. Begin by doing some research. This might include:

- *Determining your market.* Where are the jobs and employment situations you're interested in? Who and where are your potential employers?

- *Determining what you need to get the hot job you want.* Do you need additional skills, education, training, or experience?

- *Determining how to differentiate yourself from other job candidates.* What can you do that sets you apart from others?

- *Determining how to catch the eye of potential employers.* How can you make yourself and your accomplishments visible to others?

Take some time to do this research. Think about these questions and any others you might come up with. Once you have the answers, it's easier to move on to the next step: Writing your plan. Your career plan will help increase your efficiency in your job search. It should help you focus on what you are doing by making your search more organized.

What should your basic plan include?

- *Your career goals.* What do you want to do? Do you want to get a new job in a hot field or do you want to find a way to make your current job hot? Do you want to explore various careers or do you know exactly what you want to do? The more specific your goals, the faster you will be able to reach them.

- *What you need to reach those goals.* Do you need to acquire new skills? Additional education? More

Bright Idea
Write down every appointment on your calendar as soon as you find out about it. Be sure to include the time as well as the date. This will ensure you don't schedule two appointments for the same time. Check your calendar every morning so you don't miss any appointments.

experience? Do you need certification? Licensing? Do you need to move to a different area? Do you need to network?

■ *Your actions.* What do you need to do to attain your goals? Do you need to go to school? Attend seminars? Network more? Take advantage of volunteer opportunities to get experience?

■ *Your timetable.* What is your timetable? What are you going to do, and when will you do it?

Bright Idea
If you aren't moving ahead as quickly as you want, do more. Actions eventually result in achievements, so keep plugging away.

The reason you develop a plan is so that you have something to follow. You are creating an organized method of searching for your hot job. If you put it in writing, you have something to refer to so that you can see your progress.

Try to set aside a specific amount of time each day to work on your career. The number of actions you take every day depends on your current employment situation. If you're unemployed, you will probably be doing more than if you are currently employed and searching for a new hot job. A good rule of thumb is to take at least three to five positive actions a day toward getting your dream job. If you can do more, all the better.

In addition, you might find it helpful to keep a daily journal of the actions you take every day to help you attain your goals. Write everything down. This is useful because it keeps all your information in one place. Here's an example of part of a journal, below.

You also need to keep track of all the specific jobs for which you apply. This section is your Action Plan. I have included a filled-in Action Plan as well as one for you to copy and use. You can also create your own, on a computer.

HOT JOB JOURNAL

<u>Monday, January 11</u>
Read daily paper.

Called John Thompson, CBA Company, 123-456-7890. Cold call, not in. Secretary Mary said he would be in on Thursday and to call back.

Called Ty Reilly, Lincoln Corp., 123-333-3333. Got name from George Wells at LB Publishing. Spoke to Mr. Reilly about opening in marketing department. He asked for a resume. Faxed resume and cover letter to 123-333-3444. Call next week.

Scanned classifieds in Monday's paper. Nothing new.

Had lunch with Harry Jones. Told me conference and event manager left at Meetings Association.

Checked out Meetings Association on the Web. Found their number, contact names, address and information about past conferences.

Went to library board meeting (networking)

<u>Tuesday, January 12</u>
Called James Tyler, Meeting Association, 123-345-6789. Told him I had heard their conference and event manager left and asked who I could talk to about applying for the job. Mentioned that while

I had been working in marketing I handled conference planning for a not-for-profit and thought my skills and experience would be a plus. He asked me to e-mail or fax my resume and call in a few days to set up an appointment to talk. I faxed resume and cover letter to 123-345-6666. Call Friday.

Called Vicki Carpenter, executive director of Mentors In Marketing and asked if I could use her for a reference for the conference manager job. She offered to write a letter of recommendation.

Read paper.

Checked daily classifieds. Nothing new.

Went on Internet to check out newspaper ads online in surrounding areas.

Went to class on developing Web pages for the Internet.

Wednesday, January 13
Met someone at the health club who worked at LBC Communications. She said that they were hiring and it was a great company to work for. She gave me the name of person to contact.

Checked out classifieds. Blind ad in marketing. Didn't answer because I wasn't sure if it was my company.

Read paper.

My boss asked me to do a presentation for an employee meeting next month. All the higher-ups will be there. Good opportunity to showcase my skills.

Called John Thompson, CBA Company, 123-456-7890. He was in. I told him I was interested in talking to him about the possibility of working at CBA. He said they didn't have any openings. I asked if he could spare a few minutes next week for an informational meeting. He said if I could make it next Monday at lunch time, he could fit me in.

Began working on redoing my resume.

Thursday, January 14
Checked out classifieds. Nothing yet.

Read daily paper. Found stories on new companies coming in to area. Got phone numbers. Will call tomorrow.

Worked on resume.

Read business journal. Found story on recruitment firm.

Called recruiter to set up appointment for Monday after work.

Friday, January 15

Checked out classifieds. Nothing new of interest. Called companies which I read about in paper yesterday. Nothing with three of them. One said to visit their HR department when they finally get here. I asked who I could send a resume to now to get the ball rolling. The receptionist put me through to Sarah Weinstock. She will be in charge of marketing department here. She asked me to fax my resume and for my phone number. She said she would call when she came to town to set up an appointment.

Read daily paper. Found a couple of news briefs regarding people who had received awards or honors. Tore them out of paper to send notes to on weekend.

Made copies of my new resume.

Saturday, January 16

Went to job fair at coliseum. Spent the day talking to recruiters. Set up second interviews for next week.

Read paper.

Checked out classifieds.

<u>**Sunday, January 17**</u>
Read Sunday paper.

Checked out classified ads. Lots of leads to follow up.

Got Sunday paper from surrounding areas to check out their classified ad section.

Wrote and sent notes to people who had stories about them in the paper last week.

Wrote and sent notes to recruiters who I spoke to yesterday.

Unofficially...
As you can see,
finding a job is a
job in itself. The
more you do, the
better your
chances of find-
ing and getting
the job you are
seeking. While it
seems like a lot
of extra work,
remember that
the end result
will be worth it.

ACTION PLAN

Job Title: Conference and Event Planner

Job Description: Planning special events for company employees, corporate trade shows, and conferences

Company Name: Magic Music Records

Company Address: 123 South Street, Record City, NY 12341

Company Phone Number: (800) 555-1111

Company Fax Number: (800) 555-2222

Contact Name: Ed Davis

Where You Heard About Job: *Billboard Magazine* ad 2/4
New York Times 2/7

Actions Taken: Called Mr. Davis, 2/8
Faxed resume, 2/8

Actions Needed to Follow Up: Call Mr. Davis on 2/15 if I don't hear anything beforehand. Check with Genice Beach for an OK to use her as a reference.

Interview Time and Date: They are interviewing for this position after March 1.

Results: _____

Comments: Mr. Davis will be at Music News Convention in NYC on 2/20

ACTION PLAN

Job Title:

_____

Job Description:

_____

Company Name:

_____

Company Address:

_____

_____

_____

Company Phone Number:

_____

Company Fax Number:

_____

Contact Name:

_____

Where You Heard About Job:

_____

Actions Taken:

_____

Actions Needed to Follow Up:

_____

Interview Time and Date:

_____

Results:

_____

Comments:

_____

Timesaver
Buy a roll of stamps, a box or two of envelopes, a ream of good-quality paper, and any other supplies you might need so that you're ready to send out letters, resumes, and other information at a moment's notice. If you plan on sending packages via priority mail, UPS, Airborne Express, or Federal Express, get supplies ahead of time from these delivery companies.

Use every idea and action you can think of to help you find and get the job you want. Here are some actions to include in your plan:

- Read the newspaper every day. Keep up on local, regional, and national news and trends. Search for stories of new businesses, new companies, people who have been promoted or received honors, and companies that are downsizing. Use every opportunity to find reasons to contact people and network.

- Read local business journals.

- Scan the classifieds of the newspaper every day. While the majority of classified ads are found on Sunday, you can never tell when an employer will place ads or for how long.

- Try to find and take a class, seminar, or workshop in which you are interested. It doesn't necessarily have to be formal training. Learning anything new helps you increase your worth in the workplace. It will also help you feel like you are doing something positive.

- Take every opportunity to network.

- Seek out search firms specializing in the industry in which you are hoping to work.

- Visit job fairs when possible.

- Market yourself.

- Talk to people about your goals and dreams.

Remember that your job search takes time and effort. Every positive action you take is a step toward the hot career you want. Be patient, but persistent. Don't give up until you get where you want to be.

New ways to sell yourself

Everybody knows what a resume is. Most people use them to try to sell themselves. A resume is a great selling piece. It lists your accomplishments and tells your story. The question is, how can you expand on that selling tool?

Many career specialists insist a resume should only be one or two pages at the most. I disagree. Your resume is your selling piece. It's what can get you the interview. If you can get your information on one or two pages, fine. If it takes you three or four, that's fine too. This doesn't mean that you should have a 10-page resume; it just means you shouldn't leave out pertinent information.

Remember that you don't have to list everything you ever did in your entire life on your resume. You are trying to sell yourself, so if you had 10 jobs over a one-year period, you might want to leave a couple of them out. It's not good to have a gap on your resume, but you don't want to look like you can't hold down a job either.

There's no law that says you can only have one resume. You might want to develop a one- or two-page resume for situations where you need a short piece, and a longer one to use in other situations. If you have held interesting jobs or have interesting hobbies, put them down. You can never tell what will catch the interviewer's eye.

Business cards

There are other things you can use to augment your resume and sell yourself. You already know networking is important. You also know that you should tell as many people as possible about your career goals and the type of job you're looking for. The

Unofficially...
You don't neces-
sarily need to
have a job to
use a business
card—anyone
can have one. As
a matter of fact,
if you don't have
a job, or are try-
ing to get a
better one,
business cards
are essential.

question is, how do you get the people you meet to remember you? Just as important, if they remember you, how can they find you?

The answer is business cards. Business cards boost your prestige. Any printing shop can prepare business cards, and office supply stores like Staples and Office Max usually have printing services too. There are a variety of card styles to choose from. Your card can be simple or sophisticated. The simple ones are usually inexpensive, probably around $20 or so for 1,000 cards. As you add options, such as different stocks, colors, or ink, the price goes up.

When you have your cards printed, order 1,000. You're probably wondering what you're going to do with 1,000 cards. The answer is, you are going to give them to everybody. Business people keep business cards. They are a networking tool. They are also wonderful to give out at job fairs, trade shows, and networking events.

What should you put on your card? At the very least, have the following:

- Your name
- Your address
- Your phone number
- Your career objective, skills, or personality traits. For example: Writer, Graphic Designer, Reporter, Buyer, Sales Manager, Personal Shopper. You might also use words such as "effective communicator," "enthusiastic," or "team player."

I've seen people use double-sided business cards and folded-over cards successfully. As these have more room, they may list key elements of your resume. Bullets can be used to highlight skills and/or accomplishments.

Brochures

You might also want to consider a brochure. A brochure is a selling piece that gives information about a product, place, or event, among other things. In this case, the brochure will have information about you. You use it to make you stand out from other job seekers. Use a brochure in addition to your resume, not in place of it. Your resume will have your full story; your brochure will illustrate key points.

Brochures, like business cards, can be simple or elaborate. There are an unlimited number of ways brochures can be designed and a limitless number of paper or stocks, folds, inks, and colors you can use. Photographs, drawings, illustrations, or other art can also be used to enhance your brochure.

You can go to a printer to have a brochure designed and printed. This can get quite expensive. There are computer software programs available that are made especially for designing brochures. With these programs, you simply type your information into the format and print it out on computer paper designed for creating brochures.

Make sure your name, address, phone number, and career objective are prominent in the brochure. Then highlight key skills, personality traits, and experience.

Ideas you might not have considered

Trying to get the attention of someone important? So is everyone else! It's time to get creative. Consider the following possibilities for getting attention:

- Eggs
- Chocolate chip cookies
- Fortune cookies

Watch Out!
Don't try to get your entire resume on a business card. It won't look good and it will be too difficult for many people to read.

Bright Idea
Your brochure can simply be a sheet of $8^1/2 \times$ 11–inch paper folded crosswise in half or in a trifold. Brochures don't need a lot of words to be effective.

- A dozen red roses
- A chocolate bar
- A mug with gourmet coffee

Now, let's see how these items can help you grab someone's attention:

- **Take a few fresh eggs.** Wash them well with warm water. Punch a small hole in the top with a needle or pin. Carefully punch another slightly larger hole in the bottom of the egg. Save the pieces of shell. Place a straw on the top of the egg over the hole and blow the contents out. This is not the neatest or the easiest job, but the results are worth it. Once the contents are out, wash the egg well and let it dry for a day or two.

    Now type the following line on your computer: "Getting the attention of a busy man [or woman] is not easy. Now that I have yours, could you please take a moment to review my resume?" Do it in small print so you can get it out of your printer in one or two lines. Cut the paper into a strip and roll the strip around a toothpick. Stick the toothpick into the larger of the openings on the egg. Carefully, pull the toothpick out. Your message should now be in the egg. Go to a craft store, buy some little plastic or felt "feet" and glue them onto the bottom of the egg. While you're at the store, buy some of those small plastic moving eyes. Glue two onto the egg too.

    Print another line on your computer that says "Break open this egg for an important message." Cut the line out of the paper into a strip and glue it to the side of the egg. Put the egg in a box padded with cotton or bubble wrap so it won't break. These are very fragile. Place a copy of your resume with a cover letter in an envelope, put everything in a box, and either mail it or hand-deliver it to the office of the person you are trying to reach. By the time the recipient breaks open the egg, they don't notice the hole on the bottom and they usually can't figure out how you got the message in there. They usually call you up just to tell you how unique your idea is or ask you how you did it. Remember, your goal is to sell yourself sufficiently to get an interview.

■ **Chocolate chip cookies.** Go to your local bakery or cookie store at the mall. Have them decorate a big pizza-sized chocolate chip cookie with the following words: "Please Read My Resume!!! — Chris Walters." Tape a copy of your resume on the inside cover of the box. On the outside of the box, tape a card that say "Getting the attention of a busy man [or woman] is not easy. Now that I have yours, could you please take a moment to review my resume?" Put another copy of your resume and a cover letter in a large envelope. State in your letter you hope he [she] enjoys the cookie while reviewing your resume. Many of the stores which personalize cookies also have a delivery or mail service available. If not, mail or deliver the cookie yourself. Leave the package with the receptionist. Chances are, you will get a call within a day or so.

■ **Fortune cookies.** These are a great way to get someone's attention. You have a couple of choices. There are companies that can put a personalized message in the small, individually wrapped cookies. The messages inside should

"

I don't think the woman I sent the blown-out egg to would ever have called me for an interview. She couldn't figure out how I got the message inside the egg and thought the idea was so ingenious she wanted to use it to help her daughter get interviews. I didn't get the job there, but the woman referred me to another company where everything worked out.
—Judy, Public Relations Coordinator

"

Watch Out!
While it's probably less expensive to make the cookies yourself, you are taking on a liability making and sending food to someone you don't know.

say something like "He [she] who interviews Karen Scanlon will have good luck." Add your phone number. Put the message, "Getting the attention of a busy man [or woman] is not easy. Now that I have yours, could you please take a moment to review my resume?" on a card and tape it to a small box. Send a couple of cookies in a box every day for two weeks. Then stop. Chances are, by the third week, if you haven't already heard from the recipient, you will. If not, call the office and ask for an appointment.

You might also find a company that makes very large fortune cookies with personalized messages. Some of these are very elaborate. They may be covered in chocolate, sprinkles, or chocolate chips. If you send a big fortune cookie, you need only send one. Wait for a call. If you don't get one in a couple of days, place the call yourself.

Watch Out!
Many people are deathly allergic to peanuts as well as regular nuts. Make sure the cookies you order or chocolate you buy does not contain nuts.

■ **A dozen roses.** This is an expensive way to go, but it does get attention! There are very few people—men or women—who will not call immediately to thank you for roses. Send a note that says, "While you're enjoying the roses, please take a moment to look over my resume being delivered under separate cover." Sign it, "Sincerely hoping for an interview," and your name.

■ **A chocolate bar.** Most everyone loves chocolate. Buy a large, good-quality chocolate bar, the best you can find. If you are very creative, you can create a wrapping with the key points of your resume placed over the original candy wrapping. If you just want to do it the easy way, fold your resume neatly and slide it into the paper wrapping. You might also try folding your resume to cover the wrapped bar. Put the candy bar in a box with the message, "Getting the attention of a busy man [or woman] is never easy. Now that I have yours, could you please take a moment to review my resume?" Make sure you send a cover letter with your resume and the candy.

- **A mug with gourmet coffee.** Here's another way to catch people's attention. Have one or more mugs printed with either your business card or key points of your resume with your name and phone number. Add a small pack of gourmet coffee, and send it with a cover letter and a full copy of your resume.

Always be prepared

In order to be able to take advantage of every opportunity that presents itself, you must always be prepared. Keep your resume updated. If you have access to a computer at home, update your resume as you acquire new skills and gain experience. If you don't have a computer at home, keep your resume on a disk and update it on a friend's computer, at a local or college library computer lab or office supply store renting computer time.

Keep stock cover letters on your computer or a disk. These are basic letters that you can tailor to the exact job for which you are applying. You personalize each letter with the person's name, company, and address, as well as the job you are applying for, and indicate why you're qualified.

You can never tell when a recruiter will call or a potential employer might want to meet. You only have one chance to make a good first impression.

Moneysaver
Make sure you have a phone credit card for making calls for job possibilities when not at home. It's less expensive and more professional than having to put change into a phone booth. While some people use prepaid phone cards, the problem is that unless you have enough time left on your card, it can cut you off right in the middle of an important sentence with a potential employer.

To be sure it's a good one, be prepared. Make sure you keep an interview wardrobe ready and waiting. You might have one or two professional outfits for this purpose. Keep them clean, pressed, and in good repair. If a button falls off, sew it back on immediately before you forget about it. If a hem sags, fix it. Be sure that you have the proper accessories at hand, including shirts, blouses, shoes, dress socks, pantyhose, bags, scarves, and ties. These, too, should be kept clean and in good repair.

If you are working, try to save up your vacation or personal days for interviewing and other job-hunting needs. It's difficult to take time off without raising questions if you don't have time saved up.

It's not a good idea to give your work number to potential employers. If you don't already have an answering machine or voice mail at home, you should seriously consider it. Check for messages a couple times a day so you can return calls promptly.

Surfing the Net—Keeping up with trends

As I discussed in Chapter 2, the Internet is a useful tool in helping you find your new hot job. Not only can you find a job, but you can find ways to make that job better.

If you don't have access to a computer at home, go to your local library or college. Most have computer labs with Internet access for patrons, students, and local residents. Generally there is no charge to use these computers.

Moneysaver
Many libraries offer free classes in using the Internet for patrons. Call your local library to find out if they are giving classes.

If you have a computer at home, try to make time every day or two to do research. You'll be surprised at what you can find. You'll get the additional benefit of becoming more proficient at using the computer for research. The ability to use the

Internet is an added skill you can bring to a new employer.

Many companies have their own Web sites. Check out vital information *before* applying for a job. Companies may regularly post employment opportunities, offer a summary of the company's mission statement, list benefits, give the company history, and provide a wealth of other information.

Do you want to check out the viability of companies you are considering? Look for company annual reports online. Is the company on the stock exchange? Check out how their stock is doing and what the trends have been for the last year.

If you have a career question and you don't know where to find the answer, try the Internet. Visit various career sites and look for a career expert. Try a career chat to "speak" online with others who are interested in the same careers you are.

The Internet makes it easy to find material on almost any industry in which you are interested. To search, enter the name of the industry you are looking for in the search engine box. Hone your results by putting in extra search criteria. For example, if you're interested in the music business, first search for "music." Then depending what you're looking for, add words such as "careers," "jobs," or "industry."

If you're looking for more information about an industry, look for the relevant trade association Web sites. These often offer links to other sites you might find interesting.

In order to be able to explain to a potential employer how you can fill her needs, you need to know as much as possible about the job. There is a treasure trove of information on the Internet giving job descriptions for almost any job you can think of.

Timesaver
When you find Web sites you like, bookmark them in Netscape or put them in the Favorites section of Internet Explorer so you can find them easily next time.

Searching for books which are available about an industry used to mean a trip to the library. Today, you can find this information in a matter of minutes online. Amazon.com, BarnesandNoble.com, and Borders.com all have searches. Books In Print is also online. Additionally, in many areas, the card catalog of your local public library is online.

There are other ways to use high-tech tools in your job search. Many companies make job applications available online. There are employers who will e-mail job applications and forms to prospective candidates. E-mail is also a fast way of sending your resume to potential employers.

Using the Internet allows you to find virtually any information you need or want for your career and your life. You just have to look.

Networking your way to the hottest careers

I discussed in Chapter 2 the importance of networking to find hidden jobs in the market. What you might not know is that networking is also essential to your career, whatever your current job level.

Networking is a skill. Like most other skills, you must practice to become better. Even if you have to push yourself, make sure you get out, go places, meet people, talk to them, and tell them about your career goals. If you're shy, I know this might be tough. However, you have to try. The payoff is big, both in your career and your personal life.

Use every contact you have to help you get interviews with companies where you're interested in working. For example, if your mother has a friend whose son knows someone in a company where you have been trying to obtain an interview, ask for help. The worst that can happen is that someone will say

Moneysaver
Instead of buying newspapers, periodicals, and business journals at the store, look for many of them online. This lets you keep up with the latest business trends across the country and around the world.

no, they don't want to or they can't help. The best that can happen is that you'll get an interview with a great company!

Networking can help you get your foot in the door, but it's up to you to prove yourself once you're in. At that time you can rely on your package of skills, talents, experience, and personality to sell yourself to an employer.

A good method of networking is to volunteer. You can volunteer for activities totally outside of your field or showcase your skills and talents by volunteering to handle tasks that are similar to those you perform at work. Either way, you will have the opportunity to meet new people. They will have the chance to see that you are an outgoing, hard worker who does a little bit extra.

There are many places to volunteer. Look around your community and seek out organizations that have platforms or causes you agree with. Here are some ideas to get you started:

- Local hospitals
- Community theaters
- Libraries
- Public schools
- Garden clubs
- Civic groups
- Children's organizations
- Senior citizen centers
- Nursing homes
- Animal shelters
- Arts groups
- Professional associations

Bright Idea
If someone is nice enough to assist you in getting an interview or even just obtains the correct name for you to call, remember your manners. Write a note thanking that person for her help. If you end up getting a job through that contact, you might even want to send another note, some flowers, or a box of candy.

Unofficially...
Networking is a two-way street. If you hear of a position someone you know might be interested in, call him and tell him about it. Refer others to potential employers. Helping others is the way to build good relationships that will help you throughout your career.

- Ambulance corps
- Any other not-for-profit groups

How do you network in these situations? You go to meetings, help in whatever ways you can, volunteer to be on committees, chair events, do publicity, or offer to sit on the board of directors.

While volunteering is rewarding on its own, making yourself visible and known to others is like an extra pot of gold at the end of the rainbow. However, it's essential that you are known for being sincere, hardworking, reliable, and a team player. You don't want others to think of you as someone who is only helping because of a desire to get ahead.

Just because you get a job, don't stop networking. Cultivate relationships with people in various fields on various levels on a continuing basis. Once you get the hang of networking, you'll find it an effective—and enjoyable—way to widen your circle.

Just the facts

- A proactive approach to your career will move it forward.
- Marketing yourself sets you apart from other job candidates.
- Use every method possible to sell yourself to potential employers.
- The Internet contains most of the information you need for your job search.
- Networking is valuable in every aspect of your career.

Success Strategies So Hot They Sizzle

PART II

The Hot Career Toolbox

Chapter 5

Y ou are very lucky. You have chosen one of the best times ever to look for a new hot career. There are a wealth of opportunities available to you today. You just have to get started.

This chapter is about using the tools in your career toolbox to help you obtain the job of your dreams. It will offer you some ideas on jump-starting your career and assessing your skills so you can shine like a star in the workplace. I'll also give you some tips and techniques to help you find and succeed in your new hot career. Many job opportunities are at your fingertips. You just have to reach out for them!

Fire up your career

Many are frustrated with a career that they feel is unchallenging. They feel their career is stagnant and in a slump. Are you one of these people? If so, you're not alone. Having company in this situation, however, does not help. Many people just continue doing nothing to improve their situation. Sometimes, the only thing you seem to be able to do is get more depressed and wait for something to happen. While this doesn't

Watch Out!
Try not to get stuck in the "nothing is going right, why bother" mode. No matter how bad things seem, try to remain positive. Remember, getting to your perfect career is hard work.

take a lot of effort, it certainly doesn't change anything.

In order to improve your career, you have to make positive changes. It's not always easy taking steps to change your career for the better, but it can be done. Firing up your career is really a matter of moving ahead in a positive fashion. Even if you feel you can only begin by taking tiny baby steps, make sure you take them. Baby steps might get you to your destination later, but they *will* eventually get you there. The urgency for you in taking these actions depends on your current employment situation. You will usually move a lot faster if you are unemployed or currently employed in a job you hate than working in a job that just doesn't do anything for you.

How do you know if you're ready to fire up your career? When you reach a fork in the road, whether in your life or your career, it's sometimes helpful to ask yourself the following questions:

- *Do you want to stay where you are or make a change for the better?* Staying where you are is often easier, but it doesn't offer you any hope of new ,exciting opportunities.

66

I knew my career was in a slump. I was collecting a paycheck, but hated what I did...I stayed until the store went out of business. Now I have to find a job quickly.
—Ann, retail shop manager

99

- *What's the worst that can happen if you stay in your current situation?* You can continue being bored, depressed, and unfulfilled.

- *What's the best that can happen if you stay in your current situation?* An opportunity might fly in the window. It's not likely, but stranger things have happened.

- *What's the worst that can happen if you make a change?* You can fail, but you probably won't.

- *What's the best that can happen?* You can succeed and find a career you love and for which you have passion.

Chances are that if you're frustrated, making a change will look like a better course of action for you than doing nothing. You need to try to find ways to transform your unchallenging career into a fulfilling one. Nothing will change until you take action.

There are a wide array of things you can do to fire up your career. Some are specific; others are more general. Here are some general ideas which you might consider:

- Look for better opportunities in your current field.

- Look for other opportunities in your current company.

- Create opportunities for yourself that might not currently exist.

- Focus on your vision for career success.

- Develop a practical action plan and follow the steps to make it happen.

- Get started now. Even small things will get you started. Once you get started, you develop a momentum which will keep you going in a positive direction.

Many people feel they are under so much pressure performing the daily tasks of their jobs and their lives that they just don't have time to devote to helping their career. This is a big mistake. In order to achieve success in your career, you need to do everything possible—continually—to make things better.

People who are not happy in their job and career are often attracted to others who share similar situations. Those who are most successful in firing up their careers have found that surrounding

Timesaver
Only you can take the initiative to change your career. You have the control. You just need to take it. Start now.

Watch Out!
While it's OK to complain occasionally about a negative aspect of your job, constant complaining is not healthy and will do nothing for your career.

themselves with others who share their passions and their dreams is the key. Try to find people who support your efforts and share your visions, ethics, and values and keep them in your closest circle.

Sometimes taking more specific steps helps improve your career. While I have briefly covered some of these in earlier chapters, they are worth noting again. Consider one or more of the following as ideas to fire up a stalled career:

- Join professional associations in your field. If you are considering changing fields, join those appropriate associations. Remember, it's not enough just to be a member. Go to meetings and make yourself visible in a positive manner. Attending professional meetings can be a valuable networking opportunity.

- Once you belong to professional associations, get their trade journals and read them. See what's happening and how it can relate to your career.

- If you have writing skills, check out the editorial calendar of trade journals to learn what articles and subjects are being planned for the coming year. Go over the list and see if any of the subjects being covered are those in which you have expertise. Call the editor to see if the article has been assigned to a writer. If not, ask about being considered for the writing assignment. If the article has already been assigned, query her interest in another article on a different subject in your area.

- Look for other opportunities to write about your industry. You will gain exposure, heightened

Bright Idea
Make copies of articles you have published and send them to colleagues, your current boss, and prospective employers. Send short blurbs about the publication of the article to the business editor of your local newspaper and business journal.

visibility, and credibility—three factors important in firing up your career.

■ Give yourself broad visibility by checking out Web sites associated with your field. Many of these sites are seeking writers for online articles. Contact the editor or administrator of the site with your qualifications and try to make a connection.

■ If you are comfortable speaking in public and you have expertise in a subject either in your field or in an unrelated hobby or cause, consider becoming a guest speaker. Public speaking makes you very visible and offers you credibility in your field. Many communities, chambers of commerce, and trade associations have speaker bureaus. If not, contact community and civic groups and nonprofit organizations to offer your services as a speaker.

■ Keep your network active. Nurture it. Don't contact people only when you need them. Make contact with them on a consistent basis. Ask what they are doing, send them congratulatory notes for accomplishments, cards for holidays and birthdays, and so on.

■ If someone offers to help you meet your career goals in any way, don't be proud. Take them up on it and say thank-you.

■ Take classes, workshops, and seminars, either in your field or a totally different one in which you might be interested.

■ Volunteer your services to a nonprofit organization or civic or community group. Nothing gives you a better feeling of self-worth than volunteering

> **"**
> The exposure I received speaking about customer service at the Business and Professional Women's dinner meeting was tremendous. Within a couple days I received three phone calls from potential employers asking if I would come in for an interview.
> —Kim, customer service supervisor
> **"**

Bright Idea
If you aren't a writer, you can still obtain visibility in your area by becoming the focus of articles written by others. Build relationships with editors, reporters, and producers. Make them aware of your expertise. Then, when they are seeking quotes, you will come to mind.

and doing for others. Volunteering your services also gives you high visibility, which is a major key in firing up your career. Give away a little of what you do best.

Let's say you're a bookkeeper. Offer to handle the bookkeeping functions for a local civic group. Let's take it one step further. You're not a bookkeeper, but are skilled in the field and interested in getting a job in that area. This is the perfect time to offer your services. It will give you needed experience and a great reference for a job. Everyone has skills that are useful to others. Determine what these are and put them to use.

Firing up your career means taking the initiative. Don't just sit back and wait for your career to get better on its own. Go on the offensive to success.

Don't wait for opportunity to knock on your door. Start now. If you wait until tomorrow, it may be too late. What does this mean to your career?

- Always be on the lookout for new opportunities. Even if you are currently employed and happy, check out the classifieds, job fairs, and network on a consistent basis.

- If you can't find the job you are interested in, don't give up. Create the one you want. This is not such a far-fetched idea. If you can illustrate a need to a potential employer and show how you can fill it, you might land the job of your dreams.

- Prepare yourself so you are always ready for every opportunity.

There are also a number of things you can do on a more emotional level to help jump-start your career. These include:

- Believing in yourself
- Believing in your self-worth
- Having a desire to succeed
- Not giving up until you get what you want

It's essential in the firing up process to determine what problems stand between you and what you want. Once you know what the problems are, you can attack them and remove the obstacles. No matter where your career is currently, it can benefit from a jump start. It can energize a stalled career or catapult one that is moving in a positive direction to success quicker than ever.

Assess yourself and your skills

Do you know what you want? Do you know what your strengths and weakness are? Can you readily identify the fields in which you are especially interested? A major tool in your career toolbox should be an accurate assessment of yourself and your skills.

How can you assess yourself and your skills? Start by trying to determine what you want to do and where you want to do it.

- *In which general industry are you interested?* Are you interested in working in health care, entertainment, sports, education, food service, television and radio, communications, insurance, gaming, law enforcement, hospitality, publishing, computers?

- *What kinds of job functions are you interested in pursuing?* Do you want to be a teacher, salesperson, agent, manager, police officer, entertainer, writer, nurse, physician, accountant, craftsperson, attorney, reporter, publicist, personal shopper, Web site developer, information specialist?

Bright Idea
Keep a calendar marked with special dates of birthdays and anniversaries of business associates and colleagues. Check it weekly so you can send out cards on a timely basis.

Bright Idea
Keep in mind that just because you have defined your goals, they are not written in stone. This is your life. You can change your mind at any time.

■ *Where do you want to be?* Where do you want to live? Are you inclined to stay in the geographic area you live in now or are you willing to relocate for the type of position you want?

Assessing your hopes for a dream job

In order to help you find your dream job, it might help to review your past jobs. Everyone remembers what they didn't like about past jobs. Perhaps it was the hours, or the boss, or the coworkers. Maybe it was the job responsibilities, or just the job itself.

It's easy to concentrate on things that make you unhappy, but it really serves no constructive purpose. Instead of focusing on the negative aspects of work, it's sometimes helpful to concentrate on the positive parts. Then you can search for careers that encompass the portions of jobs you enjoy.

Let's look at your past jobs:

■ What parts of those jobs did you like?

■ In which parts of those jobs did you excel?

■ What parts of those jobs excited you?

■ What parts of those jobs made you happy?

■ What skills did you enjoy using?

Now that you have answered these questions, you have an idea about what you are looking for.

Determining what you are looking for in your career is easier than examining yourself. What do you want out of your career? Everyone looks for something different in their dream job. What's important to you?

■ Your work environment

■ Your hours

■ Your responsibilities

Bright Idea
Your dream job will reflect the parts of past jobs you enjoyed, coupled with your skills, talents, and lifestyle requirements.

- The ability to use your skills and talents
- Your coworkers
- Your proximity to the workplace
- Your salary
- The fringe benefits
- The job content
- The power or influence of your position
- The recognition the job offers
- The intellectual stimulation the job offers
- The satisfaction the job offers

Your personal inventory

Your personal inventory can encompass a great many things. Your inventory list is what you have to offer potential employers. You might want to sit down with a pen and paper, get comfortable, and take your own personal inventory. Start with the following list and add to it as things come to mind:

- What do you like to do?
- What are you good at?
- What are your skills?
- What are your talents?
- What are your hobbies?
- What are your personality traits?
- What types of people do you enjoy working with?
- What type of environment do you want to work in?
- What is important to you?

- What are your values?
- What are your priorities?

Assessing your skills, personality traits, and talents
Your combination of skills, personality traits, and talents determine your marketability in the workplace.

Skills are things you do well. Do you know what your skills are? It's hard to sell what you have if you aren't sure what it is. You may have different types of skills. These might include:

- *Job skills.* These are skills you use while at work (such as bookkeeping).

- *Transferable skills.* These are skills you have used on one job that you can transfer to another job (such as using publishing skills to get a Web site design job).

- *Life skills.* These are skills you use in living. Problem solving, money management, time management, decision making, and interpersonal skills are examples. More specific life skills might include cooking, child rearing, and home repair.

- *Technical skills.* These are skills you have that include the use of machinery such as cars, trucks, computers, sewing machines, cameras, and word processors.

- *Hobby or leisure-time skills.* These are skills you learn and have used in hobbies or leisure-time activities you might enjoy. These skills can often be transferred and used in a new job or career.

Many people don't realize how many skills they actually have. They aren't aware of the specialized knowledge they possess. Your package of skills makes you unique. It can set you apart from other applicants and help you win the job of your dreams. Using your skills and talents will also result in you loving your job.

Make a list of your skills. What should you include? Start with skills you know you have. Think about it. What are you good at? What have you done? What can you do? Some skills are job-related; others are more general. Include everything you can think of from very basic things on up. Use the following list of skills to help jog your memory:

- Typing
- Computer proficiency
- Public speaking
- Bookkeeping
- Time management
- Analytical skills
- Verbal communication
- Writing
- Management
- Listening
- Math proficiency
- Organizational skills
- People skills
- Language skills
- Interpersonal skills
- Selling
- Copywriting
- Sewing
- Problem solving

Timesaver
It's essential to take an inventory of the skills you have. Make your list in writing so that you can update it as you obtain new ones.

Bright Idea
Make your supervisor aware of your accomplishments. It's always a good idea to either send a memo or have a talk when you update your skills or add new ones.

- Telephone skills
- Customer service skills
- Negotiating
- Teaching
- Decision making
- Shorthand
- Leadership
- Management
- Auto repair
- Computer repair
- Cooking
- Songwriting
- Fashion design

Personality traits and talents

In addition to skills, everyone has certain unique personality traits that they bring to the table when seeking a job. When assessing yourself, make a list of your special personality traits. Here's a list of some personality traits to help you get started:

- Compassionate
- Hard worker
- Energetic
- Creative
- Honest
- Positive
- Charismatic
- Flexible
- Self-starter
- Efficient

- Reliable
- Organized

Your talents are also part of what makes you unique. Do you know what your talents are? Many are reluctant to admit what their special talents are. But if you don't identify and use your talents, you'll have wasted them.

You are born with your talents. They are not acquired. They may, however, be refined. There are many talents people may have. These might include:

- Musical ability
- Artistic ability
- Mathematical ability

Let's look at a number of talents and careers that people with those talents may enjoy:

- Are you artistic? Consider a career as a set designer, museum exhibit designer, interior designer, craftsperson, makeup artist, police sketch artist, fashion or medical illustrator.

- Do you have a flair for fashion? Consider careers in clothing design, fabric design, costume design, apparel buying, personal shopping, retail clothing sales, or fashion coordination.

- Do you love crunching numbers? Think about working as a bookkeeper, accountant, or auditor.

- Do you love talking? You could work in customer service, as an order entry operator, salesperson, radio announcer, or motivational speaker.

- Do you enjoy writing? Consider working as a reporter, journalist, speechwriter, copywriter,

Unofficially...
Once you assess your skills, personality traits, and talents, use the information honestly. If you are honest with yourself, you'll be able to use this information to find a job you love.

publicist, comedy writer, book author, technical document specialist, or scriptwriter.

- Do you have a talent for creating delicious foods and baked goods? Your passion may be to work as a chef in a fine restaurant, baker, personal chef, caterer, home economist, or cookbook author or editor.

- Do you love working with flowers and plants? Consider a career as a floral designer, managing a florist shop or garden center, or teaching others how to grow plants.

- Can you spend all day on the computer? Consider working as a programmer, information specialist, Web site designer, software developer, computer or software teacher, computer consultant, or hardware or software salesperson.

- Interested in health and nutrition? A job as a nutritionist, dietician, health-food store manager, or spa chef might fit the bill.

- Do you love to exercise and work out? A job as an aerobics instructor, health club manager, or personal trainer might be up your alley.

The key to finding the job of your dreams is assessing your self and your skills and using the information to match what you have with the needs of specific jobs.

Tips of the trade

How do people find careers they love and then excel in them? In this section I'll cover a variety of tips, tricks, and techniques from people who have been successful in their quest. While I may have touched briefly on a number of these in previous chapters, they are included for your review because of their importance.

> 66
> I lost my job in sales, which was OK because I didn't like it anyway. I went to the health club to work out....While there, I realized I was envying the class instructor. I now am a certified aerobics instructor and love what I do.
> —Shari, 35, aerobics instructor
> 99

Tip #1: Love what you do and always work to improve yourself. Those who do don't stay stagnant. They understand that things can always change for the better. These people move their life and their careers in a positive direction by searching out new opportunities, keeping active, and learning as much as possible.

Tip #2: Write a personal mission statement. Most successful businesses have mission statements. Many successful people prepare these as well. Simply put, a personal mission statement declares what you want your mission in life and work to be. Seeing it in writing sometimes helps you focus on goals you might want to reach. It also assists you in clearly defining methods and actions you can take to achieve those goals.

For example, a mission statement for someone interested in working in animal rights might be:

> *My personal mission is to find ways to help animals be treated with kindness and compassion and to protect their right to be treated humanely through my work and volunteer efforts.*

As you see, it doesn't have to be very long. It just has to tell the story. This person can now go on to search for a career that will fulfill these goals.

Tip #3: Make a good impression all the time. It's essential to every stage of your career to make a good impression on others. Here are a few helpful tips to keep in mind:

- Think before you speak. Words are something you can never take back.

- Don't use foul language or curse in (or out) of the workplace.

- Don't gossip about your boss or coworkers.

Bright Idea
Your mission statement doesn't have to be very long. It can be a couple of sentences, just long enough to say what you want.

- Don't talk badly about anyone.

- Don't bad-mouth your current or past employers or companies.

- Don't give away your old company's secrets to a potential new employer.

- Dress appropriately at all times. Casual Friday does not mean wearing ripped jeans and a tee shirt.

- Always act professionally. That means everywhere, not just in the workplace. You can never tell who you might run into outside of work.

Tip #4: Find a mentor. A mentor can be a positive force in your career. How can you find one? Often, all you have to do is ask someone you admire. Most people are pleased to have someone admire them and happier still to help.

Tip #5: Become a mentor. No matter where you are in your career, chances are someone could use your help. Helping others is usually a good way to help yourself.

Tip #6: Work to overcome your fears. It's difficult, but it will pay off in the end. Fears can paralyze your career and your life. While you might be terrified to change jobs or careers, it might be the only way you can get job satisfaction. Make a commitment (and take baby steps if you have to) but keep working against your fears. You alone have the power.

Tip #7: Be willing to take risks. Be willing to succeed. You know what you have and where you are in your career. And you know what you want in a career: success, happiness, and job satisfaction, to name a few things. If you're reading this book, chances are you want more than you have. If you're not willing to risk getting out of your comfort zone to try to achieve what you want, you probably won't get it. Take risks and be willing to succeed.

Tip #8: Network, network, network. Don't ever stop. Everyone you come in contact with is a potential contact who might help spiral your career to the top.

Tip #9: Make your resume a selling tool. Your resume should entice people and make them want to interview you. Because your resume is actually a printed marketing piece—your own personal advertisement—make sure it's as perfect as possible. A powerful resume grabs the attention of potential employers and shows that you have the qualifications and experience to fill their needs.

Don't be afraid to redo your resume to fit the needs of a specific job opening. If you have access to a computer, keep your resume on file. If not, and you are using someone else's computer to do your resume, save it to a disk. Always keep a copy of the resume you sent to a specific employer for reference.

Here are some tips on making your resume a better marketing tool:

- If you are replying to a specific job opening, make the career objective on your resume as close to the job you are applying for as possible.

- If you aren't replying to a specific job opening, make your career objective more general. Don't limit yourself unnecessarily.

- Every time you make a change to your resume, check for incorrect grammar and spelling.

- Check for incorrect word usage. Common errors include using "their" for "there," "too" or "two" for "to," "effect" for "affect," "your" for "you're," and "its" for "it's."

- Don't rely solely on a spell and grammar check-er. Go over your resume yourself and then ask one or two trusted friends or colleagues to read it.

- Don't lie on your resume. People may find out and not trust anything that's written there.

- Remember to include your name, address, and telephone number in a prominent position on your resume. The top of the first page is preferred.

- Never handwrite your resume.

- Always make good-quality copies on good-quality paper.

- Never put down the names of references without asking them first.

Tip #10: Rehearse for your interview. You've found the job you've dreamed about. All that stands between you and it is the interview process. You can increase your chances by rehearsing for your interview. That way you'll be prepared for almost anything that's thrown at you.

Begin by making sure you have your perfect interview wardrobe in order. Try on the entire outfit you plan to wear, making sure it's clean and pressed. Make sure you can sit comfortably in it and move about.

Next, go over your resume. Be sure you know every detail on it. You don't want to hem and haw when an interviewer asks about a past accomplishment, experience, or employer.

Next, try to determine what the most difficult questions the interviewer might ask you will be. Will you have to explain a gap on your resume? Or will

Bright Idea
Buy large 9 × 12–inch or 11 × 14–inch envelopes so that you don't have to fold your resume when sending it out. It will arrive looking more polished and professional.

you be asked why you've held so many jobs? Do you have a black mark on your resume that might send up a red flag? Might someone ask you about a conviction many years ago? Perhaps you might be worried about answering questions regarding your career goals or what you can offer the company or why they should hire you.

Whatever the questions are that worry you, write them down on a piece of paper and then compose your answers. When doing this find ways to turn negatives into positives. For example: "I've held a great many jobs in the past. These experiences have helped me to know what I want to do with my career. That's why I'm so excited about the possibility of this position. I think I can bring a great deal of experience to the organization with what I learned."

You should also develop answers to commonly asked questions. These might include questions such as:

- Why did you leave your last job?
- What did you like most about your last job?
- What aspect of your last job did you least enjoy?
- What were your most important accomplishments in your last job?
- What can you bring to this organization?
- Why should we hire you?
- Are you a team player?
- What are your weak points?
- What are your strong points?

Once again, write your responses down on paper and read them out loud. Practice until everything flows easily and you can answer even the toughest questions without seeming nervous.

Bright Idea
Many people fail to rehearse for their interview. Enlist a mentor or friend to ask you interview questions so you can rehearse your responses.

Watch Out!
Don't ask your interviewer about salary or benefits in your first interview unless you are offered the job. Let the interviewer bring up salary and benefits first

Tip #11: Write everything down. Successful people appear to have it all together. Whether you are actively searching for your new hot career or you've found the job of your dreams and are climbing the ladder to success, don't rely on your memory. Use a notebook or daytimer to keep track of information. As soon as you make appointments, schedule meetings or interviews, tell someone you will call them back, or make any other commitment, write it down. That way there is no room for error. You won't be sitting there trying to remember if the appointment was for 1:00 p.m. on Tuesday or Thursday.

It's also helpful to write down the names of people you meet, your contacts, and any other pertinent information while it's fresh in your mind. Similarly, many find it useful to write down the content of conversations and meetings so you have something to refer to later.

High-tech tools for the job hunt and beyond

Technology has changed the entire job-search process. You may recall what it was like to look for a job just a few years ago. You probably typed your resume on a manual typewriter. If you made an error you would have to correct it with correcting paper. It never really looked clean or neat. Job seekers a few years later used an electric typewriter, this time correcting errors with correction tape or correction fluid. Depending on when you were searching for your job, you might have made copies on a mimeograph machine or brought them to a printer (when copying was much more expensive than it is today). You wouldn't have the option of constantly changing and updating your resume. It would have been too expensive.

Instead of voice mail, you'd be looking for those important messages on an outdated answering machine, one that probably would not allow you to retrieve messages from a remote location. And if you were home, you would have had to stay off the phone if you were expecting a call from a potential boss, because there was no call-waiting.

Today you have a variety of high-tech tools at your fingertips to assist you in your search for your new hot career. Let's go over a few of them and how they can help you in your job search and beyond.

- *Telephone.* The telephone is your lifeline during your job search. Make sure your home phone is in good working order. Nothing is more annoying than crackling on the line when you're trying to talk to someone.

- *Cell phone.* A cell phone can be a great way to check your messages when job hunting or to keep in touch with your office.

- *Answering machine or voice mail.* An answering machine or voice mail is essential if you are job hunting. This is especially true if you are looking for a new job while you are currently employed. If you are considering an answering machine, make sure you'll be able to retrieve messages from remote locations.

    Whether you use an answering machine or a voice-mail service, be sure to leave a professional-sounding message. It doesn't have to be complicated. Here's an example: "Hello, this is Alice Harmon. I'm sorry I can't take your call at this time. Please leave your name, phone number,

Watch Out!
Unless your cordless phone is truly high-quality, don't use it to make calls to potential employers or other business associates. If all people hear is static, that might be all they remember.

Moneysaver
If you are considering a cell phone, check the service and fees of a number of companies in your area. Fees vary greatly. Also be sure to check out promotions that can give you a free phone or free minutes.

and a message at the tone and I will return your call shortly."

Check your messages frequently and answer them as soon as possible.

- *Beeper.* This is a nice thing to have so people can get in touch with you, but it's not a necessity. If you do decide to get a beeper, check your options on buying or renting the beeper as well as programs for monthly service.

- *Computer.* A computer is by far one of the most important high-tech tools in your job search. Use it for simple tasks such as word processing for cover letters, your resume, and thank-you letters. Your computer can handle other tasks too, such as keeping track of job-hunting expenses, scheduling appointments, and keeping an action journal.

    An especially important use of your computer is the ability to go online. As noted in Chapters 2 and 4, the Internet or World Wide Web gives you access to a wealth of information, including company profiles, job openings, trends, job descriptions, career sites, and much more.

    If you don't know how to use the Internet, take some classes at a local library, school, or community college.

    Your computer also makes it possible to send and receive e-mail. E-mail is a boon for job hunters. It can be used to send your resume, cover letters, and other information quickly to potential employers.

- *Modem.* You need a modem to make the connection between your phone and computer to go online. Some computers come with internal

Timesaver
If you don't own a computer, you can still go online with Web TV, which runs through your television set. Web TV is available in many local retailers throughout the country and is not only reasonably priced, but very easy to use.

modems; others require external modems. There are also new methods of connecting to the Internet using cable-TV lines instead of phone lines.

■ *Printer.* If you have a computer, you need a printer to get the information out. There are many inexpensive printers on the market, from laser printers on down. Make sure that whatever printer you use turns out a clear, crisp document. While color is nice, it usually isn't necessary for printing business documents.

■ *Fax machine.* A fax (or facsimile) machine is a valuable tool. The prices of these machines have dropped over the years. A fax machine gives you the option of sending or receiving information almost instantly. You can fax resumes, cover letters, and job applications directly to potential employers. There are a variety of fax machines on the market in a range of prices. Some use traditional fax paper on a roll, while others use plain paper. Some computer modem packages also offer fax capability.

If you aren't ready to invest in a fax machine right now, you can usually find fax services at both large and small office supply shops. You might also find fax services at many shopping malls, supermarkets, and a variety of other businesses and stores. For a nominal charge you can send or receive faxes.

■ *Photocopy machine.* While a photocopy machine can be a great asset during the job-hunting process, most people can't afford to have a good-quality machine in their home. There are a variety of places where you might find copying

Moneysaver
When looking into the purchase of a printer, check out the cost of the tapes, ink, and toner cartridges to see which will be most economical to run.

Moneysaver
Think about buying a fax machine, scanner, or copier. Or look into "all-in-one" machines that print, copy, and fax, to save money and space in your home workplace.

Watch Out!
Don't fax a letter of application, your resume, or any other pertinent job information to a potential employer from the fax machine of your current employer unless she knows you're job hunting. The name of the business and phone number of the sending fax machine usually prints on the top of the paper that is received.

services. Don't let the price of copies be your sole reason for using a copy shop. Check out the quality of the work. If the quality is not perfect, find a new copy shop.

- *Electronic data banks (also called PDAs or Personal Digital Assistants).* These are pocket-sized (or slightly larger) portable miniature computers. They aren't necessities, but are relatively inexpensive and neat to have. Depending on the type you get, you can input names, addresses, phone numbers, and additional information. Some of them have electronic daytimers where you have the ability to input appointments, meetings, and important dates.

- *Alarm clock.* While an alarm clock certainly isn't a high-tech tool, it is something you need. Make sure you have an alarm clock that works accurately, and that you know how to set the alarm. Being late for early-morning interviews or work is a sure way *not* to get a job—or to lose the job you have.

Smart strategies

Using smart strategies in your career can make a big difference. They can help you achieve success so that you come out on top. What are smart strategies? Simple things you can and should do to help your career move in an upward direction. They are little things that can help you build a positive favorable image in other people's eyes.

There are numerous smart strategies that you can incorporate into your daily life. Let's look at a few of them.

Smart Strategy #1: Don't skimp on the little things.

- Return phone calls promptly.

- Answer your e-mail.

- Thank people who have helped you.

- Write notes to coworkers, colleagues, supervisors, and associates congratulating them on achievements, praising them, or thanking them.

- Send cards to coworkers, colleagues, supervisors, and associates for birthdays, anniversaries, engagements, condolences, etc.

- Always answer your business correspondence promptly.

Smart Strategy #2: Do a little bit more than people expect. Sure, you're busy. You have a lot of responsibilities and things to do. However, if you do a little bit more than is expected of you, people will notice. You will obtain important visibility.

Smart Strategy #3: Set standards for yourself and follow them. You have to live with yourself. Don't put yourself in a position where you do things you don't believe in. This includes stealing, lying, or covering up for others who do.

Smart Strategy #4: Be professional at all times. A professional demeanor is essential to your career. Your professional demeanor includes the way you act, conduct yourself, speak, dress, and work. Once you act unprofessionally, it's difficult to build that image again.

Smart Strategy #5: Have a good work ethic. Show your employer you have a commitment to your job and the organization. Work hard. Don't try to cut corners. Don't see if you can come in late, leave early, and take long lunches just because you think no one notices. Do the very best you can in every job you have, whether or not you like it or want to stay.

> **❝**
> On my first day of government work, I was handed a pile of papers at four in the afternoon. I took them home and read them that night. When I was prepared to discuss them the next morning, people were impressed.
> —Charles, former Washington, D.C., professional
> **❞**

Smart Strategy #6: Always be on time. Be on time for everything. This includes interviews, meetings, appointments, phone calls, and work. Get your work done on time. Don't hold other people up with your tardiness.

Smart Strategy #7: Learn how to take a compliment graciously. When someone praises you, how do you react? Do you get embarrassed? Do you downplay what you've done? Do you reply, "It was nothing, anyone could have done it?" It's often difficult for many of us to accept a compliment or recognize our professional accomplishments. Make it your new smart strategy to learn how to say "thank-you" and acknowledge what you have achieved with grace and dignity.

Smart Strategy #8: Learn how to prioritize. It's easy to get overwhelmed, whether you're searching for your new hot job or trying to move up the career ladder. You start feeling like you can't get everything done, and that makes it difficult to get anything done. This is counterproductive. Learn how to prioritize by first making a list of everything you have to do. Then decide which are the most important things you need to do. Put these things in a second list. Prioritize each task you need to handle. Then take care of them one by one.

Timesaver
Keep a notebook with a master list of everything you need to do. Make your priority list daily from this master list. Cross tasks off both lists as you accomplish them.

Smart Strategy #9: Treat people the way you want to be treated. This includes your boss, coworkers, business associates, customers, friends, and family. Respect others and you will be respected.

Smart Strategy #10: Be a team player. If you see others need help in the workplace, pitch in. Give others praise. Don't backstab coworkers. Work as a team and you will all succeed.

Shine like a star

Did you ever notice that some people appear to be more successful in their life and the workplace than others? They are the people the boss always notices. They are productive and happy. These are the people who rise to the top. Do you think that it's talent, or is it luck? Perhaps, you think, it might be a little bit of both.

Do you want to be one of these stars? I am sure you are talented enough. You might even be lucky enough. The question is—are you motivated enough?

How can you become a star in the workplace? In order to be a star you have to want to shine. Here are some tips to help you do just that:

■ Get motivated. Have a desire to be better than you are and act on it.

■ Stay visible.

■ Take the initiative. Don't wait for someone to ask you to take on a project. If you see something that you think should be done and would help make your company better, offer to handle it.

■ Know who can make things happen in your organization. Talk to them when you need something done.

■ Determine what you are good at and become an expert. Shine at what you do best.

■ If you say you're going to do something, do it in a timely fashion.

■ Give credit to others. You are part of a team.

Just the facts

■ Every career can benefit from getting fired up.

■ Assessing yourself and your skills can help you get the career you want.

> ❝
> Nothing in this world can take the place of persistence. Talent will not; nothing is more common than unsuccessful people with talent. Genius will not; unrewarded genius is almost a proverb. Education will not; the world is full of educated derelicts. Persistence and determination alone are omnipotent.
> —Calvin Coolidge
> ❞

- Using smart strategies in your career can help catapult you to the top.
- You can shine in the workplace by becoming motivated and taking the initiative.

GET THE SCOOP ON...
New hot options in the workplace ▪ Temping as
a career choice ▪ Telecommuting and your
career ▪ Finding new ways to work part-time ▪
Job sharing

Hot Career Choices

Chapter 6

The year 2000 brings a new century. It also brings hot new career choices. This chapter will cover some of the hottest career choices you have the opportunity to choose from today. It will help you decide what is hot for you and what is not. This chapter will give you the options, so you can make an informed decision about what you want to do and how you want to do it.

Have you thought about temping? Considered job sharing? Wished you could telecommute? Wanted to know what flex time was and how you might negotiate your job to include it? This chapter will answer many of your questions in these areas and more.

What's hot and what's not

When searching for your new career, it's important to know what is hot and what is not. It's also important to understand that just because a career area is not hot, doesn't mean you can't work in that field. It just means that it will be harder to find what you're looking for. As I have stressed throughout this book, sometimes it just takes a little bit of creativity and a lot of perseverance to get what you want.

What are some of the hot career areas? Computers, information and technology, health care, medical technology, communications, sales, service, education, hospitality, travel, and engineering, to name a few.

What's not so hot? Any job that a computer can do should be avoided. Many manufacturing jobs are also declining because of automation (however, in some areas, as the number of jobs declines, the quality of the remaining jobs rises).

The new hot job market requires people with a variety of talents and skills. New and updated technology has changed the way we work and the way we live. Red-hot careers will be waiting for those who see a need and find a way to fill it.

Changing the way we work

The way we work is also changing. Home businesses are very hot and getting hotter. Consultants and freelancers are also hot commodities in the workplace.

With a diminishing labor pool and low unemployment, many companies are adding perks to attract and retain workers. When searching for your new hot career, you might find some of the following:

- On-site day care
- Day care reimbursement
- Elder care
- On-site gym
- Weekly massages
- Stress-management programs
- Educational reimbursement

Watch Out!
In considering the value of perks in choosing one job over another, evaluate them on a long-range basis and with potential changing scenarios. Perks which may seem unimportant at the time, may become so in the future and vice versa.

- Concierge service
- Flex time
- On-site medical services
- On-site dental services

The hot workplace

The workplace, too, is getting hotter. It has changed a great deal over the years. Today's workplace is a lot more worker-friendly and flexible than in the past. This flexibility is often necessary to meet the challenges of people trying to balance careers, families, and life.

Whether you are faced with the challenge of being a single working parent or you and your spouse both work, child care can be a big problem. Similarly, in today's society, elder care is a growing concern.

Everyone faces challenges regarding their job and their career. What are yours?

- Do you want to spend more time with your children?
- Do you have child care challenges?
- Do you have to care for elderly parents?
- Have you lost your job as a result of layoffs or downsizing?
- Did you quit your job?
- Do you dislike your current job?
- Do you feel unchallenged in your job but aren't sure what you want to do?
- Have you just had a baby and don't want to stop working, but can't figure out how to keep working and still care for your newborn?
- Do you hate commuting every day?

Moneysaver
Consider the value of perks as part of the entire package you are offered. Decide what is worth the most to you. For example, the security of on-site child care might be worth more than a higher salary.

- Is yours a two-paycheck family where both parents must work?

How you deal with those challenges can mean the difference between success and failure in your career. No matter what your challenges, you can find ways to face them without sacrificing your career, family, or life.

Unofficially...
You're lucky that many employers are beginning to find hot new ways to help you meet some of these challenges. You are thus afforded the benefit of having more control of your time, career, and life.

With unemployment low and the labor pool dwindling, companies must find ways to attract and retain employees. As a result, corporate America is beginning to make the workplace an easier place to work by offering flexibility to employees. This flexibility can include various options that might make your work life easier and your career better. While some workplace options have been around for a while, others are newer concepts. Let's briefly look at some of these career options you might consider:

- Temping
- Telecommuting
- Flex-time work
- Part-time work
- Job sharing

Now let's go over these options in more depth.

Temping tips 2000

Twenty years ago, temping probably meant a secretarial, clerical, or receptionist position where you filled in for a day or two. Today, temping is vastly different. Many temp agencies place professional and technical people. Virtually every industry has temp placement agencies. Here are some of specialized temp agency industry possibilities:

- Secretarial, clerical, and office
- Accounting

- Marketing
- Computer programming
- Nursing
- Communications
- Advertising
- Public relations
- Food service
- Hospitality
- Banking
- Direct marketing
- Customer service
- Media
- Law
- Music
- Technology services
- Information technology
- Engineering
- Human resources
- Sales
- Cleaning services
- Banking
- Publishing

These agencies supply employers with workers to fill in for employees who are vacationing, have quit, or have been fired. They also place employees in workplaces where organizations need or want to augment the workforce.

While to many, temping means working a day here or there, today's workforce provides you with the opportunity to become a long-term temp. What that means is that you may work for a company as a

I love working as a temporary worker at the convention center. I retired from my job as an insurance sales manager four years ago...I get to meet new people every day. If I want to go on a business trip with my husband, I just call up and tell them I'm not available. —Pat, convention center temp worker

Bright Idea
The temping trend is growing by leaps and bounds. With unemployment so low, employers often need high-quality, qualified employees to fill positions quickly. For many organizations, it's easier and more efficient to use temporary labor.

Watch Out!
As a long-term temp, you are working without the security of a permanent full-time job. The company you are working for may contact the placement agency at any time and ask that you be relieved of your duties for any legal reason.

temporary employee for an extended period of time.

When you are placed by a temp agency, you are generally paid by the temp agency at an agreed-upon rate. The client company pays the agency.

Why would employers hire long-term temps? There are a number of reasons. The temp agency is responsible not only for finding people with the right skills, but for screening them as well. If there are problems with the temp employee, the organization can get rid of him without having to pay unemployment benefits. The temp agency is responsible for telling the temp employee that he is not needed. The employer also does not have to pay benefits such as health insurance, taxes, paid holidays, paid vacations, and pension plans.

Some people make a career out of temping; others use temping to open the door to new career opportunities. What do you want to do? Temping has a great many advantages. Let's look at some of them:

- If you have just graduated and are not sure what you want to do, temping allows you to try out various fields.

- If you don't like your job and want to sample other fields, temping allows you to do so.

- If you have been out of the workplace for a period of time, temping helps you move back in.

- Temping is great for people who need flexible schedules.

- Temping is ideal for people who don't want to make a commitment to a full-time permanent job.

- Temping positions often lead to permanent employment.

- Temping usually offers you the ability to learn new skills.

- Temping is often a good work option between jobs.

- Temping offers networking possibilities.

- Temping offers the opportunity to learn about the inner dynamics of various companies to see where you might want to work.

- Temping offers the ability to earn money if you've been laid off.

Temping has a great many advantages. However, there is also a downside. Before you jump on the temping bandwagon, let's consider some of the disadvantages:

- There is no job security. While you can always find another temp position, it can sometimes take between three and five days to be placed.

- You don't really have a place or position in your workplace.

- Temping jobs do not usually include fringe benefits such as health insurance, pension plans, paid vacation days, or sick days.

Here are some tips to help you get the most out of temping:

- All temp agencies are not created equal. Some have better client companies than others. It's appropriate to ask what clients the agency serves.

- Some agencies may offer perks or benefits to attract the best and the brightest talent to their agency. These may include benefits such as vacation pay, sick days, raises, bonuses, and on occasion, health insurance.

Bright Idea
If you are trained in a specialized, high-profile, or high-demand industry, you can often earn more temping than you can in a permanent position. Consider your options.

Watch Out!
Check ahead of time to see who pays the fee to the agency. Fees are usually paid by the client company for temp employees. However, you can't be too careful. Always read all documents carefully and ask questions before you sign anything.

- As a rule, the agency will be paying you, not the company for whom you are performing services. Ask about the rate of pay you will receive and when you will be paid for your services.

- Interview at a number of agencies and ask questions.

- Generally, it's OK to register with more than one agency to make sure you get the best opportunities.

- Temping gives you the opportunity to try various jobs. If you don't like the job you were placed in, ask for another assignment.

- Always do your best in every assignment. You can never tell when there will be a great permanent job possibility waiting to be filled.

- Dress professionally when going to your temporary job.

- Don't talk about other bosses or companies at your current assignment.

- Keep confidences. If you hear something in one temporary assignment, don't share it at another.

- Look for specialized temp placement agencies to match your talents.

- Take advantage of every opportunity to learn new skills while temping.

- Take advantage of networking opportunities while temping.

Bright Idea
Stop in or call your temp agency representative on a regular basis to check in and keep your name uppermost in her mind. Don't leave it to chance that she will remember you.

Telecommuting in the new millennium

With advances in high-tech tools (see Chapter 5) and the availability of lower-priced equipment, the trend toward telecommuting is quickly growing in popularity. Telephones, voice mail, computers, printers, scanners, fax machines, and modems make it both easy and possible to work from home or any other place you might be based.

Telecommuting is ideal for working mothers or fathers. Hours are often flexible. You can do your work at odd hours and still participate in your children's life. You can take the kids to Little League or pick them up from school while handling your workload before and after the traditional workday.

For many people, telecommuting is an attractive alternative to working in the office. With company mergers and takeovers moving offices to other locations, telecommuting can often mean the difference between keeping and leaving a job. Those who hate rush hour and the daily commute might also be good telecommuting candidates.

Why would employers allow you to telecommute? There are a number of benefits to the employer:

- Office space is expensive
- Reduction of certain overhead, such as rent and telephone costs
- Reduction of employee absenteeism
- Reduction of employee turnover
- Better employee efficiency
- Happier employees
- Better job satisfaction
- Less office politics

Why would you want to telecommute? Here are a number of good reasons to consider:

- You don't have to go to the office.
- You don't have to dress professionally.
- You may avoid having to deal with office politics.

Unofficially...
Telecommuting means working from home for all or part of the work week. However, you don't even have to *be* home. With a laptop and a cell phone, you can work from almost anywhere.

Moneysaver
Many companies who are telecommuter-savvy provide computers, modems, fax machines, and other equipment to their telecommuting employees. If the company you are working for does not do this, try to negotiate as much as you can.

- You don't have to deal with traffic or driving in bad weather.

- If you only have one car in your family, you can let your spouse take it to work.

- You don't have to worry about day care if your kids get sick.

- You will be there when your kids get home from school.

- If you have a cold or headache, it's easier to work at home.

- You can work more efficiently.

- You can save money on coffee breaks and lunch by having them at home.

- You can increase your job satisfaction.

While these reasons are enticing, telecommuting is not for everyone. Some people need the social interaction of others on a daily basis to be happy and function well. Others need someone standing over their shoulder to help them pace their work. Here are some things to consider before embarking on a career telecommuting:

Watch Out!
Remember that not every job is suited for telecommuting. The best possibilities for telecommuting are jobs where you can use a phone, computer, fax, and/or modem to do your work.

- Some people don't work well independently.

- There is not a lot of support when you are telecommuting.

- It can be difficult to ask questions about your work or to get instant answers.

- There are distractions working at home that you don't have in an office environment.

- It's often difficult to distinguish between work time and personal time.

- You often feel—or you *are*—out of the office loop.

There are many instances when telecommuting can be a lifesaver in your career. For example, let's say you are a new mom. Your new family responsibilities don't coincide with the traditional workday; however, you really don't want to give up your job or take a long leave of absence. Telecommuting can often allow you the opportunity to continue working at hours more convenient to your situation.

Similarly, let's say your circumstances change and you move to another city or town a distance away from your office. Telecommuting might be a way to keep a job you really like and in which you excel. Recruiting, training, and retaining employees costs employers a great deal of money. A company may therefore be willing to let you telecommute if you are a good employee.

Many companies—perhaps yours—permit some employees to telecommute. However, what if your company hasn't yet moved into the new century with this trend? How can you convince your supervisor to let you telecommute?

Probably the smartest tactic you can take to convince a supervisor to let you telecommute is to develop a written proposal. First determine whether you want to telecommute full-time or just a few days a week. Then try to come up with some concrete ideas of the benefits of telecommuting for you and the organization, as well as what it might entail. Here are some ideas about what your proposal should cover:

- Responsibilities you will handle
- Timetables you will follow
- How you will report your progress
- How the program can be evaluated

Watch Out!
When telecommuting, it's important your family, neighbors, and friends understand you are working even though you are at home. Otherwise they may distract you.

Bright Idea
Your employer will be more apt to consider telecommuting if you have been a good employee and a high performer in the past. Employers may be concerned that without the traditional work environment you might not get your work done.

> 66
>
> I'm a conference and meeting coordinator and had just changed jobs. I wanted to move to another city to be closer to my fiancé. I explained to my supervisor that when I wasn't on the road doing site inspections or at conferences all my work was handled by phone and the computer. My supervisor agreed to let me try telecommuting.
> —Cathy, conference and meeting coordinator
>
> 99

- What your work schedule will be

- How it will save the company money (for example, saving on office space or saving on not having to recruit and retrain a new employee)

- How the plan can be phased in and implemented

- Benefits to the company

- Methods and times of communication with your supervisor or others in the office

- Who will pay for and/or be responsible for equipment such as phones, computers, fax machines, modems, and additional phone lines

- Who will pay for and/or be responsible for equipping your home office

When you ask to be allowed to telecommute, you might not face as much resistance as you think. With low unemployment and a shortage of quality workers, everyone is looking for new methods to attract and retain employees. Employers are also on the lookout for ways to give employees more job satisfaction. You might, therefore, find that an employer offers telecommuting as a perk of your new hot job before hiring you. Another reason is that companies are cutting costs aggressively, and telecommuting may allow you to help your company save money.

Flex your time

Are you looking for a hot new career that lets you balance your job, family, and life? How do you work a full-time job and still be home for the kids? How do you juggle your family commitments and your job? What can you do? One answer might be flex-time scheduling. Some progressive companies are now using this method of scheduling to help attract and retain employees and improve productivity.

Bright Idea
Consider joining the American Telecommuting Association (ATA). This organization brings together others who are telecommuting and provides information and education for its members.

What is flex time? It varies from company to company. Basically, however, it's a method of scheduling that allows employees to work flexible hours. In some companies, employees work longer hours on certain days to shorten their work week. They may work 10-hour shifts, resulting in a four-day work week. In other situations, flex time might mean employees begin working earlier than traditional work hours so they can go home earlier, or working later than traditional work hours and going home later. Some Human Resources directors even develop innovative flex-time schedules to allow employees to get three-day weekends every other week.

So what can flex time do for you and your career?

- It can help you handle the challenges of child care.

- It can help you handle the challenges of adult or elder day care.

- It can help you to find time to schedule visits to the doctor, dentist, or other medical appointments.

- It can help you handle balancing assorted family time-management problems.

- It can make you feel less stressed working more hours but fewer days.

- It can give you chunks of time off by allowing you to work longer hours on certain days.

One of the objections your employer may raise to allowing flex time is that it would force the company to keep offices open longer and employ more supervisors, all of which would cost the company money. Another problem many worry about is that work might not get done. Flex time shouldn't mean fewer hours worked.

Bright Idea
Some companies offer flex time as a perk to attract and retain employees. If you are in a job or the company doesn't currently offer flex-time schedules, it doesn't mean that they won't consider the option in the future.

Not every job or company is going to allow flex-time scheduling. However, if you are interested in this possibility, it's always worth a try. It's also worth noting that there are many industries that use shifts set up similar to flex-time positions. These industries include health care, hospitality, casinos, food service, law enforcement, radio, television, and computer data entry. Specific jobs might include:

- Nurses
- Physicians
- Police officers
- Correction officers
- Customer service agents
- Telemarketers
- Casino workers
- Hotel reservationists

If you are currently interviewing for new hot jobs, discuss the possibility of flex-time scheduling with the interviewer.

Certain jobs and situations naturally lend themselves better to flex time. For example, businesses that deal with customers on both coasts or abroad might be good possibilities for flex time because flexible scheduling might mean that customers can be taken care of more hours during the day instead of the traditional 9 to 5. Companies that run 24 hours a day are also good candidates.

When proposing flex time to a superior, illustrate what the new scheduling can do for the company:

- It can help retain employees.
- It can help make the company more customer-friendly.

- It can help make the company more efficient.

- It can help make the company more productive.

- It increases job satisfaction, leading to happier, more productive employees.

Watch Out!
When you start looking at alternative ways to work—even if your salary and benefits are reduced—often your responsibilities still stay the same.

Why should your company agree to flex time? There are a number of reasons. It's important first of all for your company to realize that they are not losing anything. Think out the situation thoroughly before you talk to your supervisor. As I mentioned, put your ideas in writing. That way you can clearly show what you will be offering in the flex-time position as well as what the organization will be gaining.

If your request for flex time is rejected by your employer, don't despair. Wait a few months, work on your proposal, and bring the idea up again.

Part-time options

Part-time work is an option for many people searching for their new hot dream career. Working part-time gives you the opportunity to learn new skills or get your foot in the door. One of the great things about a part-time job is even if you are working full time, you can often find a few hours a week to try something new.

Part-timers work fewer than 40 hours a week. Some work much less, putting in only a couple of hours a day. Some individuals may just work on the weekends. The biggest downside to working part-time is that you will be earning a lot less money than you would if you worked at a full-time job.

What is working part-time worth to you? This is an important question to ask yourself. If you are working shorter hours, how will reducing your salary and/or your benefits affect you?

It's also important to realize that you often lose a lot of benefits going from a full-time job to part-time work. This is especially true when you go from a full-time salaried position to working on an hourly basis. Some of the benefits you may lose include:

- Fewer perks, if any
- No paid lunch hour
- No paid holidays
- No paid vacation days
- No paid sick days
- Fewer benefits, if any

Part-time work is valuable if you are in between jobs, looking to earn some extra money, trying to gain experience, or learning some new skills. It is not, however, a great catalyst for career success.

Share your job

Job sharing is another option you might want to consider. Job sharing is a relatively new concept in the workplace. Generally it entails two people sharing one job. While each person works fewer hours than full time, the original position that is being filled is generally classified as full time. The responsibilities, however, are split equally between the two parties.

While job sharing is similar to working part-time, it's not exactly the same. One of the problems with working part time is that it may be difficult to advance in your career because no one takes you seriously. Superiors often do not see part-timers as people committed to their job. In job sharing, however, you are seen more as someone interested in your career than as just a part-timer.

Working as a part-timer (especially if you move from a full-time position) often means you may be

Timesaver
Job sharing is helpful to many people. It is especially useful to working mothers who need or want to cut back on hours but are concerned about damaging their careers. Job sharing may also help reduce job stress.

handling full-time duties on a part-time basis and for part-time pay. For example, let's say you reduce your work week from five days to two and a half. On the days you don't go in to work, people may pile work on your desk and leave tons of messages on your voice mail. That means when you get back to the office, you have the same amount of work to complete—in less time.

On the other hand, with job sharing, your job-sharing partner is at work when you're not. He is there to handle the work and take the phone calls.

Why would an employer allow you to job-share? There are a number of reasons. These are important to know about when proposing job sharing to your company. Let's look at a few reasons employees might be tempted to consider job sharing:

- To keep a good employee

- To boost employee morale within the company

- To increase employee commitment, loyalty, and job satisfaction

- To bring a wider range of skills and experience to a job than one person might have alone

There are also a number of challenges regarding job sharing. To begin with, you need to find a job-share partner. In some companies where job sharing is already instituted, you might only have to talk to your supervisor or the Human Resources department. If job sharing is a relatively new idea to your company, you will probably have to find a partner on your own.

When looking for your partner, look for good chemistry. You need to get along with this person. You will need to be able to work together in unison, complementing each other's strong points and covering each other's weak ones.

Watch Out!
Never talk behind your job-share partner's back. If you have a problem, try to work it out between the two of you. You are supposed to be working as a team, not backstabbing each other.

Look for a job-share partner who has similar circumstances. Do you know someone in your organization who has just had a baby and wants to continue working, but can't effectively handle both tasks full-time? Do you know someone who wants to return to school to get a degree, but doesn't want to give up working? Look around your workplace and see who might be a possibility. You and a coworker might have already discussed the situation. In some situations, two people might even apply for a job jointly as a job-share position.

Before going to your supervisor or talking to a hiring manager, develop a written proposal. That way you can see the holes ahead of time and fix them. In this manner, the supervisor will see that you have thoroughly thought out the situation, including problems and solutions.

When working on your proposal, you might want to consider the following:

Watch Out!
When choosing your job-share partner, make sure neither of you are control freaks or ultra-competitive. These traits do not lend themselves well to job sharing.

- How will the responsibilities of the job be divided? Will one partner work in the morning and the other in the afternoon? Perhaps each might work two and a half days. Maybe the two partners will alternate two- and three-day work weeks. Maybe one person will work one week, and the other the next. Whatever you decide, determine the schedule ahead of time.

- Who will do what? Will each partner handle similar tasks or will each handle specialized jobs within their position?

- How will the two partners communicate and exchange information? Will you leave written notes? Perhaps make a log of important events, projects, and tasks, and how they are being handled, might work. How about having a daily or evening phone conversation to bring each other up to speed? Maybe you might want to use e-mail. Do you want to overlap your schedules so you see each other at least an hour a day? Whichever method you use, decide ahead of time, so there are no questions.

- Who will communicate with the supervisor? Will one partner be the communicator or will both be responsible for communicating?

- Who will colleagues communicate with? Who will be responsible for answering questions? Who will make decisions? Or will decisions be made jointly?

- How will each partner be compensated? Will both partners split one full-time salary? What happens if one partner has skills that are more in demand? What happens if one partner has more experience? Should each partner's salary be prorated depending on specific skills and experience? If one partner earns more, will that affect the working relationship?

- How about benefits? In some companies, part-timers and job sharers are not covered; in others they may be.

- How will the job sharers be evaluated? Will each be evaluated on his own merit, or will the two be evaluated as a team? What happens if one job sharer is performing better than the other?

After you have thought about and answered all these questions and put your proposal together, you are ready to talk to the hiring manager or your supervisor. Be sure you are clear in your commitment to making job sharing work both for the two of you and the organization.

Bright Idea
It's a good idea to use both your name and the name of your job-share partner on memos and correspondence. This helps to promote the concept that the two of you are working together in one job. For instance, you might want to sign your memos Jones/Morgan instead of just Paul Jones or Bill Morgan.

This is a great opportunity for you. Once you are job sharing, take advantage of the situation. Learn as much as you can. If your partner has skills and experience you don't have, make an effort to pick them up. Work together to learn to update your skills and gain new experiences.

It's always a good idea when you are using any new method of working to make yourself as visible as possible in a positive manner. Demonstrate together that both partners are performing well. In this manner you both will advance your careers, get raises, and be offered promotions.

Just the facts

- New hot career options make it easier for you to succeed in the workplace.

- Temping can be done in almost any industry today.

- If you can do your work with a computer, phone, and fax machine, you might be able to telecommute.

- Flex-time schedules allow you to work the same number of hours while being more convenient to your lifestyle.

- Job sharing is a good option for those who need or want to work fewer hours but are still committed to their careers.

Hot Careers in Helping and Healing

PART III

GET THE SCOOP ON...
How helping others helps your career ▪ Hot
careers in law and law enforcement ▪
Teaching options ▪ Coaching careers ▪
Opportunities at nonprofits

Hot Careers Helping Others

Chapter 7

While you can't always help everyone all of the time, in certain jobs, you have the opportunity to make a difference even if it is only to one person at a time. Do you love helping others? Do you want to make a difference in someone's life? Did you know that with the right job, you can help others and make a difference too?

This chapter will cover hot careers helping others in a variety of areas. It will give you ideas about career options, whether you want to work in law or law enforcement, education or coaching, the nonprofit sector, or even government.

What makes a career helping others hot? Maybe it's the fulfillment you feel after a day at work. Perhaps it's the job satisfaction or the respect of others for your work. Maybe the field you choose has been one you've been dreaming about entering. Or it could be like any other job you enjoy. It's fun, exciting, or has advancement opportunity.

Timesaver
If you're interested in other careers helping people, check out the next chapter on working in health care.

This chapter will give you some new hot options. You can then determine how to get the job you want.

Law and law enforcement

Does watching the television drama *The Practice* make you think that working in law just might be the perfect career choice? Have you been watching *NYPD Blue* or reruns of *Dragnet* and begun thinking that being a police officer might be a great job?

Most people who choose careers in law or law enforcement want to help people. Whether it's on an individual level (helping a parent get custody of a child from an abusive spouse), or on a larger scale (helping protect a community), there's no question that law and law enforcement careers can make a difference in people's lives.

There are many choices today for working in law and law enforcement. Each requires a myriad of different skills, traits, education, and experience. Some of them are hot; some are not. Let's look at just some of the hotter possibilities. Maybe one of them is for you.

Unofficially...
While police officers may be the first to come to mind when you think about a job in law enforcement (just as lawyers do when thinking about law), be aware that there are a wide variety of career options in these fields.

- Law enforcement officers
- Special agents
- Private detectives
- Security consultants
- Attorneys
- Paralegals
- Mediators

Now let's look at some of these careers in more depth.

Law enforcement officers

While some might think that working as a police officer could be a dangerous and unrewarding line of work, others see it as an exciting field. Anyone who has seen a police officer comforting a lost child or assisting someone in need can understand how this can be a fulfilling career.

Police officers, sheriffs, deputy sheriffs, and state police officers are all law enforcement officers. Police officers generally work within community or city police departments in small towns or large cities. Sheriffs or deputy sheriffs usually work in more rural areas. State police officers, state troopers, and highway patrol officers patrol highways and enforce motor vehicle laws as well as work with and assist other arms of law enforcement.

Police work can differ depending on the size of the community and the structure of the law enforcement agency. Those working in smaller community forces may handle more generalized duties while those working in larger, more urban departments may handle more specialized responsibilities.

The responsibilities of individual law enforcement officers vary, even within a single agency. However, the primary responsibility of every officer is the safety of the public. General duties of all law enforcement officers (regardless of specialization) include:

- Enforcing laws
- Preventing crimes
- Patrolling areas
- Solving crimes
- Community relations
- Apprehending criminals

❝

I always wanted to work in law enforcement. I started as a community patrol officer. When the opportunity arose to join the drug task force and go undercover, I jumped on it. That's when my job turned into a career.
—Undercover task force officer

❞

Bright Idea
If you're looking for a job in law enforcement, contact county and state personnel offices as well as police departments, sheriff's departments, and state police barracks to inquire about job openings and testing dates.

Police officers are expected to serve as a stabilizing force in the community. If you decide that you want to work in law enforcement, determine what direction you want to take. In smaller police departments, duties may be more general. In larger departments, police officers may have the opportunity to specialize.

Some police officers like the day-to-day interaction with the public. Others decide they want to move into a more specialized area of police work. What would interest you?

■ Homicide

■ Youth division

■ Domestic violence

■ Drugs and narcotics

■ Arson

■ Burglary

■ Training

■ Special investigations

Out of these areas of specialization, what would you like? What would make police work your hot career? Some of these areas require more training and experience than others.

Do you have an analytic mind? Are you detail-oriented? Do you like solving crimes? Would it give you job satisfaction and fulfillment to find a killer, helping give the victim's family closure? If so, consider working in homicide, the area of police work dealing with solving murders.

Would helping a child who is being abused or beaten make you feel useful? Police officers dealing with domestic violence handle situations such as spousal or child abuse. While domestic violence may be a difficult area of police work, some individuals request this area because they feel they can make a big difference to people who really need their help.

Perhaps you feel that the most fulfilling area of police work is working with youth. Officers working in the youth division may deal with youngsters in trouble and work on drug and crime prevention programs. In this division, you could make a real difference in the lives of young people.

If you enjoy gathering facts and collecting evidence for criminal cases, you might consider becoming a detective. In this type of job you interview people, look at records, observe the activities of suspects, take part in raids, and arrest suspects.

If you're interested in working as a law enforcement officer, you need a minimum of a high school diploma. Many positions either require or prefer a two- or four-year college degree. Depending on the specific job, you will either receive on-the-job training or go through the police academy.

Special agents

If you like excitement and your dream is to work in law enforcement on a grander scale, a career as a special agent might be up your alley. While there are a number of different areas in which special agents may work, the most popular are in the Federal Bureau of Investigation (FBI) and the United States Secret Service.

FBI agents investigate violations of federal laws. They deal with organized crime, espionage, sabotage, kidnapping, terrorism, theft of government property, and bank robberies.

If you look closely the next time you see the President of the United States on television, you will see dark-suited special agents close by. These people

Bright Idea
Many police departments require applicants to take civil service tests. Good test scores help you get the job. Before taking the test, go to the bookstore and get some review books so you can see the types of questions they ask and take practice tests.

Bright Idea
If you're interested in obtaining more information on a career in the FBI, check out the FBI's Web site: www.fbi.gov.

are Secret Service agents. As a member of this elite group, you are expected to guard and protect the President and Vice President of the country as well as their families. You may also be assigned to protect presidential candidates and their families, former presidents and their families, and foreign dignitaries visiting this country.

Other assignments you might receive as a U.S. Secret Service agent could be investigating counterfeiting, the fraudulent use of credit cards, and the forgery of government checks and bonds (because the Secret Service is part of the Treasury Department).

If you love excitement, get a rush out of being around political figures, and like extensive travel, this might be a good opportunity for your to pursue. You should be aware, however, that as part of the job you may be required to put your life on the line to protect someone else.

Competition is high for any special agent position. Generally, there are more applicants than positions. That doesn't mean you can't get in, but you must be highly qualified. Learn about the requirements before you apply.

Generally, the education requirements for special agents in any branch of government are more stringent than for other areas in law enforcement. In order to be considered for a job with the FBI, for example, you generally must hold a minimum of a four-year college degree. Majors might include accounting, engineering, or computer science. College graduates fluent in foreign languages are also considered good candidates, as are individuals with law degrees. Secret Service agents need a minimum of a bachelor's degree or (in lieu of the educational requirement) a minimum of three years of work experience, in which at least two are in criminal investigation.

Once accepted into any of these federal law enforcement careers, individuals go through special federal training programs.

Private detectives

Do you think it might be cool to look into other people's private lives and affairs? If so, a hot career for you might be that of a private detective.

Private detectives (also called private investigators, or P.I.s) work in the private sector conducting investigations for a variety of reasons. While most of us have heard of private detectives being used in divorce or pre-divorce situations by one or both spouses to check out possible infidelities, they do handle other types of investigations. Individuals may, for example, be retained to locate confidential information such as hidden monies or problems with former jobs. Private investigators may also be asked to locate missing persons or to investigate crimes.

Private investigators may be hired by private people, attorneys, insurance companies, employers, or a variety of other clients. Today, with computers and the Internet, private investigators have an extra resource that wasn't available years ago. Yet they still must use the "old" methods of investigation to gather some kinds of information.

Some private investigators began working as police officers. Others were intrigued with this line of work and began training with a licensed P.I. College courses in psychology, law enforcement, legal procedures, and criminology are helpful. Depending on the specific state you live in, you may need a license (most states require one). Some

Bright Idea
Whether you're looking for a job in law enforcement, law, education, government, or nonprofit organizations, you are always more marketable if you are bi- or trilingual. Consider an immersion class in another language to get you started.

states also require a police background check before granting a P.I. license.

Security consultants

People today are worried about the safety of their home, business, and family. As a result, security consultants are becoming a hot new career. Security consultants design systems to make homes and businesses more secure. Individual consultants may use simple electronic burglar alarms, or they may develop and design elaborate systems using motion detectors, video cameras, and a variety of electronic devices. In some instances, they also train clients in safety techniques. Security consultants may be retained by private individuals, stores, shopping centers, corporations, or businesses.

The demand for security consultants adept at safeguarding electronic information is growing and will continue into the millennium. If you have skills in this field and love the challenge, this might be your niche.

Lawyers

Moneysaver
If you are interested in opening your own business as a security consultant, save money by learning the ropes working with someone else first. Once you have the basics and some experience, you can move on in your career.

Even before the O.J. Simpson televised trial, it was the dream of many to become lawyers. After the trial, the prominence of the "Dream Team" prompted even more to seek this type of career.

Some want to be an attorney because of the large amount of money they believe they can earn. Others think they'll enjoy the research, critical thinking, analysis, and litigation that comes with this type of career. Some choose this career path primarily because they feel they can help others.

Lawyers have varied responsibilities depending on where they work and their specialty. These might include:

- Negotiating contracts
- Advising clients on the legal ramifications of actions
- Representing cases in court
- Performing research
- Advising government agencies
- Advising people or companies on how to handle a specific area of the law, such as tax law, estate law, or the laws regarding nonprofits
- Acting as in-house counsel for large corporations

In order to become a lawyer, you generally must hold a bachelor's degree and go through three years of law school. You then must take and pass the Bar Exam for the state in which you plan to practice. To get into law school you must take an exam called the LSAT (Law School Admission Test). Look into classes offered by reputable companies that can help you perform better and study more efficiently.

What can make your career in law your dream career? Specialization in your area of interest. Let's look at a number of possibilities.

- Criminal law
- Elder law (sizzling hot)
- Intellectual property law (sizzling hot)
- Tax law
- Family law
- Legal aid
- Public defense
- General law
- Internet and computer law (sizzling hot)

Bright Idea
Look for internships in areas in which you are interested. This will give you related experience, and these experiences and contacts will help you find a job.

Moneysaver
In a very few states you may be able to clerk for lawyers instead of attending one or more years of law school. Clerking is (in essence) studying with lawyers to get on-the-job training. Be forewarned, however, that clerking is less respected than law school.

- Entertainment law
- Corporate law

Paralegals

Bright Idea
You may be more marketable as a paralegal if you specialize in a specific field of law such as real estate, criminal, corporate, business, elder, or family law.

Are you interested in working in law, but don't really want to go through law school? Consider becoming a paralegal. This career opportunity has been growing by leaps and bounds. What exactly does a paralegal do?

Working under the direction and supervision of an attorney, paralegals perform many of the same duties as attorneys. Some of these duties can include:

- Researching prior cases
- Investigating cases for attorneys
- Analyzing facts
- Taking case histories from clients or witnesses
- Drafting legal documentation including contracts, agreements, and pleadings
- Assisting lawyers with trial preparation

Mediators are sizzling hot

Let's say you want to get a divorce. Or you have a neighbor whose dog barks continuously every night and it's driving you crazy. You want to talk, but you're not sure what to say. What's the solution? Is a lawyer always the answer? Not really. Mediators are a new alternative. A mediator is a trained individual who brings two parties together to talk about a problem and come up with possible solutions. There are different types of mediators: Some deal with divorce or family problems; some mediate disputes between neighbors, friends, or business associates. There are even mediators who deal with problems between students in schools.

Mediation is not new. There have been volunteer mediators for years. Paid mediators, however, are a relatively new concept. There are a couple of reasons for the rise in this as a new hot career:

- Many states now require that mediation services be used prior to going to court.

- Mediation usually costs a great deal less than using lawyers.

- The court system is jammed. Mediation often quickly resolves a situation, whereas the legal system could take years to solve the same problem.

Could you be a good mediator? You need the patience of a saint and great listening skills. You also need to be nonjudgmental and to allow the two parties decide what to do on their own. Mediators only guide the conversation. They let people come up with their own solutions.

Mediators may consult for corporations, schools, or individuals. There is training available through colleges, universities, and mediation organizations.

Many areas host volunteer mediation organizations. Consider volunteering to see if you think you would enjoy this type of career and to gain some experience.

Mediators sit between two people or two groups and help them make their own decision based on discussion and compromise. Some decisions reached are binding and others are not.

Arbitrators are a different job category. Arbitrators sit between two or more people or groups, listen to their problems and make a decision between the two points of view. Usually the decision is binding. An arbitrator may be likened to a judge in a courtroom.

Bright Idea
If you are interested in becoming a mediator, check out the American Arbitration Association Center For Mediation Web site at www.adr.org.

Is law right for you?

Those interested in working in law or law enforcement need certain skills and personality traits. In order to be successful in any of these careers, individuals need to possess the following basic skills and traits:

- Honesty
- Good judgment
- Responsibility
- Interpersonal skills
- Supervisory skills
- Management skills
- Leadership skills
- People skills
- Analytical skills

Gratification from education: Careers in teaching

Many agree that teaching is the most important thing you can do for anyone. As a teacher, you have the opportunity to have a great impact on those you come in contact with. Of course, another great aspect of teaching is that you learn new subjects as you teach, and you also learn a great deal about people as you teach them.

Your success in life is based on the education and training you have received. For those who love sharing knowledge of any kind, teaching can be a very hot career. There are many hot options for those interested in teaching. Let's look at a few of them.

Elementary school teachers

Do you love working with young children and seeing their excitement when they learn something new?

Consider working in elementary education. Elementary school teachers probably have more impact on youngsters than people working in any other occupation. If this is the type of career you have been dreaming about, you may teach children from kindergarten through sixth grade. Depending on your training and skills, you might teach general classes or specialize in an area such as music, art, physical education, or special education.

Secondary school teachers

Do you prefer teaching older children? Perhaps a career teaching in secondary school would be more to your liking. If you work in a junior or high school, you'll teach a specific area such as history, language, English, or social studies. If you have the talent, hot education jobs for the new century are teaching students computer technology.

In order for any teacher to be successful, she must make learning a positive experience. Those working in traditional school settings have a number of general responsibilities. These may include:

- Teaching students
- Developing lesson plans
- Developing innovative, inspiring, and interesting ways to teach subject matter
- Helping children enjoy learning
- Preparing exams and other methods of monitoring progress
- Meeting with parents to discuss student's progress

Other teaching opportunities

Today's hot careers in education also encompass a variety of other teaching possibilities. Most people

Unofficially...
Many psychologists believe that a child's personality is fully formed by the age of seven. A child's teachers may have a lot to do with shaping that personality.

are eager to learn. They seek out opportunities to garner new skills, new trades, and new things. If you are as eager to teach as people are to learn, you can have a great career.

Would working on a college campus with the hustle and bustle of academia be a dream come true for you? There are opportunities for teaching in community and junior colleges, state schools, and private colleges and universities throughout the country. However, if you are interested in this type of career, you need post-graduate education, probably a Ph.D.

Adult education teachers are yet another hot career possibility for those interested in teaching. Adult ed teachers may instruct in various areas. Some assist people to get their GEDs (Graduate Equivalency Diploma). Others help adults learn math skills or learn to read. A hot career area in this field is teaching English to people who speak other languages. Depending on the specific employment situation, adult education teachers may or may not be required to hold a graduate degree. Often knowledge and experience are sufficient.

Trainers

Are you able to motivate and inspire others? Do you like to teach people new things? Can you do so in an easy-to-understand manner? Are you comfortable speaking in front of groups of adults? If so, you might want to consider becoming a trainer, one of the hot careers for new century in the education field.

Trainers work in a variety of locations and industries. Many businesses and corporations now hire trainers to teach, motivate, and inspire their employees in the workplace. Many more are expected to do so.

With the new government welfare-to-work programs, more trainers than ever are needed to help welfare recipients learn basic work skills. While teaching, the trainer must also motivate them to employ a better work ethic so that they can not only obtain a job, but keep it.

Similarly, government agencies as well as private businesses now need the services of diversity trainers, as well as trainers who help organizations deal with sexual harassment in the workplace.

Personal trainers are sizzling hot. Personal trainers help motivate and teach people how to get in shape. Once a luxury of the rich and famous, they are now accepted as a necessity for regular people.

Competition in every industry is fierce. People can choose where they go, whose service they use, and what company they buy from. Increasingly, corporations in every industry have found that the key to success is great customer service. As a result, many bring in or employ trainers who can motivate workers to provide good customer service. As more companies see the light, there will be a greater need for trainers in this field.

Whether you are training people in technical areas such as computer software, working with people to better their customer service skills, or helping people become the best they can be, teaching others can be a great career. Depending on the specific situation, trainers may be expected to develop and implement programs in specific technical areas or more general areas. Tremendous growth is expected for trainers in every industry. Let's look at some possible industries where trainers are used that will be expanding in the new century:

- Gaming
- Food and beverage

> **66**
> It is essential that employees realize they all must work together as a team to provide the best possible service. Without every employee, the chain will be broken. A few years ago, seminars such as my SMART Customer Care Program and Stress Busters Presentations were used only by leading companies. Today they are in demand by most organizations with more than a few employees.
> —Shelly Field
> **99**

- Hospitality
- Insurance
- Customer service
- Computers
- Software
- Internet
- Sports
- Fitness
- Education
- Real estate

Unofficially...
If you are really creative, you can create a niche for yourself as a trainer in almost any industry. Consider, for example, training people to better balance their lives, get rid of stress, or control anger.

As a trainer, you have the option of being employed by a company, business, corporation, or government agency. You might also be self-employed or have your own training consulting company. You can work as a trainer full-time or pursuing a part-time career while still working at your current job.

Teach me what you know

If you have skills that others want to know, you might consider teaching classes on your own. You may be so comfortable with the subject you excel in, it's hard to recognize that you have special skills that others can benefit from. What can you teach? Anything you think others might want to know how to do, but don't know where to turn to learn. Let's look at some examples.

- Do you know how to prepare a gourmet meal?
- Are you a great baker?
- Do you know how to decorate cakes and pastries?
- Do you know how to write screenplays?
- Can you speak another language fluently?

- Can you organize things better than most?

- Can you complain to companies better than anyone else about problems you have experienced and then get results?

- Are you an expert at applying makeup or doing hair?

- Do you know how to develop and keep a budget?

- Are you a computer whiz?

- Do you know how to develop Web pages?

- Do you know how to write press releases and do publicity?

- Are you an expert at finding information on the Internet?

- Do you know how to play a musical instrument?

If you can teach, you can make a career of teaching. You might give classes in your home, other people's homes, or through a continuing education program. You might also begin this career as a part-time venture to see if you can build it up to a full-time business.

Coaching is not just in sports

Most people believe that coaches work only in the sports industry. We have all heard of coaches in baseball, basketball, hockey, and football. But did you know that you can also find coaches in a variety of other fields and industries? Let's look at a few.

- *Acting coach.* This person helps actors and actresses (or aspiring actors or actresses) become better at their craft. Acting coaches have been around for a while and are used by people interested in acting in live theater as well as television, movies, and commercials. While

Moneysaver
If you're looking for an inexpensive place to teach classes, consider asking your local community center, church, or synagogue about using one of their meeting rooms. You can often rent a room for a nominal fee.

Watch Out!
Just because you are an expert in a particular area doesn't mean that you can teach it. Some people are not good teachers.

acting coaches can be found throughout the country, the largest number are probably in the New York City and Los Angeles areas.

■ *Voice coach.* The voice coach helps people with accents, modulation, enunciation, and general vocal quality. Many people use voice coaches, including actors, actresses, television and radio personalities, corporate business people, and salespeople.

■ *Retirement coach.* Retirement coaches are a fairly new concept. With people living longer and healthier lives, retirement no longer means just gardening or playing a round of golf. Retirement coaches help those who are leaving their jobs find meaningful things to do with their lives. They help retirees develop a plan for the rest of their life, whether it be volunteer work, consulting, or another job.

■ *Job coach.* Job coaches may be hired by the employer or an employee. They assist employees in learning about and excelling at their job. For example, social service agencies that seek to employ mentally or physically challenged clients provide job coaches to ensure success on the job. Similarly, youth agencies attempting to place young people, or welfare-to-work groups placing displaced homemakers and other former welfare recipients, may also hire job coaches.

■ *Executive coach.* Sometimes, in the world of business, executives need a little push to make them more successful and catapult them to the top. Executive coaches work with managers and other executives to help them hone their skills.

- *Parenting coach.* Parents face a variety of challenges every day. Parenting coaches help them deal more effectively with those challenges. Who would use a parenting coach? Any parent, from a new mother who hasn't had any experience dealing with an infant, to parents dealing with difficult teenage problems. Social service agencies and school districts also use parenting coaches.

Bright Idea
For more information in pursuing a career as a coach, check out the International Coach Federation (ICF) Web site at www. coachfederation. org, or contact them directly at (888) 423-3131 or (888) BEMY-COACH.

- *Time management coach.* Many find it difficult (if not impossible) to balance a family, job, and life in general. Time management coaches help people better manage their time by teaching them how to make better choices at work and at home. Time management coaches may be on staff at corporations or retained as consultants. They may also consult with private individuals needing their services.

- *Fitness and nutrition coach.* Fitness and nutrition are American obsessions, so it's not surprising that fitness and nutrition coaches have sprung up everywhere. Most find it difficult to maintain an exercise and healthy eating routine necessary to staying fit and healthy. Fitness and nutrition coaches motivate individuals to exercise and be more aware of good nutrition. They are retained by corporations or individuals.

- *Etiquette coach.* The workplace is changing, and proper etiquette can be the difference between success and failure. Most of us have heard of Emily Post or Miss Manners. Etiquette coaches help teach people how to act in various situations. They don't just teach people when to say "please" and "thank you," but on the etiquette

Unofficially...
Motivational speaker Anthony Robbins is probably one of the best-known life coaches in the world. Robbins rose to the top by seeking and following the advice of successful people and has built a coaching empire that sells seminars, books, and tapes.

of foreign countries, as well as the correct manner of handling business lunches, dinners, business meetings, interviews, and any other topic of importance.

■ *Media communications coach.* Executives are often faced with the challenge of responding to questions from newspaper reporters or having microphones or television cameras thrust in front of their face. Being able to deal with the media effectively often means the difference between a public relations nightmare and a controlled situation. Media communications coaches work with people to help prepare them for dealing with the media successfully. Coaches may conduct mock interviews with individuals or prepare them in other ways so they will be ready for any and all media situations.

■ *Life coach.* Life coaches work with people to help them attain more satisfaction in all areas of their life. They may coach people on setting goals and motivate them to work toward their goals. Life coaches deal with a variety of life problems, including finances, career, family, and relationships in general.

No matter what the industry, the job of coaching in any field, as in sports, is to help people excel. Coaches inspire and motivate people to become the best at what they do. Can you be a coach? Let's look at some of the qualities you need to be successful in this type of career:

■ An expert in the field in which you want to coach

■ A motivator

■ People skills

- Communications skills
- Nonjudgmental personality

Nonprofits make the world go 'round

Would you love to assist in a cause you believe in? If so, you might consider working in the nonprofit sector. Nonprofit organizations are businesses that put any profits earned back into the cause. They are a special classification of businesses that have nonprofit status. This grants them various governmental breaks and opportunities.

Nonprofit organizations may be local, regional, national, or global. They may be large or small and have various causes and missions. Some examples you probably have heard of include:

- The American Red Cross
- The American Cancer Society
- The United Way
- The Nature Conservancy
- A local theater or public television station
- A local battered women's shelter
- The Make-A-Wish Foundation
- The American Society for the Prevention of Cruelty to Animals (ASPCA)
- The American Heart Association
- Habitat For Humanity

Nonprofit organizations encompass trade associations such as the Advertising Research Foundation (ARF), American Bar Association (ABA), and National Association of Recording Merchandisers (NARM). The nonprofit sector also includes public schools, community colleges, state colleges and universities, many social service agencies, hospitals,

Unofficially...
Many nonprofits that have "American" in their name are also organized locally, at the city and state level. Thus, there is also a New York Society for the Prevention of Cruelty to Animals.

health care agencies, museums, zoos, libraries, and a host of others groups.

Whether it be assisting people in need, doing research, making terminally ill children's wishes come true, or defending the rights of animals, each organization has a cause and a purpose.

Look around your community. There are probably dozens of nonprofit organizations or businesses. Each holds a great many employment opportunities. One might be just right for you.

Watch Out!
You should know that earnings in the nonprofit sector are generally lower than for similar jobs in the for-profit sector.

What types of career opportunities can you look for? As in every job, career opportunities in the non-profit sector have a great deal to do with your skills, personality traits, education, and personal passions. You may find that nonprofits give you greater freedom to explore different careers, or you may just want the satisfaction that comes with doing good deeds.

Career opportunities with nonprofits are diverse. Of course, nonprofit organizations require people with different skills. For example, museums might have opportunities as exhibition coordinators, exhibit designers, and tour guides. Animal rights organizations or shelters have people who take care of animals. Hospitals have jobs for those caring for patients. If you're interested in working within the nonprofit sector, find the organization whose cause you believe in and then see what types of opportunities exist there to fit in with your skills and desires.

Job-specific careers notwithstanding, there are a number of jobs most nonprofits have that are hot for the coming century.

The executive director of a nonprofit is like the president or CEO of a for-profit company. The executive director helps to develop and carry out the missions of the organization. He is in charge of virtually everything at the agency.

Fund-raising is a large part of every nonprofit organization's goals. People who are good at this task are always in demand. Fund-raising involves planning social events, making speeches, and asking people for money one-on-one. Fund-raising and development directors may be expected to locate and cultivate corporate sponsors and donors.

Special events are not only big fund-raisers for nonprofit groups, they are also used to educate and build organization support. Do you love the challenge of developing and managing events? Do you like to put together parties? Are you detail-oriented and able to handle many tasks at one time? A job as the organization's special events coordinator or director might be a hot career for you.

Whatever job you choose in helping others, I'm sure you'll find that when you help others, you also help yourself.

Just the Facts

- There are new career options outside of traditional law and law enforcement jobs.

- Teaching others can have a great impact on both your life and theirs.

- Coaching people in various industries is a hot and viable career opportunity.

- Working in the nonprofit sector gives you the opportunity to work for a cause you believe in.

- A career helping others can be fulfilling and rewarding.

Bright Idea
Getting the word out is also an important part of every nonprofit group. If your dream is to do public relations, promotion, and publicity, you might love working in the nonprofit's public relations department.

Bright Idea
A great way to work your way into a job at a nonprofit agency is by volunteering. When a job opens up, they'll already know you, and you might get to interview for the job before it's offered to the general public.

GET THE SCOOP ON...
Medical technology jobs ▪ Alternative health
care careers ▪ Careers in fitness ▪ Careers
in nutrition

Chapter 8

Hot Health Care Careers That Keep Getting Hotter

D o you enjoy making others feel better? Do you dream about improving someone's health and making their life better? Do you feel you have a calling to heal? If so, your hot new career might be in the health care field.

Are you intrigued by recent advances in medical technology? Do you wish you could be involved someway or somehow? Maybe you should consider working in medical technology.

Do you wish you could be more involved in alternative medicine? Want to know more about a career in complementary care? Are you interested in fitness? How about nutrition? This chapter will cover some new hot choices.

Some of the fastest-growing occupations in the new century will be health-related. The field of health care is booming and the trend will continue through the millennium. The field of health care includes many different jobs. Whether your dream is to become a health care professional, work in medical technology, find a career in alternative medicine, or help people become fit and healthy, there is a place for you.

What makes a career in health care hot? Maybe it's the fulfillment of making someone feel better. Perhaps it's knowing you saved a patient's life or stopped someone's pain, even if the relief was only for a short time. Could it be the joy of helping a young mother bring a new life into the world? Perhaps you hope for the job satisfaction of teaching others how to help themselves.

Whatever your reason for joining the field of health care, read on to find a variety of hot new options.

Powerful and premium health care careers

When people hear "health care," the first job that usually comes to mind is that of a physician. Want to be a doctor? It isn't easy to become one, but it can be very rewarding.

Years ago, little boys wanted to be doctors and little girls wanted to be nurses. Today, there are male nurses and female physicians. People now have choices. So do you.

Did you grow up admiring your doctor? Did you always want to be one? Do you still have the dream? People have many reasons for wanting to become physicians. What are yours?

- It's a prestigious career.

- It can be a very well paying career.

- You can save people's lives.

- You can make a huge difference in the quality of people's lives.

Bright Idea
With enough hard work, education, and perseverance, you can be anything you want to be no matter what your gender. What do you want to do? What have you been dreaming about?

- You can help people who are in need of medical care.

- Medicine can be a very fulfilling career.

As I mentioned, becoming a doctor isn't easy, by any means. But if it's your dream, go for it. Physicians can be medical doctors, referred to as M.D.s, or doctors of osteopathy, commonly referred to as D.O.s. Both are physicians who use accepted methods to treat and care for patients.

There are stringent requirements you have to meet to become a physician. These include:

- Being accepted at an accredited medical school

- Attending and graduating from an accredited medical school

- Becoming licensed by completing a licensing exam

- Going through a residency (if you want to be an M.D.)

- Going through an internship and residency (if you want to be a D.O.)

One of the things that can make a career as a physician so hot is the opportunity to specialize in an area you are interested in. Let's look at some specialties in which you might be interested:

- Allergies

- Alternative medicine

- Anesthesiology

- Cardiovascular medicine

- Child psychiatry

- Dermatology

- Diagnostic radiology

- Emergency medicine

Moneysaver
Doctors are needed in less populated areas. In some very rural areas, the community might need physicians so badly that they will offer to help pay medical school expenses in return for a guarantee you will move back after med school to practice for a specified time period.

- Family medicine
- Gastroenterology
- Gerontology (sizzling hot)
- Internal medicine
- Obstetrics and gynecology
- Oncology
- Pathology
- Pediatric cardiology
- Pediatrics
- Plastic surgery
- Psychiatry
- Public health
- Pulmonary Disease
- Radiology
- Sports medicine
- Surgery

Let's look at some of the hotter areas in more depth.

- **Emergency medicine.** Do you watch *ER* on television in awe of the professionals who save lives and wish you could be one of them in real life? Consider a career working in emergency medicine. This fast-paced specialty is growing by leaps and bounds. You need the ability to make decisions quickly and deal with stressful situations.

- **Allergies.** More and more people are beginning to understand the relationship between allergens and health. In addition to food allergies and pollens, there are environmental allergies that many people now need to deal with. The area of allergy medicine is becoming hotter than ever.

■ **Cardiovascular medicine.** Want to help people become more heart-healthy? Consider a career in cardiovascular medicine. As the population ages, people experience a higher level of cardiovascular disease.

■ **Gerontology.** If you have an interest in dealing with aging and the elderly, a sizzling-hot specialty is that of gerontology. With new technology keeping people alive longer, the elderly population is growing.

■ **Sports medicine.** As people exercise more and take part in athletics to stay fit, there are increased sports-related injuries. Sports medicine doctors care for these injuries and prescribe treatments and therapies. This is a very hot field.

Chiropractors

Do you believe that patients should be treated in a holistic manner? Do you believe that a person's overall health and well-being is controlled by exercise, diet, environment, and heredity? If so, you might want to consider a hot health career as a chiropractor.

If you've had a bad backache or couldn't turn your neck as a result of an accident, you know that you would do almost anything to rid yourself of the pain. Chiropractors are doctors who diagnose and treat patients with health problems associated with the body's muscular, nervous, and skeletal systems. They generally use natural, non-surgical methods of realigning a patient's spine to help him attain optimum health.

Bright Idea
Want to learn more about the field of sports medicine? Check out the American College of Sports Medicine Web site at www.al.com/sportsmed.

Moneysaver
If you are just opening up a new practice, consider volunteering to speak to local civic groups about the way chiropractic medicine works or why you got involved. This is like free advertising.

In order to become a chiropractor, some of the requirements you need to fulfill include:

- Attending undergraduate school
- Attending and graduating from an accredited chiropractic college
- Taking and passing a state board examination
- Becoming licensed in the state in which you work

Registered nurses

Do you enjoy caring for the sick? Do you like helping people stay healthy? Have you always wanted to be a nurse? There are a number of reasons people choose nursing as a career.

- A desire to care for ill or infirm people
- Flexible hours
- Options in working environments and specializations

Nurses may work in a variety of environments, including:

- Hospitals
- Nursing homes
- Physician's offices
- Public health agencies
- Private duty

Bright Idea
If you're not sure about nursing as a profession, consider volunteering in a hospital, nursing home, or health care facility first. This experience will give you an idea of what this career might be like.

There is a shortage of registered nurses in facilities that care for critically and terminally-ill patients. If you really want to make a difference, consider working there.

Nurses may also have areas of specialization. Some of the hotter specialties today include:

- Obstetrics
- Surgery
- Pediatrics
- Emergency medicine
- Oncology
- Anesthesia

Nurse anesthetists

Nurse anesthetists are an advanced specialty in nursing. This can be a very hot career financially. You will be working as part of a team, in operating rooms administering anesthesia and monitoring patients. To become a nurse anesthetist, you must go through an accredited program after completing your nursing degree.

Physician assistants

Think you might want to be a doctor, but you're not ready to go through years of med school, internships, and residencies? If you like helping people medically and you're willing to go through an accredited two-year program, you might want to consider becoming a physician assistant (PA).

PAs work under the supervision of physicians. However, the extent of their supervision depends on their location. In many areas of this country, doctors are not available on a daily basis. For example, rural areas or inner city clinics might just have a doctor on location two or three days a week.

Physician assistants are becoming popular. Health care is expensive. A physician assistant can provide basic medical care less expensively than an M.D.

Physician assistants perform many of the same duties as physicians. In some states they may even prescribe medicine. Their duties might include:

Bright Idea
To learn more about nursing, check out the National League for Nursing Web site at www.nln.org.

Bright Idea
If you want to learn more about a career as a physician assistant, check out the American Academy of Physician Assistants Web site at www.aapa.org.

Bright Idea
If you're thinking about becoming a PA try to get training in as many areas of specialization as possible. This will make you more marketable and employable.

- Taking medical histories
- Examining patients
- Ordering and interpreting lab tests
- Ordering and interpreting x-rays
- Preliminary diagnosing of patient illnesses
- Splinting, suturing, and casting injuries
- Recording patient's progress
- Instructing patients on care
- Ordering therapy

Therapists

There are many hot careers in therapy. Most entering the field have job offers as soon as their training is complete. Education and training requirements vary, but you usually need to complete accredited programs in your field. What kinds of therapists are hot?

- **Music therapists.** They use music to treat physical, mental, and emotional disabilities.

- **Art therapists.** They use art and art projects to treat physical, mental, and emotional disabilities.

- **Dance therapists.** They use dance to treat physical, mental, and emotional disabilities.

- **Physical therapists.** They help patients ease pain and recover from injuries, accidents, and illness.

Emergency medical technicians

Anyone who has been in an accident or had an emergency at their home knows how welcome an emergency medical technician (EMT) can be. EMTs provide emergency medical treatment to accident victims or those who are experiencing a variety of problems from heart attacks to gunshot wounds.

Unofficially...
Most PA programs require prior experience in health care. Consider a part- or full-time job in a hospital, clinic, or nursing home to obtain experience.

As an EMT you can work on a variety of levels, depending on your experience and training. The higher your level of training, the more marketable you will be in this field. Whatever level you work on, however, you will be making a big difference in the life of someone who is experiencing a medical problem.

Eating disorder counselors

Eating disorders are becoming more common and people are starting to recognize that they are serious disorders. While young girls and women are the primary victims of these illnesses, there are cases of young boys and men suffering from the same problems.

Eating disorders may encompass many illnesses. The most common are:

- Anorexia

- Bulimia

- Bingeing

Eating disorder counselors talk to patients to help them understand their condition. They try to motivate patients to change their behavior patterns. Counselors work under the supervision of doctors, psychiatrists, and psychologists.

As in many other health care careers, eating disorder counselors often experience a great deal of job satisfaction. Seeing a patient "break through" the problem and resume a normal life can be very fulfilling.

Careers in medical technology

One of the major causes of job growth in health care is the tremendous expansion of new technology. There are wide-reaching advances in equipment in the fields of laboratory analysis, imaging, laser

Bright Idea
Therapists of all types will be needed in nursing homes, rehabilitation centers, and extended-care facilities for the new millennium.

Bright Idea
Learn more about a career as an EMT by checking out the National Association of Emergency Medical Technicians Web site at www.naemt.org.

Timesaver
If you were a medic in the armed forces, you already possess valuable experience that will make it easier for you to become an EMT.

surgery, laparoscopy, and many other areas of instrumentation. These advancements in the development of equipment not only help to extend people's lives, but improve the quality of lives. This new equipment not only requires operators, but people with special skills to analyze the data produced by the new technology.

If you have empathy and compassion for people who are experiencing the traumas of cancer, you might want to consider working as a radiation therapy technologist. In this job you prepare cancer patients for their radiation treatment as well as administer the treatment. If you have the desire and personality to make people feel comfortable and less frightened about cancer and the treatment they are receiving, you can make a big difference in people's lives.

- **Electrocardiograph (EKG) technicians** operate the machines that diagnose and treat heart and circulatory problems. When people are having EKGs, they are often worried about the results. A kind, compassionate EKG technician can make all the difference to the patient.

- **Diagnostic medical sonographers** operate ultrasound equipment. The hottest area in this field is obstetrics, where you get the opportunity to give parents their first look at their unborn baby.

- **Clinical laboratory technologists** are the people who perform lab tests for patients. They make cultures of body fluids and tissue samples. As the new century arrives there will be opportunities for lab techs not only in traditional health care settings, but also in research labs searching for cures for cancer, AIDS, and other deadly diseases.

Even with new technology, machines still break. Equipment that is used in health care for diagnosing or treating patients must be in good working order at all times. If you love to fix things or are good at diagnosing problems and want to work in a hot health care career, you might become a biomedical equipment repairperson.

Careers in complementary care and alternative medicine

Careers in alternative medicine encompass professionals, paraprofessionals, and a host of others. Alternative medicine is not new. It has been around for years in many other cultures. However, it has only recently become more accepted in this country. Let's look at some hot career possibilities in the field.

Nurse-midwives

Today, with the growing interest in doing things the natural way, trained nurse-midwives have become more popular than ever. Nurse-midwives practice in hospitals, birthing centers, clinics, or private homes.

Nurse-midwives are certified professionals who have formal training. Beginning their career as registered nurses, they go through special programs to receive a Certified Nurse Midwife designation.

Nurse-midwives have a number of responsibilities. These include:

- Counseling women on nutrition during pregnancy

- Examining and caring for women prior to and during pregnancy

Bright Idea
If you're interested in a career as a nurse-midwife, check out the American College of Nurse Midwives Web site at www.acnm.org.

Moneysaver
For years, midwives assisted mothers in giving birth when doctors were not available. They had no formal medical training but did the job just the same, saving time and money and providing compassionate care to women at a lower price.

- Caring for women during labor
- Making sure there are no complications during labor
- Assisting women with delivery
- Counseling women on caring for newborns

A nurse-midwife is an advanced specialization a registered nurse can pursue. If it's your dream to help women bring new lives into the world, this can be a very fulfilling hot career.

Massage therapists

Do you believe that massage can help the body? The mind? The spirit? You might want to consider a hot career in complementary medicine as a massage therapist.

People are always on the lookout for something to make them feel better. This industry is growing, leading to career opportunities for trained people. In addition to massage, you use essential oils and a soothing environment to help patients feel better.

Massage therapists are licensed and certified individuals who are trained in anatomy and physiology, among other things. In this job, you use various forms of massage to help people reduce stress, become relaxed, relieve headaches and other ailments, and assist in treating injuries.

Unofficially...
Actress and television talk-show host Ricki Lake says that her next career is going to be as a midwife. Lake reportedly had her own child in a birthing center, with the help of a midwife, and was so impressed that she wants to help others give birth in the same manner.

Acupuncturists

You might be thinking, "How can I have a career sticking needles in people?" Let me assure you, you can. Acupuncturists are not new. Acupuncture has been used successfully for centuries in China and other Eastern countries. Bit by bit, it has spread to America. Today, many hospitals and health care centers have credentialed acupuncturists on staff.

There are also individuals in this occupation who work on their own. Some acupuncturists are physicians who add this treatment to their healing services. Others are not physicians and are trained exclusively in this ancient art.

If you are interested in helping heal people in a nontraditional career in health care, consider acupuncture. It's essential to your success (and that of your patients) that you receive the very best training you can. Generally, you also need to be licensed in the state in which you work.

Homeopathic physicians

Homeopathic physicians have been around for years. There are M.D.s, O.D.s, and N.D.s (see next section). Homeopathic physicians treat people with homeopathic remedies, while the allopathic orthodox physician uses allopathic medications. (Allopathy is the traditional medicine most people in this country use.) Homeopathy is a natural healing system based on treating like with like. As with many other natural forms of medicine, it treats the whole person instead of just the symptoms. Homeopathic doctors put a great deal of emphasis on mental and emotional symptoms as well as physical symptoms of the patient.

In order to become a licensed homeopathic physician, you need to first become a licensed M.D. or D.O. You then usually train with an established homeopath. There are a variety of schools and classes where you can learn more about the homeopathic repertoire.

Naturopathic doctors

If you're interested in helping heal people but don't really believe in mainstream medicine, think about a career as a naturopathic doctor (N.D.). This type

Bright Idea
If you're interested in learning more about a career as a massage therapist, contact the American Massage Therapy Association at www.amtamassage.org, by phone at (847) 864-0123, or by fax at (847) 864-1178.

Bright Idea
Learn more about careers in acupuncture by checking out the California Association of Acupuncture and Oriental Medicine Web site at www.acupuncture.com.

of doctor is for people who seek an alternative to traditional medicine. N.D.s treat the whole body. They may use a variety of natural remedies and herbs as well as homeopathic remedies, and alternative treatments to heal the patient.

Complementary care program coordinators

As alternative medicine and treatments become more widely accepted, many hospitals and health care facilities are beginning to augment and integrate their traditional health care with complementary care and alternative medicine programs. If you are interested in complementary care and alternative medicine, there is a great new career waiting for you.

Complementary care program coordinators develop and implement programs in complementary care and alternative medicine in hospitals and other health care facilities. Responsibilities may vary, as the job is so new. Your job may revolve around the following:

- Developing alternative-medicine programs using various accepted alternative medical practices

Unofficially...
Many celebrities have used homeopathic medicine for years. It's reported that Queen Elizabeth and her family use homeopathy. Tina Turner, one of the queens of rock and roll, also reportedly uses homeopathic medicine.

- Finding professionals in complementary care to run programs
- Promoting programs and therapies
- Teaching classes
- Conducting research on alternative and complementary care therapies
- Determining the effectiveness of programs

Depending on the state in which you live and the specific facility in which you work, complementary care programs may encompass the following:

- Yoga
- Massage therapy
- Herbal treatments
- Tai chi
- Visualization
- Touch for health
- Feng shui
- Aromatherapy
- Walking programs
- Vegetarian cooking
- Hypnotherapy
- Humor therapy
- Stress management
- Herbal therapy
- Acupuncture
- Acupressure

Wellness coordinators

In an effort to maintain people's health and to help keep health care costs down, many hospitals, health care facilities, and large corporations employ wellness coordinators. If you enjoy working around health care and love to develop and implement programs, this can be a great career for you.

Wellness coordinators develop and implement preventive health care programs. These might include health fairs, support groups, screenings, clinics, and classes, all designed to keep people healthy. For example, you might run programs to help people lose weight, eat healthier, or stop smoking. You might also run healthy-heart screenings, develop women's or men's wellness days, or stress management programs.

Bright Idea
To learn more about careers in homeopathy, contact the National Center For Homeopathy or check out the Web site at www.homeopathic.org.

Watch Out!
Some states do not allow N.D.s to practice medicine. Check the rules and regulations of the state in which you plan on living and practicing.

This type of career requires the ability to juggle a hundred tasks at once. If you are extremely organized and detail-oriented, this might be a job for you. Large corporations as well as hospitals and health care facilities are potential employers.

Fitness and nutrition

Fitness and nutrition are becoming ever more popular as a road to good health. And with good reason: Fitness and nutrition can make us healthier, help us live longer, and make us feel better. Do you want to be part of this industry? If so, you are not alone. There are more jobs than ever in fitness and nutrition—and the trend is growing.

What general characteristics should you have if you are going to work in these fields?

- Motivation
- Inspiration
- Patience
- Tact
- Compassion

How many nights have you flipped through the television channels only to see one infomercial after another selling fitness and nutrition products? Society is obsessed with becoming not only thinner, but also more physically fit. As a result, more people than ever are exercising. This leads to a need for instructors.

Personal trainers

Personal trainers are hot, hot, hot. Formerly a luxury only the rich and famous celebrities could afford, now many people use their services. Everyone wants to be in better shape and many will pay to find ways to get there.

While many people could exercise on their own, they don't. In some cases they don't know the correct way to exercise to achieve optimum results, or they lack the motivation to work out on their own. Some people don't have the time to go to formal exercise classes. Others don't want to work out in front of people they know (or don't know).

Personal trainers plan and supervise the fitness regimes for clients on a one-on-one basis. They help people attain their optimum level of fitness. Personal trainers have a number of duties. These include:

- Assessing the physical fitness levels of their clients

- Determining what clients want to accomplish; for example, do they want to lose weight, tone up, increase their stamina, or increase their physical fitness level?

- Designing fitness programs specifically for a client

- Instructing clients on proper exercise techniques

- Exercising with clients or motivating them to exercise

- Developing healthy diet plans

Do you have what it takes to be a personal trainer?

- Are you in shape yourself?

- Can you motivate others?

- Do you have the ability to teach others?

- Do you have training in fitness, exercise, physiology, and/or exercise science?

Bright Idea
Richard Simmons, who catapulted to popularity after a stint on the popular soap opera *General Hospital* years ago, is one of the more famous weight-loss gurus. Yet even Simmons stresses that without exercise, you won't lose weight and keep it off.

Watch Out!
Nobody trusts a personal trainer who is not in shape!

- Do you deal well with others on a one-on-one basis?

Personal trainers may be self-employed or employed by corporations, gyms, health clubs, or spas.

Aerobics or exercise instructors

Do you love to work out? Do you wish you could go to the gym right now? Believe it or not, some people do. If you feel this way, consider a hot career as an aerobics or exercise instructor.

In this job, you get to lead exercise classes in aerobics, Jazzercise, or calisthenics. Good exercise instructors (those who love their job) can make classes fun and enjoyable. Depending on where you work, you might teach people of different fitness levels or age groups.

A hot career possibility in this field is working in corporate fitness programs. In this environment, you develop exercise and fitness programs for employees, lead classes, teach people how to use exercise equipment, and are responsible for the gym area.

Bright Idea
Many national exercise and fitness equipment manufacturers seek representatives throughout the country. This is a good way to learn how to use exercise equipment and make contacts in the industry.

To be the best you can in this type of career, it's a good idea to get the best training possible. There are a number of colleges which offer degree programs in exercise and fitness. Some of the larger fitness chains also offer training.

Diet consultants

When was the last time you didn't hear someone talking about being on a diet, going on a diet, or needing to diet? America is filled with those who are overweight. There is tremendous opportunity for people interested in helping others who need dieting and nutrition advice.

If you're interested in entering this field and don't really have any nutritional education or training, think about working for one of the national weight loss companies, such as Weight Watchers or Jenny Craig.

While these jobs vary from company to company, they may give you the opportunity to:

- Motivate people to stay on the program

- Congratulate people when they are successful

- Give tips on weight loss, eating, and nutrition

- Bring in new customers

Dietetic technicians

With an associate's degree program approved by the American Dietetic Association and some supervised experience, you can get a job as a dietetic technician. In this career, you'll work under the supervision of a nutritionist. Your responsibilities might include:

- Talking to patients about their diets

- Teaching patients about more nutritious food choices

- Arranging and developing meal plans

- Developing educational material on diet and nutrition

Registered dieticians

If your dream is to work as a registered dietician, you must go through an accredited program recognized by the American Dietetic Association as well as supervised experience. Once you do this, you will become an R.D., or registered dietician.

Bright Idea
If you're interested in a career as an aerobics or exercise instructor, contact the International Dance-Exercise Association (IDEA) by phone at (619) 535-8979.

Bright Idea
In addition to working in health clubs, consider retirement villages and developments, nursing homes, spas, gyms, hotels, resorts, and cruise ships. All use exercise programs and need instructors.

This is a sizzling hot career which will only become more popular throughout the millennium. Where can you work? The possibilities are endless. They include:

- Hospitals
- Clinics
- Nursing homes
- Schools, colleges and universities
- Food companies
- Corporations
- Health spas
- Hotels and motels
- Restaurants
- Private practice

One of the great things about being a dietician is your ability to help people make important changes in their eating habits. This in turn helps them change their lives. In some cases, changing eating habits can even save people's lives.

Sports and fitness nutritionists

With the prevalence of professional sports teams as well as the growing importance society puts on scholastic and amateur athletics, another of the hottest careers in nutrition is the sports and fitness nutritionist. Sports and fitness nutritionists analyze the nutritional needs of athletes and counsel them on nutrition.

This specialist may work for health and fitness clubs, gyms, or in sports medicine clinics. The most sought-after jobs involve working with individual athletes and sports teams.

Moneysaver
To earn more as a dietician, consider combining two careers. If you love to speak in public, market yourself as a professional speaker on the subject of nutrition. If you love to write, write articles for magazines, newspapers, or even a book on nutrition.

This career is similar to that of a dietician. As a matter of fact, some sports and fitness nutritionists are R.D.s. However, depending on the job, you might only need a one-year program in nutrition or a bachelor's degree with a major in foods and nutrition.

Just the facts

- There are many hot career options working in health care.

- New hot career opportunities exist in alternative medicine.

- If you have the calling to help heal others, you can have a rewarding career in health care.

- Fitness and nutrition careers can only grow in the new century.

Unofficially...
Jack Lalanne was probably one of the original television exercise mavens. Lalanne began motivating people to exercise with his early-morning shows in the early 1960s. Today, he has a line of exercise equipment named after him.

GET THE SCOOP ON...
Working as surrogate kids ▪ Hot careers active
seniors ▪ Working with the elderly ▪ Careers
for retirees

Geriatrics: Gleaning Gold From the Golden Years

Chapter 9

Our elderly population is growing faster than ever before. The increase in this population has resulted in many new and varied careers. Maybe one of them is right for you. Why would you want to work with the elderly? You might want to make a difference in their lives. Or you might want to make a difference in yours.

If you have compassion and kindness and want to help people, working with the elderly can be a very fulfilling career choice. Careers working with the elderly require a multiplicity of skills, knowledge, education, and talents. What do you want to do? What have you been dreaming of?

This chapter will cover a wide array of hot careers you might want to choose. Whether it's your dream to work with the elderly in health care, home care, or social service, there is great job waiting for you. Would you prefer helping seniors be happy, have fun, and be more productive? You can find a hot career doing that too.

Are you a senior yourself who has retired and wants to reenter the workforce? Read on. There are hot careers for you too.

Bright Idea
If you want to know more about a career in elder law, check out the National Academy of Elder Law Web site at www.naela.org.

Taking care of our elderly

How many times have you heard about uncaring relatives abusing older people? Those caregivers at home may become frustrated and lose control. In other cases, unfeeling employees in nursing homes do not properly care for the elderly, knowing they will not be reported.

If you're interested in law, there's a growing specialty called elder law. Elder lawyers work on behalf of older people. Winning a case can mean the difference between a comfortable life and one filled with pain and anguish for a client. In extreme cases, an elder lawyer's assistance can mean life or death for a client who is being abused.

Geriatric assessment coordinators

Want to make a difference in the quality of life of the elderly, but you're not interested in being an attorney? Consider a new hot career choice as a geriatric assessment coordinator. In this job, your main function is to assess the physical, emotional, and mental condition of geriatric patients using exams, medical tests, and interviews with patients and their family.

After patients have been assessed, you're responsible for determining their needs and setting up a plan to fulfill those needs. This can mean helping patients or their family make decisions about living arrangements and medical problems.

This type of job requires a great deal of compassion, organization, and interpersonal skills. As a geriatric assessment coordinator you have a great deal of contact with the patient. Look for employment opportunities in the following settings:

- Hospitals

- Extended-care facilities

- Nursing homes

- Health maintenance organizations (HMOs)

- Hospices

- Geriatric clinics

Nursing home activities directors

Do you enjoy planning and coordinating activities for others? Want to enhance the lives of older people in a hospital, nursing home, or extended-care facility? Consider a career as a nursing home activities director. These individuals are responsible for making the lives of the elderly more interesting and fulfilling. While responsibilities differ from job to job, general functions usually include assessing the skill level of residents as well as developing personalized activity plans for each resident.

Activities might include games, dances, parties, shopping trips, craft or cooking lessons, and sing-alongs. Some planned activities might be done alone, while others are group activities. Most jobs also encompass the administration of budgets and some supervision of staff. One of the reasons many like this type of job is the visible difference they can see when residents become involved in activities.

66

I was working in a hospital in an administrative position and going to school taking classes in gerontology. A new job opened up in the facility as a geriatric assessment coordinator. Helping the patients and their families have a better life is more fulfilling than I could have ever imagined.
—Keith, geriatric assessment coordinator

99

Bright Idea
There are a number of colleges and universities offering degrees in gerontology. These schools often have placement offices that know of openings working with the elderly.

Watch Out!
Working with older patients can often be difficult. Some find it depressing. Make sure you can tolerate this type of setting by volunteering in nursing homes, extended care facilities, etc. before committing yourself to a job.

Extended-care facility administrators

If you want to work at the top of the ladder in an extended-care facility or nursing home, a hot job for you might be as the facility administrator. As the administrator, you are in charge of planning, policy making, and in certain situations, community outreach. One of your major responsibilities, especially today, is complying with government agencies and regulations.

Competition is usually stiff for these positions. Many extended-care facility administrators hold masters in nursing, health services administration, hospital administration, or business administration.

This is usually a high-paying job, but it does carry a great deal of responsibility. One of the great things about this type of career is that you have the power to make your facility the very best of its kind. If you've ever heard about problems in extended-care facilities that made your blood boil, in this job you can make a difference.

Personal services for the elderly

As people get older, they may not be able to do things as easily as they once did. Carrying heavy groceries, for example, can be an impossible task. As a result, a whole new range of career possibilities has opened up in the personal service area.

Bright Idea
Learn more about careers in health care facility administration by checking out the American College of Health Care Executives Web site at www.ache.org.

- **Personal shoppers.** Personal shoppers for the elderly handle grocery shopping. This is a relatively new service. If you decide you want to do this, you can make up lists of groceries for people to choose from or they may make lists for you to purchase. You make your money by charging a flat fee or a percentage of the bill.

- **Personal chefs.** Many elderly people do not eat correctly—or at all—because they can't or won't cook for themselves. Look into becoming a personal chef for seniors. Your job will be to prepare nutritious meals. This may be done either in the client's home, or meals can be delivered. You earn your money by charging a fee per meal or per week.

∎ **Personal concierges.** Most people associate concierges with good hotels. A new service being provided for seniors (as well as others) is that of personal concierge. As noted previously, many seniors can no longer handle doing the things they used to. In many cases, even if they can handle these functions, they don't want to.

Personal concierges find people to handle functions for their clients such as: mowing the lawn, doing home repairs, painting the inside or outside of the house, chauffeuring the elderly, making arrangements for trips, preparing meals, arranging to pick up visiting grandchildren from the airport, finding baby-sitters, watching or monitoring someone's home when they are on vacation, watering plants when a client is on vacation, walking a dog, and taking care of pets when clients are in the hospital or on vacation.

You may find employment in retirement communities or with personal concierge services, or be self-employed. You will make your money either by earning a salary if you are employed or charging a fee for services if you are self-employed.

Keep 'em healthy

The United States Department of Labor indicates that many of the fastest-growing occupations for the new century will be health-related. The majority of these careers involve working with the elderly. Consider these geriatric health care specialties:

- **Geriatricians.** Doctors in this field specialize in healing older patients.

- **Geriatric dentists.** Dentists specializing in this field deal with the special dental problems and gum diseases that plague the elderly. You might find your hot career in an assisted-care facility or in a private office.

- **Geriatric nutritionists.** The elderly have different nutritional needs as they get older. Nutritionists in this field help older people develop healthy diets. Your hot career might be working in an assisted-care facility, other health care facility, or recreation center.

- **Geriatric podiatrists.** As people age, they experience a variety of foot problems. Podiatrists specializing in this field handle, diagnose, and treat foot problems in the elderly. Your hot career might be working in an assisted-care facility, other health care facility, or private practice.

- **Geriatric therapists.** There are a variety of therapists who specialize in working with the elderly. Hot opportunities working with the elderly in therapy include:

    Music therapists: Individuals who use music to treat physical, mental, and emotional disabilities.

    Art therapists: Individuals who use art projects to treat physical, mental, and emotional disabilities.

Bright Idea
Check out the American Physical Therapy Association Web site at www.apta.org to learn more about a career in physical therapy.

Dance therapists: Individuals who use dance and movement to treat physical, mental, and emotional disabilities.

Physical therapists: Individuals who evaluate patient's physical therapy needs and perform physical therapies.

Occupational therapists: Individuals who help patients who have suffered illnesses or accidents to relearn skills.

- **Geriatric technologists and technicians.** Your hot career might be as an EEG technician, operating electroencephalograph machines to diagnose strokes or brain tumors or measure the effects of disease to the brain.

  You might choose a career as an EKG technician operating the electrocardiograph machine to trace an older patient's heartbeats.

  Maybe you wish to be a clinical lab technologist working with the elderly in an assisted-care facility. In this capacity you perform lab tests, examining their blood, tissue, and other body substances to determine diseases or infections.

  Cardiovascular technologists often work with the elderly in diagnosing heart disease through various tests such as electrocardiograms and ultrasounds.

Want to take care of the elderly, but you're really not interested in actual health care jobs? Read on for some hot possibilities.

Careers for surrogate kids: What to do when you're not there

Today's society is mobile. The days where families all lived in the same town and stayed there for life

Bright Idea
If you're interested in learning more about careers in occupational therapy, check out the American Occupational Therapy Association Web site at www.aota.org.

Bright Idea
If you want to work in health care and you're interested in the elderly, get a bit creative in your job search. Train for the main job category (such as physical therapist) and then look for special classes in gerontology and aging.

are long gone. Also gone are the days when large extended families lived together under one roof. While you may live in New York City, your siblings may live in Los Angeles and Chicago and your parents in Miami. What do you do when your parents need some help and you or your siblings aren't around?

A geriatric care manager serves as a type of stand-in relative when real relatives are not in close proximity or available for other reasons. If you really like helping people and enjoy dealing with seniors, this might be a great job for you.

Geriatric care managers have many responsibilities. They assist with a variety of issues ranging from medical, legal, housing, financial, and emotional issues. Individuals are generally retained when a family is not around to respond to problems and situations that might arise with an elderly relative.

Some of their duties might include:

- Visiting a client on a regular basis
- Making sure a geriatric client is eating properly
- Making sure a geriatric client is taking medications
- Making appointments for a client to see physicians
- Taking a client to physician's appointments
- Making appointments for a client to see therapists
- Taking a client to therapy appointments
- Making dental appointments for a client
- Taking a client to dental appointments
- Determining which agencies the client is eligible to use.

Watch Out!
If you are considering working in private practice as a geriatric care manager you might be required to be licensed or certified in certain states. Call your state's department of licensing to check out requirements.

- Determining which social services a client is eligible to use
- Filling out medical and insurance forms on behalf of a client
- Filling out applications on behalf of the client
- Applying for reimbursements on behalf of a client
- Paying a client's bills and keeping a client's finances in order

A particular benefit for many people in this type of career is the close bond that is often formed with clients. There are a variety of settings in which you might work as a geriatric care manager. These include:

- Private geriatric-care management firms
- Hospitals
- Home care organizations
- Private practice

Unofficially...
Some geriatric care managers with specialized training may also handle estate planning, living wills, and family trusts. However, this is the exception, not the rule.

Because this is such a new career, you'll find that education and training requirements vary from a high school diploma to an undergraduate or master's degree. In addition, many geriatric care managers working for firms are expected to have a background in social work.

Compassionate careers in social service and home care

As in health care, social service jobs have geriatric opportunities. These may be available in a variety of institutional and agency settings as well as in independent practitioner services.

Are you interested in social work and want to work with the elderly? A good area for you might be

Timesaver
Jobs for geriatric social workers are often located in state, county, or municipal government agencies. Contact state employment offices to find out about job openings.

geriatric social work. Geriatric social workers deal with aging clients and their families. These clients have unique problems and circumstances to deal with.

Geriatric social workers help seniors who have difficulties lead more productive lives. Why would a geriatric client be assigned a social worker?

- Individual clients may ask for help.
- Individuals may be referred by another agency.

As a geriatric social worker, you might work with clients who are in nursing homes, hospitals, or extended-care facilities.

Why would you want to work in this field?

- You might help a client who still lives at home stay in his home instead of being moved to an extended-care facility.
- You might help a client locate housing.
- You might help a client who needs assistance with food or nutrition.
- You might help a client find financial help.
- You might help a client who is ill or who has a spouse who is ill.
- You might help a client who doesn't have any relatives and can't handle problems on her own.

Bright Idea
If you are interested in a career as a geriatric social worker, an internship is helpful. Contact various social service agencies or the office for the aging in your area for information and job openings.

Adult day care

Most everyone has heard about day care for children. With our aging population, the need for adult day care has exploded. There are many seniors who are not sick enough to need constant care, yet can't be left alone for long periods. Adult children who are not comfortable having their parents in nursing homes often have them living in their home. However, with both adult children working, no one is home during the day to care for the aging parent.

Adult day care providers may work in adult day care centers or may provide day care in their home or that of their client. In addition to giving basic care to the elderly person, the successful day care provider must provide stimulating activities and companionship.

If you are interested in a business opportunity, you might consider a career running an adult day care service. The need for this service is growing and will continue through the century. In this capacity you care for adults who are incapable of living alone. You are responsible for preparing and serving meals as well as providing social stimulation and interaction.

Your clientele may be developed in a number of ways. You might, for example, contact local social service agencies, advertise in newspapers, or put up flyers in the area. However, as the need for this service is so great, chances are if you provide a great service, you will have more clients than you can handle.

Home health care providers

Do you enjoy helping people who are ill or infirm? Do you think you'd enjoy helping people prepare weekly menus, shop for food, and prepare meals? Would you like to perform simple medical procedures such as checking and recording vital statistics, changing dressings, and assisting with medications? If so, you might like to work as a home health care provider.

The expanding population of older adults who don't need 24-hour supervision but do require assistance has led to a multitude of opportunities for home health care providers. The trend toward home health care has also boosted the demand for

Watch Out!
You may need a state license to run your own adult day care service. You should also check with your local zoning board if you plan on having the adult day care center in your home.

Bright Idea
As a home health care provider, one of the things that you might enjoy most is providing psychological and emotional support to your clients. Sometimes, you can make a client feel better by just by being there, drinking a cup of coffee with them, and talking.

MoneySaver
Hotels and motels often charge a fee when making long-distance credit card calls as well as using pre-paid calling cards. Save money when traveling by using a phone outside the room to stay in touch with your family or friends. You might also consider a one-rate cell phone service if you make a lot of calls.

home health care providers. As changes in reimbursement to hospitals for health care costs have forced facilities to shorten stays, hospitals can no longer keep patients for extended periods.

Careers working with sweet and sassy seniors

It's important to realize that not every senior is ill or infirm. Many of today's seniors lead very active lives. There are a wealth of career opportunities in this area working with them.

Do you like to travel? Is it your dream to visit every corner of the country and perhaps even go abroad? Consider leading tours for seniors. Many travel agencies offer tours specifically geared for the senior traveler. As a tour leader, you will coordinate the tour, make sure everyone is happy and accounted for, lead tours of specific areas, and handle emergencies.

Working with seniors who are traveling often has different challenges than working with other segments of the population. For example, a person on the tour may have left medication at home and need to find a pharmacy to fill a prescription. Older people may also require physicians or other medical care. Some seniors may have trouble walking long distances and need wheelchairs to move around. The tour guide must meet these challenges with a smile.

Depending on the specific job, you may have to be an expert on the area in which you are leading the group. You might need to know local history or at least the geography of the area in which you are leading the tour.

To be a tour guide for seniors, as well as any other group, you need to be very personable, like talking to others, and have a great personality. It's also usually essential that you are detail-oriented and do not get flustered easily.

Senior tour directors

You might want to be a tour director for seniors, in which you plan the actual tour. In this type of job, you might accompany the seniors to specific locations of interest, or have a tour leader lead them.

This type of career requires the ability to do marketing as well as coordinating. You have to find the areas to visit, negotiate with hotels, airlines, bus companies, venues, restaurants, and so on. You have to determine what your group will see, what type of events they will attend, and plan all the other details of the tour. You will then have to sell the tour to the senior market.

Senior lecturers

Do you love speaking in public? Do you have expertise in some field? Consider a great career as a lecturer for the senior market. There are many places that look for speakers in this area. These might include:

- Retirement communities
- Senior centers
- Civic groups
- Senior groups, clubs, and organizations

What would anyone be interested in hearing you talk about?

- Stress management for seniors
- Dealing with HMOs
- Eating right
- Cooking healthy

Bright Idea
If you have expertise in a certain geographic area or skill, contact Elderhostel to learn about being a group leader. This will help you try out the job before you commit yourself to a full-time position. (Elderhostel is a non-profit organization catering to senior citizen travel and programs.)

- Dealing with the death of a spouse
- Dealing with an ill spouse
- Humor for seniors
- Living a healthy life
- Current events
- Living within your means

Instructor for seniors

Would you rather give classes to those in the senior market? Today everyone wants to learn something. Do you have a special skill or talent that you would like to share? Seniors often have more time than others to attend classes.

Contact retirement communities, senior centers, and schools and colleges offering continuing education classes to see what opportunities are available. You might also build a nice business for yourself teaching classes in your home, their home, or a community center. Look at your skills and talents. What can you teach seniors?

- Craft classes
- Cooking and baking classes
- Sewing classes
- Woodworking classes
- Classes in handling finances, bookkeeping, or doing personal taxes
- Exercise and fitness
- Flower arranging
- Cake decorating

Companions

Another interesting career is serving as a senior companion. This type of job varies. You may live with a senior providing basic companionship, helping them shop, making sure they eat properly, and so on.

If you enjoy traveling, there's another companion job you might really like. Many wealthy seniors hire companions to travel with them so they don't have to travel alone. In this type of job, you travel with the individual, dine with him, stay in the same hotel, sight-see, and attend functions.

Family memory biographers

Do you know your family history? Has an older relative told you stories about your family? Wouldn't it be great to have those memories preserved? Would you like to help others remember and preserve their family history? There is a way—and you can even make a hot new career out it.

Older people have many memories of the past. To save these precious memories, many hire family video biographers. These individuals talk to older family members and ask probing questions. As the older family members answer questions, they remember other situations which they discuss. The family video biographer acts as a facilitator to extract memories and preserve them.

Depending on your skills and talents, as the family memory biographer you may prepare a videotaped documentary of the elder family member's memories or may chronicle the memories in writing instead.

You may work for a company that markets this service or you may do this on a private consulting basis.

Retirement planners

Many people's lives are centered around their jobs. They may have spent most of their lives working,

Unofficially...
Unofficially, Dorothy Shapiro and Michael Gold thought preserving family memories was such a good idea, they formed a partnership and produced a tape called Video Reflections. The video explains how to tape and interview your relatives, but may also be used to learn how to tape and interview others to chronicle their memories. Martha Stewart heard about it and interviewed Shapiro on one of her television shows.

Bright Idea
If you're interested in a career as a retirement planner, contact the Center For Creative Retirement or the American Association of Retired Persons for more information at (800) 424-3410.

and when retirement comes, they don't know how to deal with it. They have no plans for life after work.

The main function of retirement planners (also discussed in Chapter 7) is to counsel retirees to help them adjust to retirement. You might work in a variety of settings including large corporations, government agencies, private retirement planning firms, or as a consultant in private practice.

Retirement planners usually meet with employees as they are nearing retirement. At that time they discuss the retiree's goals, aspirations, and dreams for the future. Some retirees, for example, look forward to travel; others may want to go back to school to obtain a degree, volunteer, or relocate.

As the retirement planner, you help future retirees make plans that take into account their age, interests, and financial situations. Many companies have retirement programs and benefit plans. The planner, in these situations, is expected to explain the benefits and drawbacks of programs so that retirees can make an educated decision.

What do you need to become a retirement planner? This is a relatively new career. Requirements vary from job to job, but generally you need some communication and counseling skills. Experience dealing with older people is a plus. A bachelor's degree is usually required and a master's degree may be preferred.

Can't deal with retirement? Read on.

Unofficially...
If you don't have a degree in gerontology but you think you might like to work as a retirement planner, take classes in gerontology, business, social work, and recreational and occupational therapy.

Careers for recovering workaholics

Let's say you've worked for years and have now retired. But you just aren't happy. You loved working. Or maybe you need or want the extra money. It was good having a nice, steady paycheck coming in every week.

It's reported that by 2020 the number of people who are 55 or older will have jumped by almost 75 percent. The working age group, however, will grow only by about 5 percent. This means there will not be enough younger workers to fill the void older workers will create when they retire. This may result in your company not pushing you to retire or might mean companies may need you to fill a void in their staff.

What can you do? What are your options? Many older workers use their talents and the skills they have garnered to become consultants. Consulting offers you the opportunity to pick and choose assignments and to work as much or as little as you want. It gives you the flexibility you may be looking for.

Do you fear that because you are an older worker, no one will want to hire you? Here are some hints that might help you find a great position:

- Be willing to work for a troubled company. They need experienced workers and younger people may be hesitant to work for them.

- Read the business section of the newspaper and find companies that have just announced layoffs. These companies often need to hire experienced workers who may not need full benefit programs.

- Look for smaller companies (these represent a large segment of the job market today). They are often looking for experienced workers.

- Part-time positions often lead to full-time jobs.

Job hunting for seniors is no different than job hunting for the rest of the population. You just may not have done it in a while. Here are some tips to remember:

Bright Idea
More and more businesses are beginning to see the value in older workers. Generally, older workers show up on time, have a good work ethic, and possess experience that can't be beat. Older workers also demonstrate a higher commitment.

Watch Out!
Try not to compare the way your present company does things to the way your past employers did things. It makes you look like you are living in the past.

Moneysaver
Age-discrimination lawsuits are often difficult to win, hard to prove, and very expensive. Consider the costs before bringing a lawsuit.

- Network, network, network. It's easier to get an interview when someone recommends you.

- Be enthusiastic. You have a lot to offer!

- Be willing to work. Don't say things like, "I hope I don't get too tired doing this."

- Keep a positive attitude. Don't be negative in the workplace.

Don't let the fact that you may be part of graying America stop you from doing what you love best. There are a wide array of careers for retirees. You just have to look.

Sometimes, the money is not the most important reason for working. Retired people may need to work to have something to do or because they need the social interaction. If that is the case for you, consider jobs in fast-food restaurants, supermarket chains, or retailer stores.

Working in an entry-level position, however, may not be your cup of tea. Remember, you have experience and you have talent. Don't let your fear stop you from applying for jobs in management. Many of the sales and service industries have good opportunities for seniors.

Consider jobs in travel and the hospitality industry. Many seniors travel. Hotels and casinos are often more than happy to have senior workers who can relate to senior travelers and guests.

Home businesses are another great career choice for seniors. Combine your skills and talents with your passions and desires. Start a home business to augment your earnings and give you the excitement of a new challenge.

Just the facts

- Working with the elderly can be a fulfilling career.

- You can work with the elderly in most areas of health care.

- Most any skill you have can be put to use working with seniors.

- There are many opportunities to work with seniors who are not ill or infirm.

- Retiring does not mean you have to stop working. There are endless possibilities. You just have to look for them.

For Creative and Talented People

PART IV

GET THE SCOOP ON...
Working with words ▪ Hot art careers ▪
Crafting a career ▪ Working with your hands ▪
Designing your career

The Creative Career Corner

Chapter 10

A re you creative? Do you wish you could use your talent in a hot new career that doesn't stifle your creativity? Well, you can. What is your talent? What can you do better than anyone else? Do you love to write? How about using your artistic ability? Is it your dream to work with your hands? Why not design spaces or places or things?

This chapter will cover a variety of ways you can have a career without giving up your creativity. It will give you options to use your talents. You just need to have faith in yourself and try. These are competitive fields, but they can be some of the most rewarding out there.

Write a story: Careers for writers

Are you a talented writer? There are many hot careers for writers in almost every industry. Some allow you to use your writing skills; others revolve around the writing skills of others. Let's look at some possibilities.

Timesaver
The greatest obstacle between you and a published book is writing it. You don't need to write it all at once. Do a little bit each day, and you won't get frustrated or exhausted.

When it comes to people who love to work with words, the number one dream is to publish a book. Is this your dream too? If so, just get started. Hundreds of publishers are responsible for publishing thousands of titles each year. One of those published books could be yours if you just start writing.

What kind of books do you want to write? The possibilities are endless. Do you want to write books for children? Teens? Adults? The decision is up to you. Books are written for virtually every age group, ranging from preschoolers to senior citizens.

Do you want to write fiction or nonfiction? Fiction books cover stories that are not true. Fiction categories you might write about include:

- Mysteries
- Romance novels (sizzling hot)
- Westerns
- Gothic romances
- Children's stories
- Historic novels
- Young adults
- Comedy
- Dramas

Nonfiction books are based on factual information. Some subjects you might write about in this area include:

- Textbooks
- Self-help, motivational, and inspirational (sizzling hot)
- Biographies
- History books
- Cookbooks

- Careers
- Business (sizzling hot)
- Medical books
- Craft books
- Reference books
- Diet books (sizzling hot)

No matter what type of book you want to write about, there are a number of steps you usually must take. These include:

- Coming up with an idea
- Developing a proposal or outline
- Writing a sample chapter
- Sending a query letter to publishers asking if they would be interested in your book

Some people use an agent to sell books instead of seeking out a publisher themselves. You still generally have to develop the proposal or outline. However, once you find an agent to represent you, he will try to sell your book for you.

So let's say you hit it lucky. Someone wants to publish your book. You have negotiated a contract and now all you have to do is write the book. Writing is lonely work. You have to be extremely organized, self-motivated, and be able to manage your time wisely. You have to sit down and get your book done. Unfortunately, no matter how good your book ideas are, they don't write themselves.

Some people write one book and never write another. Others experience great success and write many books in their lifetime. The ultimate success for most authors is having one or more books that become best-sellers. However, it is also quite exciting to walk into a bookstore and see copies of your

Bright Idea
Before you send query letters to publishers, visit bookstores and libraries to see which publishers handle the types of books you are interested in writing.

Timesaver
Save time looking for the names and addresses of publishers and the types of books they are looking for by checking out *Writer's Digest* and the *Literary Marketplace*.

book on the shelves whether or not it is a best-seller.

It's essential in this line of work to remember that although almost anyone can write a manuscript, every manuscript may not sell the first time you send it out. Rejections are common; don't take them personally. Just because a publisher does not want your book, does not mean it is not good. You have to be persistent and keep sending it out. The more persistent you are, the better your chances of success.

Let's look at a few different hot author careers.

Cookbooks

Do you love to cook and create recipes? Do you want to couple those skills with writing? Consider becoming a cookbook author. There are thousands of cookbooks published every year. One of them can be yours.

Do you have a specialty? Do you stay home on weekends creating new recipes for cheesecakes? Do you love experimenting with ways to use one special ingredient in a variety of recipes? As a cookbook author you can write a book about cooking in general or about one area of cooking.

Cookbook authors not only write the books, they must also create the recipes or at least create new ways to adapt old recipes.

Timesaver
Some cookbook authors develop collections of recipes instead of creating new ones. If they have a collection of recipes, they may already have done a lot of the necessary work.

Whatever type of cookbook you write, you are responsible for making sure each recipe is tested and assuring the ingredients and measurements are accurate. You are also responsible for writing simple, easy-to-follow instructions for each recipe. In some situations, depending on your book, you may write introductions or stories about each recipe.

While it's always nice to have your book published by a major company, many cookbook authors self-publish their books and sell them locally to specialty shops or by mail.

Children's books

Books can have a tremendous impact on children whether someone is reading to them or they are reading a story themselves. The market for children's books is tremendous.

Do you have what it takes to write books for this special audience? You do if you understand the interests, reading levels, abilities, and attention spans of various age groups of children.

All children enjoy looking at pictures as they hear or read the story, so books with illustrations are of particular interest. It doesn't matter whether you write in prose or poetry as long as the style and story are interesting to children.

Romance novels

Want a really hot career as an author? Romance novels—a special kind of fiction based on a love story embellished by problems and adventures—are hot, hot, hot. There are publishers whose specialty is romance novels. Some publishers even have different lines of romance novels so they can appeal to different age groups.

To write these novels, you have to develop great plots with interesting story lines and characters with whom readers can identify. If you can write with romantic passion, allowing readers to escape from their daily routine and reality into a fantasy world, you have it made.

There are a variety of types of romance novels:

- They may be set in a current time period.
- They may be set in different era or time.
- They may focus on first love.

Unofficially...
If you want to become a romance novelist, one of the best ways to learn the genre is by reading romance novels. Try to read a variety, including different authors and styles, to learn as much as you can.

Bright Idea
The Romance Writers of America are helpful to those aspiring to become romance novelists. The organization sponsors courses to help you learn the craft and develop your skills. Contact them at (281) 440-6885 or check out their Web site at www. rwanational.com.

Watch Out!
It's usually not a good idea to call people at a magazine to see if they're interested in an article. You're better off writing to them with your idea and about your background. You can usually find the address of the magazine's editorial department in the front of the magazine.

- They may focus on history.
- They may focus on horror.
- They may appeal to different age groups.

Romance novels are sold like most other books. You usually need to write an outline, perhaps a couple of chapters, and a query letter to editors. There are also agents who represent romance novelists. You can look for their names in the literary marketplace.

Freelance or spec article writers

Do you want to be published, but you're not quite ready to tackle a book? Consider writing articles for magazines or periodicals on a freelance or spec basis. Freelance means that you can write for anyone you want. Spec means you are writing on speculation (you only get paid after you've done the work, and only if your work is purchased). You might write an article and if a magazine wants it they will pay you, otherwise they will pass.

You can write articles about anything that you know about or you can research. If you are interested in a career in this area, check out magazines to see what types of articles they use. Then contact those magazines to find out if they use freelance articles and information about their guidelines.

Literary agents

Do you love reading other people's stories, articles, and books? When you read things, can you see their potential even in a raw state? Do you have sales ability on top of everything else?

A great career for you might be a literary agent. In this job you read and review other people's work to determine if it has sales potential. If you feel it does, it is your job to sell it to publishers or editors.

As part of your job you might make suggestions to improve your client's work or to make it more salable, as well as negotiating on their behalf.

You might work for a literary agency, or after getting some experience you might strike out on your own. However you do it, the exciting part about this career is you can be the driving force in catapulting someone's writing career to the top.

Writing and publishing for nonprofits

How often do you open your mail and find a heart-wrenching letter asking you to donate money to a worthy cause? How about looking at a brochure that tells what an organization has to offer? Do you want to make a difference and use your writing skills too? A broad gamut of internal and external publications are issued by nonprofit organizations to disseminate information about the groups and their causes. People are needed to develop and write these publications, and one of them could be you.

Depending on the organization, its size, prestige, and purpose, it may publish a variety of internal and external publications, including:

- Newsletters
- Magazines
- Brochures
- Legislative alerts
- Letters
- Press releases
- Fund-raising materials
- Marketing and promotional materials

What kind of hot jobs are available? There is a wide array of career opportunities for people with writing skills and for those interested in various

Bright Idea
Learn more about a career as a literary agent by contacting the Association of Author's Representatives at (212) 353-3709 or check out their Web site at www. aar-online.org.

Unofficially...
For other ideas
for careers with
nonprofits, see
Chapter 7.

aspects of publishing. What are your skills? Talents? Desires? Let's look at some of the hotter possibilities.

- **Publication editors.** As a publication editor, you are in charge of the development of publications needed by an organization. You might hire and supervise copywriters, reporters, and artists; as well as write articles, assign writers to projects, and edit copy.

- **Copywriters.** As a copywriter, you hold a very important position in the nonprofit organization. The words you write can mean the difference between a reader committing to the particular cause or just reading about it. Your copy can vastly improve your organization's funding, and most nonprofits are limited only by a lack of funds.

- **Reporters.** As a reporter, you cover newsworthy events and promotions sponsored by the organization, and cover events that have an impact on the organization or its cause.

- **Fund-raising publication writers.** In this position, you write fund-raising appeals in letters, brochures, leaflets, or other promotional pieces.

Timesaver
Write to the major greeting card companies to get their writer's guidelines. You'll save time if you know what the company wants from you before you start writing.

Greeting card writers

Do you spend hours looking at cards in card and gift stores? Every time you look at cards, do you think you could do better? Did you ever wonder who writes those cards? It could be you, if you want a sizzling hot career as a greeting card writer. What's your style? Can you write funny humorous cards? How about cards that are serious, or cards with a special theme?

There is no formal education for this career. Your job is to develop ideas for greeting cards and then write the words. All you need is the ability to come up with creative, unique, and imaginative lines. You can freelance for card companies or see if you can get a job as a staff writer. Your talent creating lines can push you far in this field. The more aggressive you are in selling your work, the more you can earn.

Soap opera writers

Do you watch daytime television? Do you have a favorite soap? When you watch, do you sometimes think you could write the story and the dialogue?

Daytime television is growing by leaps and bounds. Soaps have a tremendous audience. Years ago, the majority of people who watched soaps were housewives who had no job outside the home. VCRs have changed all that. Today's viewers have a diverse background.

A coveted career in television writing is that of the soap writer. These open-ended dramas use a head writer as well as a staff of other writers working under her direction. Getting to the top isn't easy, but it's worth it in fame and fortune.

As the head writer, you are responsible for developing the main story lines and creating major characters. The other writers on the team work with the main story and create mini-stories and dialogue. The writers work as a team to develop plots, outlines, and treatments that eventually turn into the dialogue viewed daily.

You can usually find the producer's name at the end of each show. You could also check the Web site of the show, or the network's Web site. Most network Web site addresses are easy to guess: For example, you can reach ABC at www.abc.com.

Bright Idea
Look at cards produced by variety of greeting card companies to see what types of cards are being sold.

Bright Idea
Want to break in, but you're not sure how? Consider developing a story line on spec and sending it to one of the soap's producers or head writers. Make sure it illustrates your talent with plenty of great dialogue, action, and excitement.

Sitcom writers

Want to write for television, but soaps aren't your thing? Do you always see a humorous spin to everything that happens? Maybe a career as a sitcom writer is up your alley. Sitcom writers work alone or in collaboration with others.

Before you write a full script, you must develop a plot outline and a treatment. This defines your characters and describes your story's events as they occur in the script. Once you have done that, you can get started writing a full script. Your script must contain the following:

- Dialogue each character speaks
- Setting of scenes
- Descriptions of sets
- Description of the movements each character should make

For a script to be successful, you need to develop characters and settings for the story. You must also introduce one or more conflicts for each story, and decide how those conflicts will be resolved. The difficult part, however, is finding ways to make the words and actions of each character funny.

Can you write humorous dialogue? Do you think you can create situations and settings others will find humorous? Then you stand a chance of being successful at this career.

One of the best ways to break into this career is by writing a script on spec for one of your favorite sitcoms. As I noted previously, spec means you write the script and then try to sell it. Send it to the producer. Even if a producer doesn't like the script, he may see potential and ask you to rewrite it or work on a different one.

Bright Idea
Contact the Writers' Guild of America to learn more about becoming a sitcom writer. Contact the WGA-West at (323) 954-1000 or check out their Web site at www.wga.org. Contact the WGA-East at (212) 767-7800 or browse their site at www.wgeast.org.

Comedy writers

Do you like comedy, but you're not comfortable writing dialogue and scripts? Think about writing comedy instead. You can write humorous material for comedians or you might even write comedic material for publications.

Many comedians don't write their own material. Instead, they rely on comedy writers to provide them with a wealth of jokes, skits, gags, and monologues which they then perform.

You have a lot of options as a comedy writer in addition to writing for other comedians:

- You can perform as a comedian yourself.
- You can write pieces for magazines or newspapers.
- You can write a humorous column in a magazine or newspaper.
- You can write a book with a humorous spin.

Speechwriters

How many times have you sat through a program where you listened to the speaker deliver a boring speech? While doing so, did you think you could have written a better one? If so, you might consider a hot career as a speechwriter.

There are few who don't remember at least a piece of Martin Luther King, Jr.'s speech in Atlanta, or one of John F. Kennedy's state-of-the-union addresses. As a speechwriter, you can create the words that impact others.

There are many executives, politicians, and other individuals who are expected to give speeches throughout their career. While they might be great orators, they aren't all great speechwriters.

Speechwriters often determine the subject matter of a speech as well as the direction the speaker wants to go. You may have to do some research to come up with facts, quotes, or other interesting information.

To be successful in this career you have to write speeches that sound as if they were written by the speaker. Speechwriters may be employed in a number of settings. These include:

- Corporations
- Industry
- Politicians
- Trade associations
- Nonprofit organizations
- Freelance

Depending on your employment situation, you may receive a salary, be on a retainer, or be compensated on a per-speech basis.

Writers in the music industry

When you think of writing, you may not think of the music industry, but there are many careers in the music industry that involve writing.

Being a songwriter is not the easiest of careers, but hearing your song on the radio or played at a concert hall is a great reward. Songwriters must be extremely talented writers. You may write the lyrics, the music, or both. Depending on your talent, you can write tunes in a variety of styles of music.

While it takes a fair amount of time to write even a short book, there are songwriters who have written hit tunes in a matter of minutes. One of the great things about being a songwriter is that you never know when one of your tunes is going to be picked up by a recording artist who can turn it into a hit.

While you might be able to get a job with a record or production company, you usually not only have to write your songs, but sell them as well.

If you have a creative thought process and musical writing talent, a hot way to break into the industry is by writing jingles for commercial products.

Artists: Putting yourself in the picture

If you're an artist, you probably create to satisfy your need for self-expression. Wouldn't it be nice to find a hot career where you can turn an avocation into a vocation? Let's look at some possibilities.

Police sketch artists and courtroom sketch artists

Want to see your sketches in newspapers, magazines, on posters, and on television? Consider a career as a police sketch artist. Usually, when someone commits a crime, there is no one standing there with a camera to snap a picture. Often, however, there are witnesses. In order to get a likeness of a suspect, police sketch artists are called in.

To do this job, you need a great deal of artistic ability as well as drawing and illustration skills. You will be talking to witnesses to obtain information on the physical characteristics of suspects and then turning those characteristics into sketches.

While police sketch artists use a variety of mediums including pen and ink, pencil, and markers, today they may also use computers to generate composites of suspects.

Do you like to sketch, but want a little more action? Think about a career as a courtroom sketch artist. In many cases, there either isn't a television camera in the courtroom where a major case is being tried or photographers are not permitted.

Courtroom sketch artists sketch witnesses and courtroom scenes for television, newspapers, and

Unofficially...
The popular song "Handyman" (which was originally recorded by Jimmy Jones and then covered by over 50 other artists, including James Taylor) was written by singer-songwriter Jimmy Jones in 1959 in only 20 minutes.

Bright Idea
The majority of good police sketch artist jobs are located in larger metropolitan areas.

magazines. This type of career also requires drawing and illustration skills as well as artistic ability. You might be on staff with television stations, magazines, or newspapers, or you could freelance.

Fashion copyists

A really cool career if you have drawing and illustration skills is working as a fashion copyist. If you love fashion, this might be an ideal job for you. You get to visit design houses, boutiques, and stores and attend fashion shows and other functions to see what people are wearing.

Fashion copyists are talented sketch artists who gather information about fashion and garments and then sketch them. Competitors or other manufacturers then use these sketches to create copies or duplicate styles. They may also use the sketches to design original garments incorporating pieces of the sketched garment.

Who uses fashion copyists?

- Pattern houses
- Custom dress shops
- Design studios
- Apparel manufacturers
- Dressmaking companies
- Theatrical wardrobe houses
- Department stores

Bright Idea
Learn more about a career in fashion illustration by contacting the Council of Fashion Designers of America at (212) 302-1821.

Fashion illustrators

Want to know about another hot career for visual artists in fashion? A fashion illustrator draws illustrations of men's, women's, or children's clothing and accessories. Do you like doing line drawings? Are you happier doing full-color renderings? You may be asked to do both to illustrate fashions in newspapers or magazines. You might also see your designs used in advertisements or in the brochures of design houses.

Working with your hands

Do you love working with your hands and wish you could find a career that uses your talents? Consider become a craftsperson. As a craftsperson you have the opportunity to work with your hands, creating unique pieces and satisfying your own need for self-expression. Craftspeople may either be self-employed or work for others.

In addition to developing, designing, and making your craft, you must find a way to sell your work. This means that you need sales skills. To be successful in this line of work, you need to create products that are unique and well-made. They also need to be either novel or necessary in order to be marketable. You need to be able to handle a number of business functions, including keeping accurate records, setting up business books, and filing any required tax forms.

Craftspeople create a variety of crafts. These include:

- Jewelry
- Quilts
- Clothing
- Sculpture
- Wall hangings
- Dolls
- Furniture
- Accessories
- Photographs

Bright Idea
There are many hot career options for craftspeople. It's easy to find your career. You need only look at your talents, skills, and passions.

Bright Idea
To learn more about a hot career in the fine arts, contact the American Artists' Professional League at (212) 645-1345 or the American Society of Artists at (312) 751-2500.

■ Pottery

■ Stained glass

Let's look at a couple of craft careers in more depth.

Sculptors

You see sculptures at museums and art galleries. Sometimes you even see them in retail stores. The people who design and make these pieces are a special type of artist. They create three-dimensional artwork. As a sculptor, you might create your pieces from a variety of media, including clay, glass, wood, and metal.

Will you create small sculptures or large ones? Will you create for museums or for corporations to place in their buildings? Abstract designs or realistic themes? The choice is up to you.

Some sculptors sell their work on their own; others retain agents who sell their work for them. You might be commissioned to do pieces, or you might sell your work to stores, boutiques, museums, or commercial art galleries. Depending on what type of sculptures you design, you might sell your work at craft fairs or art shows.

Potters

Moneysaver
Want to display your work, but don't know where to go? Consider contacting banks, libraries, hospitals, and other public institutions. They often look for artists' work to show, and will charge less than a gallery would.

Potters, like sculptors, are craftspeople who create decorative and functional art objects. Potters work with clay and glazes to create pieces either manually or with the help of a potter's wheel.

As a potter, you either sell your work on commission or at stores, boutiques, craft fairs, galleries, museums, or other retail outlets.

Makeup artists

Want to create an illusion on a different type of canvas? Makeup artists create illustrations using people's faces as their canvas. As a makeup artist you use makeup to improve or alter people's appearances. What makes this a really hot career is that you can work in a variety of settings:

- Television and film
- Theater
- Department stores
- Health spas
- Beauty shops
- Magazines
- Photographers

Make a space a better place

Is one of your favorite Sunday activities visiting museums? Do you love checking out new exhibits? Do you wish you could be a part of the action? Well, you can be. An interesting career for you might be as an exhibit designer.

Never heard of the job? That's not surprising. Most people don't put a lot of thought into how museum exhibits are planned. The truth is they must be planned very carefully. Each object, photograph, and picture needs to be placed in just the right location so that the exhibit looks perfect and is visually attractive.

What are your responsibilities in this type of job?

- Determining how and where to place documentation describing specific items
- Creating floor plans, renderings, and scale models to illustrate how and where to exhibit objects
- Determining proper lighting for desired effects
- Determining proper lighting for maintaining safety precautions

- Choosing proper colors for walls, cases, and pedestals
- Supervising exhibit installation crews
- Working on exhibits with graphic designers
- Helping to create exhibit cases and cabinets
- Unpacking objects
- When the exhibit is done, supervising the dismantling and repacking of the exhibit

Does this sound like something you might want to do? The following skills and talents are helpful in a career in this field:

- An innate sense of design and balance
- Aesthetic judgment
- Communications skills
- Creativity
- Artistic ability

Exhibit designers may work for museums or on a freelance basis. Often you can also find jobs with temporary or traveling exhibits.

Floral designers

Do you love walking into a florist shop? Does the aroma of fresh flowers make you smile? Do you love choosing, touching, and arranging flowers? There's a great career waiting for you as a floral designer.

For this type of career you need to be creative, imaginative, and have a good sense of style, balance, and color. Your work will be guided by the types of flowers, colors, and arrangements that customers request.

As a floral designer you may find employment opportunities in a variety of settings, including:

- Flower shops
- Floral departments in retail outlets
- Craft shops
- Craft departments of retail outlets
- Hotels (sizzling hot)
- Catering halls
- Freelance
- Self-employment
- Wedding consultation service (sizzling hot)

Build up a portfolio of photographs of your creative floral designs to show to prospective clients or potential employers.

Window dressers and designers

Have you ever walked along a street or mall hallway looking at some of the window displays in boutiques, shops, and department stores and thought you could have come up with more creative designs? You can if you become a window dresser.

Retail stores want to attract the attention of as many prospective customers as possible. In order to do this they feature merchandise in their store windows and showcases. Window dressers are the individuals responsible for developing creative ways to display the merchandise.

As a window dresser or designer, part of your job includes designing sketches of what your concept of the window is, to be approved by a display manager. Depending on the type of store you are designing for, you may develop window displays using mannequins, clothing, accessories, tools, furniture, books, food items, or appliances.

The coolest specialty in this area are the window dressers who are employed to design the creative

Bright Idea
If you're interested in learning more about a career in floral design, contact the Society of American Florists toll-free at (800) 336-4743.

Watch Out!
Careers in floral design in floral and craft stores may be fulfilling, but do not usually pay high salaries. If you're interested in being a floral designer and want to make big bucks, try specializing in weddings.

Bright Idea
In any career in art, you should maintain a portfolio of your most creative work. Having pictures to demonstrate your creativity and talents makes it easier to get your next job.

windows people talk about. In New York City as well as other cities across the country, many stores are known for their elaborate holiday window displays, including Saks Fifth Avenue, Bergdorf Goodman, Macy's, and Bloomingdales.

Window dressers and designers often use a variety of moving or mechanical mannequins and other objects. They may also construct displays out of materials including wood, fabric, glass, paper, and plastics.

Interior designers

Do you really want to make a space a better place? Do you love color, design, and decorating? Perhaps a career as an interior designer is waiting for you. As an interior designer you plan and develop the interiors of a variety of settings, including:

- Private homes
- Public buildings
- Offices
- Hospitals
- Restaurants
- Hotels
- Theaters
- Other commercial establishments

Bright Idea
Window dressing and designing may be easier to break into if you first go through an internship with an interior design firm or department store.

Your job entails developing designs for complete buildings, entire houses, or even a single room. After meeting with clients to get their input, you might develop designs showing furnishings, floor coverings, accessories, lighting, window treatments, main colors, and coordinating colors. You usually provide clients with drawings or sketches as well as swatches of fabrics and colors for their approval.

This can be a very hot career if you are creative, have a good eye for design and detail, and work well with others. Not only do you have to keep your clients happy, you may be expected to hire and supervise contractors or craft workers and negotiate for prices on products and services.

Architects

Do you like designing, but would rather design for the big picture? Instead of designing the inside of a building, would you like to design the outside? A hot career for you might be as an architect. Architects design buildings and other structures. As an architect you are responsible for not only the appearance of a structure, but its functionality and safety.

Depending on what type of architect you are, you might design a variety of buildings. These include:

- Homes
- Office buildings
- Apartment buildings
- Schools
- Churches
- Hospitals
- Public buildings
- Senior housing
- Theme parks

Previously, architects needed to be able to draw their designs. Today, however, computers and CAD (computer-assisted design) programs assist architects in their work by making it easier to put their energy into the designing part of the project.

Bright Idea
If you're interested in learning more about a career as an interior designer, check out the Web site of the American Society of Interior Designers at www.asid.org.

Bright Idea
Check out the American Institute of Architects Web site at www. aiaonline.com to learn more about careers in architecture.

As an architect you need not only a creative mind but great communications and interpersonal skills. These are important to be able to translate client's ideas into reality.

Just the facts

- You can have a fulfilling career using your talent and creativity.

- One of the biggest obstacles in writing a book is just getting started.

- There are a variety of career options for writers and artists.

- You don't have to give up your creativity to have a hot career.

Let's Communicate... Tell It Like It Is

D o you want to work in advertising? How about public relations or marketing? Would you rather work in the media? Have you thought about working at a newspaper, magazine, radio, or TV station?

Communication careers are sizzling hot now, no matter what area you choose. Is this the career area you've been dreaming about? If so, your options are limitless. There is a plethora of possibilities available for the new century and beyond.

The advertising, public relations, marketing, and communications industries are multibillion-dollar businesses. Their services are used by almost every type of company, industry, government entity, political group, and nonprofit organization.

This chapter will cover a variety of hot careers in the communications field. If you want to work in this area, there's a place for you. All you have to do is look.

Chapter 11

Bright Idea
Join trade associations and attend their meetings and conferences. This gives you good opportunities to network in this field.

Advertising: Careers in selling

Do you love the challenge of persuading others? Do you enjoy finding ways to make things sound enticing? If so, consider working in advertising.

Our purchasing choices in products and services, as well as everything else, are often consciously or unconsciously affected by advertising. A career in advertising gives you selling power.

Do you think you might want to be a part of this powerful industry? If so, you can work in almost any location in the country and a variety of settings. These might include:

- Advertising agencies
- Radio stations
- Television stations
- Newspapers
- Magazines and periodicals
- Corporations
- Industry
- Nonprofits
- Entertainment
- Restaurants
- Retail establishments
- Hotels

Unofficially...
The advertising industry affects each and every one of us. There isn't a day that goes by in which we don't see a commercial on television, hear one on the radio, glance at an ad in the newspaper or a magazine, or pass a billboard on the highway selling something.

What can you do in advertising? There are many hot career choices in this field depending on your skills, talents, and desires. Let's look at a few of them.

The hottest glamour careers in advertising, for many, are in agencies. While the competition is keen for these jobs, they are attainable if you are creative, talented, and pleasantly aggressive. What are the hot careers in advertising agencies? Probably the number one career most aspire to in this field is that of account executive. Other hot choices include art director, copywriter, and media planner.

Account executives

Do you want to be the one in charge? The one who comes up with the hot ideas? As an advertising account executive, you can help create the next great campaign. This is career that entails a tremendous amount of creativity as well as administrative skills. It is your job to plan and execute the client's entire advertising campaign. You are ultimately responsible for overseeing clients' accounts.

Of course there are an assortment of other responsibilities that come with the job. These might include:

- Brainstorming with your client and other members of your creative team

- Acting as a liaison between the client and agency departments

- Meeting with creative departments to bring the concepts of the advertising campaign to fruition

- Meeting with the client on a constant basis to make sure the client is satisfied and to maintain the client-agency relationship

Think about some of the products or services you currently use. What made you buy them? Usually, an ad or advertising campaign put the thought or need into your mind. Sometimes it's a catchy phrase that makes an advertising campaign successful. Maybe it's a logo that makes you automatically think of the product. It may be one ad or a series of advertisements that build on each other.

The important thing is that it is remembered by the consumer in a positive fashion.

Copywriters

Sometimes it isn't an account executive who comes up with the great idea. More often than not, the wording for the great ad you see or hear is the creation of a copywriter.

Have you ever seen a product in the store or on television and an idea for a slogan pops into your head? Something that you're sure is better than the slogan being used? Perhaps you should consider copywriting as a career choice.

Copywriters may be responsible for:

- Writing copy for print ads
- Writing copy for billboards
- Developing the scripts for television commercials
- Developing the scripts for radio commercials
- Writing the copy for brochures
- Writing the copy for sales promotion pieces
- Writing the copy for direct mail pieces
- Writing the copy for sales letters

Copywriters need to be able to write headlines as well as body copy. One of the great things about being a copywriter is you don't necessarily have to write a book to sell the product. Sometimes all you need are a few well-chosen words.

Do you have what it takes to be copywriter? You might if you have some of the following characteristics:

- You're creative.
- Your words can grab the attention of people reading or hearing them.

- Your words can set a product or service apart from similar ones.

- Your words are persuasive.

- Your words are appealing.

- Your words make people want to buy the product or service.

- Your words inspire people to take action.

As a copywriter, you might work in various settings including agencies, nonprofits, corporate advertising, or public relations departments, or even on a freelance basis.

Media planners

Do you like spending other people's money? Can you do so wisely? Do you have a broad knowledge of all areas of media? If so, you might want to look into a hot career as a media planner.

The media planner in an agency decides on the most effective media in which to place ads and commercials. This person determines which shows, magazines, newspapers, or other advertising venues will attract the type of person to whom the product or service is marketed. For example, if you were trying to attract buyers for baby products, you probably wouldn't want to put the majority of your advertising budget into commercials on MTV. Conversely, if you were trying to attract a teenage audience, MTV ads might be a good buy.

This is an important job in an advertising agency. Clients depend on your knowledge of the media to advertise their products. Your success in choosing the correct media can ensure their success in reaching the most effective audiences.

The media planner works with others in the agency as well as the client to decide what the media

Unofficially...
Who can forget Kellogg's animated character Tony the Tiger saying "Grrrreat," the Oscar Mayer bologna song spelling the name "Oscar Mayer," or the saying "Diamonds are a girl's best friend"? All are good examples of how a few choice words can stick in our mind.

Bright Idea
As mentioned in the previous chapter, no matter what type of creative career you want to get into, it's always a good idea to put together a portfolio of your best work.

objectives are. He or she then places, buys, or issues purchase requests for the advertising.

Media buyers

Advertising costs can be astronomical, depending on the specific media used. If you like to negotiate and are skilled at it, consider becoming a media buyer.

As a media buyer, you negotiate the media space and time for clients with radio or television stations, newspapers, magazines, and other media venues. Rates for advertising space can fluctuate greatly, depending on the market. The media buyer must be able to successfully negotiate for not only price, but placement.

Media researchers

Do you like to ask questions? Are you looking for an interesting hot job in an agency? Consider a career as a researcher. In this position, you research market trends and conditions to determine the needs and interests of consumers.

Graphic artists and designers

Many popular products in the marketplace have logos that are recognized worldwide. These are seen on company packaging, stationery, publications, brochures, and in advertising. These logos are created by graphic artists and designers.

Would you like a career where your work could be seen by millions? If you're creative, talented, and have artistic ability, you might want a hot career in graphics. Graphic artists and designers use their creativity and artistic talent instead of words to communicate.

In this type of career, you create graphics and other artwork that helps put the "sizzle" in packaging, publications, ads, and brochures. Of course, every graphic artist does not create a logo seen by millions, but your work can make a positive impact on a product, advertisement, or company just the same.

There are many types of employment settings for graphic artists and designers. You might work for an ad agency, corporate clients, newspapers, magazines, book publishers, manufacturers, food companies, or be self-employed.

Account research managers

Do you like to ask questions? Consider a career as an account research manager. In this position you research market trends and conditions to determine the needs and interests of consumers. You find out what would make consumers purchase something, and determine how much they are willing to pay for that product or service. You use interviews, surveys, questionnaires, and other research methods. The data you collect is then used to develop more effective advertisements, or in some instances, even new products.

In this hot job, you're also responsible for comparing and analyzing the competition's advertisements. How do you do this? You might:

- Conduct focus groups.
- Watch competitors' ads.
- Collect data.
- Study how the commercials of both your client and the competition impact the market.

You're responsible for writing reports on the information and data you've collected. This information is then used to improve your clients' advertisement strategies.

Advertising sales

Does the thought of sitting behind a desk all day drive you crazy? Do you love to see people? Talk to people? Help people? Are you a born salesperson? Are you looking for a dynamic career? If the answer to these questions is yes, consider a hot career in advertising sales. In this type of job (depending on your specific employer) you might sell advertising space on television or radio, or in newspapers, magazines, periodicals, and trade journals.

Without advertising sales people, radio stations, television stations, newspapers, and magazines would make very little money. If you are good at what you do, you are a major asset to the station or publication.

Who could you work for?

- Small local television stations
- Local cable stations
- Midsized market television stations
- Major market television stations
- Small market radio stations
- Midsized market radio stations
- Major market radio stations
- Small weekly newspapers
- Biweekly newspapers
- Midsized daily newspapers
- Large major market newspapers
- Local magazines
- Special-interest magazines
- National magazines
- Trade journals

Sometimes you are given leads to sell advertising. Other times, advertisers seek you out to buy space from your company. The most successful advertising salespeople, however, are those who can locate potential new advertisers and sell to them.

To generate new advertisers as well as keep old accounts, individuals need to be comfortable networking, going to functions, meeting new people, and asking for business. If you have the right personality for selling, you can have a very satisfying career in this field. For this type of career, you can't take rejection personally.

Some other characteristics of a great media advertising salesperson include:

- Sales ability
- Self-motivation
- A pleasant aggressiveness
- Great communications skills
- Honesty
- Persuasiveness
- Organization
- A belief in the product you are selling

Web advertising

Are you a whiz on the Web? Do you like to sell? There are many new hot careers selling advertising on the Web. While this type of career is closely related to selling ads for print media, there are a number of differences. The major one is that this is a relatively new medium that many people either don't understand or are afraid of. To be successful in this career, you need the ability to illustrate the effectiveness of Web advertising, which many see as new and unproven.

You can track the success of a business from your first appointment throughout the duration of the ad campaign in radio sales.
—Helena Manzione, sales manager, WSUL Radio

Watch Out!
In order to be successful in advertising sales, it's essential to believe in the product you are selling. You have to feel that the organization you are working with is the best in order to get someone to spend their money to advertise with your company.

Public relations: Careers in telling

The power of public relations (PR) is far-reaching. Public relations can take a bad situation and help put a better spin on it, no matter what the difficulty. It can also take a good situation and make it look great.

PR is used in a variety of settings. You can be a part of this great industry whether you live in a small town or a large city. Whether you want to work in entertainment or with a nonprofit, in the hospitality industry or corporate business, in retail or restaurants—you can find a great job in public relations.

What kinds of jobs are hot in PR? Let's look at a few of them.

Press agents or entertainment publicists

Do you love the entertainment industry? Do you dream of working around celebrities and helping maintain their popularity? Or would you prefer to work around entertainment events, making them successful?

Some of the most sought-after jobs in public relations are in the entertainment industry. These might include:

- **Record company publicists.** These individuals publicize a record label's artists and events.

- **Theatrical press agents.** These people publicize Broadway shows and other theatrical events.

- **Unit publicists.** In this career, you publicize movies and/or television shows.

- **Pro sports team publicists.** Here, you publicize pro sports teams, their games, other events, and the various team members.

- **Press agents.** These people handle the publicity and press services for a variety of celebrities, including sports stars, movie stars, television stars, recording stars, and authors.

- **Television station publicists.** Here, you handle the publicity for the television station's programs and talent.

- **Radio station publicists.** These individuals publicize the station, programs, and disc jockeys and other talent.

Press agents or publicists in the entertainment industry help create "noise" for their clients. This means they develop and implement promotions, events, or situations so the media and the public notice their clients in a positive manner. As a publicist in the entertainment industry, you have to keep your client's name in the public eye. You need to develop various ways to get publicity, media attention, and exposure.

Some of your responsibilities may include:

- Developing press kits
- Writing press releases
- Cultivating media contacts
- Talking to the media on behalf of clients
- Conducting press conferences
- Screening media interviews
- Planting stories
- Planning press parties
- Obtaining television or radio interviews for clients
- Obtaining interviews or feature stories in newspapers for clients

Political and government PR and communications careers

If you enjoy politics, working with elected officials, public service, and public relations, you might want to check out some hot political and government communications careers.

You might consider jobs as legislative aides, district managers, or office managers for elected officials. What do you do in these jobs? Responsibilities vary, depending on your boss and the structure of the organization. Generally, however, it's your job to represent someone such as a congressman/woman, senator, assemblyman/woman, or other politician. Your responsibilities might include:

- Accepting or giving awards on behalf of your boss

- Giving speeches on behalf of your boss

- Representing your boss at political functions

- Representing your boss as community or civic events

- Handling constituents' problems and answering their questions

- Presenting official proclamations to individuals, businesses, or others

- Writing and answering letters on behalf of your boss

Do you want to work in government and public relations, but want to handle more public relations duties than a legislative aide, district manager, or office manager? Another very hot career in this field is a political press secretary. What does this person do?

Basically, press secretaries working in government or politics handle the press functions for a

Bright Idea
Look for a political internship to help you break into positions in politics and government.

public official. This might include issuing statements and press briefings, conducting press conferences, writing press releases, and handling the media. Who could you work for?

- The President of the United States
- Governors
- State senators
- Congressmen/women
- Assemblymen/women
- Mayors
- City council members
- County, City, or Town Legislators
- County, City, or Town Supervisors

Special events coordinator

Do you love putting together parties? Do you enjoy developing special events? Can you multi-task without getting flustered? Want a really great fun job in public relations? Consider a job as a special events coordinator.

Special events coordinators develop events for corporations, industries, businesses, trade associations, and nonprofit groups. Successful special event coordinators are creative, innovative people whose imagination has no limits.

Whether you create a company picnic, employee recognition dinner, fashion show, costume ball, golf tournament, entertainment extravaganza, or the party of the year, you must come up with innovative ideas that make people say "Wow! This is great. I've never seen anything like this before."

You're responsible for everything from determining the theme and developing a program to finding the perfect location and decorations,

66

Working for Rep. Maurice Hinchey as his congressional representative in Sullivan County, NY, has been a very interesting position. Networking and problem solving is what I like to do best. People energize me, and I'm happiest when I'm helping constituents.
—Julie Allen, Congressional Representative to Congressman Maurice Hinchey.

99

Bright Idea
Get into the loop by volunteering to work on political campaigns. It's a great way to network and meet people.

Bright Idea
If you're interested in a career as a special events coordinator, get some experience by volunteering to chair a special event for a local civic or nonprofit group.

Unofficially...
Join a trade association such as the Public Relations Society of America, Business/Professional Advertising Association, or International Communications Association. These groups often offer seminars that are good networking opportunities as well as educational events.

choosing the best food, hiring the entertainment, and anything else necessary to make the program a success.

What are some other great hot public relations jobs?

■ Corporate public relations counselor
■ Hotel public relations manager
■ Theme park public relations director
■ Shopping center public relations director
■ Freelance publicist

Marketing careers: Locating buyers

In Chapter 4, I discussed marketing your career. In that chapter, we learned that, basically, marketing is creating and finding markets and avenues to sell a product or service.

Marketing careers are all-encompassing. They are found in every industry. They are often connected to advertising, public relations, and promotional activities. What are some of the hotter options for the year 2000 and beyond?

Shopping center, resort hotel, or hospital marketing directors

Do you love to be around shopping malls? Do you spend weekends walking around shopping centers and window shopping? Consider a great job as a shopping center marketing director.

Shoppers today have a choice. They can visit any mall they want, shop from catalogs, or buy via televised shopping channels and infomercials—they can even buy products on the Internet. The shopping center marketing director develops programs and events designed to attract potential shoppers to the mall. These programs might include entertainment events such as free concerts, contests, community events, and sidewalk sales. This is an especially hot career if you can find a position in one of the large upscale shopping centers.

Does the health care industry interest you? Do you love marketing? You might look into a career as a hospital marketing director. In order to keep hospital beds filled, health care facilities, like all other businesses, must market themselves. The hospital marketing director develops programs and events designed to build new markets and enhance the image of the facility.

This individual may, for example, develop programs for senior citizens, teenage mothers, or cancer patients, based on the demographics of the geographic location in which the health care facility is based. The marketing director may coordinate events either on site or in outreach programs such as health fairs, screenings, wellness programs, or community events.

How would you like to work in a great resort hotel? Would you like a career telling others how they can have a great vacation? Consider a career as a resort hotel director or marketing.

There are many places for people to vacation. Their choices are often based on the visibility and reputation of a resort. The director of marketing at a resort hotel oversees the marketing efforts of the property, including advertising, direct mail, sales promotion, market research, public relations, and special events. This is an especially hot career choice in some of the large tourist destinations.

Radio station promotions directors
Do you love radio? Can you see yourself promoting a station to be the best in the area? Consider a hot

career as a radio station promotions director. The greater the number of listeners a radio station has, the more the station can charge for commercials. It is in the station's best interest then to attract as many listeners as possible.

The radio station promotions director develops and implements promotions designed to create excitement, interest, and visibility for the radio station. These activities may include a variety of contests, special events, and promotions. The hottest positions for these jobs are in major and midsized markets.

Newspaper promotions managers

Do you look at daily newspapers and know you could come up with great promotions to boost their circulation or get new advertisers? If so, think about a career as a newspaper promotions manager.

Newspapers, like all other media, are competitive. They need to create visibility and interest in their publication in order to enlarge circulation, create community goodwill, and attract advertisers.

The newspaper promotions manager holds an important job in the publication. He or she must develop promotions for the newspaper designed to attract new readers and create new advertising opportunities. These may include contests, special events, and other opportunities that may lead to advertising tie-ins such as special-edition supplements.

Television and radio: Eyes and ears of the world

There is virtually no one in this country who doesn't either watch television or listen to the radio. For many, these mediums provide the news of the day, entertainment, and companionship. Some people grow up dreaming of a career in this medium. Are you one of them?

As in other careers in communications, there are unlimited opportunities in this field. What are some of the hotter possibilities?

- Television talk show host
- Television news anchor
- Television news reporter
- Radio talk show host
- Radio news director
- Radio news reporter

Let's discuss these opportunities in more depth.

Television talk show hosts

Do you think you can be the next Oprah Winfrey, Rosie O'Donnell, or Maury Povich? Television talk show hosts have great careers. They make a lot of money, get to talk about topical subjects, meet influential people, talk to top celebrities, and help many of their viewers.

Think you can't break into the big time? It can happen, but you have to work at it and have a lot of perseverance.

Want to break in, but don't know how? Start small. Find a local independent or cable station and get hired to do something on the air. Even if you are only offered a once-a-week public affairs show, take it. Get experience, send out tapes, and move up the ladder.

Television news anchors

Do you watch television news and wish you were on camera instead of looking at the screen? The television news anchor has a very hot career. In this

Unofficially...
Lisa Ling, a young television journalist, started small, worked hard, and persevered. She was awarded one of the coveted co-host positions on ABC's popular daytime talk show *The View* after applying for the job when a nationwide search for a co-host was announced.

Bright Idea
Many areas throughout the country have small local stations, independent stations, or cable stations. If you're articulate, have good communications skills, and a good on-air appearance, you stand a good chance of getting a job.

position you have the opportunity to tell your viewing audience all the news of the day. It's glamorous, it's fun, and it's hot.

Think you can't possibly break into this job? Think again. Anything is possible. You probably won't be able to start out as the news anchor for a network or even a major market newscast, but you can break in on a smaller level and move up the ranks.

Television news reporters

When you see a news story on television, do you wish you were the one on the scene as the news unfolds? If you were a television news reporter, you could be. As a television reporter, you gather information and prepare stories to inform your viewers about events and happenings on the local, state, national, and international front.

Generally, you are assigned stories to cover by an assignment editor. Television new reporters, like all other journalists, may either work in general areas or specialize. Areas of specialty might include:

- Government/politics
- Business
- Entertainment
- Health
- Consumer affairs
- Science
- Religion
- Investigative stories

If you want to break into this field, try small market television and move up as you get experience and exposure.

Radio talk show hosts

Do you love talking? Can you draw others into your conversations? Are you well-versed on one or more subjects? A great career might be waiting for you as a radio talk show host.

Radio stations have various formats. Many stations throughout the country have added either talk shows to their programming or have turned to all-talk format. Talk shows can center around almost any subject matter.

As a radio talk show host, you may be a broadcasting personality or an expert in a specific field. You may have guests on your show, have a call-in format, or a combination of the two. However your show works, you are in charge of making sure it moves along in an interesting manner. Successful people in this field have the ability to banter back and forth with guests and callers.

You might host a general-interest talk show or a show on a variety of subject areas. These might include:

- Business
- Money
- Financial planning
- Cooking and food
- Sports
- Books
- Film
- Television
- Music
- General entertainment
- Current events

Bright Idea
If you're interested in working in television, check out the Web site www.tvjobs.com for job openings throughout the country.

Bright Idea
Try to come up with something you do on your radio show that is unique and memorable. Build your radio personality and work on building up your audience.

Bright Idea
You can dramatically increase your employment prospects as a radio talk show host if you're an expert or have credentials in a specific area that is of interest to the listening audience.

- Gardening
- Child care
- Parenting
- Relationships
- Marriage
- Legal issues
- Consumer affairs
- Community affairs
- The arts
- News
- Politics

Radio station news directors

Want to work in a radio station? Is news one of your passions? Are you a leader? Consider a job as a radio station news director.

Most radio stations host news departments with reporters who cover events and happenings as well as report the news. The radio station news director is in charge of the station newsroom. What do you do in this job? Your responsibilities vary, depending on the specific station and the size of the news department. Some of your duties might include:

- Developing news stories
- Determining what stories should be covered
- Assigning reporters to stories
- Developing news programming
- Covering stories yourself

Radio news reporters

Do you have a nose for news? Do you want to work in radio? You might want to think about a career in radio news. Radio stations report local, regional, national, and international news. Radio news reporters are responsible for developing and reporting news stories. They cover events, write copy, interview people, and do investigative journalism. Depending on the size and structure of a station, news reporters may report on all types of news or specialize in areas of interest such as government, politics, economics, or entertainment.

In this position, individuals must not only be able to seek out news, they must be able to write the reports in a clear, concise, and interesting fashion. They must also be able to deliver the news in an easy-to-understand manner.

You can break into a career as a radio news reporter in most small markets, get some experience, and move on to larger areas and stations. The hottest places to work are in major markets such as New York City, Los Angeles, Chicago, Atlanta, and other large cities.

Morning show hosts

Whether people are waking up, getting ready for their day, or driving to work, many people listen to the radio in the morning. While all radio jobs are fun for people who like to work in radio, one of the hottest jobs around in this medium is the morning show host.

There are a variety of methods that stations use to format morning shows. There may be one host, or two or more. The most successful morning shows, however, are formatted to be upbeat, fun, exciting, and humorous. Morning show hosts may also introduce music, give information, talk about the day's events, and broadcast news, weather, and traffic conditions.

Bright Idea
If you're interested in a career as a radio news director, check out the Radio-Television News Directors Foundation Web site at www.spj.org.

Unofficially...
Openings for radio jobs are often advertised in the trades (trade journals for the entertainment industry) including *Radio and Records, Broadcasting,* and *Billboard.*

Watch Out!
The downside of being a morning show radio host is having to be up at the crack of dawn. If your show runs from 6 a.m. to 10 a.m., you probably have to be at the station from 5 a.m. to 11 a.m., at least. If you're not a morning person, go for a different time slot.

You can break into this career by seeking jobs at small stations, getting experience, and moving up the ranks. Make tapes of your work and start sending them out. If you have a great on-air personality, you should have no trouble moving to larger markets.

All the news that's fit to print: Print media

Do you love telling people about the day's news and events? Are you good at writing? Can your words draw people into a story so they want to read more? If so, your hot career might be working in print media.

The media plays a critical role in today's society. Newspapers inform us about local, state, national, and international news and events. They offer facts, fiction, features, criticism, and commentary.

What are the hottest career options for the coming century and beyond in newspapers?

- Editor
- Section editor
- Editorial writer
- Reporter
- Columnist
- Wire service correspondent

Daily newspapers have many different sections. These might include the following:

- Business
- Entertainment
- City
- Government
- Food

- Travel

- Fashion

- Lifestyles

- Real estate

Within each section are opportunities to become editors, assistant editors, copy editors, reporters, columnists, and more. What are the top hot jobs?

Section editors

The section editor is basically in charge of his or her section of the paper. What are the responsibilities in this job?

- Overseeing the day-to-day decisions of the department

- Overseeing the work of the reporters

- Assigning stories to reporters

- Determining the general content of the section

- Deciding which stories are most important and should be given the most coverage

- Cutting articles that are too long

- Developing headlines

- Rewriting and editing articles

What's one of the hottest sections to edit? Whether you live in a small town or a large city, no matter what the demographics, the business section is sizzling hot. As a business editor, your section can have a tremendous impact on a community.

Why the business section? There are a variety of reasons. Basically, the economics of every area are based on its business and business culture. Communities revolve around economics. The local newspaper reports on business happenings and events on a local, regional, national, and international level. In order to keep informed, everyone who is anyone in a community usually reads the business section.

This makes you, as the business editor, both popular and powerful within a community. Everyone wants to talk to you, meet with you, and tell you their story.

Says Doug Puppel, business editor of the *Las Vegas Review Journal,* "I had a personal interest in business and economics and the opportunity to report on the nation's fastest-growing community was irresistible. Within the news organization, the business editor can move to higher levels of management or take those skills to a larger market. Also, the communications skills and contacts a business journalist acquires are valuable in many industries outside of newspapers."

Editorial writers

Do you always have an opinion and a view you want to share with others? Do you like to write? Consider a career as an editorial writer.

Editorial writers are responsible for the editorial page in a newspaper. The great thing about being an editorial writer is you have the opportunity to present your point of view on a subject or issue. You might write editorials on issues facing the local circulation area or issues of a national or international focus. Depending on the size and structure of your publication, the editorial writer may write about late-breaking news events or news that is not as timely, but just as important.

Newspaper reporters

Are two of your passions news and writing? Can you find interesting angles in which to look at stories? A hot job for you might be as a news reporter.

Newspaper reporters develop and write news stories and feature articles. As part of their job, individuals gather and check facts, interview relevant people, secure comments and quotes, and cover events.

What makes this such a hot job? As a reporter you have the opportunity to be on the breaking edge of news and tell others about it. Reporters' jobs are what they make of them. There is a great deal of opportunity for talented people who know how to put an interesting angle on their articles. In this job, you get to meet new people, find out about their stories, and write interesting pieces that grab the attention of your readers.

Columnists

Is it your dream to have your own newspaper column? Many people glance through the headlines and then head directly to their favorite columnist to see what he or she has to say that day.

Newspaper columnists write regular columns for the publication. Is this the career you've been dreaming about? In this job you might be responsible for daily, weekly, or monthly columns in a variety of areas. Depending on your background and expertise, you might write about general subjects or specialize in areas such as sports, entertainment, health, advice, business, careers, or politics.

Successful columnists are known for the way they present their columns. What would your style be if

Watch Out!
Reporters do not always get to choose what news items they'll cover. As a reporter, you usually can't choose your own assignments.

Unofficially...
The hottest columnists have syndicated columns that are bought by and published in newspapers throughout the country.

this was your dream job? Some columnists may write analytical or serious pieces. Others, such as Ann Landers or her twin sister Abigail "Dear Abby" Van Buren, may give advice with punchy jabs and flowery phrases. There are others, such as Andy Rooney, who are known for their humorous columns.

Wire service reporters

Want a really hot job in reporting the news? Think about a career as a wire service reporter. Newspapers cannot afford to pay reporters to go to every area of the world to cover every story. To make sure they get the news they want, most papers subscribe to wire services. Wire services employ reporters to gather news from their area of coverage. These correspondents write stories about news happenings and then transmit the stories electronically. These are then sent out via electronic "wire" machines to publications subscribing to the wire service.

Wire service correspondents may report on various subjects or news from geographic areas. These might include:

Unofficially...
Wire service correspondents or reporters can find employment in many of the major cities throughout the world. The best-known wire services are Reuters, United Press International (UPI), and the Associated Press (AP).

- General news
- A specific locality or beat
- Entertainment news
- Health news
- Politics
- Business
- Sports

Magazines and periodicals

Magazines and other periodicals cover a vast array of subjects and interests. Today, there is virtually no subject that doesn't have its own publication. These might include:

- Consumer magazines
- Technical magazines
- Trade journals
- Regional magazines
- Corporate or company-sponsored magazines
- Sunday newspaper magazine supplements
- Fashion magazines
- Women's magazines
- Computer magazines

What are some of the hot jobs in magazine publishing?

Magazines need to fill their publications every month. Magazine staff writers are responsible for writing the stories, feature articles, and columns for these periodicals. Individuals may be assigned specific articles or develop ideas and bring them to the editorial board for approval.

To be successful at this type of job, you need the ability to develop lively, accurate, informative, understandable articles that peak the reader's interest.

Most magazines and periodicals have regular columns in their publications. If you have an area of expertise and can develop and write interesting columns, this might be a great job for you.

Many readers look for regular columns in their favorite magazines on subjects that interest them. Some magazine columnists work in other parts of the publication's editorial department as well as write columns. Others, who may be experts in a particular subject, write regular columns while holding down a job or having a career in their own area of expertise.

Just the facts

- There are a multitude of hot careers to choose from in the field of communications.

- Careers in communications can have a big impact on others.

- Almost every business can benefit from public relations.

- You can break into coveted television and radio careers by starting in smaller markets.

- Career opportunities in newspapers and magazines are available throughout the country.

Hot Careers Serving Others

PART V

GET THE SCOOP ON...

Hot hospitality careers ▪ Working on the
Love Boat ▪ Cashing in on casino careers ▪
Food service ▪ Traveling careers

Welcome to New Vistas: Hospitality and Travel Careers

Chapter 12

The hospitality and travel industries are booming and are expected to grow throughout the new century. People today often need to travel more for business and want to travel more for pleasure.

More people are using the products and services of the hospitality and travel industry than ever before. This has created a wealth of hot career opportunities. One of them may be just right for you.

Wherever you fit in these industries, your career can take you to new vistas. This chapter will discuss some of the hottest possibilities.

Your house is my house: Careers in hotels, motels, and B & B's

The lodging industry ranges from owner-operated bed and breakfast inns, spas, independent resorts, hotels, and motels to major hotel and motel chains.

Do you think you'd like to work in this industry? If so, a wide array of opportunities await you.

What can you do? Look at some of the possibilities:

- **Hotel or resort managers.** These individuals oversee the operations of a hotel or resort.

- **Convention sales managers.** These individuals book conventions into the hotel, negotiate prices, and oversee sales representatives.

- **Convention services managers.** These individuals coordinate the various departments whose services will be used when a convention is in the hotel.

- **Concierges.** These people handle the special needs of hotel guests.

- **Reservations managers.** In this job, you oversee the reservations department of a hotel as well as supervise, train, and schedule clerks and representatives to work in the reservations department.

- **Front desk managers.** These individuals oversee the front desk area, train, and schedule front desk clerks.

- **Public relations managers.** These people handle the public relations and media relations needs of the hotel. In some situations they also handle advertising responsibilities.

- **Activities directors.** In this job, you're in charge of developing and implementing activities for guests in resort hotels.

- **Special event coordinators.** These individuals help coordinate the special event needs of the hotel.

■ **Spa managers.** These individuals oversee the operations of the hotel spa and its employees.

Let's look at a few of these careers in more depth.

Hotel/resort managers

Would you like to be part of a hotel's ultimate success? Do you have management, administrative, and supervisory skills? Can you handle difficult situations with ease? Do you want to work in the hospitality industry? If so, consider a hot career as a hotel manager. In this position your efforts and actions can mean the difference between success and failure of a property.

What does the hotel manager do? Basically, he or she is responsible for overseeing all the operations of a hotel. The manager is responsible for making sure that the hotel runs smoothly and efficiently, and that it is profitable.

What else might you do in this position? Depending on the specific hotel, you might have more specialized duties. In large properties, you may oversee a staff of assistant managers and other administrative personnel. In smaller properties, your responsibilities would be more general. Whatever the size of the property, as the hotel manager, the buck stops with you. If there is a problem, you are expected to handle it.

Where can you work? There are a variety of settings. These might include:

■ Luxury hotels

■ Inns

■ Health spas

■ Hotel chains or franchises

Unofficially...
Successful hotel and resort managers stress customer service and teamwork as a priority for all hotel employees no matter what their position.

Bright Idea
To learn more about careers in hotels, contact the Council on Hotel, Restaurant and Institutional Education Web site at www.chrie.org, or the Educational Institute of the American Hotel and Motel Association at www.ahma.com.

- Privately owned hotels or motels
- Resorts
- Suite hotels

Front desk managers

Can you keep people happy even when there's a problem? Do you have supervisory skills? A good job for you might be a front desk manager.

The front desk in a hotel is the area where guests check in and out of the property. It is often the location where people have their first and last impression of a property. It's essential to the success of hotels that clerks working at the front desk be courteous, customer service oriented and efficient. The front desk manager supervises and trains the front desk clerks.

The front desk manager is also in charge of handling problems with reservations as well as complaints from guests about their rooms. What makes this job hot? A number of things:

- Jobs are available throughout the country.
- You can become a front desk manager quickly after obtaining experience at the front desk.
- You can use this job to move up the career ladder in hotel management.
- The way you handle a guest's problem regarding their reservation or room can make their trip much more pleasant. Most guests are really happy when you upgrade their room or offer them some other type of amenity.

Convention sales managers

Are you a born salesperson? Can you motivate others to sell too? Is negotiation one of your skills and your passions? Do you want to work in the hospitality industry? Consider a career as a convention sales manager in a hotel or resort.

There are countless conventions, conferences, and groups that meet in hotels. These properties make a great deal of their money from group and convention sales, where they sell blocks of rooms as well as food and beverage service at discounted prices. The job of the convention sales manager is soliciting and selling his or her specific site to these groups.

This can be a really hot job for the right person. There are always opportunities for talented, aggressive people who can produce in this field.

Resort hotel activities directors

Are you the one in your circle of friends who always thinks of something to do? Do you like to plan and coordinate activities? If so, consider a job as a resort hotel activities director.

Resort hotels offer a variety of amenities to entice guests and make sure their stays are pleasant. These may include great accommodations, good food, entertainment, health clubs, spas, and shops. Many resorts also offer guests a variety of activities to keep them occupied while at the resort. As the activities director, it's your job to develop, implement, and schedule a variety of activities for guests. What types of activities? That depends on the type of resort and its clientele. You might schedule speakers, workshops, or seminars on various subjects such as finance, relationships, floral arrangement, parenting, local points of interest, and anything else you can imagine.

You also might arrange other activities, including the following:

Bright Idea
Many large hotel chains offer training programs. Contact the major chains at their corporate offices to find out the availability of and requirements for these programs.

- Exercise classes
- Dance classes
- Golf tournaments
- Shopping expeditions
- Tours of the local area
- Tours of local attractions
- Tours of the hotel property
- Demonstrations by hotel chefs
- Fashion shows

Concierges

Are you good at handling details? Do you like to do a little bit extra for people? Are you good at customer service? Do you want to work in a luxury hotel? If so, think about a job as a concierge. Large hotels, luxury hotels, resorts, and casino hotels all offer opportunities in this area.

What will you do as a concierge?

- Provide special assistance to guests.
- Help guests obtain tickets to shows and sold-out events.
- Recommend restaurants.
- Make restaurant reservations for guests.
- Find courier services.
- Find secretarial services.
- Handle needs of VIP guests and celebrities.
- Provide other services to accommodate hotel guests with special needs.

Want to work in the hospitality industry, but have your own business? Read on for a really hot career.

Bed and breakfast inn owners

Do you enjoy having company? Do you love making homemade goodies for others? If so, consider a career as a bed and breakfast inn owner.

Bed and breakfasts (B & Bs) are springing up around the country. Do you have a quaint, romantic, and charming home in the country? A brownstone in the city? A home or large apartment located near a tourist destination? Bed and breakfast inns may be part of your home or a separate building.

What do you do as a B & B inn owner? The most important thing a B & B owner can do is make guests feel at home while providing a comfortable room for travelers or vacationers. Although rooms just need to be clean, the best bed and breakfasts are cheerful, interesting, romantic, or decorated in a unique or special manner.

The most successful bed and breakfasts prepare homemade goodies for breakfast, such as hot muffins, biscuits, breads, jams and jellies, pancakes, and waffles. Some B & B owners also prepare tea or hors d'oeuvres in the late afternoon for guests or offer dinners at an additional charge.

One of the reasons that many bed and breakfast inn owners believe this is such a hot career is because they get to meet and socialize with new, interesting people.

Hit the jackpot with a career in casinos

The gaming industry is growing by leaps and bounds. Years ago, Las Vegas was the gaming capital of the country. Today, casinos are located all over the map. There are large luxury casinos, small casinos, docked and floating riverboat casinos, and Indian gaming facilities in almost every state in the

Watch Out!
Zoning and health department regulations vary by location. Check with your local zoning board and health department to see what restrictions apply in your area.

Unofficially...
If guests will stay in your home with you, it is perfectly acceptable to use some sort of screening process. There are a number of organizations throughout the country that screen people for bed and breakfasts.

Bright Idea
Check out jobs in
the hospitality
industry at www.
hospitalityonline.
com.

union. Many of these casinos also host large luxury hotels and entertainment complexes.

Within each casino and casino hotel there are a multitude of job opportunities. The new theme casinos and casino hotels are often like miniature cities. Many of the larger ones employ thousands of people.

Think you might want to work in gaming? If so, you'll be joining a great many others who have entered this fast-moving industry. There are many jobs in casinos and casino hotels that are both on and off the gaming floor.

Let's say you want to work on the gaming floor as a dealer. Here are some of the hottest choices:

- Baccarat dealer
- Blackjack dealer
- Caribbean stud poker dealer
- Craps dealer
- Pai gow dealer
- Pai gow poker dealer
- Poker dealer
- Roulette dealer

Dealers generally need to be trained at a gaming institute, academy, or college. Many of the casinos outside of Las Vegas and Atlantic City have their own training programs. Get some experience and you can be promoted to supervisory positions on the gaming floor, such as pit manager, floorperson, or shift manager. Don't want to be a dealer, but want to work closely with the public? Consider a job as a host. This person greets guests, issues comps, and deals with customer care and guest relations.

Bright Idea
Many casinos
throughout the
country have Web
sites listing many
of their current
employment
openings.

There are also hundreds of other diverse opportunities off the gaming floor. You can find almost every type of career and job possibility at a casino or casino hotel, including those in accounting, information services, marketing, advertising, public relations, security, surveillance, and every conceivable position in the food, beverage, and hotel areas.

One of the greatest things about working in the gaming industry is that you can start out with an entry-level position and work your way up rather quickly to a top job and a hot career.

Consider attending a gaming conference to network, get information, and learn more about the industry. There are a variety of annual gaming conferences, conventions, and seminars throughout the country. These include the World Gaming Congress, IGBE Casino Management Conference, Casino Opps, National Gaming Conference, Indian Gaming Conference, and Southern Gaming Conference.

The Love Boat: Cruising careers

Do you remember the television show *The Love Boat?* It brought the lives and careers of a captain, purser, cruise director, bartender, and doctor on a cruise ship to the viewing audience for years. The success of the television show not only resulted in more people taking cruises, it also made more people aware of the potential of careers on cruise ships.

Today, cruise ship careers are still regarded as glamorous and hot by many. Are you one of them? Is it your dream to work on a real-life Love Boat? Would you love to sail the high seas on a luxury liner while getting paid to work? If so, there is a cornucopia of career opportunities just waiting for you.

> **"**
>
> I started out working for TWA in 1986 as a reservations agent. At the time the best aspect of my job was I could travel for a very nominal fee. Then I got into corporate travel which I also liked because of the incentive travel given out by the airlines as well as perks from hotels. I get to talk to a lot of interesting people every day. Itineraries can be quite challenging and I enjoy helping people meet that challenge.
> —Michele Roberts, Accounts Representative, Travel Planners, New York
>
>

Moneysaver
Save time and money by checking cruise line Web sites to find job openings and information on where to send letters of application.

What makes cruising jobs hot? You get to travel, cruise, meet a lot of great new people, and get paid for doing it.

What can you do? There is an abundance of jobs in all areas. Each managerial or administrative job on a ship has assistants and other support personnel under it. Some of the hotter on-board positions include:

- **Ship's captain.** This is the top hot career to hold on a cruise ship. The captain is one of the most recognizable employees on a cruise and the one with the most responsibility. The captain is in command of the ship. What he or she says, goes.

- **Hotel manager.** The hotel manager on a cruise is expected to do just what a hotel manager on land does—manage the hotel. The hotel in this case is not land-based, but floating.

- **Chief purser.** The purser on a cruise ship has a great many responsibilities. He or she makes sure the ship is cleared through foreign ports as well as supervises the accounting of revenue from casino shops, handles personnel functions for the crew, and a variety of other duties.

- **Food and beverage manager.** This individual oversees the food and beverage service of the ship's dining rooms, bars, lounges, cafes, and other food service. As food is so important on luxury cruises, this is an extremely important and hot position.

- **Chef de cuisine or executive chef.** There is no question that one of the things many people remember from a cruise is the delicious and abundant food. It's almost always time to eat on a cruise. The chef de cuisine is responsible for the food and the creative presentation.

- **Pastry chef.** The pastry chef creates the pastries and desserts everyone "oohs" and "ahhs" about throughout the cruise.

- **Bartender.** This may be just a job to some, not a career. However, many people really enjoy the interaction with passengers and wouldn't give up the setting for anything.

- **Physician.** Most cruise ships have a doctor on board to handle passenger medical emergencies as well as the health care of the crew. If you don't want a land-based practice, this might be a very hot opportunity for you.

- **Cruise director.** This individual is in charge of developing, coordinating, and scheduling activities and other entertainment. A good cruise director and his or her staff can make the difference between guests having an good cruise and a forgettable one. This can be a fun, hot job for people who enjoy the setting and the responsibilities.

- **Entertainers.** Depending on the size of the ship and its entertainment, there are many opportunities for entertainers. Cruises host a variety of entertainment ranging from lounge bands, piano bars, orchestras, Las Vegas–style revues, comedians, magicians, singers, dancers, bands, show groups, and anything else that will entertain the guests.

- **Hostess.** The hostess on a cruise works as a sort of assistant to the cruise director and the captain. There are a variety of duties in this job, including handling the invitations and seating arrangements for dinner at the captain's table; conducting activities, games, tours, and lectures

Watch Out!
Glamorous as cruising careers might seem, be sure you can handle the motion of the ocean on a continuous basis before signing on.

for passengers; helping to ensure that all passengers have a good time on the cruise, and handling customer service problems.

No matter the position you aspire to on a cruise line, what can set you apart from others seeking the job?

- Your ability to work as a team member
- Your ability to offer exemplary customer service
- Great communications skills

Depending on your skills and experience, there are a variety of other cruise ship career opportunities you might want to check out. These include:

- Radio operators
- Engineers
- Passenger stewards
- Cooks
- Sous chefs
- Food servers
- Secretaries and other clerical workers
- Security staff
- Retail shop personnel
- Casino staff

Unofficially...
If you think you will be living the "Love Boat" life as a cruise ship employee, you may be in for a rude awakening. As an employee, you generally do not get the most luxurious cabins available.

Ships cruise to various locations. Some cruise rivers in the United States, while others travel to exotic locations throughout the world, such as:

- The Caribbean
- Great Lakes
- Hawaiian Islands
- The Bahamas
- Mexican Riviera

- Panama Canal
- Bermuda
- Mississippi River
- Europe
- South Pacific
- Alaska
- Islands in the Aegean Sea
- Galapagos Islands
- South America
- Ohio River
- Tennessee River
- Red Sea
- Africa
- Australia
- Transatlantic
- Canada

Watch Out!
Working on cruise ships means you are not home much of the time. You might want to rethink this as a career choice if you have children or other responsibilities that require your regular attention.

Where can you look for work? Some of major cruise lines include:

- Carnival Cruise Lines
- Chandris Celebrity Cruise Line
- Costa Cruises
- Cunard Cruise Line
- Delta Queen Steamship Company
- Disney Cruise Line
- Holland America Cruise Line
- Norwegian Cruise Line
- Princess Cruises
- Royal Caribbean Cruise Line

Unofficially...
In food service, as in many other industries, you'll probably start with an entry-level job. Get some training and experience. It will help you move up the ladder.

Food service careers: Hungry for help

With today's busy schedules, eating out is often considered a necessity, not a luxury. You'll find more people eating out today than ever before, whether they grab lunch at the office, pick up a burger and fries for the kids, or dine at a fine restaurant.

The food service industry has expanded, resulting in many hot career opportunities. Where are they located? The industry is all-encompassing. It includes:

- Restaurants
- Coffee shops
- Diners
- Fast-food operations
- Bars
- Lounges
- Specialty-food establishments
- Catering companies
- Food service division of hotels and motels
- Corporate services
- Institutional food services

What can you do in food service? It depends on where you want to work. Are you interested in cooking? Do you enjoy social interaction with the public? Would you rather be involved in management?

Let's look at some possibilities:

- Restaurant manager
- Executive chef
- Cooks
- Sous chefs
- Wine steward

- Pastry chef
- Restaurant host/hostess
- Maître d'
- Food and beverage manager
- Caterer
- Hotel catering manager
- Personal chef
- Bread baker
- Cake decorator
- Nightclub manager
- Bartender
- Food server
- Training manager

Bright Idea
If you're interested in a career in food service or restaurants, check out the Educational Foundation of the National Restaurant Association Web site at www.edfound.org.

Let's look at a few of the possibilities in more depth.

Restaurant managers

Do you want to work in food service? Are you good at motivating employees? Are you a leader? If so, consider a career as a restaurant manager. One of the great things about this career is you can enter the field in an entry-level position and climb the ladder to success rather quickly.

In this type of job, you are in charge of overseeing the operation of the restaurant, including hiring and training restaurant employees, setting up employee schedules, setting the service standards, handling customer service problems, and dealing with complaints.

Executive chefs

Are you an experienced chef? Are you creative with your culinary skills? Do you have supervisory skills?

You might consider a hot career as a restaurant's executive chef. The executive chef develops the restaurant's menu, creates recipes, and supervises the sous and pastry chefs.

The executive chef is often what makes a restaurant well-known and successful. The menu the executive chef develops and the recipes he or she creates are what bring people back to a restaurant time after time.

Caterers

Do you love to plan parties? Are you a great cook? Do you enjoy shopping for, cooking, and preparing food? Can you deal with a lot of details without stressing? A hot career for you might be in catering.

Caterers work in conjunction with clients who want to have parties or other special events. As a caterer, you meet with clients to discuss the budget, number of guests, types of food, servers needed, special requests, and other issues. Then your work begins.

You plan menus, shop, prepare food, and find ways to display it in attractive and unique ways. You may also be responsible for renting any decorations, dishes, and tables, as well as scheduling staff to work the party. The most successful caterers are those who prepare great food and have creative presentations.

Personal chefs

Do you like to cook? Does it make your day when others tell you how much they enjoyed a meal you prepared? Think about becoming a personal chef.

In this position you might work for one or more clients. There are also hot new careers for personal chefs for busy couples or business people who

Bright Idea
As a caterer, develop one or two dishes or desserts that are memorable and that no one can resist.

Timesaver
A good way to get your catering business known more quickly is to hold an open house showcasing your specialties. Invite affluent people in the community, business and community leaders, and board members of charitable organizations.

prepare a week's worth of meals that are frozen and then reheated.

Pastry chefs

Are desserts your passion? Can you create mouth-watering creations to die for? Do you wish you could spend your time preparing desserts? As a pastry chef, you could. Depending on your work setting, you may be expected to make an array of both domestic desserts and those with an international flavor, including everything from pastries, pies, cakes, and strudels to tortes, tarts, cookies, petit fours, and confections.

Wine stewards

Are you a wine connoisseur? Do you think you could develop the perfect wine cellar? If so, there might be a hot career waiting for you as a wine steward in a fine restaurant.

Good restaurants must make sure a complete range of wines are available for patrons. As the wine steward, you are responsible for selecting and ordering wines as well as storing them correctly. You might also be expected to teach the wait staff how to handle and service the wine in a correct manner.

Food servers

Whether you call them food servers, waiters, or waitresses, the job is the same. To many, this is a hot job. Why? There are a number of reasons:

- There are always jobs available.

- You can work in a variety of settings, from a fine restaurant to a coffee shop.

- You have an opportunity to make great tips if you provide good service.

- You have the opportunity to move up to a management position.

Bright Idea
Look for a pastry chef whose work you admire. Ask if he or she would consider you working as an apprentice or assistant to get experience.

Bright Idea
Contact the American Culinary Federation or the International Association of Culinary Professionals to get more information on any jobs in the culinary field by logging on to www.iacp-online.org.

- If you enjoy dealing with people, this can be a fun job.

- You can use this as a temporary job to earn money while going to school or waiting for another position to open up.

Careers in travel: Get here if you can

Whether you go by car, bus, plane, train, or boat, travel today is easier and faster than ever before. You can get to almost any destination in the country in a few hours by getting on an airplane. New cars, highways, and freeways have been built to make ground transportation safer and more comfortable than ever before. Discounts and specials make cruises, planes, and trains more affordable.

The travel industry is a vital link in all parts of our economy. Careers in this field, as in other areas of the hospitality industry, are all-encompassing. Is one of them for you? There are many opportunities depending on your skills, desires, and dreams. These might include:

- Travel agent

- Pilot

- Flight attendant

- Airline customer service clerk

- Tour guide

- Airline sales representative

- Cruise ship director

- Cruise ship activities director

- Tour director

- Travel editor

Let's take a closer look at some of these careers.

Pilots

Do you wish you had wings and could fly? When you get on a plane, do you wish you were the one in the driver's seat? As a pilot you can be.

Commercial pilots have an important job in the travel industry. They get us where we're going in a relatively quick manner. Need to go from Los Angeles to New York? Hop on an airplane and you can be there in a few short hours. Want to go to London from Chicago? Board the plane and you can be there in the time it takes to watch a movie and have a meal. There's no doubt about it, pilots fly the planes that connect the world, and make the world feel smaller.

In addition to flying the plane, pilots have a number of other duties. These might include:

- Planning their flight before takeoff

- Talking to flight dispatchers

- Talking to weather forecasters to learn about weather conditions

- Filing instrument flight plans with air traffic controllers

- Checking aircraft to ensure everything is working properly

- Checking instrument control panels

- Keeping in contact with air traffic control

- Monitoring warning devices

To become a pilot for a commercial airline, you must obtain a commercial pilot's license issued by the FAA (Federal Aviation Agency) and pass an FAA written exam.

How do you break in? Once you have your commercial FAA pilot's license, send your resume and a

Unofficially...
While the pilots most people are familiar with work for commercial airlines, there are other pilot jobs. You might fly private planes, helicopters, or other aircraft.

Bright Idea
To obtain more information about becoming a pilot, contact the Airline Pilots Association, 3375 Koapaka St. No. F238-10, Honolulu, HI 96819-1800, or the Flight Engineers' International Association (AFL-CIO) at 1926 S. Pacific Coast Hwy., No. 202, Redondo Beach, CA 90277-6145.

short cover letter to the Human Resources department of all the major commercial airlines.

Flight attendants

Do you love to travel? Are you good with people? Would you like to be the one responsible for making airline passengers feel comfortable and safe? Think you might like to be a flight attendant? If so, you join others who think this is a hot job.

To many, this is a glamorous job. You have the opportunity to travel extensively and meet a lot of new people. Depending on the airline you work for, your home base, and the routes you're assigned, you might travel to great tourist destinations, major cities, or even other countries. Once there, you usually have a layover to do what you want until your next scheduled flight. When you're away from your home base, the airline pays for your hotel accommodations and meals. What's more, you have the bonus of free or discounted travel on your off time.

There is a lot of responsibility in this job, including the following:

- Assisting passengers during flights.
- Preparing passenger cabins.
- Instructing passengers in the use of emergency equipment.
- Administering first aid.
- Calming passengers.
- Assisting passengers during an emergency.
- Serving refreshments.

Airline sales representatives

Are you interested in working for an airline, but want to stay on the ground? A good career for you might be as an airline sales representative. In this

Unofficially...
While flight attendants must be high school graduates, many airlines prefer individuals who have a college background or degree.

Timesaver
Many airlines advertise for flight attendants in newspapers in areas hosting airports. Major airlines' Web sites also offer employment opportunities. Contact the Human Resources manager of commercial airlines directly to see what their hiring procedures are.

job, you're responsible for helping potential passengers book their flights over the telephone. After determining the dates and destinations of passengers, you offer them various options regarding rates, availability, and times of travel. If they're interested, you book reservations, take credit card payments, or make other arrangements for their ticketing.

What makes this a hot job? The number one benefit for many is that you usually get to travel either for free or at a reduced cost.

Travel agents

Many people aren't aware that using a travel agent to book their travel doesn't cost anything extra. As a matter of fact, travel agents often know of specials and discounts that the average consumer does not have access to.

Do you like helping people with their travel plans? If so, a hot career for you might be as a travel agent. Your main functions are to book travel arrangements, write tickets, and put together tours. Within the scope of your job you need to determine your customer's destination, departure and return dates, and the mode of transportation they wish to use. You then use a computer to access information about available flights, prices, schedules, car rentals, hotel or motel accommodations, cruises, and so on.

There are a number of different employment settings in which to work in this career. These include:

- Major travel agencies
- Smaller travel agencies
- Corporate travel departments
- Corporate travel agencies

Bright Idea
Contact the Association of Flight Attendants by logging on to www. flightattendant-afa.org and the Transport Workers Union of America at 80 West End Ave., New York, NY 10023 for additional information on careers as a flight attendant.

66

I worked in outside sales for many years and decided to go to work for American Airlines because my immediate family and I can travel for reduced rates and enjoy ourselves. The job is fun too.
—Donna Dossey-Aust, Advantage Sales Reservations, American Airlines, Dallas–Fort Worth

99

- Travel agencies dealing mainly with tours and packages
- Airline vacation travel departments

One of the reasons many people think this is a hot career is because of the perks that travel agents enjoy. These include being invited and going on "fam" or familiarization trips to great locations and destinations. These fam trips help travel agents learn about various destinations in depth. They are usually sponsored by hotels, airlines, cruise lines, and regional organizations.

A sizzling hot specialty in this area is corporate travel agents. These individuals specialize in business travel arrangements for corporate clients.

Tour guides

Do you think you'd like a job where you vacation with others? Do you think it would be fun to go to exciting places? A hot job you might not have considered in the travel industry is a tour guide.

To be successful as a tour guide, you need to be very organized, be able to deal with a million things at once, and not get flustered when things go wrong.

As a tour guide, you:

- Go on vacation with people or meet them at their destination and guide them around an area. You might take them to museums, attractions, regional points of interest, and so on.

- Show clients points of interest in regions outside of the normal tourist areas.

- Make sure clients get on the right planes, trains, buses, and cabs.

- Make sure luggage gets to its right destination.

- Handle any problems on the tour, such as lost medications, locating physicians, and emergencies.

What makes this a hot job? You get to travel at someone else's cost and get paid for it, and you get to meet people.

Where can you find a job?

- Travel agencies

- Sight-seeing companies

- Cruise lines

- Bus lines

- Attractions

- Convention and visitors bureaus

- Self-employment

Just the facts

- There are many hot careers in the hospitality and travel industries.

- Casinos offer career opportunities both on and off the gaming floor.

- Career opportunities in food service are available throughout the country.

- Careers in the travel industry offer perks like free or reduced-cost travel.

Bright Idea
For more information about a career as a tour guide, contact the Travel Industry Association of America or the International Tour Management Institute.

GET THE SCOOP ON...
Retail careers ▪ Savvy sales careers ▪
Serving others ▪ Careers in meeting manage-
ment ▪ Money careers

Chapter 13

Hot Careers in Sales and Service

T he sales and service industries are tremendous and growing larger every day. These
industries encompass a vast array of areas
and use workers of every type. Career opportunities
are available for those with a variety of skills, talents,
experience, and educational levels.

It's important to realize that the sales and service
industries are frequently intertwined.

The millennium brings a demand for more sales
and service workers than ever before. In this chapter I'll discuss a variety of hot career choices.
Perhaps one of them is right for you.

Retailing careers: Trading on trade

Shopping is a national pastime. Those who don't
buy, browse. Retail is big. Years ago people went
shopping when they needed something. Today, people visit the mall to browse, get a bite to eat, or just
walk around, as well as to shop. A trip to the mall is
now a leisure-time activity.

Unofficially...
So far, recessions have had less of an impact on service workers than those working in manufacturing. A service job may be more secure in the long run.

Do you think you might be interested in a career in retail? There are literally thousands of opportunities available throughout the country.

If you're talented and hardworking, the retail industry offers you the opportunity to rise through the ranks quickly—even if you don't have a lot of formal training. If you're eager to climb the career ladder, this may be a hot job for you. It's not uncommon in this industry to begin a career as a sales associate and move up to an assistant or store manager.

Where are there types of employment settings in retail?

- Malls
- Shopping centers
- Boutiques
- Department stores
- Discount stores
- Specialty stores
- Grocery stores
- Privately owned shops
- Chain stores
- Convenience stores

The current explosion of purchasing power in the retail market has created a wealth of careers. The retail industry is loaded with people who have a wide array of skills and talents. Many more are needed.

What can you do in retail? Let's look at some of the possibilities. One of them might be right for you:

Bright Idea
Some larger stores may offer their employees formal training programs for upper-level jobs.

- **Store managers.** These individuals oversee a store and manage the day-to-day activities. This is a hot career in retail.
- **Assistant store managers.** These individuals help the store manager and are expected to take over when the manager is not available.

- **Sales associates.** The greatest number of opportunities in retail exist as sales associates. These individuals are responsible for assisting customers. They may welcome customers, help them find merchandise, or act as cashiers.

- **Buyers.** The success or failure of a store depends to a great extent on its merchandise. Buyers select the merchandise that is sold in a store or a specific department. Everything you see in a store is chosen by a buyer or someone acting in that capacity. In some cases, sales reps visit a buyer; in others, the buyer travels to trade shows, showrooms, and similar locations to see merchandise.

  Requirements vary from job to job. A college degree in retailing or business may be preferred.

- **District managers.** These individuals are responsible for stores in a specific area. For example, the district manager may be responsible for all the stores in New York state.

- **Department managers.** The department manager is responsible for a specific department in a store. For example, the department manager in Sears may be responsible for the electronics department.

- **Personal shoppers.** Many people don't have the time or the inclination to shop. Personal shoppers make shopping a more pleasant experience for these customers. For those with busy lifestyles, anything a store can do to make shopping more efficient is valuable.

  Personal shoppers basically make shopping easier. If customers don't have the time to shop for birthday gifts or business gifts, the personal

Bright Idea
Contact the National Association of Realtors (NAR) to learn more about careers in real estate. They can be reached at: 430 N. Michigan Ave., Chicago, IL 60611, Phone: (800) 874-6500, Fax: (312) 329-5962, Web site: www.realtor.com.

Bright Idea
If you enjoy shopping, being a personal shopper (shopping for others) might be a hot career for you.

shopper shops for them. For example, the shopper may be given a list of people a customer must buy gifts for with a price range. The individual is then expected to pick out the perfect gift.

Depending on the store, a customer can call in advance with a request; for example, for a black suit in a size 10–12. The personal shopper goes out on the sales floor, finds the suit and accessories, and has them ready for the customer to try on.

Other responsibilities of the personal shopper include having gifts wrapped and delivered and sending reminder notes to customers for birthdays, anniversaries, or holidays. This is a really hot job if you love a store environment and shopping.

■ **Advertising directors.** How do you know what products a store is featuring or what's on weekly specials? Potential customers often look at ads in the local paper, or hear commercials on the radio or see them on television. The ad director is responsible for creating and placing advertisements for a store. In some cases, the advertising director may work with an advertising agency (see Chapter 11 for more about careers in advertising).

■ **Marketing directors.** The marketing director is responsible for finding new customers and new ways to market to existing customers. The marketing director develops and creates promotions, special events, and contests, all designed to bring shoppers into a store.

■ **Customer service managers.** There is a great deal of competition in retail. If customers are not satisfied, they can shop someplace else. The customer service manager is responsible for the customer service department of a store. These individuals handle customer complaints, returns, or problems with products or services. They also help create goodwill with customers. In many cases, the manager overrides a store policy to make a customer happy. The customer service manager is expected to supervise the customer service clerks or representatives.

> Giving the customer 100% of the service they pay for, plus a smile, is what retail is all about.
> —Ed Jackson, Manager, El Portal Luggage, Las Vegas, NV

- **Window decorators.** Interesting, unique, or exciting store window displays attract attention. Displays that use merchandise sold in a store are a good way to showcase new products. The window decorator is responsible for creating the displays seen in store windows. The windows of some major stores, such as Tiffany's, are famous.

- **Merchandisers.** Merchandisers do for a store what window decorators do for a store window. (In some situations, the merchandiser is also the window decorator.) Merchandisers develop interesting ways to display store merchandise. They may install freestanding displays or showcases or create and develop wall displays of merchandise.

- **Alteration experts or tailors.** Because everyone does not fit into one size, better stores have either an alteration expert or tailor on-site to alter the clothing purchased there.

- **Security managers.** One of the big problems in retail is loss prevention. The security manager develops methods to help stop shoplifting, both by customers and employees. The security manager also supervises security guards.

Bright Idea
There is a large turnover in retail sales. If you see a store in which you're interested in working, go in and ask for an application.

One of the great things about working in retail is you have the opportunity to find employment in a store selling merchandise in which you're interested. What do you enjoy being around? Check out some hot possibilities.

- Clothing
- Records, CDs, cassettes
- Videos
- Books
- Sports and exercise equipment
- Jewelry
- Linens
- Fabric
- Crafts
- Computers, software, and office supplies
- Electronics
- Groceries and other food products
- Appliances
- Health and beauty aids
- Shoes
- Furniture
- Cards and gifts
- Hardware and building supplies
- Pets and pet supplies

To find out if you're cut out for a career in retail, answer these questions:

- Do you enjoy shopping?
- Do you like browsing?
- Do you enjoy wandering through stores just to see what's new?

Unofficially...
Retail salespeople who are knowledgeable about specialty products such as computers and software are always in demand.

- Do you enjoy seeing the way items are arranged and displayed?

- Do you enjoy helping people make decisions?

- Are you a people person?

- Are you enthusiastic?

- Do you love to see new products?

- Do you have a lot of energy?

If you answered "yes" to most of these questions, you might enjoy a career in retail. If you want to work in retail, there almost always is a job available. You can get an entry-level job, gain experience, and move up the ladder to more exciting and higher-paying positions.

Sales: Selling everything careers

Are you a born salesperson? Could you sell the Brooklyn Bridge? If so, consider a hot career in sales. Sales careers encompass much more than working in a retail environment. They can also involve selling a variety of products or services in different settings.

There is always a need for talented salespeople. The great thing about working in sales is you can virtually sell anything in any industry. That includes products as well as services. You can sell on the retail or wholesale level, handle direct sales, or do telemarketing. What are some hot possibilities?

- Automobiles

- Radio advertising

- Television advertising

- Print advertising

- Real estate

- Pharmaceuticals

- Computers

Bright Idea
Include on your resume any special training, talents, or interests when seeking a job in retail. It's a bonus for stores selling specific items to have people who are informed about those items. For example, if you enjoy crafts, you would be a valuable employee for a craft store or department.

Watch Out!
You usually have to spend a great deal of time on your feet in retail. If you have a bad back or cannot stand for a long time, this might not be a good career choice.

- Office supplies

- Paper products and cleaning supplies

- Food and groceries

- Manufacturers' products in any industry

- Talent

- Hospitals and health care services

- Books and other literary works

- Trade show and conference exhibit space

- Investments and securities

Let's look at a few options in greater depth.

Automobile salespersons

People either love being an auto salesperson or hate it. For some, it's a hot career to sell a big-ticket item like a car to people who want or need one. Today, leasing is also a popular option for many people, making it easier than ever to obtain a car.

Bright Idea
If you're interested in a career in auto sales, the more people you know, the more successful you can be. Join associations, civic groups, and nonprofit organizations, and network, network, network. Give your card to everyone.

There is a great deal of competition among dealerships as well as among makes and models of cars. In order to be successful in this career, you have to be a great salesperson with just the right amount of aggressiveness without seeming obnoxious. If people feel comfortable with you and feel you are giving them a good deal, you have them hooked. In some dealerships one of the perks of this job may be the use of a demo car.

Radio, television, or print advertising salespersons

I touched on careers in this field in Chapter 11. Basically what you should know is that if you can sell, there are always jobs available wherever you are in the country. Every area has newspapers, magazines, radio stations, and cable or television stations. This type of career gives you great mobility.

Real estate agents or real estate brokers

Do you love looking at homes? Can you see their potential? Do you want to sell a really big-ticket item? Consider a hot career as a real estate agent or broker. In this type of career, you represent a real estate broker (if you aren't one yourself) in selling, buying, renting, or leasing properties. These properties may include:

- Residential homes
- Apartments
- Land
- Businesses
- Commercial properties
- Office space

What are some of your responsibilities?

- Finding potential buyers and sellers
- Showing properties to potential buyers
- Negotiating between the buyer and seller
- Working with the buyer, seller, and their attorneys until the sale is completed

Most real estate agents are seller's agents who represent the seller in the transaction. In this type of transaction, when a deal is completed, the seller pays the commission. However, a trend for the new century is the buyer's agent, who represents the buyer. When you find a house or other type of property for a client and the transaction goes through, the *buyer*, not the seller, pays the commission.

Insurance agents

Are you interested in the insurance industry? Do you like sales? Consider a career selling insurance. Insurance sales agents may sell a variety of types of insurance. These include:

Watch Out!
You generally need a valid driver's license for this type of job so that you can drive potential clients around looking at homes. Some jobs require that you use your own car.

- Life insurance

- Health insurance

- Disability insurance

- Property/casualty insurance

- Auto insurance

- Homeowner's insurance

- Business insurance

What do you do in this type of job? In addition to selling insurance policies you might do the following:

- Explain options to clients.

- Help clients choose the correct types of policies for them.

- Obtain information from clients.

- Quote rates on policies.

- Handle background paperwork.

- Make sure forms are filled out and signed correctly.

- Assist clients in settling claims.

Timesaver
Learn more about careers in the insurance industry by contacting the National Association of Professional Insurance Agents at (703) 836-9340 or visit their Web site at www.pianet.com.

Manufacturer's representatives

Looking for a career in sales that has great employment prospects for the new century? Consider becoming a manufacturer's representative. Manufacturers of every type require representatives to sell their products to retail stores, wholesale outlets, organizations, institutions, and government agencies.

What do you do in this type of job?

- Make sales calls and appointments by telephone.

- Look for new clients.

- Write letters and send product literature to customers.

- Visit established or potential customers on sales calls.

Who can you work for as a manufacturer's rep? Industries in all fields need highly motivated people. These include:

- Clothing
- Food (retail and wholesale)
- Automobile parts
- Office equipment and supplies
- Pharmaceuticals
- Electronics
- Household supplies

No matter what type of product you are selling, you'll find the following tips useful in developing a sales pitch and strategy:

- Learn everything you can about the product you are selling.
- Learn everything you can about competitors' products.

Booking agents

Is it your dream to work in entertainment? Do you have sales skills? Do you like talking on the phone— a lot? A great career opportunity for you might be as a booking or talent agent.

In this career, your general job is to secure work for entertainers and performing artists. To do this you must sell the services of the talent you represent. Where do you sell these services?

- Venue managers
- Talent buyers
- Promoters

What else do you do? A lot of your job is done on the phone, calling people to secure engagements, looking for possible venues, and negotiating contracts. You might work for a booking or talent

Bright Idea
There are various credentialing options available for insurance agents, depending on the type of insurance you are selling. If credentials are available, take the courses and complete any requirements.

Bright Idea
Contact the Manufacturer's Agents National Association at (949) 659-4040 or visit their Web site at www. manaonline.org to learn more about careers in this field.

Bright Idea
Look for and take classes, seminars, and workshops in selling and sales techniques. The ability to sell is useful in any career.

agency. While the big ones are in Los Angeles and New York, there are agencies located throughout the country.

You might represent a variety of talent, including the following:

- Musicians
- Recording artists and singers
- Dance groups
- Models
- Actors and actresses

What kind of personality traits and skills help make you a good salesperson in any industry?

- Sales skills
- Communications skills
- Confidence
- Personability
- Perseverance
- Enthusiasm
- Organization skills
- Ability to multi-task
- Reliability
- Motivation
- Aggressiveness

Can I be of service? Careers in service

"Service" encompasses a variety of careers in a wide variety of industries. A cornucopia of exciting careers exists in the service industry. Maybe one is right for you.

Let's look at a few possibilities:

- Law enforcement officer
- Lawyer

- Paralegal
- Accountant
- Bookkeeper
- Hairstylist
- Manicurist/nail technician
- Nanny
- Secretary
- Administrative assistant
- Bounty hunter
- Repossessor
- Private investigator

Bright Idea
Take classes in public speaking. The ability to speak comfortably and effectively in public can help you give better presentations in front of groups as well as give you the confidence to speak in any situation.

People working in the service industry perform a variety of services for others. I've already discussed a number of service-oriented careers such as law enforcement officers, attorneys, and paralegals in Chapter 7. Let's look at a few other service-oriented careers in more depth.

Accountants

Do you enjoy seeing things add up? Are numbers your thing? If so, you might consider a hot career as an accountant. What do you do in this career?

- Maintain financial records.
- Conduct audits.
- Prepare financial reports.
- Prepare tax returns.
- Advise clients on tax matters.

You might work in a variety of areas, including public accounting, management accounting, internal auditing, or government accounting.

Where can you work?

- Public accounting firms
- Federal, state, or local government

- Corporations in any industry
- Hotels
- Self-employment

What kind of education do you need to become an accountant? A bachelor's degree in accounting is the minimum. A master's may be helpful.

To make yourself the most marketable in the accounting industry, become a CPA or certified public accountant. CPAs are state-licensed. You must usually take and pass a four-part exam prepared by the American Institute of Certified Public Accountants in order to obtain CPA designation.

Hairstylists

Do you want to make people feel better about themselves? Do you think you might want to be a hairstylist? In this career your major function is styling people's hair. To be successful you need to have great communications skills. In this way you can find out exactly what your customers want. Knowing what someone wants so you can do it can mean the difference between having a satisfied customer and one who will never return.

You might have your own salon or work in a commercial styling salon or beauty shop. But did you know there are other options? Consider the following:

Bright Idea
A new trend in salons is renting out styling chairs. The salon offers the equipment needed to do your job and you bring your clientele.

- Spas
- Department stores
- Luxury hotels
- Casino hotels
- Cruise ships
- Hospitals
- Nursing homes and extended-care facilities

- Television stations
- Movie studios
- Theatrical productions

Bounty hunters, repossessors, collectors

Here are some interesting career possibilities in the service industry that you might not have thought about.

When people are arrested, they usually need to put up bail to get out of jail. If they don't have the money, they may find a bond agent to post the bail for them. If the person who has been arrested doesn't show up for a court date or skips town, the bond agent doesn't get his or her money back and is stuck paying the entire bond.

In instances like this, bond agents often retain bounty hunters or bail enforcement agents. In some cases, the bond agent is also a bounty hunter. As a bounty hunter, it's your responsibility to track down fugitives and bring them back for the trial. In order to do this, though, you have to find them. This may entail using various methods of investigation, interviews, and surveillance to locate fugitives. Depending on the specific job, a fair amount of travel is often required. For those that thrive on excitement, this can be a very hot job.

If bounty hunting is a little too exciting for you, consider a career handling collections or repossession. What you do in this field depends on the specific company for which you work. Some of your duties may include:

- Collecting money
- Repossessing automobiles or merchandise
- Locating people who have skipped bail
- Investigation

Moneysaver
With today's busy lifestyles, many men and women find it difficult to find time to go to the salon to get their hair styled. You might want to fill this need by going to their home or place of business to style their hair. Although it may be more difficult to find clientele, the start-up costs will be very low.

With careers in these areas, it's important to remember that this is not the old-time Wild West! There are laws that must be followed, and rules and regulations to which you must adhere.

If you're interested in a career in these fields, it's helpful to take classes or seminars in criminal investigation. You should also learn as much as you can about surveillance and legislation regarding criminal apprehension.

Let's get together: Trade shows, meetings, and conferences

Trade shows, meetings, and conferences are big business in both the sales and service areas. Many associations and businesses hold these shows regularly. Whether they sell information or products, trade shows, exhibitions, conferences, and conventions offer a cavalcade of career opportunities. Let's look at some of the hotter possibilities:

- **Trade show directors.** These individuals coordinate the trade shows. In this high-profile job you might search out a location; negotiate rates for accommodations, food, and services; or determine the content of the show.

- **Conference managers.** These individuals handle the conferences within a trade show. Depending on the job, the conference manager may also be the trade show director. Says Brian Vargas, Vice President of US Trade Shows at Gem Communications, "I've been selling trade shows for 20 years. The trade show industry encompasses both sales and service. You not only have to sell the show to exhibitors, you have to keep them happy so they'll return next year. As Vice President of US Trade Shows of the world's largest gaming industry event, the World Gaming Congress, I have the ultimate responsibility not only of assuring the show has the best seminars, speakers, and exhibits, but coordinating everything as well. I love what I do because every year brings something new."

■ **Speaker coordinators.** Many conferences have programs, seminars, luncheons, or dinners that require speakers. The speaker coordinator is responsible (among other things) for locating speakers, negotiating rates, coordinating their requirements, and developing programs.

■ **Sales representatives.** Sales representatives are the individuals responsible for selling space to exhibitors at trade shows. In addition to sales, there is a great deal of customer service necessary in this position in order to be successful. It's essential to keep exhibitors happy so that they will return to the next event.

Help 'em grow rich: Careers in banking and investment

Money—it makes the world go 'round. And if you can help people grow rich or at least learn how to make ends meet, you can have a really hot career. Everyone wants to have enough money to take care of themselves and their family. Most people want to be rich. Today, more than ever, people are trying to find ways to save and invest their money so whatever they have can work for them and grow.

Would you like to work in an industry where you can help people do this? There are a wealth of opportunities working in the banking and investment areas. Maybe one is right for you. The banking and investment industries use both sales and service.

> **❝**
> I specialize in handling reposession. I like this type of work because I can track a person who thinks he or she outsmarted someone else. I can help my clients recover their losses. I've tracked down everything from cars to boats to airplanes and heavy equipment. This is a great career. You get to meet a lot of intereting people from the richest to the poorest. I like the thrill of the chase.
> —Donald C. Morse, Jr., Recovery Agent, Accu Search, Trenton, NJ
> **❞**

What are your options? If you want to work in banking, some of the hotter possibilities include:

- **Bank tellers.** These are the people who assist customers in depositing or withdrawing their money.

- **Customer service representatives.** In this position, among other things, you open accounts and sell loans or investments.

- **Operations managers.** In this job you might make sure the branch in which you work is in compliance with federal regulations and bank policies, as well as handling the day-to-day operations of the bank. In some settings, this job may be referred to as a back office manager.

- **Personal bankers.** Personal bankers are the individuals you usually see in private offices or sitting prominently at desks in the bank. In this position, you are responsible for an array of duties depending on the structure of the specific bank, including serving customers, opening new accounts, referring people to the bank's investment center, and handling miscellaneous problems and customer service.

Think you might want to work in the investment and securities end of the money industry? There are a slew of sizzling hot careers there too.

What are some other possibilities?

- **Portfolio managers.** These individuals make decisions on buying or selling stocks in a company's portfolio.

- **Financial analysts.** These individuals study companies and their performance. Based on this information, they then recommend the buying and selling of stocks.

■ **Securities brokers or stockbrokers.** These individuals advise clients, and buy and sell securities, stocks, annuities, mutual funds, and other investments for their customers. Says Lloyd Barriger of Barriger and Barriger, Inc., a securities brokerage firm, "The financial industry is so huge and diverse that it will offer virtually unlimited opportunities for innovative people to carve out lucrative careers."

■ **Investment banking managers.** These individuals advise corporate clients on acquisitions, lending and borrowing, corporate issues, and creating securities.

Administrative careers are abundant in this field, as are clerical positions. Opportunities include everything from back-office jobs to operations, processing, and customer credit checks.

Just the facts

■ There are thousands of career opportunities available in retail.

■ If you are a talented salesperson, you can always find a good job.

■ The sales and service industries are often intertwined.

■ Trade shows, meetings, and conferences are big in both the sales and service areas.

■ The banking and investment industries encompass both sales and service.

> 66
> Being a meeting planner is like being a juggler trying to keep a lot of balls up in the air at the same time achieving balance, poise, and professionalism. I love it—especially when all the rehearsals (planning) result in a successful performance (meeting) pleasing the audience (attendees)!
> —Ellen B. Ackerman, Conference Manager, Gem Communications
> 99

Computers, Information, and Technology

GET THE SCOOP ON...
Cool computer careers ▪ Working with the Web ▪
Computer training ▪ Making money with
sizzling sites

PART VI

Hot Careers in the Information Age

C an you remember when only those business-es on the cutting edge had computers? Do you remember when most people didn't own one?

The price of computers has dropped dramatic-ally, making them available to almost everyone. They speed work at all levels, from the boardroom to the stockroom. They even help students work more effi-ciently.

Today, computers are used for both work and play. The World Wide Web has opened up new vistas for youngsters and seniors and everyone in between. Just by accessing the Internet, you can expand your boundaries. Many are now buying via the Internet as well as selling.

It is essential, no matter what type of career you're interested in today, to be comfortable using a computer. Careers using computers are all-encompassing. They are found in almost every industry and require different skills, education,

Bright Idea
If you like to move around and enjoy new challenges, the computer field is perfect for you. Many computer careers allow you to work on a contract basis. For example, a company might contract you to develop a program or create a Web site. When you've done that, you can seek another project with another company.

and talents. This chapter will cover some hot possibilities using the computer keyboard. Maybe one is right for you.

New computing careers

Do you love working on a computer? Is your computer an extension of you? Would you like to compute a new hot career? Well, you can. Careers using computers cover a wide range of options. Let's look at some of them:

- Technical documentation specialist
- Computer service technician
- Data processing director
- Programming manager
- Computer system operations manager
- Word processor operator
- Systems analyst
- Computer programmer
- Computer salesperson

Now let's look at a few of these in more depth.

Technical documentation specialists

If you've ever read through some of the instructions that came with your computer and thought you could do a better job writing them, you might consider a job as a technical documentation specialist.

Can you take hard-to-understand information and explain it so people can understand it? Do you like to write? If so, this might be a career for you. In this job, you write the manuals, operating instructions, and documents for computer hardware and software. If you're good at your job, you are able take information that is difficult to understand and put it into everyday language that everyone can understand.

There are always jobs for skilled, talented technical documentation specialists who can make software and hardware easy to use. Where can you find employment? You might work on a per-project basis or be a self-employed contractor. You might also be an employee of a hardware manufacturer, software developer, software manufacturer, or computer book publisher.

Word processor operators

Can you believe that you used to have to erase mistakes when you typed? Things have changed dramatically. Do you like to type? You might consider a job as a word processor operator. In this job, your main function is to process text. You might type letters, forms, documents, or anything else that appears in print. After you type the information, you check it for correct style, spelling, punctuation, and grammar.

What makes this a hot job? If you have word processing skills and are a quick, accurate typist who knows how to use a computer, you can usually find employment anywhere in the country.

What types of industries use word processors? Pretty much any industry where a lot of typing is required. You might work with:

- Law offices
- Book publishers
- Government agencies
- Health care facilities
- Insurance agencies
- Real estate companies
- Colleges and universities
- Manufacturers

Timesaver
As I've said about any creative career, put together a portfolio of your work to show to employers illustrating your writing methods. Remember to bring it with you when meeting with potential employers. If you prepare it before you start looking for a job, you'll thank yourself later.

Bright Idea
The more software programs you're familiar with, the more marketable you are. Take classes, seminars, or workshops in a variety of software applications.

An added benefit of this type of job is that you can often find work with temp agencies. This means that even if you are laid off from one job, are searching for employment in another industry, or are looking for part-time employment, you have a way to earn money.

Computer systems operations managers

Many companies have large computer systems. The computer systems operation manager is in charge of the daily operations of that computer system, as well as scheduling and overseeing a staff and vendor communications. This is an important job. Today, when companies are so dependent on computers, or the entire business of a corporation is linked to their computer system, it's essential for everything to be in top working order. If the system is down or not working properly, it's difficult to take care of anything in an efficient manner.

Systems analysts

Do you know more about computers than almost anyone you know? Does everyone always ask your advice about computers, systems, and software? Are you good at analyzing problems? A hot career for you might be as a systems analyst.

What do you do in this type of job?

Moneysaver
You can often get software training for free or for a nominal charge from temp agencies eager to have trained workers available.

- Meet with managers or owners of businesses to find out what types of requirements they have regarding their computers, peripherals, and software.

- Design computer systems to meet clients' requirements.

- Meet with programmers to develop programs for a system.

- Prepare cost analyses of various computer systems.

- Debug systems.

- Create computer solutions.

This job is more important than ever before. More businesses than ever are computerized. Many of these businesses have multi-user systems. The large number of home businesses that use computers also adds to the need for systems analysts.

In this type of job, you might be self-employed or hired on a contractual basis by a variety of companies. A great number of jobs are available with hardware and software manufacturers. Other employment settings might include:

- Other manufacturers

- Government agencies

- High-tech companies

- Banks

- Sales-based companies

Computer programmers

Did you ever wonder how computers know what to do? It appears that they have their own language, and in fact, that's true. Do you want to be the one who tells the computer what it should do? You can if you're a computer programmer. In this job, you write the instructions for the computer to follow in computer language. The instructions are known as the computer programs or software. There are a variety of special computer languages programmers use, depending on the type of program they are writing.

In this type of job, you might be a systems programmer or an applications programmer. Systems

Bright Idea
Learn more about careers in this field by contacting the Association for Systems Management. You can check out their Web site at www.infoanalytic.com.

Bright Idea
For more information on careers in this field, contact the International Association for Computer Information Systems at (405) 744-8632 or visit their Web site at www.iacis.org.

programmers are responsible for taking care of software that controls the computer system. Applications programmers are responsible for developing programs to handle specific tasks.

As a programmer you might develop software for almost any type of application. You could develop a program to handle the services of television shopping or a youngster's computer game. But writing programs is just the beginning of your job. Before you're done, you must test them to make sure they have no bugs and work properly.

Software is needed in almost every industry. This means you can seek employment in industries in which you have an interest. Computer programmers may work full-time or handle specific projects for companies on a consulting basis.

Computer salespersons

Is selling one of your talents? Do you love to be around all the newest computer equipment and show it to others? A career as a computer salesperson might be right up your alley.

There are a number of employment settings you might consider as a computer salesperson. The first setting that comes to mind is working in a computer store. You might also work in the computer department of a department store or office machine or supply store.

Unofficially...
If you live in an area hosting a catalog sales center, consider selling computers over the phone.

Selling computers by phone takes a lot of patience. Many people who call up don't know what they want and don't have a computer sitting right in front of them to see. Some computer salespeople selling over the phone get a great deal of satisfaction helping people choose and buy systems.

Wherever computer salespeople work, the most successful are well-versed in their products. They know how everything works, what the advantages and disadvantages of each product are, and can honestly answer questions in an informative and easy-to-understand manner.

Computer service technicians

Do you want to save the day? Become a computer service technician. People who have computers that have "crashed," don't start, don't work, or are generally on the blink will regard you as a hero if you can fix their machine. Want to be loved? People who don't back up their work who have crashed systems might even ask you to marry them if you can only bring back their data!

What are your main functions as a computer service tech?

- Diagnosing problems

- Testing equipment

- Repairing computers and peripherals

- Performing preventative maintenance of computers and peripherals

- Installing memory

- Installing equipment and peripherals in people's homes or businesses

Where can you look for work?

- Computer stores or stores with computer departments

- Computer or peripheral manufacturers

- Corporations that want an on-site technician

- Computer maintenance companies

- Self-employment

Moneysaver
Many employers provide formal training in computers for their employees. This is an opportunity to enhance your earning potential while getting paid.

Home businesses and computers

Home businesses are also benefiting from the computer revolution. There are literally hundreds of ways you can make money with a home computer. These include:

- Data processing services
- Desktop publishing
- Word processing
- Information brokering
- Graphic services
- Newsletter publishing
- Publicity services
- Accounting services
- Bookkeeping services
- Online catalog business
- Computer trainer
- Web page design
- Software trainer

There are also an array of home businesses that use the computer, but are not based on a computer. For example, you might use your computer to keep records for a beauty shop, boutique, or gardening and landscaping business that you operate out of your home.

Other computer careers

Computers are now used in almost every industry. If you want to be more productive, efficient, and creative, just look around you—there are opportunities everywhere:

- Want to work in *fashion*? Many fashion designers now use computer technology. With the click of a mouse, they can change the neckline of a dress or the color or pattern of a fabric. Pattern drafting, too, can now be accomplished with a computer and the proper software program.

- Want to work in the *music industry?* Considering doing some work as a copyist? What used to be a time-consuming job can now be accomplished with a computer and notation program. Some talented people even record songs with the help of MIDI technology.

- Want to work in *auto sales?* Many auto dealers can locate the exact location of the perfect car for a potential customer with the click of a mouse. Many auto repairs are also diagnosed with the help of computers.

- Want to work in *publishing?* Virtually every newspaper and magazine today is written, laid out, and produced with the aid of computers.

- Considering working in *retail?* In some of the larger retail outlets, computers are used to tell exactly how many of a product are available in each store throughout the country. Even smaller stores are now becoming computerized.

Telecommuting careers

As discussed in Chapter 6, telecommuting is growing in popularity. As you may remember, telecommuting is essentially working from home for all or part of the work week.

Whether you use a desktop computer with all the peripherals or just a laptop, remember, telecommuting careers generally involve a computer. Some hot possibilities include:

- Graphic designer
- Newsletter editor

Bright Idea
Continue your training even after you're employed, and even if you're self-employed. Get as much training in as many areas as possible. This will make you more marketable.

- Book editor
- Copywriter
- Researcher

The Web awaits

The World Wide Web has changed the way we communicate and the way many of us live and work. The Internet has created a wide array of jobs and opportunities for many people. Let's look at a few possibilities:

- Web site designer
- Webmaster
- Web programmer
- Trainer
- Online news producer
- Web advertising sales
- Web site maintainer
- Web site editor
- Web site evaluator

Now let's look at a few of these possibilities in more depth.

Web site designers

Everyone wants a presence on the Web. It's the place to be. Did you ever notice while surfing the Web, that some sites are exciting and others just "blah"? Do you ever look at sites and think you could create a better one? As a Web site designer you can—and you can get paid well for your work.

As a Web designer, you develop and create the "look" and the graphic design for the site. Depending on your design and ideas, you might use programs such as Photoshop or Adobe Illustrator to

Unofficially...
There is a tremendous demand for talented and creative Web site designers. Gone are the days businesses just needed a site. Today, they need a *great* site. Who do you call to handle the task of creating a great site? A Web designer.

develop graphics. You determine the colors, graphics, and look of the whole set. You work with a Webmaster (unless you are also the Webmaster) to put the whole site together. Your creativity is what can make a site sparkle and shine or just be mildly functional.

You might work for a Web site development company or be self-employed. Possible clients include:

- Restaurants
- Shopping centers
- Department stores
- Music groups
- Manufacturers
- Banks
- Insurance companies
- Politicians
- Hotels and motels
- Florists
- Boutiques
- Travel agents
- Real estate companies
- Specialty food companies
- Craftspeople
- Colleges and universities
- Schools
- Tourist attractions
- Radio stations
- Newspapers
- Magazines

- Trade associations
- Hospitals and health care facilities

Webmasters

Do you want to put together Web sites? Do you want to be in charge? Become a Webmaster. These people are in demand and can make a lot of money.

What do you do as a Webmaster? A lot depends on your skills and your talent. Your main job is putting together the entire Web site. You may work with a designer or you may be the Web designer. You'll probably also do the programming, although you may work with a Web programmer on all or part of the site.

Once you put together the site, it's your job to test it to make sure everything works and the links and the site itself are bug-free. You may or may not be responsible for maintaining the site.

Maintenance is an important part of a Web site. An effective site is one in which people keep coming back and checking it out. In order for that to happen, the site must be updated regularly. Some companies use contests or tips of the day or other promotions to build interest in their site. Others promote their Web site through e-mail.

Online news producers

Do you like to write? Many newspapers today put the print version of their publication online. Some have also begun creating new online publications. These may consist of a combination of articles from the printed version of the paper as well as news gathered and written by reporters, editors, journalists, and news producers.

To do this type of job you need the ability to write in a manner that attracts attention. You also need to know your audience. Are you writing for people in the business community? Students? A specific industry? Every aspect of your client's business will affect the way you write.

As an online producer, you might:

- Write content for online newspaper sites.
- Look for clever original content.
- Conduct online forums.
- Be responsible for a daily news page.
- Develop and write articles.
- Take wire copy and post it to the Web.

Internet shopping

You can now buy almost anything on the Internet. Many established catalog companies have added Internet sites. Other companies have developed and created sites selling everything from books, clothes, and jewelry to food and travel or cars and homes. This industry has created many new job possibilities.

In addition to developing Web sites and maintaining those sites, there are a wealth of opportunities. What can you do?

- Become a buyer searching for unique and innovative products.
- Develop new and better ways to sell products.
- Develop new markets to sell products.
- Write descriptive copy for products.
- Publicize the site.
- Market the site.

Web ads

There are many ways to make money on the Web. Some talented and creative people put together

> 66
> The great thing about this job is that it's in an industry full of possibilities for aspiring writers...The key to success is flexibility. Titles, responsibilities, personnel, and management change frequently, so be prepared to reinvent yourself constantly.
> —Bruce Kohl, online news producer, Boston Herald.com
> 99

Unofficially...
To sell advertising, you need to develop a site that attracts attention, find ways to bring people back consistently, and most importantly, have the ability to sell.

Watch Out!
Develop your Web site and get it online before you approach advertisers. Otherwise you will be setting yourself up for failure. People will tell you they might be interested at a later date after they see how your site looks. You will have lost the initial impact of your sales pitch.

sites on a variety of subjects and then sell banner ads. If your site is dynamic, informative, and gets a lot of "hits," you can make a great deal of money.

What will you be selling? First, you need to sell the idea of advertising on your site to companies and businesses. Then you have to sell them the actual advertising.

Who can you sell to? It depends on the type of site you have, its subject matter, and its content. If you develop a great site that has mass appeal, you can often attract national advertisers. However, you might need to begin your venture with smaller, local or regional advertisers.

Check out Web sites similar to yours and see what types of ads they have on their site. You have to sit down and think who would benefit from advertising on your site. Remember, it's not what they can do for you, it's what you can do for them. Let's look at a couple of examples:

- Are you thinking about a site where you put together information on alternative and complementary medicine? You might try contacting vitamin companies, herb manufacturers, alternative-care products, and health food stores to see if they're interested in advertising on your site.

- Are you considering developing a site about parenting and child care? Try contacting companies who sell products for children as well as companies selling products or services to the parents. On a more local level, consider contacting child day care centers, local supermarkets, and newspapers.

- Want to put together the world's largest dessert recipe site? Look for manufacturers of products that are used in desserts, supermarket chains, even airlines might be a possibility.

- Thinking about a site full of crafting advice and projects? Potential advertisers might be craft magazines, craft product manufacturers, craft stores, department stores with craft departments, and any similar businesses that you can find.

How should you approach potential advertisers? Look for companies and businesses that might profit from advertising on your site. Then call them and ask who their marketing director is. Depending on your sales skills, you can try to speak to the individual and pitch your proposal, or you could send a proposal in writing and then follow up with a call.

You need to have great sales skills and believe in your product. You also need to illustrate to your potential advertisers how being on your site can benefit them. To gain confidence, try preparing mock sales calls and practicing a number of times before making actual sales calls.

You might also want to put together a press kit on your site. It should describe the content, numbers, and demographics of the type of people who visit and other pertinent information to send to potential advertisers. Any promotion you do that gets your site attention will help you sell ads.

Selling advertising on your own site takes some practice. For some people it may be hard to start off selling your own product. If this is the case, you might want to consider selling ad space for an established company first.

Selling Web advertising is like selling anything else. If you have great sales skills and can explain the benefits of advertising on a site, you can get in on

Watch Out!
It's important to come up with a realistic price ahead of time for people to pay to advertise on your site. Don't get to the point where people say they might be interested, only to have you say, "I haven't come up with a price yet. What do you think it's worth?"

the ground floor of this new opportunity. Where can you find a job? Many newspapers, radio stations, television stations, and magazines have Web sites that sell advertising space.

Browse the Web and check out the banner ads you see on various sites. This should help give you an idea of the types of sites or companies you can contact for employment possibilities.

Explain it to me

Children today may have computers in the class-room from the time they are in kindergarten. Depending on your age, you might have grown up using computers too. Some people, however, are new to computers and very intimidated by them. They may not be sure how to use a computer, soft-ware, or peripherals. Others may be comfortable with computers, but need instruction in using new software packages or making the most of their sys-tem. Whatever the situation, training has become big business in the computer industry, resulting in career opportunities for those skilled in teaching others. Could one of them be you?

Computer and software trainers

Do you enjoy teaching others? Do you know more about computers than most people? Can you explain how to use hardware so people don't get frustrated? If so, consider a hot career as a com-puter or software trainer.

The market for computer and software trainers is growing and will continue to expand into the new century as new computers and software applications come out.

Teaching is a talent, and good teachers are rare. If you can teach people how to use computers and software, you will be giving them a skill that can enrich their life and career. How do you teach others skills in computer usage or new software? You might use a variety of teaching methods and aids to help people grasp subject matter:

- You might work one-on-one.
- You might work in a classroom situation where each student has a computer.
- You might use overhead transparencies.
- You might use slides.
- You might use videos.

Where would you work? You might be self-employed working as a consultant, or you might be employed by computer stores, corporations, software or hardware manufacturers, or computer training centers.

Who might use the services of computer and software trainers?

- Seniors with no prior knowledge of computers (especially those in senior centers)
- Children attending after-school programs
- Children at school
- Corporations teaching employees new software applications
- Temp agencies teaching potential employees computer usage and software applications
- Software manufacturers
- Computer stores that want to provide an extra service
- Computer training centers that need trainers

Bright Idea
If you are self-employed, become friends with employees in computer stores in your area. They will often either rec-ommend you or let you put your business card or fliers in their store.

Internet trainers/Web trainers

While it can be hard to remember life without the World Wide Web, it's actually relatively new. As each day goes by, more and more people want to log on, but don't know how.

As an Internet or Web trainer, you would help people to:

- Become more comfortable using the Internet.
- Learn how to install, use, and download various browsers.
- Learn how to use various search engines.
- Learn how to surf efficiently to find what they're looking for.
- Become familiar with chat rooms.
- Become familiar with sending and receiving e-mail

As an Internet or Web trainer, you might be self-employed or work for continuing ed programs, computer stores, Internet service providers (ISPs), community colleges, or a variety of other employers.

Trainers of Web page design

There are a vast number of people and businesses who want to have their own Web site. Many people today wants a presence on the Web. Some go to professional Web site developers; others decide they want to create their own Web sites.

This has created a need for people to teach others how to create, develop, and design Web pages and sites. Trainers may give classes on basic Web creation using Web page design programs or offer students instruction on how to create sites using HTML, one of the Web's programming languages.

Where can you work? You might be self-employed or act as a consultant. Schools, community colleges,

Bright Idea
If you're self-employed, con-sider contacting local senior cen-ters to find potential clients. Many seniors are intimidated by computers but eager to get online so they can chat with friends or their children.

and continuing ed facilities often look for people to teach in this area. Internet service providers and computer training centers also offer opportunities.

Data processing training managers

Many large companies have data processing training managers on staff to handle the training needs of the staff who work with computer functions.

In this job, your function is to make sure every member of the company who deals with computers knows exactly how to use them. You might conduct training classes or work one-on-one with people. You may also determine what types of additional training are needed and develop computer operations manuals, training videos, or other training materials.

Depending on the size and structure of the company you work for, you might have one or more trainers working under you. Where could you work? Pretty much any setting that is largely computerized, including hotels, banks, insurance companies, and large corporations.

Just the facts

- Most jobs today require some level of computer literacy.

- Computers and the Internet have changed the way we live and work.

- Careers using computers are available in every industry.

- A significant portion of all home businesses use the computer.

- Teaching and training in the computer field is big business.

Bright Idea
Many people are more comfortable learning about computers at home sitting at their own computer. There is a growing need for people to offer one-on-one training for any capacity of computer usage in people's homes.

GET THE SCOOP ON...

Cool conservation careers ▪ Working in the environment ▪ Biology careers ▪ Sizzling science careers ▪ Engineering options

The Environment, Sciences, and Engineering

T he environment is one of our most precious assets. Over the years, however, we have often misused our resources. Preserving the environment in the best shape possible is important to future generations. Remedying problems and attempting to replenish and reconstitute a healthy environment are important as well.

Important, too, is the increase in new technology and scientific advances. The complexity of today's society has resulted in a plethora of career possibilities.

In this chapter I'll discuss careers in areas including conservation, the environment, science, biology, and engineering. Perhaps one of them is right for you.

What about the environment?

Do you have a concern for the environment? Do you want to work in this exciting and essential field? Opportunities are endless and increasing every day.

351

What can you do? Depending on your skills, talent, education, desires, and dreams, there are a multitude of hot possibilities working in this area. These include:

- Environmentalists
- Engineers
- Technicians
- Technologists
- Scientists
- Educators
- Attorneys
- Physicians
- Nurses
- Landscape architects
- Farmers
- Horticulturists
- Public relations and communications specialists
- Writers
- Fund-raisers
- Environmental managers

Within these general areas you might work in a variety of settings, including:

- Governmental agencies
- Corporations
- Private industry
- Environmental organizations
- Research laboratories
- Schools, colleges, and universities

Let's explore a few specific careers working in conservation and the environment in depth.

Environmentalists

Are you interested in helping to prevent and control pollution? Would you like to solve environmental problems? A hot career for you might be as an environmentalist.

The environment is becoming more and more polluted. Your main function in this career is to help prevent pollution of the air, land, and water. Within the scope of your job you may perform a number of duties. These include:

- Conducting research to control pollution that has previously occurred
- Conducting research to stop pollution from occurring
- Developing methods to deal with conserving natural resources
- Lobbying
- Testifying in front of legislative committees and other groups
- Speaking to groups and organizations about preventative measures of controlling pollution and saving the environment
- Preparing reports
- Performing inspections of polluted sites

As an environmentalist you might specialize in a few different areas, depending on your interests. These include:

- Preservation of wildlife
- Land and range conservation
- Contamination of water
- Removal of hazardous or toxic wastes

Where would you work as an environmentalist?

Bright Idea
If you're still in college, volunteer with a nonprofit environmental agency or group to get on-the-job experience in this field.

- Governmental agencies
- Mining corporations
- Chemical companies
- Oil companies
- Nonprofit groups and organizations
- Environmental consulting firms
- Private industry

How can you become an environmentalist? A bachelor's degree is the minimum requirement for most jobs in this field. Majors might include environmental science, natural sciences, environmental engineering, civil engineering, environmental studies, engineering management, political science, or even liberal arts. If you're interested in senior positions, you might be required to continue on with a graduate degree.

Environmental technicians

Do you want to help prevent the pollution of water? Do you want to help treat water that is already polluted? Consider a career as an environmental technician.

In this type of job, your main functions are helping to prevent water pollution and treating waste water. Within the scope of the job you might perform a number of duties. Depending on the specific employment setting, you might do the following:

- Take samples of water or sewage.
- Test samples to see if they are polluted.
- Treat sewage with chemicals to break it down.
- Operate equipment to control waste into plants.
- Operate equipment to remove solid waste.
- Monitor equipment.

Bright Idea
Learn more about becoming an environmentalist by contacting the National Association of Environmental Professionals at (904) 251-9901 or log on to their site at www.enfo.com/naep.

- Record data at wastewater plants.
- Prepare reports concerning data at wastewater plants.
- Perform field tests on streams, lakes, and industrial wastewater.

  Where do you work in this career?

- Government agencies
- Foreign agencies responsible for pollution control
- Equipment manufacturers
- Sewage treatment plants
- Companies that manufacture pollution control equipment

How can you become an environmental technician? This is one of those jobs where you might need just a high school diploma and get on-the-job training. Other positions might require or prefer a college background or degree. Consider an associate's or bachelor's degree program in either environmental technology and wastewater technology.

Environmental managers

With all the building that goes on every year, someone is needed to make sure the water, air, and soil are polluted as little as possible. As an environmental manager, you come up with plans to minimize the pollution caused by building new facilities. You might also develop remedial plans for situations that have already occurred or develop environmental impact reports when stores or companies expand. Your report could mean the difference between a corporation expanding or not expanding in a community.

Bright Idea
To learn more about career opportunities in this field, check out the National Registry of Environmental Professionals Web site at www.nrep.org.

Environmental attorneys

Want to work in law, but you're also concerned about the environment? Here's a solution. Consider a career as an environmental attorney.

What do you do? First you become an attorney, then you specialize. Environmental attorneys might deal with a variety of clients ranging from corporations to the government.

Environmental analysts

Does working to help the environment excite you? Do you like to develop solutions? Consider a hot career as an environmental analyst.

What do you do in this job? Your main function is determining what is problematic with the air, water, and Earth and then developing solutions. Why is this a hot career? In this type of position you have the power to help people find solutions. For example, many areas in the country are cancer clusters (people living in those areas are far more likely to get cancer than people living in other areas). Environmental analysts are the individuals who work to find what is causing the cluster in specific areas. Could it be chemicals running into the water from a manufacturing plant? Might it be airborne contaminants? It is up to the analysts to locate the problem and find ways to solve it.

Where would you work?

Bright Idea
Check out the Environmental Law Institute Web site at www.eli.org to learn more about careers in this field.

- Federal environmental protection agencies
- State environmental protection agencies
- Local environmental protection agencies
- Private consulting groups

Environmental engineers

Do you think it might be exciting to supervise the cleanup of environmental contamination? Would you like to develop solutions to environmental concerns? If so, you might enjoy working as an environmental engineer.

In this career, you use the skills of environmentalists as well as those of chemical and civil engineers to determine exactly how complex environmental problems as well as solutions affect your client.

What will you deal with as an environmental engineer?

- Oil spills

- Chemical spills

- Dumping of toxic or hazardous waste

There are a multitude of functions you might handle depending on your specific employment situation. You might deal with the remediation of man-made environmental contamination, or determine what environmental problems exist as well as the consequences for not dealing with the remediation.

Where will you work as an environmental engineer?

- Government agencies

- Public utilities

- Private industry

- Waste-disposal companies

- Chemical industrial corporations

- Energy industry

- Manufacturing industry

- Engineering firms

How do you become an environmental engineer? Generally, you should obtain a bachelor's degree in environmental engineering. Also consider

Bright Idea
Want to learn more about careers for environmental analysts? Check out the National Registry of Environmental Professionals Web site at www.nrep.org.

Watch Out!
Depending on the state in which you live and work and your employment situation, you may need a license or other credentials to work in the environment.

a major in environmental studies, civil engineering, chemical engineering, engineering management, or general engineering. You might also need a master's degree or Ph.D. for senior, research, or teaching positions.

Careers for biologists

Did you enjoy biology in high school? Are you interested in studying living organisms and their relationship to their environment? If so, you might want to work as a biologist. In this field, you can specialize in an area in which you have an interest, including:

- *Zoology.* Zoologists study all aspects of animals including their origin, behavior, diseases, and life processes.

- *Microbiology.* Microbiologists study the growth and characteristics of microscopic organisms. Working in this area you might be asked to investigate bacteria, algae, or fungi.

- *Biochemistry.* Biochemists study the chemical composition of living things. These individuals work in both biology and chemistry. This is a hot career, especially in pharmaceuticals, biotechnology, and environmental protection.

- *Aquatic biology.* Aquatic biologists study plants and animals living in water environments. Specialists in this field include marine biologists (those who study saltwater organisms) and limnologists (who study freshwater organisms).

- *Computational biology.* There are many new careers that merge the latest advances in computer science and biology. Computational geneticists, for example, map the human

Bright Idea
Check out the Web site of the American Academy of Environmental Engineers at www.enviro-engrs.org/address.htm to learn more about careers in this field.

genome (the genetic code that determines the structure of humans).

- *Botany.* Botanists explore plants and their environment. In this career you might study the causes and cures of plant diseases.

- *Physiology.* Physiologists study the life functions of plants and animals.

- *Ecology.* Ecologists study the relationship of organisms and their environment.

How do you break into a career as a biologist? A bachelor's degree is the minimum requirement; however, advanced degrees are often required or preferred for many teaching or research positions.

Careers for scientists

Are you interested in science? There is a cornucopia of careers in this area to consider. These include:

- Meteorologists

- Chemists

- Geologists

- Geophysicists

- Physicists

- Astronomers

- Agricultural scientists

Let's look at some of these in more depth.

Meteorologists

Will it be cold or hot outside? Will it be sunny or cloudy? These are the questions many people want answers to so they can plan what to wear and their activities. The first thing many people do when they wake up in the morning is flip on the television or radio and wait for the weather report. Others catch

Unofficially...
Within microbiology, there is a very hot career as a medical microbiologist. Medical microbiologists study the relationship between organisms and disease as well as the effect of antibiotics on microorganisms. Their research is very important in the creation of new medicines.

Bright Idea
Learn more about a career as a biochemist by contacting the American Society of Biological Chemists at (301) 530-7145.

66

Not all careers in science require a science degree. A just-the-humanities-ma'am student who never took physics and barely glanced at an equation in college, I reverentially entered publishing upon graduation. But my inner science dilettante always lurked. When an opportunity at the copy desk of *Scientific American* appeared, I jumped at the chance. The reward? The most fascinating—and best—job I've ever had.
—Myles McDonnell, Copy Editor, *Scientific American*

99

the weather report on the 11 o'clock news before they go to bed.

Does the weather amaze you? Does it interest you for reasons other than what you're going to wear tomorrow? If so, you might consider a hot career as a meteorologist. Who hires meteorologists? Probably the largest employer of meteorologists in this country is the National Oceanic and Atmospheric Administration. Some of these employees work for the National Weather Service in various locations throughout the country.

Where else could you work?

■ Cruise companies

■ Colleges or universities

■ Ski resorts

■ Airlines

■ Nonprofit organizations

■ Engineering companies

■ Department of Defense

■ Research departments of various companies

■ Private weather consultants

■ Radio stations

■ Television stations

Every weather reporter on television and radio is not a meteorologist. In some cases, they are just reading the forecast prepared by the meteorologist. Many of the popular weather reporters on television, however, are also meteorologists.

There are a number of specialties of meteorologists. These include:

■ Syoptic or operational meteorologists

■ Physical meteorologist

■ Climatologists

Meteorologists who specialize in forecasting the weather are known as syoptic or operational meteorologists. What do you do in this type of job?

- Study the atmosphere and its elements.
- Accumulate data on air pressure, humidity, temperature, and wind velocity.
- Forecast long- and short-term weather predictions.

Do you think you'd prefer specializing in research? Those who do this are known as physical meteorologists. In this job, individuals study things such as:

- Weather phenomena
- Chemical and physical properties of the atmosphere
- The transfer of atmospheric energy
- The transmission of light, radio, and sound waves

Climatologists analyze past weather records including wind, sunshine, rainfall, and temperature for specific geographic regions. This information is then used when planning the size of heating and cooling systems in buildings.

To become a meteorologist, you generally need a minimum of a bachelor's degree with a major in meteorology or a closely related field to get an entry-level job. Also consider a bachelor's degree in any area with a minimum of 20 semester hours of meteorology courses. Other helpful courses include college physics, computer science, physical science, and calculus.

There are many civil service positions in meteorology. Contact the U.S. Civil Service Examiners in

Bright Idea
Look for an internship or apprenticeship in meteorology to get valuable on-the-job training. Contact the American Meteorological Society to find out if they know of any possibilities.

Watch Out!
There are only a
few colleges that
offer degrees in
meteorology or
atmospheric sci-
ence. Check with
the National
Weather Service
to see what
courses are cur-
rently required to
make sure that
the college you
want to attend
offers the
required classes.

Washington, D.C., to find out about test dates and openings.

Chemists

Are you interested in searching for and using chemicals? Do you like working in research and development? Perhaps a hot career for you would be working as a chemist.

All physical things are composed of chemicals. Chemists are responsible for developing a variety of things. These include:

■ Drugs

■ Electronic components

■ Synthetic fibers

■ Paints

Chemists also do research to develop ways to save energy and reduce pollution.

What else could you do as a chemist? You might be the one to do research that catapults advances in medicine, agriculture, food processing, or a variety of other areas. You might work in production and quality control in chemical and manufacturing plants.

Do you want to work as a chemist? There are a number of subdivisions in this area. You might work as:

Watch Out!
To become any
type of chemist,
you generally
need a minimum
of a bachelor's
degree in chem-
istry. However, if
you're interested
in teaching or
research, you will
probably need a
doctorate.

■ **Analytical chemists.** If you choose this area of chemistry, you determine the structure, composition, and nature of substances as well as develop analytical techniques. One of the reasons this area is so hot is that you identify the presence and concentration of chemical pollutants in the air, water, and soil.

■ **Organic chemists.** If you choose this field, you study the chemistry of various carbon compounds. This is the area to work if you're interested in developing new drugs, plastics, or fertilizers.

- **Inorganic chemists.** In this field you research elements other than carbon. This is the area to work if you're interested in researching and developing electronic components.

- **Physical chemists.** In this field you study the physical characteristics of atoms and molecules. If you choose this area of chemistry, you might be responsible for developing new and better energy sources.

Bright Idea
For more information about careers in chemistry, contact the American Chemical Society Career Services Department.

Geologists and geophysicists

Do you want to help in the search for natural resources and look for solutions to environmental problems? Your hot career might be as a geologist or geophysicist.

What's the difference between a geologist and a geophysicist?

- **Geologists** study the composition, structure, and history of the earth's crust. In this job you work on finding out how rocks were formed and what has happened to them since their formation.

- **Geophysicists** use the principles of physics and math to study the earth's surface as well as its internal composition. This might include ground and surface waters, atmosphere, oceans, and the magnetic, electrical, and gravitational forces affecting Earth.

Geologists and geophysicists study the physical aspects and history of the Earth. What does this mean you will do?

Bright Idea
To obtain additional information about a career as a geologist, contact the American Geological Institute at (702) 379-2480 or the Geological Society of America at (303) 447-1133 or log on to their Web site at www.geosociety. org.

- Identify and examine rocks.

- Study information collected by remote sensing instruments.

- Conduct geological surveys.

- Construct maps.

- Use instruments to measure the earth's gravity and magnetic field.

- Analyze information collected through seismic prospecting.

- Search for oil.

- Search for natural gas.

- Search for minerals.

- Search for underground water.

Why is a career as a geophysicist hot? In this line of work you can study, preserve, and assist in the cleanup of the environment. You might design and monitor waste-disposal sites, protect water supplies, and reclaim contaminated land and water to comply with federal environmental rules. With today's growing and necessary interest in the environment, this is a vital and important job.

Want to get into one of these fields? A bachelor's degree in geology or geophysics will help you obtain an entry-level job; if you want a higher-level job, continue your education and go for a master's degree.

Bright Idea
For more information about a career as a geophysicist, contact the American Geophysical Union at (202) 462-6900 or their Web site at www.agu.org, or the Society of Exploration Geophysicists at (918) 497-5500 or their Web site at www.seg.org.

Agricultural scientists

Do you like working with the principles of biology and chemistry? Do you want to help farmers find ways to improve their crops? Do you want to help find ways to produce healthier food products? A hot career for you might be in the field of agricultural science.

What can you do? That depends what field you select. Do you think you might want to work as an agricultural scientist in food science? In this job you might do the following:

- Develop better ways of preserving, processing, packaging, storing, and delivering foods.
- Perform research.
- Analyze food content.
- Search for substitutes to harmful additives in food.
- Develop new foods.
- Enforce government regulations.
- Inspect food processing areas to ensure sanitation, safety, quality, and waste management.

Would you prefer to work as an agricultural scientist in plant sciences? In this career area you might do the following:

- Study plants and their growth in various soils.
- Help food producers find ways to grow food while conserving natural resources and maintaining the environment.
- Find ways to increase productivity in plants.
- Study genetic engineering to develop crops resistant to pests and drought.

Do you think you might want to work as an agricultural scientist in the soil sciences? In this job you can help farmers and others determine the best use of their land. These individuals study the chemical, physical, biological, and mineral composition of soils in relation to plant and crop growth. You might do the following:

- Study the relationship between different types of soil and fertilizers or crop rotation.

- Work to ensure environmental quality and efficient land use.

Would you prefer working in the animal sciences area of agricultural science? In this type of job you develop better ways of producing and processing meat, poultry, eggs, and milk. You might study the genetics, nutrition, reproduction, and development of domestic farm animals.

Engineering a career

If you're interested in science and math and like developing solutions to problems, consider a career in engineering. What do engineers do? That depends on the area in which they work. Generally engineers design a variety of products, machines, systems, and processes. Within the scope of their job, engineers make sure the things they design are as efficient as possible.

Engineering careers are diverse, with many hot careers in a variety of specialties and subspecialties. These include:

- **Civil engineers** design and supervise the construction of roads, tunnels, bridges, water supply and sewage systems, airports, and buildings. Hot career specialties in this field are in the environmental and construction areas.

- **Electrical engineers** design, develop, test, and supervise the manufacture of electrical and electronic equipment. The hot career areas in this field are computer electronics and electrical equipment manufacturing. They account for more than one-quarter of all engineers working in this country.

- **Mechanical engineers** plan and design tools, engines, machines, and mechanical equipment. As a mechanical engineer, you may design the tools that other engineers use in their work.

- **Industrial engineers** decide the most effective ways for a company to use people, machines, materials, information, and energy to make products. Industrial engineers, unlike most others in the field, are concerned with increasing a company's productivity through the management of people and methods of business organization.

- **Mining engineers** locate, extract, and prepare metals and minerals for the manufacturing industries. As a mining engineer, you ensure that a mine is run in an efficient, safe, economical, and environmentally sound manner. You may also work on solutions for water and air pollution or land reclamation.

- **Petroleum engineers** look for and produce oil and natural gas. If you like exploring, this might be an area for you. Once you find a reservoir containing oil or natural gas, it's your job to develop the most profitable and efficient production methods.

- **Nuclear engineers** perform research on nuclear energy and radiation. As a nuclear engineer, you might be on a team that designs and develops medical uses for radioactive materials used to diagnose and treat medical problems.

- **Materials engineers** develop new types of metal alloys, ceramics, composites, and other materials. As a materials engineer, you might develop ceramic tiles for space shuttles or parts of a plane.

Bright Idea
Internships are a great way to obtain experience in this field. When looking for an internship, try to find one with a civil engineer working in the specialty in which you're interested.

- **Chemical engineers** solve problems involving the production or use of chemicals. One hot career specialty in chemical engineering is working in pollution control.

- **Aerospace engineers** design, develop, test, and help manufacture commercial and military aircraft, spacecraft, and missiles.

Here are some places to look for more information on the engineering career you're interested in:

- For more information about a career as a petroleum engineer, contact the Society of Petroleum Engineers at (972) 952-9393.

- Interested in learning more about working as a nuclear engineer? Contact the American Nuclear Society at (708) 352-6611.

- The Society for Mining, Metallurgy and Exploration, Inc., will send you information on careers as mining engineers if you call (303) 973-9550. You might also check out their Web site at www.smenet.org.

- The American Society of Mechanical Engineers and the American Society of Heating, Refrigeration, and Air-Conditioning Engineers, Inc., will send you additional information on careers in mechanical engineering. Contact the ASME toll-free at (800) THE-ASME or the ASHRAE at (512) 255-3146.

- If you are interested in learning more about careers in industrial engineering, contact the Institute of Industrial Engineers at (770) 449-0460 or check out their Web site at www.iienet.org.

- Contact the Institute of Electrical and Electronic Engineers at (212) 419-7900 for

Moneysaver
Often employers in the engineering field pay educational reimbursement for their employees to take classes, workshops, or seminars to keep up with trends in technology.

information on careers in electrical and electronics engineering.

- For more information on career opportunities for civil engineers, contact the American Society of Civil Engineers toll-free at (800) 548-2723 or visit their Web site at www.asce.org.

- To learn more about career opportunities in chemical engineering, contact the American Institute of Chemical Engineers at (212) 591-7338 or visit their Web site at www.aiche.org, or additional information may be obtained by contacting the American Chemical Society, Career Services division toll-free at (800) 227-5558, or visit their Web site at www.acs.org.

- To learn more about career opportunities as an aerospace engineer, contact the American Institute of Aeronautics and Astronautics toll-free at (800) NEW-AIAA or visit their Web site at www.aiaa.org.

- JETS-Guidance (Junior Engineering Technical Society) offers information on a variety of engineering careers. Contact them at (703) 548-0769 or visit their Web site at www.jets.org.

Are you interested in working in engineering but don't have the degree? Consider working as an engineering technician. Most specialties in engineering have technician positions available. What do technicians do? While more limited in scope than full-fledged engineering jobs, technicians still use the principles and theories of science, engineering, and math to solve problems and develop solutions. Engineer technicians, working under the direction of engineers, assist with research and development or work in production or inspection.

Just the facts

- You can find a hot career helping to protect the environment.

- The need for scientists and engineers in the future will exceed that of the past.

- There are a variety of careers in engineering to choose from.

- Employment settings for scientists, biologists, and engineers are diverse.

You're So Lucky...Careers
Everyone Wants

GET THE SCOOP ON...
How to get the best boss ▪ Home businesses ▪
Are you ready for a career at home? ▪
Hot home career options

PART VII

The Best Boss
Ever—You

Chapter 16

Want the best boss ever? You can have that boss if you start your own home business and work for yourself. Home businesses are a growing trend. According to the United States Department of Labor, there are more home businesses today than ever before. Whether you choose to make a full-time or part-time commitment, a home business can make a major difference in your life.

Financially, a home business can allow you to add to the income of a traditional career or it can allow you to make your income grow more than you ever imagined while you were working for someone else. Emotionally, the satisfaction resulting from bringing a home business from inception to fruition and then catapulting it to success can mean everything.

This chapter will discuss hot home careers. Wherever your interests lie, there are a plethora of possibilities just waiting for you to choose from.

Unofficially...
A home business career does not mean working at home all the time. Many home businesses sell products or services outside the home. For example, a cleaning service may be based at home, but the actual work is performed outside of the home.

Home is where your headquarters is

It is estimated that over 30 million people today are already involved in a home business of some kind. They reportedly earn an average of approximately $50,000 annually, with 20 percent earning more than $75,000 per year. Many succeed in their first year. If you want it, one of them can be you!

There are a number of different categories of those working at home. Loosely based, these include:

- *Full-time self-employed.* This includes those whose main career is their home business.

- *Part-time self-employed.* This includes those who are working part-time at their home business without any other means of income, as well as those who have a part-time home business in addition to their full-time traditional job.

- *Telecommuters.* This includes people who work from home all or part of the time. They do not necessarily have a home business and may work for someone else.

Working from home, you face challenges that you don't have to deal with in a traditional job. These may vary depending on the type of home business you have. Some of these challenges include:

- **Maintaining a professional image.** What does that mean? We all know how it sounds when the kids start crying, the dog doesn't stop barking, or neighbors begin arguing loudly so everyone who calls can hear the commotion.

  With a home-based business, associates, colleagues, and customers may call at any time. You want them to see you as a professional so they will believe that you are handling their business in a professional manner. You therefore need to find ways to maintain a positive professional image. You can begin by keeping your business phone in a room away from the kids, the barking dog, and, hopefully, the screaming neighbors, and always answer the phone in a businesslike manner. Your professional image is reinforced by the quality of your work and by your calm and professional demeanor.

- **Family.** Can you keep your business life and your family separate in the same location? You'll need to set boundaries for when you are working. A home business is just that, a business.

- **Household distractions.** Can you keep the kids and your spouse from asking for things on a constant basis while you are working? Can you stop yourself from turning on the television and watching the soaps when you should be working? Can you find a way to make sure neighbors and family members understand you are working, not just home? If not, everyone will be asking you to run errands during the day while they are at "work" and you are at "home."

- **Home-family balance.** It's important in a home business (as in any career) to find the right balance between your work and your family. If you work *all* the time, you're probably ignoring your family. If you don't work enough, your business will suffer. Balance is the key.

- **Isolation.** You may feel isolated working by yourself. At home, you don't have the workplace coffee breaks or camaraderie. To help make this easier, it's important to make time to join associations, attend their meetings, have lunch with colleagues or business associates, and continue to network with others.

Is a home business for you?

Why do people want to go into a home-based business? There are many reasons:

- Tired of the long, tiring commute to work
- Job or workplace stress
- Pressures of a large office
- Lack of recognition in the workplace
- A desire for more quality time at home
- Lack of job security
- Dislike of current job

Today more than ever, people are worried about job security. When you lose a job, don't like your job, or want to make more money than you can possibly make in a job, a home business is a great way to go. A home business has other significant advantages over other options:

- There are lower start-up costs and reduced overhead. A spare room, your den, attic, basement, or even the kitchen table can be your office.

- Technology makes it more feasible to operate a business at home. You don't have to visit an outside office to communicate with anyone in the world. There are modems, faxes, computers, inexpensive copiers, and telephone equipment.

Sizzling hot reasons to have your own home business

What's so hot about having your own home business?

- You are your own boss—the best boss ever.

- You set your own hours.

- You decide when you go on vacation.

- You decide when and if to expand your business.

- You choose the business, services, and products that interest you.

- You determine your target income and find ways to meet that goal.

- You have the opportunity to build a business that you can leave to your children or your spouse.

- You have the opportunity to build a business that you can sell at a later date.

- You can obtain tax benefits.

- You put your efforts toward attaining your own personal freedom and financial goals instead of making someone else rich.

Your home office

What do you need in your home office? It depends on the type of business you have. If your business does not require customer contact in your home, you need not worry about a "formal" office.

There are some things you will need, however:

- **Telephone.** A separate line is nice but not necessary, as long as the phone is always answered in a professional manner and the line is not kept busy.

- **Answering machine or voice mail.** This is essential to be sure you don't miss important business calls when you're out. Check your messages frequently and return calls promptly.

Watch Out!
Whether you use
a computer, word
processor, or
typewriter, your
correspondence
should look as
professional as
possible. If you
can possibly
avoid it, try not
to handwrite
letters or
proposals.

- **Computer and printer.** Computers and printers are useful in handling business correspondence, billing, keeping records, and so on. You can often rent computers if you are trying to keep your initial overhead down.

- **Modem and Internet access.** Although not an absolute must (depending on the business), this is becoming more and more necessary to do research and correspond with people.

- **Fax machine.** This is another helpful device in getting and sending information to potential clients. If you don't have one, don't despair. Many office supply stores, groceries, and other stores have fax services.

- **Photocopy machine.** These are a bit expensive for many small home businesses that are just starting out. You can often rent the machines. Your fax machines might also double as a copier, or you can go down to the local office supply store, Kinko's, or even your library to make copies.

- **File cabinets.** You should have a place for all your business correspondence. Whether you keep it in a file cabinet, drawer, or closet, make sure everything is neat and orderly. It's essential to know where your business records are and to be able to find them easily.

- **Stationery, letterhead, and business cards.** You can often create great-looking designs right on your own home computer. You can also visit a local print shop. Check a couple of shops to compare prices and quality of work before making a decision.

The home career challenge

Are you ready for a career at home? You might want to answer these questions first:

- Are you tired of worrying about layoffs?

- Are you tired of worrying about insecurity in the job market?

- Do you want to gain more control over your life?

- Do you want to gain more financial stability in your life?

If the answer to these questions is "yes," you may be ready for a career at home.

Are you a risk taker? In order to be successful in a home business, you have to be willing to take a risk. Right before most people start a home business, they usually tell their friends or family and inevitably someone says. "You know, I don't know if that's such a good idea."

Then they give you the "What if's":

- What if you aren't successful?

- What if it doesn't work?

- What if you lose your shirt?

- What if you don't make enough money?

And the list goes on. Then they give you the "What are's":

- What are you, crazy?

- What are you going to do if you quit your job?

- What are you going to do if you can't get your job back?

- What are you going to do if the sky falls in?

Then they give you every reason in the world your idea won't work. These are better known as the

Bright Idea
If you don't have a computer, go to your local Kinko's or other office supply store and use their equipment for a nominal fee. Keep your information on disks. This will save you time typing and retyping information. Colleges and libraries also have computers you might use either free or for a small charge.

Watch Out!
If you have teenagers who like to stay on the phone for long periods of time, you will need an extra line for your business. Call-waiting may help. However, when you place a business call, you might want to deactivate the call-waiting feature so that no other calls can get through.

"You don't's":

- You don't have enough money.
- You don't have enough education.
- You don't have enough training.
- You don't have enough this, or enough that.

These are followed by the "You're too's":

- You're too young.
- You're too old.
- You're too lazy.
- You're too successful in your current job.

If none of these work, people often simply say, "You can't do this or you can't do that," "You're out of your mind," or "You're a pipe dreamer." If you can stand your ground after you've you heard all these, be ready for friends, family, or relatives telling you horror stories of others who have given up everything (or at least the job they had and hated) to start their own business who wound up losing everything and becoming bag people.

First of all, you have to remember that some people don't want you to be successful. A lot of people are jealous of other people's success. What would happen, after all, if you attained success in your own business and they are still stuck in their job?

You can't listen to others. You have to listen to yourself. If *you* think it's a good idea, try it. What do you have to lose?

Many successful people go against the advice of their friends, family, and sometimes even their employer when they start a home business. Successful home business owners are usually very independent. And you know what? When you are left to achieve success on your own, you can do it on your own.

Will you be successful working at home? Answer these questions to see:

- Is the skill, service, or product you want to sell highly marketable?

- Do you have an important reason to work at home?

- Do you mind working long hours if it means ultimate success?

- Can you set a work schedule for yourself and stick to it?

- Are you disciplined?

- Are you motivated?

- Are you comfortable working alone?

- Do you have a supportive family?

- Will your family and friends respect your work time?

- Are you willing to work and develop new skills?

- Are you willing to take risks?

- Are you willing to try new things even if you are scared?

- Are you able to manage your finances while waiting for the checks to come in?

The more "Yes" responses you have to these questions, the better your chances of success working at home.

Finding your niche

You are probably familiar with some of the most successful entrepreneurs of the last century. A great many of them were like you and me. What did they have in common?

- They saw a need.

- They had an idea.

Watch Out!
Doing nothing is the worse risk of all. If you do nothing, nothing can happen. If you do *something,* something might—and it just might be good.

Unofficially...
Martha Stewart was filming her television show from her home in Connecticut (which was not zoned for commercial or business use). Reportedly, neighbors began complaining that the television crews were disturbing the neighborhood and Ms. Stewart had to go to court to find a way to continue filming from that location.

Bright Idea
Check with your insurance agent to get any additional coverage you might need for your new business.

- They had a desire to see it work.
- They wanted to make money.
- They wanted to succeed.

So they started a business at home with a little bit of money and an idea. And it's important to note that the idea was not necessarily always a unique one. Many successful people use ordinary ideas as seeds for what eventually become major businesses.

Remember, however, that you can't do everything from your home. A lot has to do with your local zoning. You need to check with the local zoning officials before you get started and tell them what you want to do and see if it's possible. Also, health departments are becoming more strict. If you are planning on beginning a business preparing food, talk to the local board of health *ahead* of time to see what requirements they have.

Do you have a seed of an idea? If so, maybe it's time to grow your own home business. Your business doesn't have to turn into a major corporation to be a success. Remember, success is what you want. You can start and run a business from home and expand it as much or as little as you want.

Do you currently have a job and you're not sure you want to get into a home-based business? That's the beauty of a home business. It gives you flexibility. You can begin a part-time home business and continue running it part-time until it is so profitable that it just doesn't make any sense to continue working your regular job anymore.

Are you unemployed? Have you been downsized? A home business is an immediate answer to your problem. Why you start a home-based business is not important. What is important is that you have an opportunity to be as successful as you want.

Home businesses are not new. They have been around for years. Today, however, they are more acceptable than ever. Let's look at a couple of examples of people who started home-based businesses and experienced real success.

Do you know Amanda Smith? You might not know her, but I bet you have heard of her. Amanda, like many of us, had recipes her family had handed down over the years. In the early 1900s, she took those recipes and, like we all do, changed them around, added a little bit of this and a little bit of that. Everyone told Amanda her pies were the best in the world. Everyone told her they were so good she should sell them. Has anyone said that to you about your baked products? Did you do anything?

Well, Amanda did. She listened and took action. She baked pies at home, packed them into the back of her car, and sold them to customers in her local area. The more she baked, the more she sold. As a matter of fact, Amanda baked pies at home for seven years until she retired.

Do you know what company Amanda started? You might have even eaten some of her products. Amanda started Mrs. Smith's Homemade Pies. Could you have your own pie company? You might be able to if you take action.

It's important to realize that you have to work at success and never give up your dream. What would you think of a husband who brought his wife some secondhand candy-making equipment instead of a box of candy? One day a man named Russell did just that. He told his wife that he wanted them to start making and selling candy. Neither of them had experience in this field, but Russell didn't give up. Together the husband-and-wife team eventually

Unofficially...
Do you want to know about another home business success story? Steve Jobs and a partner began the Apple Macintosh computer company in the 1970s in Steve's parents' garage.

developed a recipe for candy that was pretty good. However, success was not in the cards at that time.

Unfortunately, by the time they came up with the recipe, World War I was going on. During this time, sugar was being rationed, and this made a candy business very difficult.

Russell and his wife moved to another state and tried again. Success once again eluded them. Russell found it necessary to begin working for another candy maker. During this time, he developed a famous ice cream confection, the "Eskimo Pie." Russell sold his interest in the Eskimo Pie for a reported $30,000 and decided to reach for his dream again.

Russell still wanted his own candy company. He didn't give up. So once again, he and his wife began another candy company. This time, the couple experienced a tremendous success. We know the business as Russell Stover Candies.

Lane Bryant was begun by a young widow and mother named Lena Bryant who reportedly pawned a pair of diamond earrings her late husband had left her for money for a sewing machine. George Parker created the classic board game Monopoly at home while he was ill, and later started the Parker Brothers Game Company with his brother. There are countless other examples of business that began like this. One of the success stories can be yours.

What is the common thread all these people had? An idea, some luck, and, most importantly, a strong will to succeed! They didn't give up, and neither should you.

How can you determine what your home business should be? The first thing you need to do is find something you like to do. What is your passion?

What are you willing to put a lot of time into and still enjoy doing? Many home businesses are built on things people have done as hobbies and then turned into money-making ventures. Successful home business owners not only love what they do, they see a need and find a way to fill it.

One of the truths most successful home business owners share is that they can't wait to get up in the morning to work on their business and they hate to stop working at night. This passion, love, and desire to succeed is what catapults a home business to the top.

Can you find your niche? What do you love to do?

- Work with children?
- Work with food?
- Work with people?
- Work with computers?
- Work with numbers?
- Work with words?
- Work with crafts?
- Work around animals?
- Do you like to shop?
- Do you like to cook?
- Do you like to bake?
- Do you like to organize?
- Do you like to have company?

Sit down with a pen and a pad and try to figure out what you like to do, who or what you enjoy working with, and what makes you happy. As I have asked you to do previously, write down your answers. It's often easier to see what you want when it's written down in front of you.

Unofficially...
Why is it essential to love what you do? Because you will be spending a lot of time doing it. Home businesses take a lot of time, but in the end, the results are worth it.

Watch Out!
Don't forget sales tax. If you are selling a product, you have to find out what the requirements are for collecting sales tax and then you have to collect it. You'll probably have to apply for a state sales tax number to collect sales tax.

Moneysaver
When you are working for someone else, the employer pays half of your Social Security tax. When you are your own boss, *you* get to pay all of it. The good news is half the amount you pay for Social Security tax is tax-deductible.

Hot home careers

When you own your own business, you are your own financial department. You will have to pay estimated taxes every quarter. Don't underestimate what your taxes will be or you may end up with a penalty. You must report your income to the IRS. Not declaring income is fraudulent and you could go to jail. Luckily, you only pay taxes on your profits, not on your total earnings. What you have to do is take the maximum deductions possible. Keep accurate records. Some people hire an accountant to handle their business; others do it on their own.

That said, let's look at some possible home businesses. However, don't let this list limit you. Instead, let it get you thinking about what you could do to have the hottest home business around.

- **Bed and breakfast inn owners.** As noted in Chapter 12, this is a wonderful business if you have one or more spare bedrooms, like to entertain, and enjoy company. You provide a charming, unique, or romantic bedroom, some gourmet goodies for breakfast, and perhaps even some company for the guests. If you want, you can even offer appetizers or dinner for an extra charge. The most successful bed and breakfasts offer quaint, romantic, and charming rooms in locations travelers or vacationers often visit.

    What's so hot about owning a bed and breakfast inn? You have the opportunity to meet new people, entertain, and have company all while getting paid. You can decorate rooms and choose accessories so they are unique and charming, and it's a tax deduction.

Don't despair if you live in the city and still want to have a bed and breakfast. Large apartments or brownstones with extra bedrooms are becoming popular bed and breakfast sites in popular cities.

Moneysaver
Scout the tag and estate sales to find an array of antique and unusual furniture, throws, flatware, dishes, and serving pieces to help decorate your bed and breakfast while saving tons of money.

- **Animal-related home businesses.** Do you love animals? Pets are a good idea on which to base a home business. There are an array of businesses you can get into related to pets. Once again, it's important to be creative. Think of your skills, talents, and desires. What can you do? Consider doggie day care, pet-sitting, or even a pet hotel. Or you might want to create tee shirts with pet photos on them, bake gourmet dog treats, make gourmet dog or cat food, or start a dog-training business.

- **Pet-sitter service.** If you like dealing with pets, this is currently very hot and is expected to get hotter. Many people don't want to leave their beloved pet in a kennel. They prefer to leave their pet in a home setting (and the pet probably prefers this too). In this business, you care for people's pets in their home or yours while they are on vacation or away from home or work.

- **Doggie day care.** In this spin-off of child care, you care for people's dogs during the day while people are at work. You will provide exercise, stimulation, affection, and food. It is a sizzling hot job.

- **Adult day care service.** as noted in Chapter 8, in this job, you care for adults who can't be left alone during the day. You provide social stimulation, care, and interaction as well as prepare and serve meals.

- **Tailors/seamstresses.** If you can sew and alter clothing, this can be very lucrative. Many people buy clothing that either doesn't fit properly or needs to be shortened, lengthened, let out, or taken in, and they will pay a premium for good, personalized work.

- **Personal concierge service.** If you like paying attention to detail and doing things for people, this might be the hot home business for you. Basically, you are like the concierge in a hotel, but you offer similar services on an individual basis. You perform a variety of duties to make people's lives easier, such as running errands, waiting for repair people, bringing in the car for repair, finding nannies or baby-sitters, making reservations, booking trips, and so on. You can serve both individual and corporate clients.

- **Child-care service.** With the tremendous number of working women, child-care services are essential. Many people offer a child-care service in their home, affording them the opportunity to have a business and be with their own children as well.

- **Image consulting.** In this business you assist clients in choosing clothing, accessories, and makeup. Potential clients might be business people who are moving up the corporate ladder. Other clients might include people who are in television or other professions that require frequent personal public appearances.

- **Information broker service.** In this service, you locate information and other data for your clients. You might do this using a computer, the Internet, databases, through interviews, or other searches. Clients may include small businesses or large corporations. They may be writers, students, public relations businesses, advertising agencies, or other individual professionals.

■ **Home instruction service.** This is a good business for those who enjoy teaching new skills to people at home. It can encompass teaching anything from cooking and baking to sewing, computer skills, or any other skill you have that others might want. Hot possibilities include how to repair things around the house, cooking, building Web pages, and using computers, but let your imagination run wild—anything is possible.

■ **Bookkeeping and accounting service.** In this job you handle bookkeeping services and accounting needs for individuals or small businesses. You may also maintain business records and, depending on your expertise, prepare tax forms.

■ **Personal trainers.** As a personal trainer you visit clients in their home or office or they come to you. It's your job to help them attain their optimum fitness level by coaching them in exercise and nutrition.

■ **Desktop publishing business.** If you are a computer whiz and have an understanding of graphics and a sense of style, this might be the business for you. You might develop layouts and design brochures, fliers, letters, pamphlets, booklets, reports, or posters. Developing the layout and design of newsletters is very hot.

■ **Word processing service.** Many people either can't type, don't want to, or don't have a

Bright Idea
If you want to become a personal trainer, contact large corporations that host company gyms to find potential clients.

Moneysaver
If you already have a computer and a printer, you can start a desktop publishing or word processing business with very low overhead.

computer to do the work. In this type of business you might type a variety of documents or correspondence. You need a computer, a good word processing program, and a decent printer. You also need the ability to type quickly and accurately. There are a variety of clients you can target, including students, writers, small businesses, researchers, attorneys, physicians, and temp agencies. Many people combine this business with a desktop publishing business.

■ **Webmaster service.** Everyone wants a presence on the Web today, but many people don't know how to put together a Web page. Large companies may charge $25,000 or more to develop a site, making it unfeasible for many smaller companies. You might begin a business developing simpler Web pages at a lower cost or develop basic sites and for an additional fee teach people how to maintain them. This and other computer careers are covered in Chapter 14.

■ **Personal shoppers.** Are you a shopaholic? Here's a way to shop for others and get paid for it. You might have heard of stores offering personal shopper services. There are also people who have personal shopping businesses. Your clients might be corporate people or individuals who don't like to shop or don't have time to shop. You might be asked to choose gifts, clothing, even groceries. Use your imagination. You might just build up a lucrative hot home business.

■ **Publicity service.** Many small businesses can't afford a full-time publicist. Similarly, many large businesses are interested in outsourcing publicity and public relations duties. In this job you write press releases, put together press kits, and obtain publicity for your clients using a variety of methods.

- **Marketing service.** Similar to a publicity service, you are responsible for marketing products, services, or people. Many people combine this with a publicity or public relations business.

- **Rent-a-husband service.** Many households have jobs that are too small for a general contractor but still need to be handled. Even though there may be a husband in the house, he may not be handy or have the time to fix things. The rent-a-husband service handles small repairs, cleans out garages, paints, puts up wallpaper, mows the lawn, helps move, and so on. (Please note that any of these jobs can also be handled by a woman. The service is just known as "rent-a-husband.")

- **Rent-a-wife service.** Similarly, many households have jobs that require a woman's touch. These include everything from helping a young girl (whose mother cannot be present) pick out a prom dress to cooking, cleaning, sewing, baking, and decorating. (As mentioned in the previous selection, this work can also be done by a man, but the service is known as "rent-a-wife.")

- **Personal secretary service.** Many small businesses don't have enough work for a full-time secretary, but still may require secretarial services.

- **Craftsperson.** Do you like to create things? Are you artistic and skilled? A craft business can be lucrative if you create good-quality products and have a flair for sales. The types of products you can make are limitless. Whether you create

Bright Idea
If you want to start up a publicity service, contact your local newspaper and offer to write a regular column discussing methods small businesses can use to obtain publicity. This will place your name and company in the public's eye.

Bright Idea
Promote your gift basket service by donating baskets to high-visibility events and nonprofit auctions and raffles.

baskets, silk flower arrangements, sculpture, leather work, quilts or batik, fabric crafts, pottery, or folk art, you can have a career as a craftsperson. It's important to recognize that creating the product is only the first step. You also need to find methods to market and sell your wares.

- **Gift basket service.** Gift baskets are hot and getting hotter. As the owner of a gift basket service, you design and arrange visually pleasing gift baskets. Successful services develop interesting themes or use unique products. Some gift basket services use commercially produced items, foods, and gifts; others use a combination of homemade goodies, handcrafted gifts, and commercially produced items. Your clients may include small businesses or corporations, offices, and individuals.

- **Floral designers.** In this business you use silk or fresh flowers (or a combination) to produce attractive and unique floral designs. You might sell your products at craft fairs or to stores, shops, and boutiques, or fill special orders for clients.

Bright Idea
A tutoring service is a great idea for a retired teacher or anyone who is home-schooling their own children.

- **Tutoring service**. Many children and teenagers need help to understand their schoolwork. As a tutor, you help students with math, a language, science, or to excel in any subject. You might advertise in a local paper or put up fliers at the library. The best advertising for this type of business, however, is word of mouth from satisfied parents and their children.

- **Upholsterer.** If you are skilled in upholstering, this is a great home business. As an upholsterer, you redo chairs, couches, or a variety of furniture. Successful upholsters build up their business making slipcovers, window treatments, and accessories as well. If you want to go into the upholstering business, remember that you'll need a van or truck to transport the furniture back and forth.

■ **Cleaning service.** Whether you choose to specialize in cleaning homes, offices, or both, this is a hot business. There is a tremendous demand for this service almost every place in the country. The beauty of this service is you can make it as large or small as you want. You can either make your business a one-person operation, taking on only as much work as you can handle alone, or you can hire others to handle more clients. Your clients may include corporate executives, banks, physician's offices, law offices, stores, families where both spouses work, and single-person households.

To succeed in this job, develop a checklist to ensure that all work the client wants done is performed satisfactorily. Call clients to make sure they're happy with the work, especially if you have hired others to help you. You may need to be bonded or require other certification to go into people's homes or offices.

■ **Event planning service.** If parties and special events are your thing and you like to organize, consider an event planning service. In this type of business, you develop and implement special events and parties from inception through fruition.

Depending on your clients and projects, you might be responsible for corporate meetings,

Bright Idea
Build a clientele for any type of business that might be used by corporate accounts by sending fliers and other promotional literature to corporations, banks, insurance companies, and other local businesses. Don't forget to include doctors, dentists, lawyers, and other professional people.

sweet sixteen parties, showers, weddings, corporate parties, high school reunions, bar mitzvahs, fund-raising events, golf tournaments, or an array of other events. You need to be detail-oriented and creative to come up with interesting and unique themes.

- **Gardening service.** Many people want beautiful gardens, but either don't like to garden or don't have time for the task. If you love working outside and enjoy working with flowers, this is a great business. How can you get clients? Drive around your area and get the addresses of homes with big yards. Send promotional literature announcing your service. You might also consider corporate clients to handle gardens outside their offices and businesses.

- **Personal chef service.** Do you like to cook, but don't want to get into the whole catering thing? Consider a hot home career as a personal chef. There is an expanding market for personal chefs and it's expected to grow tremendously. Why do people use personal chefs? They may work hard all day and not feel like coming home and cooking. They may not want to eat out frequently. They may have special dietary needs or personal likes and dislikes. Or they may not be able to cook for themselves.

What you do as a personal chef depends on your specific situation; but you generally prepare meals either in your client's home or in another kitchen. Many personal chefs prepare a week's worth of meals that may be frozen and reheated during the week.

As part of your job, you meet with clients and discuss their dietary requirements as well as their personal likes and dislikes. You might prepare main dishes or you might be asked to cook full meals.

Think you live in an area where you might not have enough clients? Get creative. People might not give loads of parties all winter, but everyone has to eat dinner every night. What about preparing and delivering meals to families of working mothers? What about preparing five nights of meals, freezing them, and delivering them to families so that all that needs to be done is to pop them in the oven? What about preparing meals for seniors and selling the service to their adult children who don't live in the area? You need a hook or an angle for success. Look for it instead of giving up.

- **Dessert service.** Do you prefer baking instead of cooking? Do people invite you to their party so you will bring dessert? There's a great market for bakers too.

To get clients, you might want to give a tasting party. Send out invitations to people you think are potential clients and let them know you have embarked on a new venture. Prepare samples of your baked goods and let everyone taste them. Make sure you also develop brochures or at least simple photocopied sheets of your service, products, and prices. You might also try peddling your desserts to better restaurants in your area.

Want to try another idea to get potential clients to know your product? Volunteer to bake desserts or your specialty for a nonprofit fundraiser. The trick is letting people know what you do and what your business is. The expense and

Moneysaver
In most localities, you can't use your primary kitchen to prepare food for commercial use. Churches, synagogues, and other nonprofit groups often rent out their kitchens at a nominal charge.

Bright Idea
A great way for people to get to know you and your services is by holding an open house with samples of your food for community leaders, prominent citizens, and corporate business people.

time you spend in donating or volunteering is as useful as advertising. And remember, people trust their own experience more than any advertisement.

Put a new spin on a baking business. Start a dessert delivery service. Are pies, cakes, or cookies your specialty? Bake some, then put a slice of cake, piece of pie, or couple of cookies on a paper plate, add a plastic fork, and put them into a pretty bag with a flier telling about your products, pricing structure, phone, and fax number. Obtain new customers by delivering these samples to office buildings in your area. Let people in offices order their mid-afternoon snacks or desserts to take home.

▪ **Catering service.** Do you love to cook? Does your food make people's mouths water? Consider a hot home business in catering. Why is catering such a hot home career? The most important reason is because if you really enjoy cooking, catering gives you the opportunity to turn a hobby into a business. There's also a great need for caterers today. Many people who enjoy entertaining either don't have time to prepare food or don't like to cook.

You can specialize in various types of parties or events or even types of cuisine. Some caterers handle cocktail parties, while others handle weddings and other large events. The choice is yours.

There are many ways to make money at home; you just need the desire and commitment. There is a great deal of support for home business owners, including magazines, associations, and books.

Today, people don't look down on those who run home businesses, they envy them.

It's important to remember that even in your own home business, things might go wrong. Even if you are the best boss ever, you might get on your own nerves at times. Things will get better. Think and act positively. Be dedicated. You have to be willing to put in extra time. This is your business, your success. You will see the fruits of your labors if you try hard enough. Don't give up and don't give in. If you give up, you're never going to get what you want. And guess what? Someone else who didn't give up will. You have to hang on to your dreams and believe in yourself. You can be successful in your home business career, but you have to try or it won't happen.

Moneysaver
You can start a catering business with relatively low overhead. While it's nice to have industrial equipment and cookware, it's not essential. To avoid huge start-up costs, you can often rent important items such as dishes, china, glassware, and silverware.

Just the facts

- You need to determine if you will be successful in a home business.

- A home business can be the answer to layoffs, downsizing, and unemployment.

- A home business offers you opportunities you might not have working for someone else.

- You need to be willing to put in time and effort to make your business succeed.

- Choose a home business you love using your skills, talents, and dreams.

GET THE SCOOP ON...
Pleasing others to please yourself ▪ Working in
customer service ▪ Entertaining people ▪
Becoming a star in your own space ▪
Sporting careers

People Pleasers

S ome people like to please others. It makes them happy. Did you know that there are a whole slew of people-pleasing careers in various industries where you can actually get paid to make people happy? You might consider, for example, a hot career in customer service. Working in this area, you might take people who are disgruntled with a product or service and help them become happier and more satisfied with the item.

Would you prefer working in entertainment? The main job of entertainers is to keep people entertained and to make them happier. A good entertainer is always a people pleaser.

Or have you always dreamed of working in the sports industry? You just have to look at a stadium full of fans to realize that those in the sports industry are people pleasers.

This chapter will cover a plethora of people-pleasing careers. Check them out. One of them might be yours for the taking.

Careers in customer service

Do you believe the old adage, the customer is always right? If so, consider a hot career in customer service. Customer service is very important to business today.

There is a great deal of competition in every industry. The difference between customers returning and going to a competitor can mean the difference between success and failure to any business. Good customer service is often the answer.

What types of industries use customer service? Every industry needs it. Here are a few possibilities:

- Hospitality

- Travel

- Food and beverage

- Retail

- Banking

- Insurance

- Health care

- Real estate

What type of jobs can you find working in customer service?

- Customer service manager

- Customer service training manager

- Customer service trainer

- Quality assurance representative

- Mystery shopper

- Customer service representative

- Customer service training consultant

Let's look at these careers in more depth.

- **Customer service managers.** The customer service manager is in charge of handling the customer service needs of a company. In this job you may supervise a staff or be a one-person department. In some situations, you are expected to write either internal or external customer service materials. Depending on the specific employment setting, you may handle customer complaints either in person, by phone, or via mail. You might do this yourself or supervise a staff of customer service reps.

■ **Customer service training managers.** In this job you develop interesting and innovative programs for trainers and/or employees of the company. Depending on the specific job, you may be responsible for overseeing a staff. In smaller companies, you may also be expected to present programs.

■ **Customer service trainers.** In this job you train others in the company to give the best possible customer service. You need to be able to speak in front of groups in a confident, interesting, and motivational manner.

■ **Quality assurance representatives.** In this job you make sure the products and/or services of a company are up to par. You may conduct inspections, interviews, and surveys and report your results.

■ **Mystery shoppers.** This is a neat job. What do you do? Depending on your employer, you get to shop in stores or perhaps visit restaurants, hotels, or other locations to see what kind of service you receive. No one in the store or other location knows you are working. As a mystery shopper you evaluate how you are greeted, the quality of the service, the friendliness and helpfulness of employees, the length of time it takes

> **"**
>
> I used to work in customer service in another part of the tourism industry. I transferred my skills and now work as a customer service representative in leisure travel instead. I love my job because it's very rewarding. I enjoy talking to our guests and helping to meet their needs for their visits to our Harrahs property in Las Vegas. Even though I'm based in Memphis, I know I'm helping people all over the country plan a great time in Las Vegas.
> —Robbie Neal, Customer Service Representative, Harrahs Teleservice Center, Memphis, TN.
>
>

Bright Idea
Mystery shoppers may be employed by consulting firms or work for the companies themselves. There are full- and part-time jobs available. Contact the corporate offices of large retail companies to see if there are jobs available.

to check out, and so on. You then fill out a form to report your results.

- **Customer service representatives.** Customer service reps are very important to a company. In this position, you are expected to represent your company and provide not only information and answers, but goodwill as well. The customer service representative is the person customers usually contact when they are billed incorrectly, have poor service, or have a problem with a product. Customer service representatives also take orders from customers. They may work in a variety of settings.

  As a customer service rep you have the power to make a customer happy. It's up to you to try to help the customer and find ways to keep them satisfied. In this type of job, you may deal with customers face-to-face or work over the phone.

  In order to be successful in this job, you must be able to stay calm, cool, and collected at all times, even when customers are irate. It's also essential to be able to listen to customers and provide answers and solutions. Sometimes you can handle the problem on your own; other times, you may need to contact another person in the company to take care of the problem.

- **Customer service training consultants.** Many companies use outside training consultants to handle their customer service training needs. In some situations, outside consultants are even used to augment company-run programs. The key in this type of position is developing interesting, informative, and effective programs. As in any other consulting business, in addition to performing your service, you need to find ways to market and sell it. If you are good at what you do and market your services, you can build up a great consulting business in this area.

In addition to actual customer service careers, there are a multitude of jobs that require customer service skills in a wide array of areas. These might include:

- Bank tellers
- Billing clerks
- Cashiers
- Counter clerks (in any industry)
- Rental clerks (in any industry)
- Credit clerks
- Dispatchers
- Financial services sales representatives
- Flight attendants
- Pilots
- Food and beverage service workers
- Restaurant managers
- Office clerks
- Receptionists
- Secretaries
- Hotel and motel desk clerks
- Hotel and motel managers
- Insurance agents
- Manufacturer's representatives
- Wholesale sales representatives
- Messengers
- Real estate agents

Bright Idea
If you are interested in becoming a customer service consultant, consider specializing in a specific area. For example, you might specialize in the customer service needs of telephone call centers, the hospitality industry, or the health care industry.

66
It takes hours to get a customer, and just seconds to lose one.
—Anonymous
99

- Recreation workers
- Reservation agents
- Transportation ticket agents
- Retail sales workers
- Retail store managers
- Securities sales representatives
- Casino employees
- Telephone operators
- Travel agents

What type of personality traits and skills do you need to provide good customer service?

- Patience
- Listening skills
- Communications skills
- Calmness
- Good judgment
- People skills

Standing ovations: Entertaining careers

Keeping customers happy is one way to be a people pleaser. Want to be a people pleaser in another industry? Consider the entertainment industry.

Are you a born entertainer? The main job of entertainers is pleasing people. Nothing is more gratifying and fulfilling to an entertainer than performing and having people enjoy the performance. Even a seasoned pro loves a standing ovation!

What can you do if you want to be an entertainer? Well, a great deal of that has to do with your talent:

- Can you sing?
- Can you dance?
- Can you act?

Unofficially...
While the television shopping channel QVC's name stands for quality, value, and convenience, they are best known for their great customer service.

- Are you good at telling jokes and funny stories?
- Can you perform magic tricks and illusions?
- Can you play an instrument?
- Can you juggle?

Once you know where your talents lie, you can decide what you want to do and determine if and how you can make a living doing it.

For example, let's say you can sing. What are some of your options in entertainment?

- Lounge singer
- Backup singer
- Club singer
- Opera singer
- Chorus singer
- Singer in recording group
- Solo recording artist
- Singer in show group
- Singer in theatrical performance
- Singer of jingles (in commercials)
- Singing telegram messenger

Where can you find employment?

- Nightclubs and lounges
- Cruise ships
- Hotels and motels
- Casinos
- Bars
- Coffeehouses and cafes
- Opera houses
- Concert halls
- Private functions

66

I've been playing the piano since I was 5 years old in Philadelphia. I consider myself very lucky and successful too. For the past eight years I've been living and performing in Las Vegas. I have two steady jobs at local restaurants here and I'm free to take extra bookings when they come along. I do something I love on a daily basis and get paid for it too.
—David Morris, Entertainer at the Golden Gate Casino and Piero's, Las Vegas, NV

99

- Recording studios
- Singing messenger services
- Theaters
- Dinner theaters

Many aspiring singers hold down jobs in other industries while honing their craft. They may work in the daytime, for example, and then perform in clubs at night. Others obtain jobs singing at parties or private events on the weekends or during holiday periods.

There are also individuals who make demos, send them out to producers and record companies, or present showcases in an effort to attract the attention of people who can help them attain success.

Can't sing? Prefer to act? What are your options?

- Daytime or soap opera actor/actress
- Nighttime television actor/actress
- Television extra
- Movie or film actor/actress
- Movie extra
- Broadway theater actor/actress
- Dinner theater actor/actress
- Television commercial actor/actress

Remember that in any facet of entertainment, you usually have to pay your dues. Most people are not overnight sensations. It's also important to know that you don't necessarily have to be a top recording artist to earn a living in the music business or star in a Broadway show to make a living acting. This is not to say that it wouldn't be nice; it just doesn't have to be. There are many singers and musicians who earn good livings performing in dinner clubs or hotel lounges.

Bright Idea
Remember that the better known you are as an entertainer and the more you are in demand, the greater your compensation. If you can't afford a publicist, be your own press agent. Keep your name in the public eye in a positive manner as much as possible.

Take it from the pros. Says Earl Nesmith, singer/musician, "I was the musical director of a famous 1950s recording group for several years. I play keyboards and sing. I finally decided that I wanted to travel less and play more of the type of music I wanted to play. For the last eight years I have performed in the Helmsley Hotel in Sarasota, Florida. I make a comfortable living and am having more fun than ever before. Instead of traveling all over to perform for people, now I stay in one place and people from all over the world come and see me perform there."

Every entertainer is not going to be famous, and just because an entertainer is not famous does not mean he or she is not successful. Many build up large loyal followings and become stars in their own right.

Success in entertainment, as in everything else, is relative. For some, having the opportunity to work full-time and make a living as an entertainer is success enough. To others, the need for celebrity status is necessary to feel successful.

What are some of the qualities that make people successful entertainers no matter what the area?

- Talent
- Stage presence
- Confidence
- The ability to please an audience
- Charisma
- Dedication
- Ability to perform in front of an audience
- Ability to deal with rejection
- Versatility

Singing is my greatest joy. It fills my soul and sets me free. I would do it for nothing, but it's a hell of a lot better to get paid for it.
—Carrie Dean, Singer

■ Reliability

■ Perseverance

In addition to careers revolving around singers, musicians, actors, and actresses, what are some other hot options to please people as an entertainer? Let's look at a few possibilities:

■ Magician

■ Comedian

■ Celebrity impersonator

■ Clown

■ Dancer

■ Motivational speaker

■ Acrobat

■ Circus act

Now let's look at a few of these in more depth.

Magicians

If you've ever heard the "oohs" and "ahhs" when a magician performs an illusion, you know that good magicians are certainly people pleasers. Are you an amateur magician, looking to turn your passion into a career?

Well, if you work at it, it can happen. You need to put an act together and then practice, practice, practice. Nothing is worse than having an audience member yell out, "I see how you did that." Once you have your act developed, try it out on your family and friends. Once you feel ready, start looking for bookings.

How can you find bookings?

■ Place small ads in the entertainment section of your local newspaper.

■ Look in the newspaper and phone book for leads on clubs you might contact.

- Call entertainment directors of hotels.

- Contact hotel convention sales managers. They may know of conventions that are looking for an act.

- Contact trade associations to inquire about entertainment needs for their annual meetings or conventions.

- Consider putting up fliers at a local party store.

- Look for a booking agent.

What else should you do? It's a good idea to put together a brochure and/or press kit about your act, places you have appeared, and perhaps some testimonials from satisfied clients. Make sure you include a professional 8 × 10 photo of yourself. You can send your brochure to potential clients after you have spoken to them, or you can send brochures cold, without contacting the potential client first.

When you do get hired, be careful. Make sure you have a written agreement or contract with the people or organization hiring you to perform. Among other things, contracts should specify the date, time, and length of the engagement, as well as the address where it will be held. It should also stipulate your fee and how and when you will be paid.

You might want to speak to an attorney and have him or her draw up a basic contract for you to use. Without a signed agreement, you don't have a leg to stand on if someone doesn't pay your fee.

Want to get a full-time job as a magician? If you live in an area with magic shops that's a good possibility. Many magic shops hire magicians to work as sales associates. As an extra benefit, you get to see all the new magic tricks and illusions when they arrive. You might even get a store discount.

Unofficially...
Most successful magicians have more than just good technique. Many, such as Penn and Teller, use a "patter" (prepared monologue) which is as important as the magic tricks themselves.

Moneysaver
Get free exposure for yourself and your act by volunteering your services to a local nonprofit fund-raiser. Not only will you showcase your act to everyone attending the event, your name will probably appear in all the pre-event and post-event publicity.

Comedians

They say that laughter makes the world go 'round. Do you like to make people laugh? Were you the class clown in school? Do you think you might want a career as a comedian?

Comedians often begin their careers in comedy clubs. Comedy clubs or "open mikes" (in which anyone can come on stage) offer great opportunities to get experience working in front of an audience as well as working out new material. Even established comedians often appear at comedy clubs to try out new acts.

Motivational speakers

Let's say you can't sing, you don't act, and while you can tell a few jokes, you really couldn't make an act out of it. Is there any other way you can entertain?

You can if you have a talent for talking. Do you motivate others? Inspire them? Do people tend to be riveted by what you say? You might want to consider a hot career as a motivational speaker.

While everyone wouldn't look at motivational speakers as entertainers, in essence, that is exactly what they are. Motivational speakers are very hot in today's society. One of the best-known is Anthony Robbins, creator of the Personal Power program. Robbins travels around the world motivating people to be their personal best. And when he does, a charisma surrounds him everywhere he goes.

What makes a good professional motivational speaker?

- You are comfortable speaking in front of a group.
- You have one or more interesting topics you can talk about.

- You can move an audience with your words.

- You are inspirational.

- Your speeches are interesting and motivational.

- Your presentations are entertaining.

Celebrity impersonators

Do you look like a celebrity? Do you want to capitalize on it? If so, you might consider becoming a celebrity imposter or look-alike. There are impersonators of actors, actresses, politicians, singers, and every other public figure you can think of.

In this type of career you generally work on a freelance basis, although there are hotels and theaters that produce reviews using celebrity look-alikes. You may appear at private parties, conventions, trade shows, and special events. Sometimes you are asked to take photos with guests, walk around and mingle, or pose in exhibit booths.

Cities hosting large conventions and trade shows often offer many opportunities for celebrity impersonators. Contact the Convention Bureau in your area for information on conventions coming to your city.

If you look *and* sound like a celebrity, you are even more marketable. Singers are especially marketable because they can perform complete shows of the stars they are impersonating.

Some popular celebrities who are often impersonated include:

- Elvis

- Barbra Streisand

- Sonny & Cher

- Marilyn Monroe

- The President

Bright Idea
There's a difference between a true pro and an amateur speaker. If you need some pointers and extra confidence speaking in front of groups, consider joining a local Toastmasters club before jumping into this type of career.

Timesaver
There are many talent agencies throughout the country specializing in booking celebrity look-alikes and imposters. Check your local Yellow Pages under "Talent Agencies" or "Booking Agencies" for leads.

Unofficially...
There are a number of Elvis impersonators performing around the country who are earning over one million dollars annually.

There are a wide array of careers in the entertainment industry. Whether you choose to be an actual entertainer, work in one of the many support services, or in another area of the industry entirely, you will be helping to please others.

Goals you can achieve: Sporting careers

Whether people are participating in sports or watching them, sports are a form of entertainment. Sporting activities are people pleasers.

What are some of the most coveted careers in sports?

- Professional baseball player
- Professional football player
- Professional basketball player
- Professional hockey player
- Professional soccer player

People in these careers tend to enjoy fame, fortune, and everything that goes with it. How hard is it for everyday people to become involved in these careers? Well, it's not easy, that's for sure. Competition is stiff in professional sports. But that doesn't mean if you have talent in these areas, you shouldn't try.

Every sports star started somewhere. Why can't you? Where would Michael Jordan, Wayne Gretzky, Mark McGwire, Sammy Sosa, or Mia Hamm be if they thought they couldn't make it? Where would their careers be if they never tried?

What can you do to improve your chances?

- Practice, practice, practice.
- Attend clinics, camps, and workshops to hone your skills.

- Try to find a coach or mentor to help you make contact with the pros, agents, or scouts.

- If you are in college, get on the team. Scouts and agents often check out college teams.

Professional boxing is another hot sports career. This is another one of those careers where if you make it, you can have multimillion-dollar paydays.

Today, opportunities even exist for women. Most successful professional fighters start out as amateurs and work their way up the ranks before they turn pro. Your chances of becoming a professional boxer are actually better than becoming a pro in most of the other spectator sports.

Want to really make someone happy? Become a professional scout. These individuals seek out athletes for professional sports teams. You travel all over looking for new talent. When you find it, you make the athlete happy as well as the team for which you work.

Are you good at business? Are you a great negotiator? Want to make a sports star really happy? Become a professional sports agent. In this type of career, you act on behalf of athletes and negotiate deals for them. Among other duties, you negotiate big deals for sports stars' contracts, as well as those mega-buck product endorsements. In return, you usually get a percentage of your client's income. If you represent major sports stars, this can be a very lucrative career.

What are some other hot careers in the sports industry that are people pleasers?

- Coach
- Sportswriter

Bright Idea
Looking for the names and addresses of professional sports teams? Log on to www.hoovers.com. For example, go to www.hoovers.com/lists/baseball.html for pro baseball teams. Also check out league sites, such as www.nfl.com and www.nhl.com.

Bright Idea
If you have your heart set on a hot career in pro sports, attend a college that puts an emphasis on their sports program, and then get on the team.

- Newspaper or magazine sports editor
- Sports publicist
- Sports photographer

From professional athletes to teachers, coaches, writers, store owners, therapists, agents, and managers, the sports industry has hundreds of job opportunities. You might have to use your creativity to find a hot career, but if you really want it, it's worth the effort.

Just the facts

- Careers that make others happy may also please you.

- If you believe the customer is always right, consider a career in customer service.

- You can have a hot career in the music industry even if you aren't a top recording artist.

- There are a wide array of careers in entertainment for you to choose from.

- There are many opportunities to work in the sports industry other than as a professional athlete.

GET THE SCOOP ON...
Meeting people in the workplace ▪ Working with
animals ▪ Careers working with kids ▪
Hot careers everyone wants

Looking for Love in All the Right Places

There are all kinds of love. There is romantic love, the love you feel for your family, the love you feel for your friends, the love for pets or other animals, the love of a job…and the list goes on. You can find love almost everywhere you look—if you look in the right places.

Did you know you can look for love even when you work? You spend a great deal of time at work every day. The workplace is a great environment to begin new relationships, whether they be platonic or romantic. You might even meet a potential spouse.

Are you an animal lover? Would it make you happy to have a career working with animals in some capacity? Do you wish your career could involve preventing animals from being exploited or hurt? Would it surprise you to find out that there are many careers that make a difference in the well-being of animals?

Maybe it's kids that pull at your heartstrings. Is it a dream of yours to work with children in some

Chapter 18

415

Unofficially...
Meeting people is a numbers game. The more people you meet, the better your chances of forging a friendship.

manner? There are some interesting options. You just have to look.

Perhaps you simply wish you had a career you couldn't help but love. In this chapter I'll cover some hot possibilities in all these categories. Maybe one will be right for you.

Hot careers meeting people to like and people to love

Studies have shown that the more social contact and relationships people have, the longer and healthier their lives. One of the fringe benefits of many jobs is the ability to meet others. Let's look at a couple of scenarios:

1. You're single. After spending eight or more hours at work, you want to relax, meet new people, or go out. Today, however, it's becoming increasingly difficult to meet new people with similar interests. The bar scene may be fine for some, but you're tired of it. What can you do?

2. You're not single. You may be married, engaged, or in a committed relationship. But you still want to meet new people and make new friends. Where can you meet others?

One way to get around these problems is to meet people either at work or through work. Whether your job offers you the opportunity to meet more people in general or meet more interesting people, it certainly is an added fringe benefit.

One of the most important aspects of any relationship, whether platonic or romantic, is to have things in common. Whether the common threads of a relationship are goals, interests, or values, certain employment settings offer great opportunities to meet people who share something that's important to you.

What are some examples of places you can work where you can meet more people? Look around and you'll find those places:

- **Large corporations.** Just by virtue of their size, these companies offer more opportunities to meet people.

- **Hospitals.** Health-care facilities employ a lot of people with different skills, talents, and education.

- **Cruise lines.** If you like to travel, this affords you the opportunity to do so, and to meet other employees as well as interesting new people every time a cruise takes off.

- **Casinos.** Casinos employ large numbers of people in all adult age groups, in jobs both on and off the gaming floor. People who work in casinos are generally customer service–oriented and enjoy being in a hospitality setting (and enjoy people).

- **Resorts.** Resorts, especially large ones, employ people in a variety of areas, in all skill and education levels.

- **Executive search firms.** Even if your organization is small, working in this environment enables you to meet people searching for better jobs as well as potential employers. A bonus is that you know the background of the people you meet.

- **Schools.** Schools usually have a turnover every school year leading to the requirement for new teachers, counselors, and other workers. The need for new employees means there are new people to meet every year.

- **Colleges and universities.** The world of academia is one unto itself. If you're interested in meeting people who value education and like the campus life, this might be the work setting for you.

- **Bookstores.** People who work in bookstores generally enjoy reading. Those who visit bookstores usually like to read, too. Many bookstores even have events such as mixers or singles nights where people can get together.

- **Outside sales in any industry.** Outside salespeople get to meet a lot of different people. Hopefully, you are working in an industry in which you have an interest.

- **Health clubs.** Today, a lot of people visit health clubs not only to exercise and get fit, but to socialize. Working in a health club or gym, you meet others interested in health and fitness.

- **Advertising or public relations agencies.** If you're looking for other creative people with whom to socialize, agencies—especially mid- to large-sized ones—are filled with creative people.

- **Meeting planners.** These individuals meet new people while traveling to do on-site inspections at sites such as hotels, conference centers, and restaurants. They also meet all their conference attendees, speakers, seminar presenters, and vendors.

- **Tour group escorts.** If you want to meet new people and travel too, you might enjoy a job as a tour escort. If you are single and want to meet other singles, consider working for an organization that arranges singles tours.

■ **Television or radio show guest coordinators.** This is an exciting job if you want to meet people who have probably done interesting things.

If you want to meet new people in your workplace, there are some things you can do to increase your chances:

■ Take advantage of every opportunity.

■ Many companies have employee activity programs; make sure you participate.

■ Go to employee picnics and other social functions.

■ Don't be afraid to say hello to someone you don't know.

■ Bring in homemade goodies to share with your coworkers.

Meeting people at work or through work is a good idea not only for social contacts, but for your career. The more people you meet, the more opportunities you have to network. It's also wise to give business cards to everyone you meet. If you are interested in forging a more personal type of relationship, write your home phone number on the card. It's OK to ask a business associate or client if they would like to get together after work to socialize. To make the situation more comfortable, if you don't know someone well you might say, "Let's go out after work for dinner, Dutch treat." With this approach there is no awkwardness afterwards on who pays the check.

Another great way to get to know more people in your company is to offer to help collect information for the employee newsletter.

Whatever happens, don't talk about coworkers or your supervisor to others in your workplace. It's unprofessional and will probably get back to them.

Watch Out!
Some people feel that office romances are not a good idea. If you are dating a coworker, remember it's important to always act professionally in the workplace.

Careers for animal lovers

Do you love being around animals? Would you like to have a career where you could make a difference in their lives? There are many careers that involve working with animals. What would you like to do? What are your dreams and desires? Once you determine those, you can make sure you have the skills, education, and training needed to get a job in your chosen field.

Veterinarians

Has it always been your dream to work as veterinarian? When you were younger, did you bring home stray animals in need of assistance and nurse them back to health?

Veterinarians work with animals of various sizes. Some take care of domestic animals such as dogs and cats; others work more with farm animals or wild animals.

Many vets perform general veterinary medicine. What do they do? Vets have a multiplicity of functions and duties. These might include:

- Giving animals annual checkups
- Administering tests
- Giving immunizations
- Performing examinations to diagnose illness
- Prescribing treatment
- Performing surgery
- Spaying or neutering animals
- Setting bones
- Handling preventative medicine

Vets can work in a variety of settings:

- Private practice
- Veterinary clinics

Bright Idea
Volunteer to work on employee events in your workplace. This will give you a greater chance to meet new people as well as make you visible so others will want to meet you too.

- Animal shelters
- Animal refuges
- Zoos
- Sanctuaries

To become a vet, you must attend and graduate from an accredited college of veterinary medicine as well as pass a state board examination in the state in which you intend to practice.

Veterinary technicians

Want to work closely with animals, but don't really want to go through six years of veterinary school? Consider a job as a vet technician. In this job, you assist vets, much the way nurses help doctors.

What do you do as a vet technician? That depends on your specific job and your training. In many cases you perform many of the same functions as vets, with the exception of diagnosing medical problems, performing surgery, and prescribing medications. However, you work with the veterinarian assisting in these functions.

Some of your other responsibilities might include:

- Monitoring animals and reporting any problems to the vet
- Keeping tabs on an animal's physical symptoms
- Keeping tabs on an animal's psychological attitude
- Comforting animals in physical or emotional pain
- Giving animals special attention
- Preparing animals for surgery

Bright Idea
To be successful in veterinary medicine, you need a genuine commitment to working with and helping animals. You should also be compassionate, sensitive, and have a way with animals.

Bright Idea
To learn more about careers in veterinary medicine, contact the American Veterinary Medical Association (AVMA) toll-free at (800) 248-2862 or on the Web at www.avma.org, or the Association of Veterinarians for Animal Rights (AVAR) at (530) 759-0208, or on the Web at www.envirolink. org/arrs/avar/ avar-www.htm.

- Assisting with anesthesia and surgery
- Drawing blood
- Administering tests
- Collecting specimens to check for diseases

  Where can you work?

- Animal hospitals
- Clinics
- Veterinary offices
- Zoos
- Shelters
- Humane societies
- Sanctuaries

Careers in animal rights

A living thing does not have to be a human being to have feelings. It has been proven that animals have feelings and experience many of the emotions that we do. What does this mean?

- They experience joy.
- They experience happiness.
- They experience emotional pain.
- They experience physical pain.

Do you think you might want to work in the animal rights field? People who love animals usually feel that animals, like people, should have the right to live their lives with dignity. They also believe that animals have the right to live without being subjected to cruelty, abuse, unnecessary pain, or exploitation. If you share these ideals, you might be a prime candidate to work in the field.

Think there aren't any paying jobs in animal rights? Think again. There are a variety of jobs available that use a multitude of skills. In order to succeed in this field, you need the dedication to treat animals humanely and compassionately, and to stop their abuse and exploitation.

Basically, any job you have working on behalf of animals is working in animal rights. Working for animal rights does not necessarily mean you are an activist, throwing paint on people's fur coats or letting test animals out of their cages. What it means is you are working to make sure animals aren't abused or exploited.

Where can you find a job working in animal rights? There are a number of settings:

- Animal rights organizations

- Humane societies

- Animal shelters

- Sanctuaries

- Animal refuges

If you want to work in animal rights, become a member of one or more animal rights organizations, humane societies, animal shelters, or rescue leagues. These memberships help you make important contacts in the industry.

Let's look at some specific career areas in these organizations:

- Administration

- Public relations

- Publishing and writing

- Fund-raising and development

- Organization membership

- Research and investigation

- Education and outreach

Bright Idea
If you are just entering the field, it's often easier to locate a position in a smaller animal rights organization to get experience, get on-the-job training, and make contacts. You can then move up to a larger or more prestigious organization.

Watch Out!
It takes 40 dead raccoons, 120 non-target animals, and 2,400 hours of agony to make one raccoon coat! It takes 60 dead mink, 180 non-target animals, and 3,600 hours of agony to make one mink coat! It takes 42 dead foxes, 126 non-target animals, and 2,520 hours of agony to make one fox coat! (Information provided by Friends of Animals)

Bright Idea
Internships are very useful when preparing for a career in the administration of animal rights organizations. Contact organizations you are interested in working with to see if internships are available.

- Special events
- Business and finance
- Law
- Grants
- Lobbying
- Personnel and human resources
- Clerical

Now let's look at a few of these areas in more depth.

- **Administration.** Animals rights organizations are usually classified as nonprofit organizations. They are not publicly owned. Money earned by the organization is put back into the organization to pay for services, buy equipment, or run the organization.

    One of the main items on the agenda for animal rights organizations is determining what their issues, causes, and platforms will be. The function of the administration of an animal rights organization is making sure the organization runs efficiently while developing ways to meet its specific policies and goals.

    What types of jobs are available in the administration of an animal rights organization?

    Executive director. This is an important position in the animal rights organization. As the executive director, you have a direct liaison with the board of directors. You work with them to develop policies and issues as well as carry out the orders of the board. You are also ultimately responsible for the overall management of the organization.

Assistant executive director. This individual assists the executive director to fulfill the responsibilities of the organization. Depending on the organization and its structure, the assistant director may supervise the fund-raising, public relations, lobbying, or volunteer force. The assistant executive director may also be responsible for making many of the day-to-day decisions.

Field directors. Not every organization has field directors, but those that do employ them to manage satellite offices in other parts of the country or the world.

Administrative assistants. In this position you may work with the executive director, the assistant executive director, field director, or department head. What do you do in this job? Responsibilities vary, but basically you assist with coordinating the services of the specific department, handle clerical or secretarial duties, and possibly do research.

Directors or managers of departments. You may be the manager or director of the public relations department, be in charge of volunteers, fund-raising and development, or any other area.

■ **Public relations.** Almost every organization uses public relations in one form or another. The PR department of an animal rights organization is expected to help spread the word about its issues, goals, and projects. The public relations department is responsible for developing press releases, feature stories, and special request articles for the media. The staff may also develop and write newsletters, magazines, and internal

Bright Idea
When considering which animal rights organizations to work with, choose one with causes and issues that you strongly believe in.

and external publications. In some instances, the PR department is asked to write speeches and put together informational kits, press kits, and other media for the general public. They may also arrange press conferences or be official spokespeople for the organization.

The staff size of the PR department may vary, depending on the size and structure of the group. Positions in this area include:

Public relations director

Assistant public relations director

Promotion staffer

Publicist

Writer

Photographer

- **Writing and publishing.** In many organizations, there is a department dedicated to writing and publishing a gamut of internal and external publications. These might include:

Newsletters

Magazines

Brochures

Annual reports

Legislative alerts

Leaflets

- **Fund-raising and development.** As animal rights organizations are not usually publicly funded, they depend to a great extent on donations and contributions. Fund-raising departments of large animal rights organizations may employ a director, one or more assistants, and staff members. Smaller groups may have just a director of fund-raising to handle that chore. What does the fund-raising staff do?

Develops and implements fund-raising programs

Seeks annual gifts from individuals

Seeks annual gifts from corporations

Seeks grants

Writes grants

■ **Research and investigation.** Animals are often mistreated, abused, or exploited. In some cases someone sees the problem and decides to help by calling an animal shelter, humane society, the Society for the Prevention of Cruelty to Animals (SPCA), or other animal rights organization. Organizations usually have a research and investigation office that looks into these problems. While laws, rules, and regulations exist to protect animals in this country, many are ignored or violated. The research and investigation department does a number of things when they receive a call:

They investigate the charge.

They look into the laws to see if they are being violated.

They make authorities aware of the situation.

They press charges which help effect change.

Depending on the size, structure, and budget of a group, it may be a one-person office or there may be an entire staff.

Possible jobs in this area include:

Director of research and investigation

Assistant director of research and investigation

Bright Idea
Contact the National Society of Fund Raising Executives (NSFRE) for more information about a career in fund-raising and development. You can call toll-free (800) 666-FUND or log on to their Web site at www.nsfre.org.

Unofficially...
Bob Barker, host
of television's
game show *The
Price Is Right*,
gave up a lucra-
tive contract as
host of a tele-
vised beauty
contest because
fur coats were
given away as
prizes. Barker
further promotes
animal rights by
ending every
show by telling
people to help
control the pet
population by
spaying or neu-
tering their pets.

Investigator

Caseworker

Researcher

No matter which area of an animal rights organization you are interested in, you will be making a
tremendous difference in the lives of animals. If you
truly love animals, this is a very fulfilling career area
in which to work.

Careers working with animals in shelters

There are a number of other careers you might consider if you enjoy working with animals. These
include:

- **Shelter director.** This individual is in charge of
  the administration of a shelter and its operation,
  including working with the board of directors to
  develop policies, philosophies, and programs.

- **Shelter manager.** This individual is responsible
  for the operation of the shelter. In this capacity,
  the manager hires, trains, and supervises the
  staff, maintains the facility, makes sure adop-
  tions are done according to policy, and ensures
  that investigations are handled correctly.

- **Humane educator.** This is a very hot job that
  enables you to make a huge difference in the
  way people treat animals. The humane educator
  is responsible for teaching people how to treat
  animals in a caring and compassionate manner.
  Humane educators may do presentations in a
  number of settings, including schools or meetings of civic groups. They may also appear on
  television and radio shows or write columns for
  the print media talking about the care and treatment of animals. In many cases, humane educators develop programs for people of all ages and

walks of life on the humane treatment of animals.

Hot careers working with kids

Do you have a special place in your heart for children? Would it make you happy to have a career working with them? There are many career options, depending on your skills, talents, education, and desires.

What would you like to do? No matter what industry you're interested in working in, there's usually a way you can work with kids.

- Interested in becoming a doctor? Want to work with children? You can have a hot career as a pediatrician.

- Is nursing your dream career? Wish you could work with kids? Think about specializing in pediatric nursing.

- Want to work in a resort? Consider becoming a director of children's activities.

- Do you like to write? You might think about writing children's books.

- Are you a talented artist? Nothing makes a children's book more appealing than great pictures. Consider becoming an illustrator.

- Want to work in law enforcement? Juvenile officers can often make the difference between kids getting in trouble and staying out of trouble.

- Interested in law? You might want to specialize in protecting the rights of children.

- Do you want to work in interior design? You might want to carve out a career in designing nurseries and children's rooms.

Watch Out!
There is a difference between working with animals and being involved in animal rights. There are jobs that have contact with animals, but you might be asked to do unpleasant things. For example, some animal shelters kill the animals they house or send them to animal testing labs.

Bright Idea
Read parenting and children's magazines to get more ideas of careers working with children. Sometimes you just need to see a need that you can fill to come up with a great idea.

- Are you a crafter? Come up with some unique products, toys, clothing, or furniture for infants, babies, toddlers, or older children.

As you can see, all you have to do is think about the concept a little and get creative. You can find a way to develop a career working with children.

Let's discuss a few other possibilities. Are you interested in teaching? There are a vast array of opportunities in this area. We already covered some of them in Chapter 7.

In addition to teaching in a secondary or high school, you may want to teach in a preschool venue. If you love young children and want to help mold their minds in a positive way, this is a great opportunity to do so. Nothing is more gratifying than seeing a youngster's excitement when he learns something.

Let's say you want to teach children in a less traditional fashion. Consider offering classes for children in areas in which you have expertise, such as cooking, baking, sewing, repairing things, crafts, or playing an instrument.

Child care is another very hot option, whether you're running a child-care service from your home or working in someone else's. What do you do in this type of career? Responsibilities include:

- Keeping children safe
- Reading to children
- Planning and executing activities that stimulate children's minds
- Serving meals and/or snacks
- Playing with children

Want some other options working with youngsters? Here are some possibilities:

- Children's photographer
- Children's party planner
- Director of children's camp
- Director of children's educational programs at a museum

What else can you do? You might want to be a nanny. Families hire nannies to help care for their children for a variety of reasons:

- Parents may both work long hours.
- The family may be a single-parent household with the single parent working long hours.
- Both parents may travel extensively.
- The parents may want or need help caring for their children.

What do you do as a nanny? Basically you live in and care for the children in a household. You may travel with the family while they are on vacation or while the parents are on business trips or stay home with the kids. You really need to be good with kids as well as enjoy being around them to be successful in this type of career.

Because nannies spend a great deal of quality time with children, they often develop strong bonds with them. In many situations, nannies become part of the family and stay in contact with the children they've cared for even after they have grown up. While it's not essential to go to "nanny school," it may be helpful. Not only will you get valuable training, but families tend to contact schools when they are looking for a suitable nanny.

Careers you can't help but love

We've talked about all types of careers in this book. What I've stressed throughout is the importance of

Bright Idea
There are employment services you can contact to find work especially geared towards nannies.

Bright Idea
To find out more about becoming a nanny, contact the American Council of Nanny Schools at (517) 686-9417 or the National Academy of Nannies toll-free at (800) 222-NANI.

finding a job you love. I've also mentioned a number of times that all people's ideas of the ideal job are not the same. A career you might love might be one your neighbor would not.

Every career has advantages and disadvantages. Even the best careers have a couple of negatives to deal with. But if you're doing something you love, the negatives are always easier to deal with.

Finding a career you love means putting your dreams and desires together with your skills, talents, and training; taking action; and then not giving up. Everyone has a dream of a career they wish they were involved with, one they're sure they would love. To some, they're fantasy careers. Just remember that if you have a dream and a goal and work toward attaining it, nothing is impossible.

Do you ever look at someone and say to yourself, "Oh, is he [or she] lucky. I'd love to have his [or her] job!" If you're like most others, you probably have. If you could be doing any job in the world, what would it be? One that was exciting? One that made you a fortune? One that made you famous? There are a number of careers many think they couldn't help but love. Let's look at a few of them:

- A top recording artist
- A hot rock-and-roll singer
- A hot country singer
- A lead daytime soap opera actor/actress
- A sizzling hot television actor/actress
- A movie star
- Television talk show host
- Author of a best-selling book
- Model

- Host on QVC or other cable shopping channel

- The head writer of a number one soap opera

- A successful writer of hit sitcoms

    You might say, no one can get these jobs. They're unattainable. Well you're wrong. Elton John, Ricky Martin, Madonna, Michael Jackson, Janet Jackson, the Backstreet Boys, and others have all attained success as top recording artists. Mick Jagger has been a hot rock-and-roll singer for years. Collin Raye, Vince Gill, Shania Twain, and Wynonna are all hot country singers.

    Should I go on? Who hasn't heard of Susan Lucci, the daytime soap opera actress; or television stars Bill Cosby, Michael J. Fox, and Jimmy Smits? Movie stars from John Wayne to Marilyn Monroe attained success on the silver screen and many more continue to do so every year.

    Here are some other careers people can't help but love:

- **Location managers.** As a location manager, you search for the perfect locations for television shows or movies. You also negotiate fees to use the location as well as obtain permits.

- **Contestant coordinators.** Did you ever wonder how television game shows get their contestants? In this job you work for producers of television game shows, finding contestants, fielding, screening, testing, and interviewing applicants, arranging mock games, and telling them about the rules.

- **Tour managers for a recording act.** As tour manager, you travel with the band all over the country and possibly the world. You handle their arrangements and help decide who gets

Unofficially...
Do you know who Kathy Levine is? How about Steve Bryant, Bob Bowersox, Mary Beth Roe, or Pat James Dimentri? Together they have probably told more people in America about more products and been responsible for millions of dollars in sales. Who are these people? Some of the most popular hosts on television's QVC.

66
Persevere. Don't give up. The reason most people fail is that they gave up one day too early.
—Shelly Field
99

Bright Idea
For more information on careers for the creative, see Chapter 10.

close to the act and who doesn't. You take care of all the problems, go to all the parties, deal with the media, and coordinate everybody and everything. It's an exhausting job, but it's more fun than you can imagine.

- **Comedians.** Do you like to make people laugh? Do you like to entertain? Comedians have the opportunity to make others laugh by telling jokes, performing skits, or telling stories.

- **Motivational speakers.** You travel around the country, inspiring and motivating others to be the best they can be and getting paid for it.

- **Singing messengers.** If you are an entertainer at heart, this is a fun job. You work for a messenger service delivering messages to recipients while singing.

- **Ring conductors.** You know how when you go to the circus there's a person who introduces acts into the ring? This is the ring conductor.

- **Ring announcers.** The ring announcer works in a boxing ring, announcing the contenders in a boxing match as well as the results. Probably the most well-known ring announcer is Michael Buffer.

Bright Idea
For more information on becoming a clown, contact Clowns of America toll-free at (888) 522-5696 or on the Web at www.clown.org, or contact the Ringling Brothers and Barnum & Bailey Clown College.

- **Clowns.** You may work in a circus or may be self-employed doing shows. The great part of your job is you always make people happy. You dress up in costume and perform routines or skits.

- **Advice columnists.** Is everyone always asking for your advice? Do you like to write? Ann Landers, Dear Abby, and Miss Manners are famous for giving advice. You can write great columns too.

- **Crossword puzzle creators.** These individuals create the puzzles and the clues.

- **Chocolatiers.** If your passion and talent is chocolate, this can be a great job. You create chocolate confections. Not only will you love your job, everyone will love you.

- **Candy makers.** In this job you make all types of candy and confections, from chocolate to taffy to brittles. This is another job where everyone adores you.

- **Ice cream tasters.** Do you love ice cream? As an ice cream taster, it's your job to ensure quality control as well as work with new flavors being developed.

Rosie O'Donnell, Regis Philbin, Kathie Lee Gifford, Leeza Gibbons, Oprah Winfrey, Maury Povitch, Sally Jesse Raphael, Jay Leno, and David Letterman have all attained success as talk show hosts.

None of these people gave up and neither should you. No matter what job you are searching for, what your career aspirations are, or what type of job you think you want, go after it.

Just the facts

- Some workplaces offer more opportunities for meeting new people than others.

- Take advantage of every opportunity to meet new people at work and through your job.

- You can have a hot career working with animals.

- There are an array of career opportunities working in animal rights.

- If you're creative, you can find a career working with children in many industries.

- You can have a career you can't help but love if you work at it and don't give up.

Glossary

action plan   Specific actions you plan on taking to achieve a goal.

advertising red book   This book has the names, addresses, and phone numbers of advertising agencies all over the world. Other information includes the volume of business each agency handles annually. Its formal name is the *Standard Directory of Advertising Agencies*.

Arbitron ratings   A rating service for television and radio stations that illustrates the percentage of the population viewing or listening to specific shows or stations. Commercials on television and radio are often based on Arbitron ratings.

Associated Press (AP)   A news wire service. See also **wire services**.

b & w glossy   Designates a black-and-white photograph used for reproduction purposes in newspapers or magazines.

bio   Short for biography.

blind ad   Advertisements found in the classifieds that don't mention a company name.

book   A portfolio or collection of artwork or writing samples used to illustrate talent to prospective clients or employers.

brochure   A selling piece that gives information about a product, place, or event (among other things). You can use a brochure with information about yourself to help make yourself stand out from other employees.

buyer's agent   A term used in real estate transactions. Buyer's agents represent the buyer, not the seller. Most agents are seller's agents. When a real estate transaction goes through, the *buyer,* not the seller, pays the commission.

C.P.A.   Certified public accountant.

career fair   An event or gathering of one or more companies used to meet, interview, and hire employees. Career fairs also consist of professionals in a variety of careers gathering in a location such as a school or college to help others explore careers in various areas.

career objective   This is what you want your career to accomplish. It's okay to have different career objectives on different resumes for different types of jobs.

career plan   A plan to help you move your career in a positive direction.

classifieds   The section of a newspaper containing advertisements for employment opportunities.

complementary care   A form of medicine and treatment that complements traditional therapies.

cross platforms   In computers, software that is compatible with PC technology as well as Macintosh.

dailies   Newspapers published on an everyday basis.

direct mail advertising   Advertising and promotional materials mailed to consumers.

downsized Refers to being let go from a company when it is tightening up for financial or other reasons.

EEG Electroencephalograph; measures the effects of strokes and disease on the brain.

EKG Electrocardiogram; diagnoses a patient's heart.

elder care Taking care of older adults.

executive search firm A company that hires high-level employees for businesses or corporations.

feature story An article or human interest story about a specific subject feature in a newspaper or magazine or on a radio or television station.

five Ws of press releases Information that should be included when writing a press release: who, what, when, where, and why.

flex time A category of work in which your working hours are not fixed.

freelance writing Writing on an independent or freelance basis (as opposed to a permanent job).

getting motivated Having a desire to be or do something better and acting on it in a positive fashion.

graphics Artwork, photographs, drawings, and so on, used in brochures, advertisements, or other publications.

head hunters Recruiters.

hidden job market Jobs that are not advertised in the traditional manner.

hobby or leisure-time skills These are skills you learn and have used in hobbies or leisure-time activities. These skills may often be transferred and used in a new job or career.

hot job journal A journal you keep of the positive actions you take daily to obtain a better job or improve the job you currently have.

HTML Hypertext Markup Language, used in writing Web pages.

Internet search engine Site that allows you to search for specific information on the Internet or find a specific Web site. Some search engines use software that searches for words you type into the search engine; others are directories that provide lists of Web sites under cascading topical headlines.

job hopping Job-hoppers are those who frequently change jobs.

job satisfaction Enjoying your job.

job sharing Two people sharing the job of one person.

job skills Skills you use in a job.

L.P.N. Licensed practical nurse.

lateral career change Taking a job on the same career level instead of moving upwards. People often make a lateral change to learn new skills or for more job satisfaction.

law clerk A lawyer who works for a judge on county, state, and federal levels doing his or her research.

life skills These are skills you use in living. Problem solving, money management, time management, decision making, and interpersonal skills are examples. More specific life skills might include cooking, child rearing, and home repair.

LSAT Law School Admission Test.

media The media includes newspapers, magazines, radio stations, and television stations.

mentor A person who can help guide your career and your life.

millennium One thousand years.

Monday-Morning Blues club People who often get depressed at the beginning of the work week because they don't enjoy their job are said to belong to this club. Also see **TGIF.**

Net   The Internet.

networking   Meeting people and making contacts.

news editor   This is the person you contact at a newspaper, radio, or television station to see if she is interested in a specific news story. You might, for instance, contact the news editor to see if the paper wants to cover a speech you are giving at a trade show.

outplacement programs   A program offered to employees of a specific company who are leaving the company.

part-time job   A job in which you don't work full-time.

paying your dues   Paying your dues may mean that you have to take a job that you don't like for a short time to obtain experience, training, or new skills, so that you can get to the job you really want.

podiatrist   A doctor who cares for feet.

portfolio   A collection of artwork or writing samples used to illustrate talent and potential to prospective clients or employers.

PR   Public relations.

practice interviews   These can be either mock (practice) interviews or those you go on where you don't really care if you get the job. Practice interviews are used to get experience in the interviewing process and help build confidence.

press kit   A promotion kit containing photographs, promotional materials, and publicity on a person, product, or service. Usually used by publicists or public relations people to publicize clients.

prioritizing   Determining what tasks are most important to handle first.

programming languages Used to write computer programs.

promo Short for promotion.

PSAs Public service announcements.

R.N. Registered nurse.

recruiter A person whose job it is to hire people for companies.

resume A written selling piece detailing your accomplishments.

Reuters A news wire service. See also **wire services.**

seller's agent A term used in real estate transactions. Seller's agents represent the seller, not the buyer. Most agents are seller's agents. When a real estate transaction goes through, the *seller,* not the buyer, pays the commission.

severance package A package offered when an employee is fired, laid off, or let go from a job that may include pay, benefits, and services. Under certain circumstances, people who resign may also receive severance packages.

severance pay Pay you receive when you are fired, laid off, or let go from a job.

spec. Speculation. Writers often do articles on spec, which means they write the article before an editor has agreed to buy it.

stock resume cover letter A letter that is generic in nature and can easily be changed for each specific job for which you apply.

surf the Net Looking for information on the Internet.

taking the initiative Not waiting for someone to ask you to handle a project. If you see something that you think should be done and that would help make your workplace or company better, offer to handle it or at least make the suggestion.

talent Talent is what you are born with. You can embellish on talent.

team player Working well with your coworkers toward a common goal.

technical skills These are skills you have that include the use of machinery, such as cars, trucks, computers, sewing machines, cameras, or word processors.

telecommuter An employee who works all or part of the work week from home.

telecommuting Working all or part of the time from home.

temp agencies Employment agencies that specialize in finding work for temporary employees and filling temp positions for companies.

temping A work classification in which you have a temporary position at a company.

TGIF Thank God It's Friday.

tooting your own horn Telling people about your accomplishments.

trades Magazines, newspapers, and other publications that deal with specific industries.

transferable skills These are skills you have used on one job that you can transfer to a new job.

UPI United Press International. See also **wire services.**

URL Universal Resource Link. An address on the Internet.

virtual job fair A job fair you view on the World Wide Web.

Webmaster The person who develops and puts together Web sites.

weeklies Newspapers published once a week (as opposed to a daily publication).

wire services   News-gathering services such as UPI, AP, and Reuters, that, for a fee, provide the media with news stories.

World Wide Web (WWW)   The Internet's multimedia form (as opposed to e-mail).

Resource Guide

The following is a listing of trade associations, unions, and organizations you might find useful in obtaining information on the careers discussed in this book. Names, addresses, and phone numbers are included so that contact can be made for information regarding membership, conferences, seminars, internships, or career guidance. Fax numbers, Web site addresses, and e-mail addresses are also included when available. Web sites can provide you with a wealth of information with the click of a mouse.

Appendix B

Academy of Country Music (ACM)
6255 Sunset Blvd.
Suite 923
Hollywood, CA 90028
Phone: (213) 462-2351
Fax: (213) 462-3253

Accreditation Council for Accountancy and Taxation (ACAT)
1010 N. Fairfax St.
Alexandria, VA 22314-1574
Phone: (703) 549-2228
Fax: (703) 549-2984
Toll-Free: (888) 289-7763
E-mail: info@acatcredentials.org
URL: www.acatcredentials.org

Accrediting Bureau of Health Education Schools (ABHES)
803 W. Broad St.
Suite 730
Falls Church, VA 22046
Phone: (703) 533-2082
E-mail: abhes@erols.com
URL: abhes.org/accredit.html

Accrediting Council on Education In Journalism and Mass Communications (ACEJMC)
Stauffer/Flint Hall
University of Kansas
Lawrence, KS 66045
Phone: (785) 864-3986
URL: www.ukans.edu/~acejmc

Acoustical Society of America (ASA)
500 Sunnyside Blvd.
Woodbury, NY 11797
Phone: (516) 576-2360
Fax: (516) 576-2377
E-mail: asa@aip.org

Actors and Others for Animals (A&O)
11523 Burbank Blvd.
North Hollywood, CA 91601-2309
Phone: (818) 755-6323
Fax: (818) 755-6048

Actors' Equity Association (AEA)
165 W. 46th St.
New York, NY 10036
Phone:(212) 869-8530
Fax: (212) 719-9815
E-mail: aeisenberg@actorsequity.org

Advertising Club of New York (ACNY)
235 Park Ave. S., 6th Floor
New York, NY 10003
Phone: (212) 533-8080
Fax: (212) 533-1929

Advertising Research Foundation (ARF)
641 Lexington Ave.
New York, NY 10022
Phone: (212) 751-5656
Fax: (212) 319-5265
E-mail: email@arfsite.org
URL: www.arfsite.org

Advertising Women of New York (AWNY)
153 E. 57th St.
New York, NY 10022
Phone: (212) 593-1950
Fax: (212) 759-2865
E-mail: awny85@aol.com

Aerobics Center (see Cooper Aerobics Center)

Aerobics and Fitness Association of America (AFAA)
15250 Ventura Blvd.
Suite 200
Sherman Oaks, CA 91403
Phone: (818) 905-0040
Fax: (818) 990-5468
Toll-Free: (800) 446-AFAA
URL: www.afaa.com

Affiliated Advertising Agencies International (AAAI)
2289 South Zanadu Way
Aurora, CO 80014
Phone: (303) 671-8551

African Wildlife Foundation (AWF)
1400 16th St. NW
Suite 120
Washington, DC 20036
Phone: (202) 939-3333
Fax: (202) 939-3332
Toll-Free: (800) 344-TUSK
E-mail:
awfwash@igc.apc.org
URL: www.awf.org

Air Conditioning Contractors of America (ACCA)
1712 New Hampshire Ave.
NW Washington, DC 20009
Phone: (202) 483-9370
Fax: (202) 588-1217
URL: www.acca.org

Air Transport Association of America (ATA)
1301 Pennsylvania Ave.
Suite 1100
Washington, DC 20004-7017
Phone: (202) 626-4000
Fax: (202) 626-4166
URL: www.air-transport.org

Airline Pilots Association
3375 Koapaka St.,
No. F238-10
Honolulu, HI 96819-1800

Alaska Wildlife Alliance
P.O. Box 202022
Anchorage, AK 99520-2022
Phone: (907) 277-0897
Fax: (907) 277-7423
E-mail:
alaskawa@igc.apc.org

Alliance for Animals
232 Silver St.
Boston, MA 02127
Phone: (781) 648-6822
Fax: (617) 269-0455

Allied Pilots Association (APA)
P.O. Box 5524
Arlington, TX 76005
Phone: (972) 988-3188
Fax: (972) 606-5668
Toll-Free: (800) 323-1470

American Academy of Actuaries
1100 17th St. NW, 7th Floor
Washington, DC 20036
Phone: (202) 223-8196
Fax: (202) 872-1948

American Academy of Environmental Engineers (AAEE)
130 Holiday Ct., No. 100
Annapolis, MD 21401
Phone: (410) 266-3311
Fax: (410) 266-7653
E-mail: aaee@ea.net
URL: www.enviro-engrs.org

American Academy of Physician Assistants (AAPA)
950 N. Washington St.
Alexandria, VA
22314-1552
Phone: (703) 836-2272
Fax: (703) 684-1924
E-mail: aapa@aapa.org
URL: www.aapa.org

American Advertising Federation (AAF)
1101 Vermont Ave. NW
Suite 500
Washington, DC 20005
Phone: (202) 898-0089
Fax: (202) 898-0159
URL: www.aaf.org

American Anti-Vivisection Society (AAVS)
801 Old York Rd.
Suite 204
Jenkintown, PA 19046
Phone: (215) 887-0816
Fax: (215) 887-2088
Toll-Free: (800) SAY-AAVS
E-mail:
aavsonline@aol.com
URL: www.aavs.org

American Artists Professional League (AAPL)
47 5th Ave.
New York, NY 10003
Phone: (212) 645-1345

AACSB—The International Association for Management Education
600 Emerson Rd.
Suite 300
St. Louis, MO 63141-6762
Phone: (314) 872-8481
Fax: (314) 872-8495
URL: www.aacsb.edu

American Association for Adult and Continuing Education (AAACE)
1200 19th St. NW
Suite 300
Washington, DC 20036
Phone: (202) 429-5131
Fax: (202) 223-4579
URL:
www.albany.edu/aaace

American Association for the Advancement of Science (AAAS)
1200 New York Ave. NW
Washington, DC 20005
Phone: (202) 326-6400
URL: www.aaas.org

American Association of Advertising Agencies (AAAA)
405 Lexington Ave.
18th Floor
New York, NY 10174-1801
Phone: (212) 682-2500
Fax: (212) 682-8391
URL: www.actuary.org/

American Association of Blood Banks (AABB)
8101 Glenbrook Rd.
Bethesda, MD 20814
Phone: (301) 907-6977
Fax: (301) 907-6895
E-mail: aabb@aabb.org
URL: www.aabb.org

American Association for Clinical Chemistry (AACC)
2101 L St. NW, Suite 202
Washington, DC 20037
Phone: (202) 857-0717
Fax: (202) 887-5093
Toll-Free: (800) 892-1400
E-mail: info@aacc.org
URL: www.aacc.org

American Association of Colleges of Osteopathic Medicine (AACOM)
5550 Friendship Blvd.
Suite 310
Chevy Chase, MD
20815-7231

Phone: (301) 968-4100
Fax: (301) 968-4101

American Association of Colleges of Pharmacy (AACP)
1426 Prince St.
Alexandria, VA 22314
Phone: (703) 739-2330
Fax: (703) 836-8982
E-mail: prtaacp@aol.com
URL: www.aacp.org

American Association of Colleges of Podiatric Medicine (AACPM)
1350 Piccard Drive
Suite 322
Rockville, MD 20850
Phone: (301) 990-7400
Fax: (301) 990-2807
E-mail:
aacpmas@aacpm.org
URL: www.aacpm.org

American Association of Dental Examiners (AADE)
211 E. Chicago Ave.
Suite 760
Chicago, IL 60611
Phone: (312) 440-7464
Fax: (312) 440-3525

American Association of Dental Schools (AADS)
1625 Massachusetts Ave. NW
Suite 600
Washington, DC 20036
Phone: (202) 667-9433
Fax: (202) 667-0642
E-mail: aads@aads.jhu.edu
URL: www.aads.jhu.edu

American Association of Homes and Services for the Aging (AAHSA)
901 E Street NW
Suite 500
Washington, DC
20004-2001
Phone: (202) 783-2242
Fax: (202) 783-2255
E-mail:
members@aahsa.org
URL: www.aahsa.org

American Association of Medical Assistants (AAMA)
20 N. Wacker Dr.
Suite 1575
Chicago, IL 60606-2903
Phone: (312) 899-1500
Fax: (312) 899-1259
Toll-Free: (800) 228-2262
URL: www.aama-ntl.org

American Association of Nurse Anesthetists (AANA)
222 S. Prospect
Park Ridge, IL 60068-4001
Phone: (847) 692-7050
Fax: (847) 692-6968
URL: www.aana.com

American Association for Paralegal Education (AAFPE)
P.O. Box 40244
Overland Park, KS 66204
Phone: (913) 381-4458
Fax: (913) 381-9308
E-mail: sabanske@aol.com

American Association for Respiratory Care (AARC)
11030 Ables Lane
Dallas, TX 75229-4593
Phone: (972) 243-2272
Fax: (972) 484-2720
E-mail: info@aarc.org
URL: www.aarc.org

American Association of Retired Persons (AARP)
601 E St. NW
Washington, DC 20049
Phone: (202) 434-2277
Fax: (202) 434-2320
Toll-Free: (800) 424-3410
URL: www.aarp.org/

American Bar Association (ABA)
750 N. Lake Shore Dr.
Chicago, IL 60611
Phone: (312) 988-5000
Fax: (312) 988-5528
Toll-Free: (800) 285-2221

American Bed and Breakfast Association (ABBA)
P.O. Box 1387
Midlothian, VA
23113-8387
Phone: (804) 379-2222
Fax: (804) 379-1469
Toll-Free: (800) 769-2468

American Board of Registration of EEG and EP Technologists (ABRET)
P.O. Box 916633
Longwood, FL 32791
Phone: (407) 788-6308

**American Cetacean
Society (ACS)**
P.O. Box 1391
San Pedro, CA 90733
Phone: (310) 548-6279
Fax: (310) 548-6950
E-mail: acs@pobox.com
URL: www.acsonline.org

**American Chemical
Society (ACS)**
1155 16th St. NW
Washington, DC 20036
Phone: (202) 872-4600
Fax: (202) 872-4615
Toll-Free: (800) 227-5558
E-mail: meminfo@acs.org
URL: www.acs.org

**American Chiropractic
Association (ACA)**
1701 Clarendon Blvd.
Arlington, VA 22209
Phone: (703) 276-8800
Fax: (703) 243-2593
Toll-Free: (800) 986-4636
URL: www.amerchiro.org

**American Choral
Directors Association
(ACDA)**
P.O. Box 6310
Lawton, OK 73506
Phone: (405) 355-8161
Fax: (405) 248-1465
URL: www.ACDAonline.org

**American College of
Health Care
Administrators (ACHCA)**
325 S. Patrick St.
Alexandria, VA 22314
Phone: (703) 739-7900

Fax: (703) 739-7901
Toll-Free: 888-88A-CHCA
E-mail: info@achca.org
URL: www.achca.org

**American College of
Healthcare Executives
(ACHE)**
1 N. Franklin
Suite 1700
Chicago, IL 60606-3491
Phone: (312) 424-2800
Fax: (312) 424-0023
URL: www.ache.org

**American College of
Nurse-Midwives (ACNM)**
818 Connecticut Ave.
Suite 900
Washington, DC 20006
Phone: (202) 728-9860
Fax: (202) 289-9897
E-mail: info@acnm.org
URL: www.midwife.org

**American Compensation
Association (ACA)**
14040 N. Northsight Blvd.
Scottsdale, AZ 85260
Phone: (602) 951-9191
Fax: (602) 483-8352
E-mail: aca@acaonline.org
URL: www.acaonline.org

**American Composers
Alliance (ACA)**
170 W. 74th St.
New York, NY 10023
Phone: (212) 362-8900
Fax: (212) 362-8902
E-mail:
ACA@composers.com
URL: www.composers.com

American Correctional Association (ACA)
4380 Forbes Blvd.
Lanham, MD 20706-4322
Phone: (301) 918-1800
Fax: (301) 918-1900
Toll-Free: (800) 222-5646
URL:
www.corrections.com/aca

American Council of Nanny Schools (ACNS)
c/o Joy Shelton
Delta College
University Center, MI 48710
Phone:(517) 686-9417
Fax: (517) 686-8736

American Council on Pharmaceutical Education (ACPE)
311 W. Superior St.
Suite 512
Chicago, IL 60610
Phone: (312) 664-3575
Fax: (312) 664-4652

American Counseling Association (ACA)
5999 Stevenson Ave.
Alexandria, VA 22304-3300
Phone: (703) 823-9800
Fax: (703) 823-0252
Toll-Free: (800) 347-6647
URL: www.counseling.org

American Craft Council (ACC)
72 Spring St., 6th Floor
New York, NY 10012-4019
Phone: (212) 274-0630
Fax: (212) 274-0650
E-mail: council@
craftcouncil.org

American Culinary Federation (ACF)
10 San Bartola Dr.
P.O. Box 3466
St. Augustine, FL 32085-3466
Phone: (904) 824-4468
Fax: (904) 825-4758

American Dance Therapy Association (ADTA)
2000 Century Plaza
Suite 108
Columbia, MD 21044
Phone: (410) 997-4040
Fax: (410) 997-4048
E-mail: adta@aol.com
URL: www.ADTA.org

American Dental Assistants Association (ADAA)
203 N. LaSalle St.
Suite 1320
Chicago, IL 60601-1225
Phone: (312) 541-1550
Fax: (312) 541-1496
Toll-Free: (800) SEE-ADAA
E-mail: ADAA1@aol.com
URL: www.members.aol.
com/adaa1/index.html

American Dental Association (ADA)
211 E. Chicago Ave.
Chicago, IL 60611
Phone: (312) 440-2500
Fax: (312) 440-7494
E-mail:
publicinfo@ada.org
URL: www.ada.org

American Dental Hygienists' Association (ADHA)
444 N. Michigan Ave.
Suite 3400
Chicago, IL 60611
Phone: (312) 440-8900
Fax: (312) 440-6780
Toll-Free: (800) 243-ADHA
E-mail: mail@adha.net
URL: www.adha.org

American Design Drafting Association (ADDA)
P.O. Box 11937
Columbia, SC 29211
Phone: (803) 771-0008
Fax: (803) 771-4272
E-mail: national@adda.org
URL: www.adda.org

American Dietetic Association (ADA)
216 W. Jackson Blvd.
Suite 800
Chicago, IL 60606
Phone: (312) 899-0040
Fax: (312) 899-1979
URL: www.eatright.org

American Federation of Government Employees (AFGE)
80 F St. NW
Washington, DC 20001
Phone: (202) 737-8700
Fax: (202) 639-6441
E-mail: communications@afge.org

American Federation of Musicians of the United States and Canada (AFM)
1501 Broadway, Suite 600
New York, NY 10036
Phone: (212) 869-1330
Fax: (212) 764-6134

American Federation of State, County, and Municipal Employees (AFSCME)
1625 L St. NW
Washington, DC 20036
Phone: (202) 452-4800
URL: www.afscme.org

American Federation of Teachers (AFT)
555 New Jersey Ave. NW
Washington, DC 20001
Phone: (202) 879-4400
Fax: (202) 879-4545
Toll-Free: (800) 238-1133
E-mail: online@aft.org
URL: www.aft.org/

American Federation of Television and Radio Artists (AFTRA)
260 Madison Ave.
New York, NY 10016
Phone: (212) 532-0800
Fax: (212) 545-1328

American Forests
910 17th St. NW, No. 600
Washington, DC 20006
Phone: (202) 955-4500
Fax: (202) 955-4588
Toll-Free: (800) 368-5748
E-mail: member@amfor.org
URL: www.amfor.org

American Fund for Alternatives to Animal Research (AFAAR)
C/o Dr. Ethel Thurston
175 W. 12th St., No. 16-G
New York, NY 10011
Phone: (212) 989-8073
Fax: (212) 989-8073

American Geological Institute (IGI)
4200 King Street
Alexandria, VA
22302-1502
Phone: (702) 379-2480
URL: www.sba.gov

American Geophysical Union (AGU)
2000 Florida Ave. NW
Washington, DC 20009
Phone: (202) 462-6900
Fax: (202) 328-0566
Toll-Free:
(800) 966-AGU1
E-mail:
service@kosmos.agu.org
URL: www.agu.org

American Geriatrics Society (AGS)
770 Lexington Ave.
Suite 300
New York, NY 10021
Phone: (212) 308-1414
Fax: (212) 832-8646
Toll-Free: (800) 247-4779
E-mail: info.amger@
americangeriatrics.org
URL: www.
americangeriatrics.org

American Guild of Music (AGM)
250 Village Dr., No. 353
Downers Grove, IL
60516-3048
Phone: (630) 769-6154

American Guild of Musical Artists (AGMA)
1727 Broadway
New York, NY 10019
Phone: (212) 265-3687
Fax: (212) 262-9088

American Guild of Organists (AGO)
475 Riverside Dr.
Suite 1260
New York, NY 10115
Phone: (212) 870-2310
Fax: (212) 870-2163
Toll-Free: (800) AGO-5115
E-mail: info@agohq.org
URL: www.agohq.org

American Guild of Variety Artists (AGVA)
184 5th Ave.
New York, NY 10010
Phone: (212) 675-1003

American Health Care Association (AHCA)
1201 L St. NW
Washington, DC 20005
Phone: (202) 842-4444
Fax: (202) 842-3860
URL: www.ahca.org

American Health Information Management Association (AMRA)
919 N. Michigan Ave.
Suite 1400
Chicago, IL 60611
Phone: (312) 787-2672
Fax: (312) 787-9793
URL: www.ahima.org

American Horse Protection Association (AHPA)
1000 29th St. NW, T100
Washington, DC 20007
Phone: (202) 965-0500

American Hotel & Motel Association (AH&MA)
1201 New York Ave. NW
Suite 600
Washington, DC
20005-3931
Phone: (202) 289-3100
Fax: (202) 289-3199
E-mail: info@ahma.com
URL: www.ahma.com

American Humane Association (AHA)
63 Inverness Dr. E.
Englewood, CO 80112
Phone: (303) 792-9900
Fax: (303) 792-5333
URL:
www.americanhumane.org

American Institute of Aeronautics and Astronautics (AIAA)
C/O Michael Lewis
1801 Alexander Bell Dr.
Suite 500
Reston, VA 20191-4344
Phone: (703) 264-7500
Fax: (703) 264-7551
Toll-Free: (800) NEW-AIAA
E-mail:
customerserv@aiaa.org
URL: www.aiaa.org

American Institute of Architects (AIA)
1735 New York Ave. NW,
Washington, DC 20006
Phone: (202) 626-7300
Fax: (202) 626-7421

American Institute of Baking (AIB)
1213 Bakers Way
P.O. Box 3999
Manhattan, KS 66505-3999
Phone: (785) 537-4750
Fax: (785) 537-1493
E-mail: mailbox@
aibonline.org
URL: www.aibonline.org

American Institute of Biological Sciences (AIBS)
1444 I St. NW, Suite 200
Washington, DC 20005-2210
Phone: (202) 628-1500
Fax: (202) 628-1509
E-mail: jkolder@aibs.org
URL: www.aibs.org

American Institute of Certified Public Accountants (AICPA)
1211 Avenue of the
Americas
New York, NY 10036-8775
Phone: (212) 596-6200
Fax: (212) 596-6213
Toll-Free: (800) 862-4272
URL: www.aicpa.org

American Institute of Chemical Engineers (AICHE)
3 Park Avenue
New York, NY 10016
Phone: (212) 591-7338
Fax: (212) 752-3294
Toll-Free: (800) 242-4363
URL: www.aiche.org

American Institute of Chemists (AIC)
515 King St., Suite 420
Alexandria, VA 22314
Phone: (703) 836-2090
Fax: (703) 836-2091
E-mail: sdobson@
clarionmr.com
URL: www.theaic.org

American Institute of Graphic Arts (AIGA)
164 5th Ave.
New York, NY 10010
Phone: (212) 807-1990
Fax: (212) 807-1799
Toll-Free: (800) 548-1634

American Institute of Physics (AIP)
1 Physics Ellipse
College Park, MD 20740-3843
Phone: (301) 209-3100
Fax: (301) 209-0843
URL: www.aip.org

American Library Association (ALA)
50 E. Huron St.
Chicago, IL 60611
Phone: (312) 944-6780
Fax: (312) 280-3255
Toll-Free: (800) 545-2433
URL: www.ala.org

American Marketing Association (AMA)
250 S. Wacker Dr., Suite 200
Chicago, IL 60606
Phone: (312) 648-0536
Fax: (312) 993-7542
Toll-Free: (800) 262-1150
E-mail: info@ama.org
URL: www.ama.org

American Massage Therapy Association (AMTA)
820 Davis St., Suite 100
Evanston, IL 60201-4444
Phone: (847) 864-0123
Fax: (847) 864-1178
E-mail: info@inet.
amtamassage.org
URL: www.amtamassage.org

American Medical Association (AMA)
515 N. State St.
Chicago, IL 60610
Phone: (312) 464-5000
Fax: (312) 464-4184
URL: www.ama-assn.org

American Medical Technologists (AMT)
710 Higgins Rd.
Park Ridge, IL 60068
Phone: (847) 823-5169
Fax: (847) 823-0458
Toll-Free: (800) 275-1268
E-mail: amtmail@aol.com

American Meteorological Society (AMS)
45 Beacon St.
Boston, MA 02108-3693
Phone: (617) 227-2425
Fax: (617) 742-8718
E-mail: amspubs@
ametsoc.org
URL: www.ametsoc.org/AMS

**American Music
Conference (AMC)**
5790 Armada Drive
Carlsbad, CA 92008-4391
Phone: (760) 431-9124
Fax: (760) 438-7327
E-mail:
info@amc-music.com
URL: www.amc-music.com

**American Music Festival
Association (AMFA)**
12450 Whittier Blvd.
Whittier, CA 90602
Phone: (562) 945-5610
Fax: (562) 945-7520

**American Music
Scholarship Association
(AMSA)**
441 Vine St., Suite 1030
Cincinnati, OH 45202
Phone: (513) 421-5342
Fax: (513) 421-2672

**American Music Therapy
Association**
8455 Colesville Rd.
Suite 1000
Silver Spring, MD 20910
Phone: (301) 589-3300
Fax: (301) 589-5175
E-mail:
info@musictherapy.org
URL:
www.musictherapy.org

**American Newspaper
Publishers Association
Foundation (ANPAF)**
The Newspaper Center
11600 Sunrise Center
Reston, VA 22091
Phone: (703)648-1000

**American Nuclear Society
(ANS)**
555 N. Kensington Ave.
La Grange Park, IL 60526
Phone: (708) 352-6611
Fax: (708) 352-0499

**American Nurses
Association (ANA)**
600 Maryland Ave. SW
Suite 100 W.
Washington, DC
20024-2571
Phone: (202) 651-7000
Fax: (202) 651-7001
Toll-Free: (800) 637-0323
URL: www.nursingworld.org

**American Occupational
Therapy Association
(AOTA)**
4720 Montgomery Lane
P.O. Box 31220
Bethesda, MD 20824-1220
Phone: (301) 652-2682
Fax: (301) 652-7711
E-mail: praota@aota.org
URL: www.aota.org

**American Optometric
Association (AOA)**
243 N. Lindbergh Blvd.
St. Louis, MO 63141
Phone: (314) 991-4100
Fax: (314) 991-4101
URL: www.aoanet.org

**American Osteopathic
Association (AOA)**
142 E. Ontario St.
Chicago, IL 60611
Phone: (312) 202-8000
Fax: (312) 202-8200
Toll-Free: (800) 621-1773

American Physical Therapy Association (APTA)
1111 N. Fairfax St.
Alexandria, VA 22314
Phone: (703) 684-2782
Fax: (703) 684-7343
Toll-Free: (800) 999-2782
URL: www.apta.org

American Podiatric Medical Association (APMA)
9312 Old Georgetown Rd.
Bethesda, MD 20814
Phone: (301) 571-9200
Fax: (301) 530-2752
URL: www.apma.org

American Red Cross National Headquarters (ARC)
8111 Gatehouse Rd.
Falls Church, VA 22042
Phone: (202) 737-8300

American Registry of Diagnostic Medical Sonographers (ARDMS)
600 Jefferson Plaza
Suite 360
Rockville, MD 20852-1150
Phone: (301) 738-8401
Fax: (301) 738-0312
Toll-Free: (800) 541-9754
E-mail: sloper@ardms.org
URL: www.ardms.org

American Registry of Radiologic Technologists (ARRT)
1255 Northland Dr.
St. Paul, MN 55120
Phone: (612) 687-0048

American Society for Clinical Laboratory Science (ASCLS)
7910 Woodmont Ave.
Suite 530
Bethesda, MD 20814
Phone: (301) 657-2768
Fax: (301) 657-2909
URL: www.ascls.org

American Society for Information Science (ASIS)
8720 Georgia Ave.
Suite 501
Silver Spring, MD 20910-3602
Phone: (301) 495-0900
Fax: (301) 495-0810
E-mail: asis@asis.org
URL: www.asis.org

American Society for the Prevention of Cruelty to Animals (ASPCA)
424 E. 92nd St.
New York, NY 10128
Phone: (212) 876-7700
Fax: (212) 876-9571
URL: www.aspca.org

American Society for Training and Development (ASTD)
P.O. Box 1443
1640 King St.
Alexandria, VA 22313
Phone: (703) 683-8100
Fax: (703) 683-8103

**American Society of
Agricultural Engineers
(ASAE)**
2950 Niles Rd.
St. Joseph, MI 49085-9659
Phone: (616) 429-0300
Fax: (616) 429-3852
E-mail: hq@asae.org
URL: www.asae.org

**American Society of
Artists (ASA)**
P.O. Box 1326
Palatine, IL 60078
Phone: (312) 751-2500

**American Society of
Biological Chemists
(ASBC)**
9659 Rockville Pike
Bethesda, MD 20814
Phone: (301) 530-7145

**American Society of Civil
Engineers (ASCE)**
1801 Alexander Bell Dr.
Reston, VA 20191-4400
Phone: (703) 295-6000
Fax: (703) 295-6222
Toll-Free: (800) 548-2723
E-mail:
webmaster@asce.org
URL: www.asce.org

**American Society of
Clinical Pathologists
(ASCP)**
2100 W. Harrison
Chicago, IL 60612
Phone: (312) 738-1336
Fax: (312) 738-1619
Toll-Free: (800) 621-4142

**American Society of
Composers, Authors, and
Publishers (ASCAP)**
1 Lincoln Plaza
New York, NY 10023
Phone: (212) 621-6000
Fax: (212) 724-9064
URL: www.ascap.com

**American Society of
Cytopathology (ASC)**
400 W. 9th St., Suite 201
Wilmington, DE 19801
Phone: (302) 429-8802
Fax: (302) 429-8807
E-mail:
asc@cytopathology.org

**American Society of
Electroneurodiagnostic
Technologists (ASET)**
204 W. 7th St.
Carroll, IA 51401-2317
Phone: (712) 792-2978
Fax: (712) 792-6962
E-mail: aset@netins.org
URL: www.aset.org

**American Society of
Heating, Air
Conditioning, and
Refrigeration**
1105 Nothingham Hill
Round Rock, TX 78681
Phone: (512) 255-3146

**American Society of
Health System
Pharmacists (ASHP)**
7272 Wisconsin Ave.,
Bethesda, MD 20814
Phone: (301) 657-3000
Fax: (301) 657-1251

American Society of Interior Designers
608 Massachusetts Ave. NE
Washington, DC 20002-6006
Phone: (202) 546-3480
Fax: (202) 546-3240
E-mail asid@asid.org
URL: www.asid.org/

American Society of Magazine Editors (ASME)
919 3rd Ave.
New York, NY 10022
Phone: (212) 872-3700
Fax: (212) 906-0128

American Society of Mechanical Engineers (ASME)
345 E. 47th St.
New York, NY 10017
Phone: (212) 705-7722
Fax: (212) 705-7674
Toll-Free: (800) THE-ASME
E-mail:
infocentral@asme.org
URL: www.asme.org

American Society of Music Arrangers and Composers (ASMAC)
P.O. Box 11
Hollywood, CA 90078
Phone: (818) 994-4661
Fax: (818) 994-6181
E-mail:
tpi97@ix.netcom.com

American Society of Music Copyists (ASMC)
P.O. Box 2557
Times Square Station
New York, NY 10108
Phone: (212) 246-0488

American Society of Pension Actuaries (ASPA)
4350 N. Fairfax Dr.
Suite 820
Arlington, VA 22203
Phone: (703) 516-9300
Fax: (703) 516-9308
E-mail: aspa@pixpc.com
URL: www.aspa.org

American Society of Radiologic Technologists (ASRT)
15000 Central Ave. SE
Albuquerque, NM 87123
Phone: (505) 298-4500
Fax: (505) 298-5063
Toll-Free: (800) 444-2778
URL: www.asrt.org

American Society of Travel Agents (ASTA)
1101 King St.
Alexandria, VA 22314
Phone: (703) 739-2782
Fax: (703) 684-8319
URL: www.astanet.com

American Society on Aging (ASA)
833 Market St.
Suite 511
San Francisco, CA 94103-1824
Phone: (415) 974-9600
Fax: (415) 974-0300
E-mail:
info@asa.asaging.org
URL: www.asaging.org

American Therapeutic Recreation Association (ATRA)
P.O. Box 15215
Hattiesburg, MS 39404
Phone: (601) 264-3413
Fax: (601) 264-3337
Toll-Free: (800) 553-0304
E-mail: admin@atra-tr.org
URL: www.atra-tr.org

American Veterinary Medical Association (AVMA)
1931 N. Meacham Rd.
Suite 100
Schaumburg, IL 60173-4360
Phone: (847) 925-8070
Fax: (847) 925-1329
Toll-Free: (800) 248-2862
URL: www.avma.org

Animal Allies
P.O. Box 7040
Fairfax Station, VA 22039-7040
Phone: (703) 978-4462
Fax: (703) 425-6328
E-mail: allies@erols.com

Animal Legal Defense Fund (ALDF)
127 4th St.
Petaluma, CA 94952-3005
Phone: (707) 769-7771
Fax: (707) 769-0785
URL: www.aldf.org

Animal Rights International (ARI)
P.O. Box 214,
Planetarium Sta.
New York, NY 10024
Phone: (212) 873-3674
URL: www.ari-online.org

Animal Rights Mobilization
P.O. Box 805859
Chicago, IL 60680
Phone: (312) 381-1181
Fax: (312) 381-1182
E-mail: kayarm@earthlink.net

Animal Welfare Institute (AWI)
P.O. Box 3650
Georgetown Sta.
Washington, DC 20007
Phone: (202) 337-2332
Fax: (202) 338-9478
E-mail: awi@animalwelfare.com
URL: www.animalwelfare.com

Anti-Cruelty Society
157 W. Grand Ave.
Chicago, IL 60610
Phone: (312) 644-8338
Fax: (312) 644-3878
URL: www.anticruelty.org

Ark II—Canadian Animal Rights Network
P.O. Box 687, Sta. Q
Toronto, ON
Canada M4T 2N5
Phone: (416) 223-4141
Fax: (416) 730-8550

Art Directors Club (ADC)
250 Park Ave. S.
New York, NY 10003-1402
Phone: (212) 674-0500
Fax: (212) 460-8506
E-mail: adcny@interport. net
URL: www.adcny.org

Association for Business Communication (ABC)
Baruch College
17 Lexington Ave.
New York, NY 10010
Phone: (212) 387-1620
Fax: (212) 387-1655

Association for Computing Machinery (ACM)
One Astor Plaza
1515 Broadway
New York, NY 10036
Phone: (212) 869-7440
Fax : (212) 944-1318
E-mail:
ACMHELP@acm.org
URL: www.acm.org

Association for Computing Machinery, Special Interest Groups On Programming Languages (SIGPL)
One Astor Plaza
1515 Broadway
New York, NY 10036
Phone: (212) 869-7440
Fax: (212) 944-1318
E-mail:
ACMHELP@acm.org
URL: www.acm.org

Association for Gerontology in Higher Education (AGHE)
1030 15th St. NW
Suite 240
Washington, DC 20005
Phone: (202) 289-9806
Fax: (202) 289-9824

Association for Systems Management (ASM)
P.O. Box 38370
Cleveland, OH
44138-0370

Association for Women In Communications
1244 Ritchie Hwy., Suite 6
Arnold, MD 21012-1887
Phone: (410) 544-7442
Fax: (410) 544-4640
E-mail: pat@womcom.org

Association of American Law Schools (AALS)
1201 Connecticut Ave. NW
Suite 800
Washington, DC
20036-2605
Phone: (202) 296-8851
Fax: (202) 296-8869
E-mail: aals@aals.org
URL: www.aals.org

Association of American Medical Colleges (AAMC)
2450 N St. NW
Washington, DC 20037
Phone: (202) 828-0400
Fax: (202) 828-1125
E-mail:
webmaster@aamc.org
URL: www.aamc.org

Association of American Veterinary Medical Colleges (AAVMC)
1101 Vermont Ave.
Suite 710
Washington, DC 20005
Phone: (202) 371-9195
Fax: (202) 842-0773
E-mail: aavmc@aavmc.org
URL: www.aavmc.org

Association of Authors' Representatives (AAR)
10 Astor Place, 3rd Floor
New York, NY 10003
Phone: (212) 353-3709
URL: www.aar-online.org

Association of Computer Professionals (ACP)
9 Forest Dr.
Plainview, NY 11803
Phone: (516) 938-8223
Fax: (516) 938-3073
URL: www.acp-inter.org

Association of Flight Attendants (AFA)
1275 K St. NW
Washington, DC 20005-4090
Phone: (202) 712-9799
Fax: (202) 712-9798
Toll-Free: (800) 424-2401
URL: www.flightattendant-afa.org

Association of Ground Water Scientists and Engineers (AGWSE)
601 Dempsey Rd.
Westerville, OH 43081
Phone: (614) 898-7791
Fax: (614) 898-7786
Toll-Free: (800) 551-7379
URL: www.h20-ngwa.org

Association of Local Air Pollution Control Officials (ALAPCO)
444 N. Capitol St. NW
Suite 307
Washington, DC 20001
Phone: (202) 624-7864
Fax: (202) 624-7863

Association of Physician Assistant Programs (APAP)
950 N. Washington St.
Alexandria, VA 22314
Phone: (703) 548-5538
Fax: (703) 684-1924

Association of Schools and Colleges of Optometry (ASCO)
6110 Executive Blvd.
Suite 510
Rockville, MD 20852
Phone: (301) 231-5944
Fax: (301) 770-1828
E-mail: mwall@opted.org
URL: www.opted.org

Association of Surgical Technologists (AST)
7108-C S. Alton Way
Suite 100
Englewood, CO 80112-2106
Phone: (303) 694-9130
E-mail: ast@ast.org
URL: www.ast.org

Association of Talent Agents (ATA)
9255 Sunset Blvd.
Suite 930
Los Angeles, CA 90069
Phone: (310) 274-0628
Fax: (310) 274-5063
E-mail: agentassoc@aol.com

Association of Theatrical Press Agents and Managers (ATPAM)
1560 Broadway
New York, NY 10036
Phone: (212) 719-3666
Fax: (212) 302-1585
E-mail: atpam@erols.com

Association of University Programs in Health Administration (AUPHA)
1110 Vermont Ave. NW
Suite 220
Washington, DC
20005-3500
Phone: (703) 524-5500
Fax: (703) 525-4791

Association of Veterinarians for Animal Rights
P.O. Box 208
Davis, CA 95617-0208
Phone: (530) 759-0208
Fax: (530) 759-8116
E-mail: avarc@igc.apc.org
URL: www.envirolink.org/arrs/avar/avar-www.htm

Beauty Without Cruelty U.S.A. (BWC)
175 W. 12th St., No. 16-G
New York, NY 10011
Phone: (212) 989-8073

Bide-A-Wee Home Association
410 E. 38th St.
New York, NY 10016
Phone: (212) 532-6395
Fax: (212) 532-4210

Broadcast Music, Inc. (BMI)
320 W. 57th St.
New York, NY 10019
Phone: (212) 586-2000
Fax: (212) 956-2059

California Association of Acupuncture and Oriental Medicine
1231 State St., Suite 208-A
Santa Barbara, CA
93101-2629
Phone: (805) 957-4384
Fax: (805) 957-4389
Toll-Free:
(888) HEAL-NOW
E-mail: caaom@sb.net

Cardiovascular Credentialing International (CCI)
4456 Corporation Lane
Suite 120
Virginia Beach, VA 23462
Phone: (804) 497-3380
Fax: (804) 497-3491
Toll-Free: (800) 326-0268
E-mail: ccircvt@nettek.net

Career College Association (CCA)
750 1st St. NE, Suite 900
Washington, DC 20002
Phone: (202) 336-6700
Fax: (202) 336-6828
E-mail: cca@career.org
URL: www.career.org

Casino Management Association
3172 N. Rainbow
Suite 254
Las Vegas, NV 89108-4534
Phone: (702) 593-5477
Fax: (702) 837-5353
E-mail:
lasvegascma@juno.com
URL: www.cmaweb.org

Casualty Actuarial Society (CAS)
1100 N. Glebe Rd., Suite 600
Arlington, VA 22201
Phone: (703) 276-3100
Fax: (703) 276-3108
E-mail: office@casact.org
URL: www.casact.org

Center for Marine Conservation (CMC)
725 DeSales St. NW
Suite 600
Washington, DC 20036
Phone: (202) 429-5609
Fax: (202) 872-0619

Cetacean Society International (CSI)
P.O. Box 953
Georgetown, CT 06829
Phone: (203) 544-8617
Fax: (203) 544-8617
E-mail: 71322.1637@
compuserve.com
URL: elfi.com/csihome.html

Choreographers Guild (CG)
256 S. Robertson
Beverly Hills, CA 90211
Phone: (310) 275-2533
Fax: (213) 653-5608

Choreographers Theatre (CT)
94 Chambers St.
New York, NY 10007
Phone: (212) 227-9067
Fax: (212) 227-5895

Citizens to End Animal Suffering and Exploitation (CEASE)
P.O. Box 440456
Somerville, MA 02144

Phone: (617) 628-9030
Fax: (617) 628-9034

Civil Service Employees Association (CSEA)
143 Washington Ave.
P.O. Box 125
Albany, NY 12210
Phone: (518) 434-0191
Fax: (518) 462-3639
Toll-Free: (800) 342-4146

Clowns of America, International (COAI)
P.O. Box 6468
Lees Summit, MO
64064-6468
Toll-Free: (888) 522-5696
E-mail: barnettd@tgn.net
URL: www.clown.org

College of Osteopathic Healthcare Executives (COHE)
5550 Friendship Blvd.
Suite 300
Chevy Chase, MD
20815-7201
Phone: (301) 968-2642
Fax: (301) 968-4195

Committee on Accreditation for Respiratory Care
1701 W. Euless Blvd.
Suite 300
Euless, TX 76040
Phone: (817) 283-2835
Fax: (817) 354-8519
Toll-Free: (800) 874-5615
E-mail:
richwalker@coarc.com

Council for Early Childhood Professional Recognition (CECPR)
2460 16th St. NW
Washington, DC 20009
Phone: (202) 265-9090
Fax: (202) 265-9161
Toll-Free: (800) 424-4310
URL: www.cdacouncil.org

Committee for Humane Legislation (CHL)
2000 P St. NW, No. 415
Washington, DC 20036
Phone: (202) 296-2172
Fax: (202) 296-2190

Committee to Abolish Sport Hunting (C.A.S.H.)
P.O. Box 562
New Paltz, NY 12561
Phone: (914) 255-4227
Fax: (914) 256-9113
E-mail: wildwatch@
worldnet.att.net

Communications Workers of America, Local 4478 (CWA)
1464 Temple Rd.
Bucyrus, OH 44820
Phone: (419) 562-3535

Computer Aided Manufacturing International (CAM-I)
3301 Airport Fwy., No. 324
Bedford, TX 76021-6032
Phone: (817) 860-1654
Fax: (817) 275-6450

Computer and Communications Industry Association (CCIA)
666 11th St. NW
Suite 600
Washington, DC 20001
Phone: (202) 783-0070
Fax: (202) 783-0534
E-mail: ccianet@gte.net
URL: www.ccianet.org

Contact Center
P.O. Box 81826
Lincoln, NE 68501
Phone: (402) 464-0602
Fax: (402) 464-5931
Toll-Free: (800) 228-8813

Cooper Aerobics Center
12200 Preston Rd.
Dallas, TX 75230
Phone: (214) 239-7223
E-mail: coopermail@
cooperaerobics.com
URL:
www.coopercenter.com

Council for Advancement and Support of Education (CASE)
1307 New York Ave. NW
Suite 1000
Washington, DC 20005
Phone: (202) 328-5900
Fax: (202) 387-4973

Council of Fashion Designers of America (CFDA)
1412 Broadway, Suite 2006
New York, NY 10018
Phone: (212) 302-1821
Fax: (212) 768-0515

**Council on Chiropractic
Education (CCE)**
7975 N. Hayden Rd.
No. A-210
Scottsdale, AZ 85258-3246
Phone: (602) 443-8877
Fax: (602) 483-7333

**Council on Hotel,
Restaurant, and
Institutional (CHRIE)**
1200 17th St. NW
Washington, DC
20036-3097
Phone: (202) 331-5990
Fax: (202) 785-2511
E-mail:
alliance@access.digex.net

**Council on Social Work
Education (CSWE)**
1600 Duke St., Suite 300
Alexandria, VA
22314-3421
Phone: (703) 683-8080
Fax: (703) 683-8099
URL: www.cse.org

**Country Dance and Song
Society (CDSS)**
132 Main St.
P.O. Box 338
Haydenville, MA
01039-0338
Phone: (413) 268-7426
Fax: (413) 268-7471
E-mail: office@cdss.org
URL: www.cdss.org

**Country Music
Association (CMA)**
Music Cir. South
Nashville, TN 37203-4312

Phone: (615) 244-2840
Fax: (615) 726-0314

**Culinary Institute of
America (CIA)**
433 Albany Post Rd.
Hyde Park, NY 12538
Phone: (914) 452-9600

**Data Processing
Management Association,
Pittsburgh Chapter
(DPMA-P)**
P.O. Box 2004
Pittsburgh, PA 15230
Phone: (412) 227-1013
Fax: (412) 456-7602
E-mail: 76523.3221@
compuserve.com

**Defenders of Animal
Rights**
14412 Old York Rd.
Phoenix, MD 21131-1415

Defenders of Wildlife
1101 14th St., NW
Suite 1400
Washington, DC 20005
Phone: (202) 682-9400
Fax: (202) 682-1331
E-mail:
defenders@defenders.org
URL: www.defenders.org

**Dental Assisting National
Board (DANB)**
216 E. Ontario St.
Chicago, IL 60611
Phone: (312) 642-3368
Fax: (312) 642-8507
Toll-Free:
(800) FOR-DANB

Direct Marketing Association (DMA)
1120 Avenue of the Americas
New York, NY 10036-6700
Phone: (212) 768-7277
Fax: (212) 768-7353
E-mail: dma@the-dma.org
URL: www.the-dma.org

Doris Day Animal League (DDAL)
227 Massachusetts Ave. NE
Suite 100
Washington, DC 20002
Phone: (202) 546-1761
Fax: (202) 546-2193
E-mail: ddal@aol.com
URL: www.ddal.org

Earth Island Institute (EII)
300 Broadway, Suite 28
San Francisco, CA 94133
Phone: (415) 788-3666
Fax: (415) 788-7324
E-mail: earthisland@earthisland.org
URL: www.earthisland.org

Educational Foundation of the National Restaurant Association (EFNRA)
1200 17th St. NW
No. 1400
Washington, DC 20036-3097
Phone: (202) 331-5900
Toll-Free: (800) 765-2122
E-mail: isal@restaurant.org
URL: www.restaurant.org

Educational Institute of the American Hotel & Motel Association (AH&MA)
1201 New York Ave. NW
Suite 600
Washington, DC 20005-3931
Phone: (202) 289-3100
Fax: (202) 289-3199
E-mail: info@ahma.com
URL: www.ahma.com

Electronic Industries Association (EIA)
2500 Wilson Blvd.
Arlington, VA 22201
Phone: (703) 907-7500
Fax: (703) 907-7501
URL: www.eia.org

Environmental Industry Council (EIC)
529 14th St. NW, Suite 655
Washington, DC 20045
Phone: (202) 737-3018
Fax: (202) 737-8406

Environmental Law Institute (ELI)
1616 P St. NW, Suite 200
Washington, DC 20036
Phone: (202) 939-3800
Fax: (202) 939-3868
E-mail: law@eli.org
URL: www.eli.org

Environmental Management Association
530 W. Ionia St., Suite D2
Lansing, MI 48933-1062
Phone: (517) 485-5715
Fax: (517) 371-1170

Environmental Protection Agency (EPA)
401 M St. SW
Washington, DC 20460
Phone: (202)382-2973

Farm Animal Reform Movement (FARM)
P.O. Box 30654
Bethesda, MD 20824
Phone: (301) 530-1737
Fax: (301) 530-5747
Toll-Free: (800) 632-8688
E-mail: farm@farm.org
URL: www.farm.org

Farm Sanctuary-East (FSE)
P.O. Box 150
Watkins Glen, NY 14891
Phone: (607) 583-2225
Fax: (607) 583-2041
E-mail:
farmsanc@servtech.com
URL:
www.farmsanctuary.org

Flight Engineers' International Association (FEIA)
1926 S. Pacific Coast Hwy.
No. 202
Redondo Beach, CA
90277-6145
Phone: (310) 316-4094

Friends of Animals (FOA)
777 Post Rd., Suite 205
Darien, CT 06820
Phone: (203) 866-5223
Fax: (203) 656-0267
E-mail: foa@igc.apc.org
URL:
www.friendsofanimals.org

Friends of the Sea Otter (FSO)
2150 Garden Rd., B4
Monterey, CA 93940
Phone: (831) 373-2747
Fax: (831) 373-2749
E-mail: seaotter@
seaotters.org
URL: seaotters.org

Fund for Animals
200 W. 57th St.
New York, NY 10019
Phone: (212) 246-2096
Fax: (212) 246-2633

Geological Society of America (GSA)
3300 Penrose Place
P.O. Box 9140
Boulder, CO 80301-9140
Phone: (303) 447-2020
Fax: (303) 447-1133
Toll-Free: (800) 472-1988
E-mail: web@geosociety.org
URL: www.geosociety.org

Gerontological Society of America (GSA)
1275 K St. NW, Suite 350
Washington, DC 20005
Phone: (202) 842-1275
Fax: (202) 842-1150
URL: www.geron.org

Gospel Music Association (GMA)
1205 Division St.
Nashville, TN 37203
Phone: (615) 242-0303
Fax: (615) 254-9755
Toll-Free: (888) 242-0303
E-mail: gmatoday@aol.com
URL:
www.gospelmusic.org

**Gospel Music Workshop
of America (GMWA)**
3908 W. Warren Ave.
Detroit, MI 48208
Phone: (313) 898-6900
Fax: (313) 898-4520
E-mail: slpuddie@
worldnet.att.net
URL: www.ghwa.org

**Graphic Artists Guild
(GAG)**
90 John St., Suite 403
New York, NY 10038-3202
Phone: (212) 791-3400
Fax: (212) 791-0333
E-mail: paulatgag@aol.com
URL: www.gag.org

Greenpeace U.S.A. (GP)
1436 U St. NW
Washington, DC 20009
Phone: (202) 462-1177
Fax: (202) 462-4507
Toll-Free: (800) 326-0959
E-mail: info@wdc.
greenpeace.org
URL: www.greenpeace.org

Greyhound Friends
167 Saddle Hill Rd.
Hopkinton, MA 01748
Phone: (508) 435-5969
Fax: (508) 435-0547
E-mail: ghfriend@tiac.net
URL: www.greyhound.org

**Greyhound Pets of
America**
P.O. Box 2433
La Mesa, CA 91943-2433
Phone: (619) 443-0940
Fax: (619) 443-0130
URL:
www.greyhoundog.org

**Hair International/
Associated Master Barbers
and Beauticians of
(HI/AMBBA)**
124-B E. Main St.
P.O. Box 273
Palmyra, PA 17078-1712
Phone: (717) 838-0795
Fax: (717) 838-0796
E-mail: hairint@nbn.net
URL:
www.hairinternational.com

**Health Insurance
Association of America
(HIAA)**
555 13th St. NW
Suite 600 E.
Washington, DC
20004-1109
Phone: (202) 824-1600
Fax: (202) 824-1722

**Hooved Animal Humane
Society (HAHS)**
P.O. Box 400
Woodstock, IL 60098-0400
Phone: (815) 337-5563
Fax: (815) 337-5569
E-mail:
hahs@megsinet.net
URL:
www.chicweb.com/hahs

**Humane Farming
Association (HFA)**
1550 California St.
Suite 6
San Francisco, CA 94109
Phone: (415) 771-2253
Fax: (415) 485-0106
URL: www.hfa.org

Humane Society of the United States (HSUS)
2100 L St. NW
Washington, DC 20037
Phone: (202) 452-1100
Fax: (202) 778-6132
E-mail: hsusceo@
ix.netcom.com
URL: www.hsus.org/
Primary Contact: Paul G.
Irwin, Pres.

In Defense of Animals (IDA)
131 Camino Alito, Suite E
Mill Valley, CA 94941
Phone: (415) 388-9641
Fax: (415) 388-0388

Independent Insurance Agents of America (IIAA)
127 S. Peyton
Alexandria, VA 22314
Phone: (703) 683-4422
Fax: (703) 683-7556
Toll-Free: (800) 221-7917

Information Technology Industry Council (ITI)
1250 Eye St. NW, Suite 200
Washington, DC 20005
Phone: (202) 737-8888
Fax: (202) 638-4922
URL: www.itic.org

Institute for Certification of Computing Professionals (ICCP)
2200 E. Devon Ave.
Suite 247
Des Plaines, IL 60018
Phone: (847) 299-4227
Fax: (847) 299-4280
Toll-Free: (800) U-GET-CCP

E-mail: 74040.3722@
compuserve.com
URL: www.iccp.org

Institute of Certified Financial Planners
3801 East Florida Ave.
Suite 708
Denver, CO 80210-2571
Phone: (303) 759-4900
Fax: (303) 759-0749
Toll-Free: (800) 322-4237

Institute of Certified Travel Agents (ICTA)
148 Linden St.
P.O. Box 812059
Wellesley, MA 02482
Phone: (781) 237-0280
Fax: (781) 237-3860
Toll-Free: (800) 542-4282

Institute of Electrical and Electronics Engineers (IEEE)
3 Park Ave.
New York, NY 10016
Phone: (212) 419-7900
Fax: (212) 752-4929

Institute of Environmental Science (IES)
University of Orange
Free State
P.O. Box 339
Bloemfontein 9300
Republic of South Africa
Phone: 27 51 70711

Institute of Industrial Engineers (IIE)
25 Technology
Park/Atlanta
Norcross, GA 30092
Phone: (770) 449-0460
Fax: (770) 263-8532
URL: www.iienet.org

Institute of Internal Auditors (IIA)
249 Maitland Ave.
Altamonte Springs, FL 32701-4201
Phone: (407) 830-7600
Fax: (407) 831-5171
E-mail: iia@theiia.org
URL: www.theiia.org

International Alliance of Theatrical Stage Employees (IATSE)
1515 Broadway, Suite 601
New York, NY 10036
Phone: (212) 730-1770
Fax: (212) 921-7699

International Association for Computer Information Systems (IACIS)
C/o Dr. G. Daryl Nord
Oklahoma State University
College of Business Administration
Stillwater, OK 74078
Phone: (405) 744-8632
Fax: (405) 744-5180
E-mail: dnord@okway.okstate.edu
URL: www.iacis.org

International Association for Financial Planning (IAFP)
5775 Glenridge Dr. NE
Suite B-300
Atlanta, GA 30328-5364
Phone: (404) 845-0011
Fax: (404) 845-3660
Toll-Free: (800) 945-IAFP
URL: www.iafp.org

International Association of Assembly Managers (IAAM)
4425 W. Airport Fwy.
Suite 590
Irving, TX 75062
Phone: (972) 255-8020
Fax: (972) 255-9582
E-mail: iaam.info@iaam.org
URL: www.iaam.org

International Association of Business Communicators (IABC)
1 Hallidie Plaza, Suite 600
San Francisco, CA 94102
Phone: (415) 433-3400
Fax: (415) 362-8762
E-mail: leader-centre@iabc.com
URL: www.iabc.com

International Association of Culinary Professionals (IACP)
304 W. Liberty St., Suite 201
Louisville, KY 40202
Phone: (502) 581-9786
Fax: (502) 589-3602
Toll-Free: (800) 928-4227
E-mail: iapl@hqtrs.com
URL: www.iacp-online.org

International Association of Culinary Professionals Foundation (IACP)
304 W. Liberty St., Suite 201
Louisville, KY 40202
Phone: (502) 587-7953
Fax: (502) 589-3602
E-mail: ellenm@hgtrs.com
URL: www.gstis.net/epicure

International Association of Tour Managers—North American Region (IATM-NAR)
65 Charnes Dr.
East Haven, CT
06513-1225
Phone: (203) 466-0425
Fax: (203) 787-6384
E-mail: gdomp@callnet.com

International Brotherhood of Electrical Workers (IBEW)
1125 15th St. NW
Washington, DC 20005
Phone: (202) 833-7000
Fax: (202) 467-6316
URL: ibew.org

International Chiropractors Association (ICA)
1110 N. Glebe Rd.
Suite 1000
Arlington, VA 22201
Phone: (703) 528-5000
Fax: (703) 528-5023
E-mail: chiro@erols.com
URL: www.chiropractic.org

International Council on Hotel, Restaurant, and Institutional (CHRIE)
1200 17th St. NW
Washington, DC
20036-3097
Phone: (202) 331-5990
Fax: (202) 785-2511
E-mail:
alliance@access.digex.net

International Dance-Exercise Association (IDEA)
6190 Cornerstone Court E.
San Diego, CA 92121
Phone: 619-535-8979

International Executive Housekeepers Association (IEHA)
1001 Eastwind Dr., Suite 301
Westerville, OH 43081-3361
Phone: (614) 895-7166
Fax: (614) 895-1248
Toll-Free: (800) 200-6342
E-mail: excel@ieha.org
URL: www.ieha.org

International Foundation of Employee Benefit Plans (IFEBP)
18700 W. Bluemound Rd.
P.O. Box 69
Brookfield, WI 53008
Phone: (414) 786-6700
Fax: (414) 786-8670
Toll-Free: (888) 334-3327
E-mail: pr@ifebp.org
URL: www.ifebp.org

International Fund for Animal Welfare (IFAW)
411 Main St.
Yarmouthport, MA 02675
Phone: (508) 362-6268
Fax: (508) 362-5841

International Primate Protection League (IPPL)
P.O. Box 766
Summerville, SC 29484
Phone: (843) 871-2280
Fax: (843) 871-7988
E-mail: ippl@awod.com
URL: www.ippl.org

International Society for Animal Rights (ISAR)
965 Griffin Pond Rd.
Clarks Summit, PA
18411-9214
Toll-Free: (800) 543-ISAR
E-mail: ISAR@aol.com

International Society for Clinical Laboratory Technology (ISCLT)
917 Locust St., Suite 1100
St. Louis, MO 63101-1413
Phone: (314) 241-1445
Fax: (314) 241-1449
E-mail: isclt@aol.com

International Wildlife Coalition (IWC)
70 E. Falmouth Hwy.
East Falmouth, MA 02536
Phone: (508) 548-8328
Fax: (508) 548-8542
Toll-Free: (800) 548-8704
E-mail:
lwcadopt@ccsnet.com
URL: www.lwc.org

International Wildlife Rehabilitation Council (IWRC)
4437 Central Pl., Suite B-4
Suisun, CA 94585-1633
Phone: (707) 864-1761
Fax: (707) 864-3106
E-mail: iwrc@inreach.com
URL: iwrc-online.org

Internet Professionals Association (IPA)
P.O. Box 92
Passumpsic, VT 05861

Junior Engineering Technical Society (JETS)
1420 King St., Suite 405
Alexandria, VA
22314-2794
Phone: (703) 548-5387
Fax: (703) 548-0769
E-mail: jets@nae.edu
URL: www.jets.org

Last Chance for Animals
8033 Sunset Blvd., No. 35
Los Angeles, CA 90046
Phone: (310) 271-6096
Fax: (310) 271-1890
Toll-Free: 888-ANIMALS
E-mail: info@lcanimal.org
URL: www.lcanimal.org

Mail Advertising Service Association International (MASA)
1421 Prince St.
Alexandria, VA 22314
Phone: (703) 836-9200
Fax: (703) 548-8204
Toll-Free: (800) 333-6272

Manufacturers' Agents National Association (MANA)
23016 Mill Creek Rd.
P.O. Box 3467
Laguna Hills, CA 92654
Phone: (949) 859-4040
Fax: (949) 855-2973
E-mail: mana@
manaonline.org
URL:
www.manaonline.org

Marketing Research Association (MRA)
1344 Silas Deane Hwy.
Suite 306
P.O. Box 230
Rocky Hill, CT
06067-0230
Phone: (860) 257-4008
Fax: (860) 257-3990
E-mail:
email@mra-net.org

Medical Group Management Association (MGMA)
104 Inverness Terr. E.
Englewood, CO
80112-5306
Phone: (303) 799-1111
Fax: (303) 643-4439
Toll-Free: (888) 608-5601
URL: www.mgma.com

Music Critics Association of North America (MCA)
7 Pine Ct.
Westfield, NJ 07090
Phone: (908) 233-8468
Fax: (908) 233-8468
E-mail: beethoven@
prodigy.com

National Academy of Nannies, Inc. (NANI)
1681 S. Dayton St.
Denver, CO 80231
Toll-Free: (800) 222-NANI

National Academy of Elder Law Attorneys (NAELA)
1604 N. Country Club Rd.
Tucson, AZ 85716-3102
Phone: (520) 881-4005
Fax: (520) 325-7925
E-mail: info@naela.com
URL: www.naela.org

National Academy of Recording Arts and Sciences (NARAS)
3402 Pico Blvd.
Santa Monica, CA 90405
Phone: (310) 392-3777
Fax: (310) 399-3090

National Academy of Songwriters (NAS)
6255 Sunset Blvd.
Suite 1023
Hollywood, CA 90028
Phone: (213) 463-7178
Fax: (213) 463-2146
Toll-Free: (800) 826-7287
E-mail: nassong@aol.com
URL: www.nassong.org

National Accrediting Commission of Cosmetology Arts and Sciences (NACCAS)
901 N. Stuart St., No. 900
Arlington, VA 22203
Phone: (703) 527-7600
Fax: (703) 527-8811
E-mail: naccas@erols.com
URL: www.naccas.org

National Association for Humane and Environmental Education (NAHEE)
P.O. Box 362
East Haddam, CT
06423-0362
Phone: (860) 434-8666
Fax: (860) 434-9579
E-mail: nahee@nahee.org
URL: www.nahee.org

National Association for Practical Nurse Education and Service (NAPNES)
1400 Spring St., Suite 330
Silver Spring, MD 20910
Phone: (301) 588-2491
Fax: (301) 588-2839
E-mail: napnes@
bellatlantic.net

National Association of Activity Professionals (NAAP)
P.O. Box 23909
Jackson, MS 39225
Phone: (601) 853-3722
Toll-Free: 601-853-3536
E-mail: NAAP1@aol.com

National Association of Alcoholism and Drug Abuse Counselors (NAADAC)
1911 Fort Myer Dr.
Suite 900
Arlington, VA 22209
Phone: (703) 741-7686
Fax: (703) 741-7698

Toll-Free: (800) 548-0497
E-mail: naadac@well.com
URL: www.naadac.org

National Association of Boards of Pharmacy (NABP)
700 Busse Hwy.
Park Ridge, IL 60068
Phone: (847) 698-6227
Fax: (847) 698-0124

National Association Broadcast Employees and Technicians— (NABET-CWA)
501 3rd St. NW, 8th Floor
Washington, DC 20001
Phone: (202) 434-1254
Fax: (202) 434-1426
E-mail: nabetcwa@aol.com

National Association of Broadcasters (NAB)
1771 N. St. NW
Washington, DC 20036
Phone: (202) 429-5300
Fax: (202) 429-5343

National Association of County Training and Employment (NACTEP)
C/o National Association of Counties
440 1st St. NW, 8th Floor
Washington, DC 20001
Phone: (202) 393-6226
Fax: (202) 393-2630
E-mail: gorten@
spaceworks.com

National Association of Emergency Medical Technicians (NAEMT)
408 Monroe St.
Clinton, MS 39056
Phone: (601) 924-7744
Fax: (601) 924-7325
Toll-Free: (800) 34-NAEMT
E-mail: naemthq@aol.com

National Association of Environmental Professionals (NAEP)
6524 Ramoth Dr.
Jacksonville, FL 32226-3202
Phone: (904) 251-9900
Fax: (904) 251-9901
E-mail: naep@ilnk.com
URL:
www.enfo.com/naep

National Association of Government Employees (NAGE)
317 S. Patrick St.
Alexandria, VA 22314
Phone: (703) 514-0300
Fax: (703) 519-0311
E-mail: nage@erols.com
URL: www.nage.org

National Association of Health Underwriters (NAHU)
1000 Connecticut Ave. NW
Suite 810
Washington, DC 20036
Phone: (703) 276-0220
Fax: (703) 841-7797
E-mail:
kcorcoran@nahu.org
URL: www.nahu.org

National Association of Home Based Businesses (NAHBB)
P.O. Box 30220
Baltimore, MD 21270
Phone: (410) 363-3698
URL:
www.homebusiness.com

National Association of Legal Assistants (NALA)
1516 S. Boston, Suite 200
Tulsa, OK 74119
Phone: (918) 587-6828
Fax: (918) 582-6772
E-mail: nalanet@nala.org
URL: www.nala.org

National Association of Legal Secretaries International(NALS)
314 E. 3rd. St., Suite 210
Tulsa, OK 74120
Phone: (918) 582-5188
Fax: (918) 582-5907
URL: www.nals.org

National Association of Life Underwriters (NALU)
1922 F St. NW
Washington, DC
20006-4387
Phone: (202) 331-6000
Fax: (202) 835-9601

National Association of Personnel Services (NAPS)
3133 Mt. Vernon Ave.
Alexandria, VA 22305
Phone: (703) 684-0180
Fax: (703) 684-0071
E-mail: info@napsweb.org
URL: www.napsweb.org

National Association of Plumbing-Heating-Cooling Contractors (NAPHCC)
180 S. Washington St.
P.O. Box 6808
Falls Church, VA 22040
Phone: (703) 237-8100
Fax: (703) 237-7442
Toll-Free: (800) 533-7694
E-mail:
naphcc@naphcc.org
URL: www.naphcc.org

National Association of Professional Geriatric Care Managers (PGCM)
1604 N. Country Club Rd.
Tucson, AZ 85716-3102
Phone: (520) 881-8008
Fax: (520) 325-7925

National Association of Professional Insurance Agents (NAPIA)
400 N. Washington St.
Alexandria, VA 22314
Phone: (703) 836-9340
Fax: (703) 836-1279
E-mail:
piaweb@pianet.org
URL: www.pianet.com

National Association of Realtors (NAR)
430 N. Michigan Ave.
Chicago, IL 60611
Fax: (312) 329-5962
Toll-Free: (800) 874-6500
URL: realtor.com

National Association of Recording Merchandisers (NARM)
9 Eves Dr., Suite 120
Marlton, NJ 08053

Phone: (609) 596-2221
Fax: (609) 596-3268
URL: www.narm.com

National Association of Schools of Music (NASM)
11250 Roger Bacon Dr.
Suite 21
Reston, VA 20190
Phone: (703) 437-0700
Fax: (703) 437-6312
URL:
www.arts-accredit.org

National Association of Social Workers (NASW)
750 First St. NE
Suite 700
Washington, DC
20002-4241
Phone: (202) 408-8600
Fax: (202) 336-8312
Toll-Free: (800) 638-8799
E-mail: info@naswdc.org
URL: www.naswdc.org

National Association of Substance Abuse Trainers and Educators (NASATE)
1521 Hillary St.
New Orleans, LA 70118
Phone: (504) 286-5234

National Association of Webmasters (NAW)
9580 Oak Pkwy.
Suite 7-177
Folsom, CA 95630
Phone: (916) 929-6557
Fax: (916) 929-1721
E-mail: wbc@naw.org
URL: www.naw.org

National Audubon Society (NAS)
700 Broadway
New York, NY 10003
Phone: (212) 979-3000
Fax: (212) 353-0377
URL: www.audubon.org

National Board for Certified Counselors (NBCC)
3 Terrace Way, Suite D
Greensboro, NC 27403-3660
Phone: (336) 547-0607
Fax: (336) 547-0017
Toll-Free: (800) 398-5389
E-mail: nbcc@nbcc.org
URL: www.nbcc.org

National Board for Respiratory Care (NBRC)
8310 Nieman Rd.
Lenexa, KS 66214
Phone: (913) 599-4200
Fax: (913) 541-0156

National Center for Homeopathy (NCH)
801 N. Fairfax St., Suite 306
Alexandria, VA 22314
Phone: (703) 548-7790
Fax: (703) 548-7792

National Child Care Association (NCCA)
1016 Rosser St.
Conyers, GA 30012
Phone: (770) 922-8198
Fax: (770) 388-7772
Toll-Free: (800) 543-7161
E-mail: nccallw@nccanet.org
URL: www.nccanet.org

National Commission on Certification of Physician Assistants (NCCPA)
2845 Henderson Mill Rd. NE
Atlanta, GA 30341
Phone: (404) 493-9100

National Conference of Personal Managers (NCOPM)
46-19 220 Place
Bayside, NY 11361

National Cosmetology Association (NCA)
3510 Olive St.
St. Louis, MO 63103
Phone: (314) 534-7982
Fax: (314) 534-8618
Toll-Free: (800) 527-1683
E-mail: nca-now@primary.net
URL: www.nca-now.com

National Council for Accreditation of Teacher Education (NCATE)
2010 Massachusetts Ave. NW
Suite 500
Washington, DC 20036-1023
Phone: (202) 466-7496
Fax: (202) 296-6620
E-mail: ncate@ncate.org
URL: www.ncate.org

National Council for Therapeutic Recreation Certification (NCTRC)
P.O. Box 479
Thiells, NY 10984
Phone: (914) 639-1439
Fax: (914) 639-1471

National Education Association (NEA)
1201 16th St. NW
Washington, DC 20036
Phone: (202) 833-4000
Fax: (202) 822-7767
URL: www.nea.org

National Environmental Health Association (NEHA)
720 S. Colorado Blvd.
Suite 970, S. Tower
Denver, CO 80246-1925
Phone: (303) 756-9090
Fax: (303) 691-9490
E-mail:
neha.org@juno.com
URL: www.neha.org/beckyr

National Federation of Federal Employees (NFFE)
1016 16th St. NW
Suite 300
Washington, DC 20036
Phone: (202) 862-4400
Fax: (202) 862-4432

National Federation of Licensed Practical Nurses (NFLPN)
1418 Aversboro Rd.
Garner, NC 27529-4547
Phone: (919) 779-0046
Fax: (919) 779-5642
Toll-Free: (800) 948-2511
URL: www.nflpn.com

National Federation of Paralegal Associations (NFPA)
C/o Lu Hangley
P.O. Box 33108
Kansas City, MO
64114-0108
Phone: (816) 941-4000
Fax: (816) 941-2725
E-mail:
info@paralegals.org
URL: www.paralegals.org

National Health Council (NHC)
1730 M St. NW, Suite 500
Washington, DC 20036
Phone: (202) 785-3910
Fax: (202) 785-5923
E-mail:
info@nhcouncil.org

National Humane Education Society (NHES)
521-A E. Market St.
Leesburg, VA 22075
Phone: (703) 777-8319
Fax: (703) 771-4048
E-mail:
natlhumane@aol.com

National Lawyers Guild (NLG)
126 University Place
New York, NY 10003-4538
Phone: (212) 627-2656
Fax: (212) 627-2404
E-mail: nlgno@nlg.org
URL: www.nlg.org

National League for Nursing (NLN)
61 Broadway, 33rd Floor
New York, NY 10006-2701
Phone: (212) 989-9393
Fax: (212) 989-2272
Toll-Free: (800) 669-9656
URL: www.nln.org

National Newspaper Association (NNA)
1525 Wilson Blvd.
Suite 550
Arlington, VA 22209
Phone: (703) 907-7900
Fax: (703) 907-7901
Toll-Free: (800) 829-4662
E-mail: info@nna.org
URL: www.nna.org

National Oceanic and Atmospheric Administration Personnel Office
14th St. & Constitution Ave. NW
Room 6013
Washington, DC 20230
Phone: (202) 482-6090
Fax: (202) 482-3154
URL: www.noaa.gov

National Paralegal Association (NPA)
P.O. Box 406
Solebury, PA 18963
Phone: (215) 297-8333
Fax: (215) 297-8358

National Registry of Environmental Professionals (NREP)
P.O. Box 2099
Glenview, IL 60025
Phone: (847) 724-6631
Fax: (847) 724-4223
E-mail: nrep@primenet.com
URL: www.nrep.org

National Restaurant Association (NRA)
1200 17th St. NW
Washington, DC 20036
Phone: (202) 331-5900
Fax: (202) 331-2429
E-mail: isal@restaurant.org
URL: www.restaurant.org

National Retail Federation (NRF)
325 7th St. NW, Suite 1000
Washington, DC 20004-2802
Phone: (202) 783-7971
Fax: (202) 737-2849
Toll-Free: (800) NRF-HOW2
E-mail: nrf@nrf.com
URL: www.nrf.com

National Safety Council (NSC)
1121 Spring Lake Dr.
Itasca, IL 60143-3201
Phone: (630) 285-1121
Fax: (630) 285-1315
URL: www.nsc.org

National Society of Fund Raising Executives (NSFRE)
1101 King St., Suite 700
Alexandria, VA 22314
Phone: (703) 684-0410
Fax: (703) 684-0540
Toll-Free:
(800) 666-FUND
E-mail: aserv@nsfre.org
URL: www.nsfre.org

National Society of Professional Engineers (NSPE)
1420 King St.
Alexandria, VA 22314
Phone: (703) 684-2800
Fax: (703) 836-4875
Toll-Free: (888) 285-6773
E-mail: customer.
service@nspe.org
URL: www.nspe.org

National Society of Public Accountants (NSPA)
1010 N. Fairfax St.
Alexandria, VA
22314-1574
Phone: (703) 549-6400
Fax: (703) 549-2984
Toll-Free: (800) 966-6679
E-mail: NSA@wizard.net
URL: www.nsa.org

National Student Nurses' Association (NSSA)
55 W. 57th St., Suite 1327
New York, NY 10019
Phone: (212) 581-2211
Fax: (212) 581-2368
E-mail:
NSNA@NSNA.ORG

National Therapeutic Recreation Society (NTRS)
22377 Belmont Ridge Rd.
Ashburn, VA 20148
Phone: (703) 858-0784
Fax: (703) 858-0794
Toll-Free: (800) 626-6772
E-mail: ntrsnrpa@aol.com
URL:
www.NRPA.org/NRPA

National Weather Service Employees Organization (NWSEO)
601 Pennsylvania Ave.
Suite 900
Washington, DC 20004
Phone: (703) 293-9651
Fax: (202) 628-1948

National Wildlife Federation (NWF)
8925 Leesburg Pike
Vienna, VA 22184
Phone: (703) 790-4000
URL: www.nwf.org

National Wildlife Rehabilitators Association (NWRA)
14 N. 7th Ave.
St. Cloud, MN 56303-4766
Phone: (320) 259-4086
E-mail:
nwra@cloudnet.com
URL:
www.cloudnet.com/nwra/
main.html

The Nature Conservancy (TNC)
4245 Fairfax Dr.
Suite 100
Arlington, VA 22203-1606
Phone: (703) 841-5300
Fax: (703) 841-1283
Toll-Free: (800) 628-6860
URL: www.tnc.org

Newspaper Association of America Foundation
1921 Gallows Rd.
Suite 600
Vienna, VA 22182
Phone: (703) 902-1725
URL: www.naa.org

Nuclear Medicine Technology Certification Board (NMTCB)
2970 Clairmont Rd.
Suite 935
Atlanta, GA 30329
Phone: (404) 315-1739
Fax: (404) 315-6502
E-mail: board@nmtcb.org
URL: www.nmtcb.org

Opticians Association of America (OAA)
10341 Democracy Lane
Fairfax, VA 22030
Phone: (703) 691-8355
Fax: (703) 691-3929

People for the Ethical Treatment of Animals (PETA)
501 Front St.
Norfolk, VA 23510
Phone: (757) 622-PETA
Fax: (757) 622-0457
E-mail:
peta@norfolk.infi.net
URL: www.peta-online.org

Performing Animal Welfare Society (PAWS)
P.O. Box 849
Galt, CA 95632
Phone: (209) 745-7297
Fax: (209) 745-1809
E-mail:
paws@capaccess.org
URL:
www.envirolink.org/arrs/paws

Physicians Committee for Responsible Medicine (PCRM)
P.O. Box 6322
Washington, DC 20015
Phone: (202) 686-2210
Fax: (202) 686-2216
E-mail: pcrm@pcrm.org
URL: www.pcrm.org

Professional Secretaries International
10502 NW Ambassador Dr.
P.O. Box 20404
Kansas City, MO
64195-0404
Phone: (816) 891-6600
Fax: (816) 891-9118
URL: www.main.org/psi

Promotion Marketing Association of America (PMAA)
257 Park Ave. S.,
11th Floor
New York, NY 10010-7304
Phone: (212) 420-1100
Fax: (212) 533-7622
E-mail:
pmaa@pmaalink.org
URL: www.pmaalink.org

Public Relations Society of America (PRSA)
33 Irving Place, 3rd Floor
New York, NY 10003-2376
Phone: (212) 995-2230
Fax: (212) 995-0757
Toll-Free:
(800) WER-PRSA
URL: www.prsa.org

Radio Advertising Bureau (RAB)
261 Madison Ave.,
23rd Floor
New York, NY 10016
Phone: (212) 681-7200
Fax: (212) 681-7223
Toll-Free: (800) 232-3131
URL: www.rab.com

Recording Industry Association of America (RIAA)
1330 Connecticut Ave.
Suite 300
Washington, DC 20036
Phone: (202) 775-0101
Fax: (202) 775-7253
E-mail:
webmaster@riaa.com
URL: www.riaa.com

Refrigeration Service Engineers Society (RSES)
1666 Rand Rd.
Des Plaines, IL
60016-3552
Phone: (847) 297-6464
Fax: (847) 297-5038
E-mail:
rses@starnetinc.com
URL: www.rses.org

Robotics International of the Society of Manufacturing Engineers (RI/SME)
One SME Dr.
P.O. Box 930
Dearborn, MI 48121-0930
Phone: (313) 271-1500
Fax: (313) 271-2861
URL: www.sme.org/ri

Romance Writers of America (RWA)
3707 F.M. 1960 West
Suite 555
Houston, TX 77068
Phone: (281) 440-6885
Fax: (281) 440-7510
E-mail: info.
rwanational@aol.com
URL:
www.rwanational.com

Sales and Marketing Executives International (SMEI)
5500 Interstate North
Pkwy. #545
Atlanta, GA 30328
Phone: 770-661-8500
Fax: 770-661-8512
E-mail: smeihq@smei.org
URL: www.smei.org

Scientists Center for Animal Welfare (SCAW)
7833 Walker Dr.
Suite 340
Greenbelt, MD 20770
Phone: (301) 345-3500
Fax: (301) 345-3503
E-mail: scaw@erols.com

Screen Actors Guild (SAG)
5757 Wilshire Blvd.
Los Angeles, CA 90036-3635
Phone: (213) 954-1600
URL: www.sag.com

Screen Composers of America (SCA)
2451 Nichols Canyon
Los Angeles, CA 90046-1798
Phone: (213) 876-6040
Fax: (213) 876-6041

Shelly Field Organization (motivational seminars and presentations)
P.O. Box 711
Monticello, NY 12701
Phone: (914) 794-7312

Small Business Administration (SBA)
1441 L St. NW
Washington, DC 20416
Phone: (202) 653-6832
URL: www.sba.gov

Society for Animal Protective Legislation (SAPL)
P.O. Box 3719
Georgetown Sta.
Washington, DC 20007

Phone: (202) 337-2334
Fax: (202) 338-9478

Society for Human Resource Management (SHRM)
1800 Duke St.
Alexandria, VA 22314-3499
Phone: (703) 548-3440
Fax: (703) 836-0367
Toll-Free: (800) 283-7476
E-mail: shrm@shrm.org

Society for Mining, Metallurgy, and Exploration (SME)
P.O. Box 625002
Littleton, CO 80162-5002
Phone: (303) 973-9550
Fax: (303) 973-3845
Toll-Free: (800) 763-3132
E-mail: sme@smenet.org
URL: www.smenet.org

Society for Technical Communication (STC)
901 N. Stuart St.
Suite 904
Arlington, VA 22203-1854
Phone: (703) 522-4114
Fax: (703) 522-2075
E-mail: stc@stc-va.org
URL: www.stc-va.org

Society of Actuaries (SOA)
475 N. Martingale Rd.
Suite 800
Schaumburg, IL 60173-2226
Phone: (847) 706-3500
Fax: (847) 706-3599
URL: www.soa.org

Society of American Florists (SAF)
1601 Duke St.
Alexandria, VA 22314-3406
Phone: (703) 836-8700
Fax: (703) 836-8705
Toll-Free: (800) 336-4743

Society of Diagnostic Medical Sonographers (SDMS)
12770 Coit Rd.
Suite 708
Dallas, TX 75251
Phone: (972) 239-7367
Fax: (972) 239-7378
Toll-Free: (800) 229-9506
E-mail: sdms@sdms.org
URL: www.sdms/org

Society of Exploration Geophysicists (SEG)
P.O. Box 702740
Tulsa, OK 74170
Phone: (918) 497-5500
Fax: (918) 497-5557
URL: www.seg.org

Society of Illustrators (SI)
128 E. 63rd St.
New York, NY 10021
Phone: (212) 838-2560
Fax: (212) 838-2561
E-mail: society@
societyillustrators.org
URL: www.
societyillustrators.org

Society of Nuclear Medicine (SNM)
1850 Samuel Morse Dr.
Reston, VA 20190-5316
Phone: (703) 708-9000
Fax: (703) 708-9777
URL: www.snm.org

Society of Petroleum Engineers (SPE)
222 Palisades Creek Dr.
Richardson, TX 75080
Phone: (972) 952-9393
Fax: (972) 952-9435
E-mail:
spedal@spelink.spe.org

Society of Professional Audio Recording Services (SPARS)
4300 10th Ave. N.
Lake Worth, FL 33461
Phone: (561) 641-6648
Fax: (561) 642-8263
E-mail: spars@spars.com
URL:
www.spars.com/spars/

Society of Wine Educators (SWE)
8600 Foundry St.
Mill 2044
Savage, MD 20763
Phone: (301) 776-8569
Fax: (301) 776-8578
E-mail: vintage@erols.com

Society of Women Engineers
120 Wall St., 11th Floor
New York, NY 10005-3902
Phone: (212) 509-9577
E-mail: hq@swe.org
URL: www.swe.org

Soil Science Society of America (SSSA)
677 S. Segoe Rd.
Madison, WI 53711
Phone: (608) 273-8080
Fax: (608) 273-2021
E-mail:
input@agronomy.org
URL: www.agronomy.org

Songwriters Guild of America (SGA)
1500 Harbor Blvd.
Weehawken, NJ
07087-6732
Phone: (201) 867-7603
Fax: (201) 867-7535
E-mail:
songnews@aol.com
URL: songnews.org

Special Libraries Association (SLA)
1700 18th St. NW
Washington, DC
20009-2514
Phone: (202) 234-4700
Fax: (202) 265-9317
E-mail: sla@sla.org
URL: www.sla.org

The Cousteau Society (TCS)
870 Greenbrier Cir.
Suite 402
Chesapeake, VA 23320
Phone: (757) 523-9335
Fax: (757) 523-2747
Toll-Free: (800) 441-4395
E-mail: cousteau@infi.net
URL: www.cousteau.org

The Newspaper Guild (TNG-CWA)
501 3rd St. NW, 2nd Floor
Washington, DC
20001-2760
E-mail: lgildersleeve@
cwa-union.org
URL: www.newsguild.org

The One Club
32 E. 21st St.
New York, NY 10010
URL: www.oneclub.com

Transport Workers Union of America (TWU)
80 West End Ave., New
York, NY 10023
Phone: (212) 873-6000
Fax: (212) 721-1431

United Food and Commercial Workers International Union (UFCW)
1775 K St. NW
Washington, DC 20006
Phone: (202) 223-3111
Fax: (202) 466-1562
URL: www.ufcw.org

United Scenic Artists
16 W. 61st St., 11th Floor
New York, NY 10023
Phone: (212) 581-0300
Fax: (212) 977-2011

United States Department of Agriculture— Forest Service (USDA-FSVP)
P.O. Box 96090
Washington, DC 20090
Phone: (203) 235-8855
URL: www.usda.gov

United States Department of Labor
200 Constitution Ave. NW
Room S-1032
Washington, DC 20210
Phone: (202) 693-4650
URL:http//www.dol.gov

U.S. Office of Personnel Management and the Veterans Administration
1900 E St. NW
Washington, DC
20415-0001
Phone: (202) 606-1800
URL: www.opm.gov/veterans/index.htm

Veterans Administration
810 Vermont Ave.
Washington, DC 20420
Phone: (202) 233-2741
URL: www.va.gov

Volunteer Lawyers for the Arts (VLA)
1 E. 53rd St., 6th Floor
New York, NY 10022
Phone: (212) 319-2787
Fax: (212) 752-6575
E-mail: vlany@bway.net

Water Environment Federation (WEF)
601 Wythe St.
Alexandria, VA
22314-1994
Phone: (703) 684-2400
Fax: (703) 684-2492
Toll-Free: (800) 666-0206
URL: www.wef.org

Women In Communications, Inc. (Now known as Association for Women In Communications)
1244 Ritchie Hwy.
Suite 6
Arnold, MD 21012-1887
Phone: (410) 544-7442
Fax: (410)544-4640
E-mail: pat@womcom.org

Writers Guild of America, East (WGAE)
555 W. 57th St.
New York, NY 10019
Phone: (212) 767-7800
Fax: (212) 582-1909
E-mail: info@wgaeast.org
URL: www.wgaeast.org

**Writers Guild of America,
West (WGA)**
7000 W. Third St.
Los Angeles, CA
90048-4329
Phone: (213) 550-1000
Fax: (213) 782-4800
URL: www.wga.org

Recommended Reading List

Acting careers

Acting in Television Commercials for Fun and Profit by Squire Fridell; Crown, 1995.

An Actor's Guide: Your First Year in Hollywood by Michael Saint Nicholas and Michael Saint Nichols; Allworth Press, 1996.

Career Opportunities In Theater and The Performing Arts by Shelly Field; Facts On File, 1999.

Getting the Part: Thirty-Three Professional Casting Directors Tell You How to Get Work in Theater, Films, Commercials, and TV by Judith Searle; Limelight Editions, 1995.

How to Be a Working Actor: The Insider's Guide to Finding Jobs in Theater, Film, and Television by Mari Lyn Henry and Lynne Rogers; Back Stage Books, 1994.

The Film Actor's Complete Career Guide: A Complete, Step-By-Step Checklist of All the Things Actors Seeking Film Careers Can and Should Do, and When by Lawrence Parke; Acting World Books, 1992.

Your Film Acting Career: How to Break into the Movies & TV & Survive in Hollywood by M. K. Lewis and Rosemary R. Lewis; Gorham House Pub., 1997.

Advertising careers

Career Opportunities In Advertising and Public Relations by Shelly Field; Facts On File, 1997.

Airline pilot careers

Airline Pilot Technical Interviews: A Study Guide by Ronald D. McElroy; Cage Consulting, Inc., 1999.

Animals and animal rights careers

An Unspoken Art: Profiles of Veterinary Life by Lee Gutkind; Henry Holt & Company, Inc., 1997.

Careers As An Animal Rights Activist by Shelly Field, Rosen Press, 1993.

Opportunities in Veterinary Medicine Careers by Robert E. Swope and Sarah Beth Mikesell; Vgm Career Horizons, 1993.

The Veterinarian's Touch: Profiles of Life Among Animals by Lee Gutkind; Henry Holt, 1998.

Artist careers

100 Best Careers For Writers and Artists by Shelly Field; Arco, 1997.

Banking and finance careers

Investment Banking Firms, an Industry Guide for Job Seekers by Ed Shen, Vault Reports Staff, Edward Shen, and H. S. Hamadeh; VaultReports.com, 1998.

Job Seekers Guide to Wall Street Recruiters by Christopher W. Hunt and Scott A. Scanlon; John Wiley & Sons, 1998.

Resumes for Banking and Financial Careers by Vgm Career Horizons (editor); Vgm Career Horizons, 1993.

The Fast Track: The Insider's Guide to Winning Jobs in Management Consulting, Investment Banking, and Securities Trading by Mariam Naficy; Broadway Books, 1997.

Business careers

Business School Companion: The Ultimate Guide to Excelling in Business School and Launching Your Career by H. S. Hamadeh, Andy Richard, and Andrew Richard; Princeton Review, 1996.

Clown careers

Rodeo Clown: Laughs and Danger in the Ring (Risky Business) by Keith Elliot Greenberg; Blackbirch Marketing, 1995.

Comedy careers

A Biography of the Early Popular Stage Comedian by Armond Fields; McFarland & Company, 1999.

How to Be a Working Comic: An Insider's Guide to a Career in Stand-Up Comedy by Dave Schwensen; Back Stage Books, 1998.

My Life As a Fifth-Grade Comedian by Elizabeth Levy; HarperTrophy, 1998.

Computer careers

Careers for Computer Buffs & Other Technological Types by Marjorie Eberts, Margaret Gisler, and Maria Olson (contributor); Vgm Career Horizons, 1999.

Career Opportunities in Computers and Cyberspace by Harry Henderson; Facts on File, Inc., 1999.

The Complete Idiot's Guide to a Career in Computer Programming by Jesse Liberty; Alpha Books, 1999.

Cover letters

101 Best Cover Letters by Jay A. Block and Michael Betrus; McGraw-Hill, 1999.

175 High-Impact Cover Letters by Richard H. Beatty; John Wiley & Sons, 1996.

201 Killer Cover Letters by Sandra Podesta, Andrea Paxton (contributor); McGraw-Hill, 1996.

Cover Letters (National Business Employment Weekly Premier Guides series) by Taunee S. Besson, Perri Capell, and Tannee S. Besson; John Wiley & Sons, 1999.

Cover Letters for Dummies by Joyce Lain Kennedy; IDG Books Worldwide, 1996.

Cover Letters That Blow Doors Open: Job-winning cover letters by Anne McKinney (editor); PREP Publishing, 1999.

Dynamic Cover Letters: How to Sell Yourself to an Employer by Writing a Letter That Will Get Your Resume Read, Get You an Interview, and Get You The Job by Katherine Hansen and Randall Hansen; Ten Speed Press, 1995.

Gallery of Best Cover Letters by David F. Noble; Jist Works, 1999.

The Complete Idiot's Guide to the Perfect Cover Letter by Susan Ireland; Alpha Books, 1997.

The Perfect Cover Letter by Richard H. Beatty; John Wiley & Sons, 1996.

Culinary careers

Becoming a Chef: With Recipes and Reflections from America's Leading Chefs by Andrew Dornenburg and Karen Page; John Wiley & Sons, 1995.

Careers for Gourmets and Others Who Relish Food by Mary Donovan; Vgm Career Horizons, 1992.

Dining Out: Secrets from America's Leading Critics, Chefs and Restaurateurs by Andrew Dornenburg and Karen Page; John Wiley & Sons, 1998.

The Making of a Chef: Mastering Heat at the Culinary Institute of America by Michael Ruhlman; Henry Holt & Company, Inc., 1997. (This one is more like journalism than career advice, but it does make a fun read.)

Opportunities in Culinary Careers by Mary Deirdre Donovan; Vgm Career Horizons, 1997.

Opportunities in Restaurant Careers by Carol Caprione Chmelynski; Vgm Career Horizons, 1998.

Customer service careers

Customer Service Representative by Kathryn A. Quinlan; Capstone Press, 1999.

Success as a Customer Service Representative by Lloyd Finch; Crisp Publications, Inc., 1998.

Entertainment careers

100 Best Careers In Entertainment by Shelly Field; Arco, 1995.

Career Opportunities In Theater and The Performing Arts by Shelly Field; Facts On File, 1999.

Career Opportunities In The Music Industry by Shelly Field; Facts On File, 1996.

Environmental careers

Careers Inside the World of Environmental Science (Careers and Opportunities) by Robert Gartner; Library Binding, 1995.

Guide to Graduate Environmental Programs compiled by Student Conservation Association Staff; Island Press, 1997.

The Complete Guide to Environmental Careers in the 21st Century by Kevin Doyle; Island Press, 1998.

Health care careers

Career Opportunities in Health Care (Career Opportunities series) by Shelly Field; Facts On File, 1998.

Directory of Schools for Alternative and Complementary Health Care by Karen Rappaport (editor); Oryx Press, 1998.

Planning Your Career In Alternative Medicine by Dianne J. B. Lyons; Avery Publishing Group, 1997.

Resumes for Nursing Careers (Vgm Professional Resumes series) by Robert T. Teske et. al.; Vgm Career Horizons, 1996.

The Nurses' Career Guide: Companion Workbook by Zardoya E. Eagles; Sovereignty Press; 1997.

Home business, freelancing, and consulting

101 Home Office Success Secrets by Lisa Kanarek; Career Press, 1994.

Directory of Home-Based Business Resources (Where to Find What You Want to Know series) by Priscilla Y. Huff; Pilot Books, 1997.

Finance and Taxes for the Home-Based Business by Charles P. Lickson, Regina Preciado (editor), and Bryane Miller Lickson (contributor); Crisp Publications, Inc., 1997.

Home-Based Travel Agent: How to Cash in on the Exciting New World of Travel Marketing by Kelly Monaghan; Intrepid Traveler, 1999.

How to Start A Home-Based Photography Business, 2nd Edition by Kenn Oberrecht; Globe Pequot Press, 1996.

How to Start a Home Based Travel Agency by Joanie Ogg and Tom Ogg; Tom Ogg & Associates, 1997.

How to Start Your Own Business on a Shoestring and Make Up to $500,000 a Year by Tyler Gregory Hicks; Prima Publishing, 1998.

J.K. Lasser's Tax Deductions for Small Businesses, 2nd Edition by Barbara Weltman; Macmillan Publishing, 1997.

J.K. Lasser's Taxes Made Easy for Home-Based Business by Gary W. Carter, Ph.D.; Macmillan Publishing, 1997.

J.K. Lasser's Year-Round Tax Strategies 1998 (Serial) by David S. De Jong, Ann Gray Jakabcin, and David S. DeJong; Macmillan Publishing, 1997.

Moneymaking Moms: How Work at Home Can Work for You by Caroline Hull and Tanya Wallace; Citadel Press, 1998.

Start and Run a Profitable Tour Guiding Business: Part-Time, Full Time, at Home, or Abroad: Your Step-By-Step Business Plan by Barbara Braidwood, Susan M. Boyce, and Richard Cropp; Self Counsel Press, 1996.

The Complete Idiot's Guide to Making Money in Freelancing by Christy Heady and Janet Bernstel; Alpha Books, 1998.

The Complete Idiot's Guide to Starting a Home-Based Business by Barbara Weltman; Alpha Books, 1997.

Internet job search

110 Best Job Search Sites on the Internet by Katherine K. Yonge; Linx Education Pub., Inc., 1998.

Career Exploration on the Internet: A Student's Guide to More Than 300 Web Sites! by Elizabeth H. Oakes (editor); Ferguson Publishing, 1998.

Electronic Resumes & Online Networking: How to Use the Internet to Do a Better Job Search, Including a Complete, Up-To-Date Resource Guide by Rebecca Smith; Career Press, 1999.

Internet Resumes: Take the Net to Your Next Job! by Peter D. Weddle; Impact Publications, 1998.

Job Searching Online for Dummies by Pam Dixon; IDG Books Worldwide, 1998.

Resumes in Cyberspace: Your Complete Guide to a Computerized Job Search by Pat Criscito; Barrons Educational Series, 1997.

The 1999 WetFeet Insider Guide to Jobs in the Computer Software Industry by Steve Pollock and Gary Alpert; WetFeet Press, 1999.

Interviews

10 Minute Guide to Job Interviews by Dana Morgan; Alpha Books, 1998.

100 Winning Resumes for $100,000+ Jobs: Resumes That Can Change Your Life! by Wendy S. Enelow; Impact Publications, 1997.

Best Answers to the 201 Most Frequently Asked Interview Questions by Matthew J. Deluca and Mathew J. DeLuca; McGraw-Hill, 1996.

The Complete Idiot's Guide to the Perfect Interview by Marc A. Dorio; Alpha Books, 1997.

Conquer Interview Objections by Robert F. Wilson and Erik H. Rambusch (contributor); John Wiley & Sons, 1994.

Get Hired!: Winning Strategies to Ace the Interview by Paul C. Green; Bard Press, 1996.

Interview Power: Selling Yourself Face to Face by Tom Washington; Mount Vernon Press, 1995.

The Interview Kit/How to Answer over 500 Tough Interview Questions by Richard H. Beatty; John Wiley & Sons, 1995.

Job Interviews for Dummies by Joyce Lain Kennedy; IDG Books Worldwide, 1996.

Law careers

Alternative Careers for Lawyers by Hillary Mantis; Princeton Review, 1997.

The Lawyer's Career Change Handbook: More Than 300 Things You Can Do With a Law Degree by Hindi Greenberg; Avon Books, 1998.

What Can You Do With a Law Degree?: A Lawyers' Guide to Career Alternatives Inside, Outside & Around the Law by Deborah Arron; Niche Press, 1999.

Law enforcement careers

Careers in Criminal Justice by W. Richard Stephens, Jr.; Allyn & Bacon, 1999.

Guide to Careers in Federal Law Enforcement: Profiles of 225 High-Powered Careers & Sure-Fire Tactics for Getting Hired by Thomas Ackerman; Rhodes & Easton, 1999.

Leisure and recreation

Community Leisure and Recreation: Theory and Practice by Les Haywood (editor), Maurice Mullard, and Hugh Butcher; Butterworth-Heinemann, 1994.

Meetings, conferences, conventions and special events

Organizing Special Events and Conferences: A Practical Guide for Busy Volunteers and Staff by Darcy Campion Devney; Pineapple Press, 1993.

The Comprehensive Guide to Successful Conferences and Meetings: Detailed Instructions and Step-By-Step Checklists by Leonard Nadler and Zeace Nadler; Jossey-Bass Publishers, 1987.

Miscellaneous career guide

100 Best Careers For The 21st Century by Shelly Field; Arco, 1996.

Motivation and inspiration

100 Ways to Motivate Yourself by Steve Chandler; Career Press, 1996.

Awaken the Giant Within: How to Take Immediate Control of Your Mental, Emotional, Physical & Financial Destiny! by Anthony Robbins and Frederick L. CoVan; Fireside, 1993.

Brighten Your Day With Self-Esteem: How to Empower, Energize & Motivate Yourself to a Richer, Fuller, More Rewarding Life (Personal Development series) by William J. McGrane and Miriam Burkart (editor); Markowski International, 1996.

Don't Sweat the Small Stuff—and it's all small stuff by Richard Carlson; Hyperion, 1997.

Don't Sweat the Small Stuff at Work: Simple Ways to Minimize Stress and Conflict While Bringing Out the Best in Yourself and Others by Richard Carlson; Hyperion, 1998.

Reinventing Yourself: How to Become the Person You've Always Wanted to Be by Steve Chandler; Career Press, 1998.

Unlimited Power: The New Science of Personal Achievement by Anthony Robbins, Joseph McClendon, Jason Winters (Introduction), and Kenneth H. Blanchard; Fireside, 1997.

You Can Be Happy No Matter What: Five Principles For Keeping Life in Perspective by Richard Carlson and Wayne W. Dyer; New World Library, 1997.

Music careers

Career Opportunities In The Music Industry by Shelly Field; Facts On File, 1996.

Publicity

Bulletproof News Releases: Help at Last for the Publicity Deficient by Kay Borden; Franklin Sarrett Publishers, 1994.

The Complete Guide to Publicity: Maximize Visibility for Your Product, Service, or Organization by Joe Marconi; Ntc Business Books, 1999.

Public relations careers

Career Opportunities In Advertising and Public Relations by Shelly Field; Facts On File, 1997.

Resumes

100 Best Resumes for Today's Hottest Jobs by Ray Potter; Macmillan Publishing, 1998.

101 Best Resumes by Michael Betrus, Jay A. Block; McGraw-Hill, 1997.

101 Quick Tips for a Dynamite Resume by Richard Fein; Impact Publications, 1998.

1500+ Keywords for $100,000+ Jobs by Wendy S. Enelow; Impact Publications, 1998.

Better Resumes for Executives and Professionals, 3rd Edition by Robert F. Wilson and Adele Lewis; Barrons Educational Series, 1996.

Designing the Perfect Resume: A Unique 'Idea' Book Filled With Hundreds of Sample Resumes Created Using Wordperfect Software by Pat Criscito; Barrons Educational Series, 1996.

Gallery of Best Resumes: A Collection of Quality Resumes by Professional Resume Writers by David F. Noble; Jist Works, 1994.

Heart & Soul Resumes: 7 Never-Before-Published Secrets to Capturing Heart & Soul in Your Resume by Chuck Cochran and Donna Peerce; Consulting Psychologists Press, 1998.

Professional Resumes for Executives, Managers, and Other Administrators: A New Gallery of Best Resumes by Professional Resume Writers by David F. Noble; Jist Works, 1998.

Resumes for Dummies by Joyce Lain Kennedy; IDG Books Worldwide, 1998.

Resumes for Scientific and Technical Careers (Vgm's Professional Resumes) by Kathy Siebel (editor); Vgm Career Horizons, 1993.

Resume Magic: Trade Secrets of a Professional Resume Writer by Susan Britton Whitcomb; Jist Works, 1998.

Resume Power: Selling Yourself on Paper, 5th Edition by Tom Washington; Mount Vernon Press, 1996.

Resume Winners from the Pros: 177 of the Best from the Professional Association of Resume Writers by Wendy S. Enelow (editor); Impact Publications, 1998.

Retailing careers

Opportunities in Retailing Careers by Roslyn Dolber; Vgm Career Horizons, 1996.

Retailing Career Starter: Move Ahead in This Fast Growing Field by Valerie Lipow; Learning Express, 1998.

Sales careers

Opportunities in Telemarketing Careers (VGM Opportunities) by Anne Basye; Vgm Career Horizons, 1994.

Science and engineering careers

A Ph.D. Is Not Enough: A Guide to Survival in Science by Peter J. Feibelman; Pereus Press, 1994.

Alternative Careers in Science: Leaving the Ivory Tower by Cynthia Robbins-Roth (editor); Academic Press, 1998.

Jump Start Your Career in BioScience by Chandra B. Louise; Peer Productions, 1998.

Opportunities in Biological Science Careers (VGM Opportunities) by Charles A. Winter and Kathleen Belikoff; Vgm Career Horizons, 1998.

The Scientist As Consultant: Building New Career Opportunities by Carl J. Sindermann and Thomas K. Sawyer (contributor); Plenum Press, 1997.

To Boldly Go: A Practical Career Guide for Scientists by Peter S. Fiske; American Geophysical Union, 1996.

Tomorrow's Professor: Preparing for Academic Careers in Science and Engineering by Richard M. Reis; IEEE, 1997.

Speaking careers

Confessions of an American Speaker: If B.S. Were Concrete, I'd Be Route 66 by Bob Basso; Sligo Press, 1998.

The Zig Ziglar Difference: How the Greatest Motivational Speaker of the Century Has Changed Lives—And How He Can Change Yours by Juanell Teague and Mike Yorkey (editors); Berkley Pub. Group, 1999.

Special event management

The Complete Guide to Special Event Management: Business Insights, Financial Advice, and Successful Strategies from Ernst & Young, Advisors to the Olympics, the Emmy Awards, and the PGA Tour by Richard L. Van Kirk and G. Young Ernst; John Wiley & Sons, 1992.

Sports careers
Career Opportunities In The Sports Industry by Shelly Field; Facts On File, 1998.

Travel and tourism careers
100 Best Careers In Casinos and Casino Hotels by Shelly Field; Arco, 1997.

Careers in Travel, Tourism, and Hospitality by Marjorie Eberts, Linda Brothers (contributor), and Ann Gisler (contributor); Vgm Career Horizons, 1997.

Career Opportunities In Casinos and Casino Hotels by Shelly Field; Facts On File, 2000.

Contact: Customer Service in the Hospitality and Tourism Industry by Donald M. Davidoff; Prentice Hall College Division, 1994.

Dictionary of Travel, Tourism and Hospitality by S. Medlik; Butterworth-Heinemann, 1996.

Guiding Your Entry into the Hospitality, Recreation, and Tourism Mega-Profession by Jack B. Samuels and Reginald Foucar-Szocki; Prentice Hall College Division, 1998.

Hospitality and Tourism Careers: A Blueprint for Success by Carl Riegel and Melissa Dallas; Prentice Hall College Division, 1998.

The Intrepid Traveler's Complete Desk Reference by Sally Scanlon and Kelly Monaghan; Intrepid Traveler, 1997.

Travel (Careers Without College) by Robert F. Miller and Peggy J. Schmidt; Petersons Guides, 1993.

Travel Perspectives: A Guide to Becoming a Travel Agent by Ginger Todd and Susan Rice; Delmar Pub., 1996.

Writing careers

100 Best Careers For Writers and Artists by Shelly Field; Arco, 1997.

1998 Guide to Literary Agents: 500 Agents Who Sell What You Write (serial) by Don Prues and Chantelle Bentley (editors); Writer's Digest Books, 1998.

1999 Writer's Market (Annual) by Kirsten Holm, Donya Dickerson, and Don Prues (editors); Writer's Digest Books, 1998.

Book Editors Talk to Writers by Judy Mandell; John Wiley & Sons, 1995.

How to Be Your Own Literary Agent: The Business of Getting a Book Published by Richard Curtis; Houghton Mifflin, 1996.

How to Write Attention-Grabbing Query & Cover Letters by John Wood; Writer's Digest Books, 1996.

How to Write Irresistible Query Letters by Lisa Collier Cool; Writer's Digest Books, 1990.

Literary Agents: What They Do, How They Do It, and How to Find and Work With the Right One for You by Michael Larsen; John Wiley & Sons, 1996.

Magazine Editors Talk to Writers by Judy Mandell; John Wiley & Sons, 1996.

Writer's Digest Handbook of Magazine Article Writing by Jean M. Fredette; Writer's Digest Books, 1990.

Writer's Guide to Book Editors, Publishers, and Literary Agents, 1999–2000: Who They Are! What They Want! And How to Win Them Over! by Jeff Herman; Prima Publishing, 1998.

Statistics

All information in this section is from the U.S. government's Bureau of Labor Statistics. For more statistics, see the Bureau of Labor Statistics Web site at stats.bls.gov.

TABLE 1. EMPLOYMENT BY MAJOR INDUSTRY DIVISION, 1986, 1996, AND PROJECTED 2006 (NUMBERS IN THOUSANDS)

Industry	1986	1996	2006
Total[1]	111,374	132,352	150,927
Nonfarm wage and salary[2]	98,727	118,731	136,318
Goods producing	24,538	24,431	24,451
Mining	778	574	443
Construction	4,810	5,400	5,900
Manufacturing	18,951	18,457	18,108
Durable	11,200	10,766	10,514
Nondurable	7,751	7,691	7,593
Service producing	74,189	94,300	111,867
Transportation, communications, utilities	5,247	6,260	7,111
Wholesale trade	5,751	6,483	7,228
Retail trade	17,878	21,625	23,875
Finance, insurance, and real estate	6,275	6,899	7,651
Services[2]	22,346	33,586	44,852
Federal government	2,899	2,757	2,670
State and local government	13,794	16,690	18,480
Agriculture[2]	3,327	3,642	3,618
Private household wage and salary	1,235	928	775
Nonagricultural self-employed and unpaid family workers[4]	8,085	9,051	10,216

(1) Employment data for wage and salary workers are from the BLS Current Employment Statistics (payroll) survey, which counts jobs, whereas self-employed, unpaid family workers, agricultural, and private household data are from the Current Population Survey (household survey), which counts workers.

(2) Excludes SIC 074,5,8 (agricultural services) and 99 (nonclassifiable establishments), and is therefore not directly comparable with data published in Employment and Earnings.

(3) Excludes government wage and salary workers, and includes private sector SIC 08, 09 (forestry and fisheries).

(4) Excludes SIC 08, 09 (forestry and fisheries).

TABLE 2. EMPLOYMENT BY MAJOR OCCUPATIONAL GROUP, 1986, 1996, AND PROJECTED 2006 (NUMBERS IN THOUSANDS)

Occupational Group	1986	1996	2006
Total, all occupations	111,375	132,353	150,927
Executive, administrative, and managerial	10,568	13,542	15,866
Professional specialty	13,589	18,173	22,998
Technicians and related support	3,724	4,618	5,558
Marketing and sales	11,496	14,633	16,897
Administrative support, including clerical	20,871	24,019	25,825
Service	17,427	21,294	25,147
Agriculture, forestry, fishing, and related	3,661	3,785	3,823
Precision production, craft, and repair	13,832	14,446	15,448
Operators, fabricators, and laborers	16,206	17,843	19,365

TABLE 3. THE 10 INDUSTRIES WITH THE FASTEST EMPLOYMENT GROWTH, 1996–2006 (NUMBERS IN THOUSANDS OF JOBS)

Industry Description	1996	2006	Growth Number	Growth Percent
Computer and data processing services	1,208	2,509	1,301	108
Health services, nec.	1,172	1,968	796	68
Management and public relations	873	1,400	527	60
Miscellaneous transportation services	204	327	123	60
Residential care	672	1,070	398	59
Personnel supply services	2,646	4,039	1,393	53
Water and sanitation	231	349	118	51
Individual and miscellaneous social services	846	1,266	420	50
Offices of health practitioners	2,751	4,046	1,295	47
Amusement and recreation services, nec.	1,109	1,565	457	41

TABLE 4. THE 10 OCCUPATIONS WITH THE FASTEST EMPLOYMENT GROWTH, 1996–2006 (NUMBERS IN THOUSANDS OF JOBS)

Occupation Employment Change, 1996–2006	1996	2006	Number	Percent
Database administrators, computer support specialists, and all other computer scientists	212	461	249	118
Computer engineers	216	451	235	109
Systems analysts	506	1,025	520	103
Personal and home care aides	202	374	171	85
Physical and corrective therapy assistants and aides	84	151	66	79
Home health aides	495	873	378	76
Medical assistants	225	391	166	74
Desktop publishing specialists	30	53	22	74
Physical therapists	115	196	81	71
Occupational therapy assistants and aides	16	26	11	69

Press release concerning home work

Internet address: http://stats.bls.gov/newsrels.htm

Technical information: (202) 606-6378 USDL 98-93

Media contact: 606-5902, Wednesday, March 11,
     1998

WORK AT HOME IN 1997

More than 21 million persons did some work at
home as part of their primary job in May 1997, the
Bureau of Labor Statistics of the U.S. Department of
Labor reported today. The overall number of persons doing job-related work at home did not grow
dramatically between 1991 and 1997, but the number of wage and salary workers doing paid work at
home did.

These findings are from a special supplement to
the May 1997 Current Population Survey (CPS), the
monthly survey of about 50,000 households that
provides data on the nation's labor force. The information presented here pertains to persons
employed in nonagricultural industries who were at
work during the May 1997 survey reference week
and indicated that they do some job-related work at
home. Similar data were last collected in the CPS in
May 1991. Highlights of the 1997 survey include:
More than half of those working at home were wage
and salary workers who were not paid expressly for
their time worked at home. About 17 percent, however, were wage and salary workers who were paid
for the hours they put in at home. Virtually all the
remainder were self-employed workers, nearly two-
thirds of whom had home-based businesses. Nearly
9 of 10 workers doing paid work at home were in
"white-collar" occupations. More than 4.1 million

self-employed persons were working in a home-based business. About 6 in 10 used a computer for the work they did at home. Wage and salary workers who were paid for working at home averaged nearly 15 hours per week at home; those who weren't paid worked about 9 hours at home. Workers in home-based businesses worked 23 hours per week at home, on average. Of those who worked at a second job, 37 percent did at least some of their work at home.

Pay status, industry, and occupation

While the number of persons reporting work at home grew by only 1.5 million since 1991, there was a sharp increase in the number of persons who were paid for working at home. In 1997, 3.6 million wage and salary workers—about 3.3 percent of all wage and salary workers—were paid for the work they did at home. In 1991, only 1.9 million wage and salary workers—1.9 percent of the total—were doing work at home for pay.

Of the 3.6 million wage and salary workers doing paid work at home, 88 percent were in "white-collar" occupations. Nearly a million of these workers were in professional specialty occupations, slightly more than the number of executives and managers. Sales and administrative support occupations also had large numbers of paid home workers.

By industry, about 1.6 million wage and salary workers in the services industry were doing paid work at home, about 44 percent of the total; more than half a million in manufacturing were paid for work at home. All of the major industry groups except mining had significant numbers of workers doing paid work at home.

The number of persons who were simply "taking work home from the office"—that is, wage and salary workers who were not being officially compensated for the work they did at home—was 11.1 million. This was a modest decline from 1991, when 12.2 million wage and salary workers worked at home without being paid for that work. As with those paid, persons who were not paid for the work they did at home were overwhelmingly employed in white-collar occupations. Teachers were especially likely to do unpaid work at home; 2.8 million teachers reported doing so in 1997. From an industry perspective, services had the largest number of unpaid home workers (6.1 million), followed by manufacturing (1.5 million).

About 6.5 million self-employed persons did some work at home in May 1997, more than half of all the self-employed who were at work during the survey reference week. More than 4.1 million of the self-employed indicated that they were working in home-based businesses. This was the first time that the CPS had contained questions specifically designed to gather information on home-based businesses. Managers and professionals accounted for 1.7 million, or two-fifths, of those working in home-based businesses. Sales, service, and precision production occupations also had large numbers of such workers. In terms of industry, 2.1 million persons, or about half, were working in services, while construction and retail trade accounted for 726,000 and 532,000 workers, respectively.

Demographics

More than 70 percent of persons who did some work at home in 1997 were in married-couple families.

Women and men were about equally likely to work at home. The work-at-home rate for married parents was about the same as the rate for married persons without children. Whites were more than twice as likely to be engaged in some form of home-based work as either blacks or Hispanics.

Computer use

Just under 60 percent of those who worked at home in 1997 used computers. Among wage and salary workers, computer use was about the same for those who were paid for work done at home (63.3 percent) as for those doing unpaid work at home (61.6 percent). Paid home workers were more likely to use a modem for their work at home (43.2 percent) than were unpaid home workers (32.8 percent). Also, 23.2 percent of paid home workers used a telephone line that was furnished by their employer. Only 54.4 percent of self-employed home workers used a computer for work done at home.

Work at home on a second job

Of the 8 million persons who worked on a second job in May 1997, 37 percent did at least some of that work at home. Men with a second job were slightly more likely than women to work at home on that job, and married people were substantially more likely to work at home than unmarried people. Married parents were about as likely to work at home on a second job as married persons without children. However, single parents, and especially single mothers, had higher work-at-home rates than single workers without children.

A total of 23.3 million persons were engaged in work at home on either a first or second job in May

1997, including 21.5 million who worked at home on their primary job and 3 million who did work at home on a second job. About 1.2 million persons had two jobs and worked at home on both.

Information in this release will be made available to sensory-impaired individuals upon request. Voice phone: (202) 606-STAT; TDD phone: 202-606-5897; TDD message referral phone number: (800) 326-2577.

Career and Job
Web Sites

The following are career and job Web sites you might want to check out. Some are helpful in locating hot job possibilities, while others provide career advice or additional resources. This list is only a beginning. There are many more sites you can find while you surf the Net.

1st steps in the job hunt:
www.interbiznet.com/hunt

100 Careers In Cyberspace:
www.globalvillager.com/villager/csc.html

Access Careers & Jobs Resources:
www.hawk.igs.net/jobresources

Achievement Corporation: www.acorp.co.uk

Advertising and Media Jobs Page:
www.nationjob.com/media

Airbase: www.airforce.com

Airline Employment Assistance Corps:
www.ww2.csn.net/AEAC

America's Employers:
www.amaericasemployers.com

America's Job Bank: www.ajb.dni.us

American Management Association:
tregistry.com/ama.htm

Asian Career Web Home Page: www.rici.com/acw

Asia-Net, Inc.: www.asia-net.com

Best Jobs In USA: www.bestjobsusa.com

Boldface Jobs: www.boldfacejobs.com

Bridgepath: www.bridgepath.com

Broadcast Employment Services:
TV Jobs-www.tvjobs.com/index_a.htm

Career Center For Developers:
dev.careercenteral.com

Career Center:
www.netline.com/career/career.html

Career Crafting: www.careercraft.com

Career Exchange: www.careerexchange.com

Career Expo: www.www.eos.net/careersex

Career Mosaic: www.careermosaic.com

Career Net: www.careers.org

Career Planning Process:
www.www.cba.bysu.edu/class/webclass/nagya/
career/process.html

Career Resource Center: www.careers.org

Career Resumes: www.branch.com/cr/cr.html

Career Shop: www.tenkey.com

CareerCity: www.adamsonline.com

CareerMart: www.careermart.com

CareerPath.com: www.careerpath.com

Careers Accounting: www.accounting.com

Careers: www.webplaxzxa.com/pages/Careers/
123Careers/123Careers.html

CareerWEB: www.cweb.com

Colossal List of Career Links:
www.emory.edu//CAREER/Links.html

Computer Jobs Store: www.computerjobs.com

Computer Work: www.Computerwork.com

Contract Employment Weekly Online:
www.ceweekly.wa.com

Cool Works: www.coolworks.com/showme

CyberFair: www.career.com/cyberfair.html

Developers.net: www.developers.net,
www.developers1.net

DICE (Data processing Independent Contractors):
www.dice.com

E-Span: www.espan.com

Employment Channel Online: www.employ.com

Employment Resources On The Internet:
members.iquet.net/-swlodin/jobs

EngineeringJobs.com: www.engineeringjobs.com

Fast Company: www.fastcompany.com/career

Federal Jobs Digest: www.jobsfed.com

Findlawjob.com: www.find-lawjob.com

GET A JOB: www.getajob.com

Good Works: www.tripod.com/work/goodworks

Hard@Work: www.hardatwork.com

High Technology Careers:
www.hightechcareersx.com

HiTech Careers: www.hightechcareer.com/hitech

Hoover's Online: www.hoovers.com

Hot Jobs: www.hotjobs.com

Insurance Career Center: www.connectyou.com/talent

Internet Fashion Exchange: www.fashionexch.com

Job Resource: www.thejobresource.com

Job Search Resources: cadserv.cadlab.vt.edu/bohn/Job_Search.html

JobBank USA: www.jobbankusa.com

JobCenter: www.jobcenter.com

JobHunt: www.job-hunt.org

Jobs & Careers Online: www.servonet.com/jobs

Jobs.com: www.2-Jobs.com

JobSmart: jobsmart.org/index.htm

JobTrak: www.jobtrak.com

JobWeb: www.jobweb.org

Marketing Classifieds: www.marketingjobs.com

Monster Board: www.monster.com

National Business Employment Weekly: www.nbew.com

National Diversity Journalism Job Bank: www.newsjobs.com

Online Career Center: www.occ.com

Online Sports Career Center: www.onlinesports.com/pages/CareerCenter.html

Recruiters Online Network: www.ipa.com

Resume'Net: www.resumenet.com

Riley Guide: www.dbm.com/jobguide

Salary Calculator: www.homefair.com/homefair/calc/salcalc.html

Science Professional Network: www.recruit.sciencemag.org

Shelly Field: www.shellyfield.com

Silicon Valley Employment Opportunities:
www.netview.com/jobs

Summer Jobs: www.summerjobs.com

TechCareers:
www.techweb.com/careers/careers.html

Telecommuting Resources: www.cisc.com/tele.html

TOPjobs USA: www.topjobsusa.com

Virtual Job Fair: www.vjf.com

Wanted Technologies: www.wantedtech.com

What Color Is Your Parachute: The Net Guide:
washingtonpost.com/parachute

Which Job Fair Is Right For You?:
www.psijobfaira.com/a-fair.html

Work: www.4work.com

World Wide Web Employment Office:
www.harbornet.com/biz/office/annex.html

A

E

F

The *Unofficial Guide*™ Reader Questionnaire

If you would like to express your opinion about finding a hot career or this guide, please complete this questionnaire and mail it to:

The *Unofficial Guide*™ Reader Questionnaire
IDG Lifestyle Group
1633 Broadway, floor 7
New York, NY 10019-6785

Gender: ___ M ___ F

Age: ___ Under 30 ___ 31–40 ___ 41–50
___ Over 50

Education: ___ High school ___ College
___ Graduate/Professional

What is your occupation?
_____

How did you hear about this guide?
___ Friend or relative
___ Newspaper, magazine, or Internet
___ Radio or TV
___ Recommended at bookstore
___ Recommended by librarian
___ Picked it up on my own
___ Familiar with the *Unofficial Guide*™ travel series

Did you go to the bookstore specifically for a book on hot careers? Yes ___ No ___

Have you used any other *Unofficial Guides*™?
Yes ___ No ___

If Yes, which ones?
_____
_____
_____

What other book(s) on hot careers have you purchased? _____

_____

_____

Was this book:
___ more helpful than other(s)
___ less helpful than other(s)

Do you think this book was worth its price?
Yes ___   No ___

Did this book cover all topics related to hot careers adequately?
Yes ___   No ___

Please explain your answer:

_____

_____

_____

Were there any specific sections in this book that were of particular help to you?   Yes ___   No ___

Please explain your answer:

_____

_____

_____

On a scale of 1 to 10, with 10 being the best rating, how would you rate this guide? ___

What other titles would you like to see published in the *Unofficial Guide*™ series?

_____

_____

Are Unofficial Guides™ **readily available in your area?**   Yes ___   No ___

Other comments:

_____

_____

_____

_____

Get the inside scoop...with the *Unofficial Guides*™!

Health and Fitness

The Unofficial Guide to Alternative Medicine
ISBN: 0-02-862526-9 Price: $15.95

The Unofficial Guide to Conquering Impotence
ISBN: 0-02-862870-5 Price: $15.95

The Unofficial Guide to Coping with Menopause
ISBN: 0-02-862694-x Price: $15.95

The Unofficial Guide to Cosmetic Surgery
ISBN: 0-02-862522-6 Price: $15.95

The Unofficial Guide to Dieting Safely
ISBN: 0-02-862521-8 Price: $15.95

The Unofficial Guide to Having a Baby
ISBN: 0-02-862695-8 Price: $15.95

The Unofficial Guide to Living with Diabetes
ISBN: 0-02-862919-1 Price: $15.95

The Unofficial Guide to Overcoming Arthritis
ISBN: 0-02-862714-8 Price: $15.95

The Unofficial Guide to Overcoming Infertility
ISBN: 0-02-862916-7 Price: $15.95

Career Planning

The Unofficial Guide to Acing the Interview
ISBN: 0-02-862924-8 Price: $15.95

The Unofficial Guide to Earning What You Deserve
ISBN: 0-02-862523-4 Price: $15.95

The Unofficial Guide to Hiring and Firing People
ISBN: 0-02-862523-4 Price: $15.95

Business and Personal Finance

The Unofficial Guide to Investing
ISBN: 0-02-862458-0 Price: $15.95

The Unofficial Guide to Investing in Mutual Funds
ISBN: 0-02-862920-5 Price: $15.95

The Unofficial Guide to Managing Your Personal Finances
ISBN: 0-02-862921-3 Price: $15.95

The Unofficial Guide to Starting a Small Business
ISBN: 0-02-862525-0 Price: $15.95

Home and Automotive

The Unofficial Guide to Buying a Home
ISBN: 0-02-862461-0 Price: $15.95

The Unofficial Guide to Buying or Leasing a Car
ISBN: 0-02-862524-2 Price: $15.95

The Unofficial Guide to Hiring Contractors
ISBN: 0-02-862460-2 Price: $15.95

Family and Relationships

The Unofficial Guide to Childcare
ISBN: 0-02-862457-2 Price: $15.95

The Unofficial Guide to Dating Again
ISBN: 0-02-862454-8 Price: $15.95

The Unofficial Guide to Divorce
ISBN: 0-02-862455-6 Price: $15.95

The Unofficial Guide to Eldercare
ISBN: 0-02-862456-4 Price: $15.95

The Unofficial Guide to Planning Your Wedding
ISBN: 0-02-862459-9 Price: $15.95

Hobbies and Recreation

The Unofficial Guide to Finding Rare Antiques
ISBN: 0-02-862922-1 Price: $15.95

The Unofficial Guide to Casino Gambling
ISBN: 0-02-862917-5 Price: $15.95

All books in the *Unofficial Guide*™ series are available at your local bookseller, or by calling 1-800-428-5331.